LIBRARY OF NEW TESTAMENT STUDIES

634

formerly The Journal For The Study Of The New Testament Supplement series

Editor
Chris Keith

Editorial Board
Dale C. Allison, Lynn H. Cohick, R. Alan Culpepper, Craig A. Evans,
Jennifer Eyl, Robert Fowler, Simon J. Gathercole, Juan Hernández Jr., John
S. Kloppenborg, Michael Labahn, Matthew V. Novenson, Love L. Sechrest,
Robert Wall, Catrin H. Williams, Brittany E. Wilson

The Scriptures in the Book of Revelation and Apocalyptic Literature

Essays in Honour of Steve Moyise

Edited by
Susan E. Docherty and Steve Smith

t&tclark
LONDON • NEW YORK • OXFORD • NEW DELHI • SYDNEY

T&T CLARK
Bloomsbury Publishing Plc
50 Bedford Square, London, WC1B 3DP, UK
1385 Broadway, New York, NY 10018, USA
29 Earlsfort Terrace, Dublin 2, Ireland

BLOOMSBURY, T&T CLARK and the T&T Clark logo are trademarks of
Bloomsbury Publishing Plc

First published in Great Britain 2023
Paperback edition published in 2025

Copyright © Susan E. Docherty, Steve Smith and contributors, 2023

Susan E. Docherty and Steve Smith have asserted their right under the Copyright,
Designs and Patents Act, 1988, to be identified as Editors of this work.

All rights reserved. No part of this publication may be reproduced or transmitted in
any form or by any means, electronic or mechanical, including photocopying,
recording, or any information storage or retrieval system, without prior
permission in writing from the publishers.

Bloomsbury Publishing Plc does not have any control over, or responsibility for, any
third-party websites referred to or in this book. All internet addresses given in this
book were correct at the time of going to press. The author and publisher regret any
inconvenience caused if addresses have changed or sites have ceased to exist,
but can accept no responsibility for any such changes.

Library of Congress Cataloging-in-Publication Data

Names: Docherty, Susan E., 1965- editor. | Smith, Steve
(New Testament scholar), editor.
Title: "The scriptures in the Book of Revelation and apocalyptic
literature" / edited by Susan E. Docherty and Steve Smith.
Description: London : T&T Clark, 2023. | Series: Library of New Testament
studies, 2513-8790 ; 634 | Includes bibliographical references and
index. | Summary: "This volume explores the reuse of scripture within
the genre of apocalyptic, with a particular focus on the Book of
Revelation, while also considering other apocalyptic texts in the New
Testament and early Jewish literature"– Provided by publisher.
Identifiers: LCCN 2022056556 (print) | LCCN 2022056557 (ebook) | ISBN
9780567695895 (HB) | ISBN 9780567710444 (PB) | ISBN 9780567695901 (ePDF)
| ISBN 9780567695925 (ePUB)
Subjects: LCSH: Bible. Revelation–Criticism, interpretation, etc. | Eschatology.
Classification: LCC BS2825.52 .S453 2023 (print) | LCC BS2825.52 (ebook)
| DDC 228/.06–dc23/eng/20230419
LC record available at https://lccn.loc.gov/2022056556
LC ebook record available at https://lccn.loc.gov/2022056557

ISBN: HB: 978-0-5676-9589-5
PB: 978-0-5677-1044-4
ePDF: 978-0-5676-9590-1
ePUB: 978-0-5676-9592-5

Series: The Library of New Testament Studies, volume 634
ISSN 2513-8790

Typeset by Newgen KnowledgeWorks Pvt. Ltd., Chennai, India

To find out more about our authors and books visit www.bloomsbury.com
and sign up for our newsletters.

This volume is presented with gratitude and affection to Professor Steve Moyise, scholar, teacher, colleague, mentor and friend.
It celebrates Steve's immense contribution over nearly three decades to deepening scholarly understanding of the ways in which Israel's scriptures are reused in the New Testament and his gift for explaining these most complex of issues so clearly and judiciously to a wide range of audiences.

Steve Moyise. Image courtesy of the University of Chichester.

Contents

List of Contributors ix
List of Abbreviations xi

Introduction: Scripture in Revelation and apocalyptic 1
   Steve Smith and Susan E. Docherty

Part 1 Reusing scripture: Methodological issues

1 Typology and eschatology: The scriptural shaping of imagery in the Book of Revelation 11
   Frances Young

2 Smells like teen spirit: Steve Moyise and G. K. Beale on the use of scripture in Revelation in the 1990s 25
   Garrick V. Allen

3 Dreaming with scripture: Revisiting the Beale-Moyise debate 41
   Benjamin Sargent

Part 2 Scriptures and interpretation in the Book of Revelation

4 Something old, something new: The origins of the Song of Moses in Rev. 15.3 53
   David M. Allen

5 Echoes from the Septuagint Psalter in the apocalyptic texture of Revelation 65
   Gert J. Steyn

6 The Old Testament background of sound and silence in the Book of Revelation 83
   Beate Kowalski

7 The reimagining of theological time: Revelation's use of the OT in defining its temporality 101
   Ian Paul

Contents

8 The *Expositio Apocalypseos* of the Venerable Bede: An example of early medieval preoccupation with construing time and its end — 117
   Paul M. Collins

9 Apocalyptic on screen – can the hermeneutical flow really be reversed? The TV drama series *Years and Years* and the Book of Revelation — 131
   Clive Marsh

Part 3 Scripture in early Jewish and early Christian apocalyptic writings

10 The Psalms in *1 Enoch* — 147
    Susan E. Docherty

11 Revelation in Johannine perspective: On seeing the glory in Jn 1.14 — 161
    Wendy E. S. North

12 The identity and destiny of 'all Israel' in Paul's apocalyptic imagination: Revisiting Rom. 11.26 — 171
    B. J. Oropeza

13 The wedding imagery of the Apocalypse and Paul — 183
    Lionel North

14 David the prophet in the first apocryphal *Apocalypse of John* — 193
    Craig A. Evans

Bibliography — 211
Index of Modern Authors — 231
Scripture Index — 235

Contributors

David M. Allen is Academic Dean at the Queen's Foundation for Ecumenical Theological Education, Birmingham, UK.

Garrick V. Allen is Senior Lecturer in New Testament Studies at the School of Critical Studies at the University of Glasgow, UK.

Paul M. Collins is a retired priest and former Reader in Theology at the University of Chichester.

Susan E. Docherty is Professor of New Testament and Early Judaism at Newman University, Birmingham, UK.

Craig A. Evans is the John Bisagno Distinguished Professor of Christian Origins at Houston Christian University in Texas, United States.

Beate Kowalski is Professor of Exegesis and Theology of the New Testament at TU Dortmund University, Germany.

Clive Marsh is Principal of the Queen's Foundation for Ecumenical Theological Education, Birmingham, UK.

Lionel North is an independent scholar and was formerly senior lecturer in the Department of Theology at Hull University, UK.

Wendy E. S. North is an honorary research fellow in the Department of Theology and Religion at Durham University, UK.

B. J. Oropeza is Professor of Biblical and Religious Studies at Azusa Pacific University, California, United States.

Ian Paul is Associate Minister at St Nic's, Nottingham, UK, and adjunct professor at Fuller Theological Seminary, United States; he publishes at www.psephizo.com.

Benjamin Sargent is Vicar of Bransgore and Hinton Admiral, Hampshire, UK.

Steve Smith is Tutor and Lecturer in New Testament Studies at St Mellitus College, London, UK.

Gert J. Steyn is Professor of New Testament Exegesis and Theology at the Theologische Hochschule Ewersbach, Germany, and Research Associate at the Faculty of Theology, University of Pretoria, South Africa.

Frances Young is Emeritus Professor of Theology at the University of Birmingham, UK.

Abbreviations

AB	Anchor Bible
ArBib	The Aramaic Bible
AUSS	*Andrews University Seminary Studies*
BECNT	Baker Exegetical Commentary on the New Testament
Bib	*Biblica*
BIS	Biblical Interpretation Series
BNT	Die Botschaft des Neuen Testaments
BNTC	Black's New Testament Commentary
BR	*Biblical Research*
BZNW	Beihefte zur Zeitschrift für die neutestamentliche Wissenschaft
CBQ	*Catholic Biblical Quarterly*
CBR	*Currents in Biblical Research*
CEJL	Commentaries on Early Jewish Literature
CGSS	Cambridge Genizah Studies Series
CNT	Commentaire du Nouveau Testament
ConBNT	Coniectanea neotestamentica or Coniectanea biblica: New Testament Series
COQG	Christian Origins and the Question of God
CQ	*Classical Quarterly*
CTJ	*Calvin Theological Journal*
DR	*Downside Review*
ECA	Early Christian Apocrypha
EDNT	Exegetical Dictionary of the New Testament
EGGNT	Exegetical Guide to the Greek New Testament
ÉJM	*Études sur le Judaïsme Médiéval*
ET	*Expository Times*
FAT	Forschungen zum Alten Testament 2. Reihe
FRLANT	Forschungen zur Religion und Literatur des Alten und Neuen Testaments
HThKNT	Herders theologischer kommentar zum Neuen Testament
HTR	*Harvard Theological Review*
IBS	*Irish Biblical Studies*
JAJS	*Journal of Ancient Judaism Supplements*
JAOS	*Journal of the American Oriental Society*
JASIMS	*Eolas: Journal of the American Society of Irish Medieval Studies*
JECH	*Journal of Early Christian History*
JETS	*Journal of the Evangelical Theological Society*
JML	*Journal of Medieval Latin*
JSJ	*Journal for the Study of Judaism*
JSNT	*Journal for the Study of the New Testament*

JSNTSup	Journal for the Study of the New Testament: Supplement Series
JSPL	*Journal for the Study of Paul and His Letters*
JSQ	*Jewish Studies Quarterly*
JThS	*Journal of Theological Studies*
LD	Lectio Divina
LHBOTS	The Library of Hebrew Bible/Old Testament Studies
LNTS	The Library of New Testament Studies
MB	Manuscripta Biblica
NCB	New Century Bible
NCBC	New Cambridge Bible Commentary
NCCS	New Covenant Commentary Series
Neot	*Neotestamentica*
NICNT	New International Commentary on the New Testament
NIGTC	New International Greek Testament Commentary
NIVAC	New International Version Application Commentary
NJJWSFI	*Nashim: A Journal of Jewish Women's Studies & Gender Issues*
NovT	*Novum Testamentum*
NTL	New Testament Library
NTM	New Testament Monographs
NTS	*New Testament Studies*
OtSt	Oudtestamentische Studiën
PEA	*Philosophy of Education Archive*
PRIA	Proceedings of the Royal Irish Academy: Archaeology, Culture, History, Literature
RivBib	*Rivista biblica*
SAN	Studio Aarhusiana Neotestamentica
SBB	Stuttgarter biblische Beiträge
SBLEJL	Society of Biblical Literature Early Judaism and Its Literature
SBLRBS	Society of Biblical Literature Resources for Biblical Study
SBS	Stuttgarter Bibelstudien
SBT	Studies in Biblical Theology
SCH	*Studies in Church History*
ScrB	*Scripture Bulletin*
SDSSRL	Studies in the Dead Sea Scrolls and Related Literature
SJSJ	Supplements to the Journal for the Study of Judaism
SJT	*Scottish Journal of Theology*
SNTSMS	Society for New Testament Studies Monograph Series
SNTU.A	*Studien zum Neuen Testament und seiner Umwelt. Serie A*
SP	Sacra Pagina
SPE	*Studies in Philosophy and Education*
SSEJC	Studies in Early Judaism and Christianity
SVTP	Studia in Veteris Testamenti Pseudepigrapha
TBN	Themes in Biblical Narrative
ThH	Théologie historique
THOTC	The Two Horizons OT Commentary

TNTC	Tyndale New Testament Commentary
TRHS	*Transactions of the Royal Historical Society*
TSAJ	Texts and Studies in Ancient Judaism
TU	*Texte und Untersuchungen*
TynBul	*Tyndale Bulletin*
USQR	Union Seminary Quarterly Review
VC	*Vigiliae christianae*
VT	*Vetus Testamentum*
VTSup	Vetus Testamentum Supplements
WBC	Word Biblical Commentary
WUNT	Wissenschaftliche Untersuchungen zum Neuen Testament
YJS	Yale Judaica Series
ZAC	*Zeitschrift für Antikes Christentum*
ZBK	Zürcher Bibelkommentare
ZECNT	Zondervan Exegetical Commentary on the New Testament
ZNW	*Zeitschrift für die neutestamentliche Wissenschaft und die Kunde der älteren Kirche*

Introduction: Scripture in Revelation and apocalyptic

Steve Smith and Susan E. Docherty

Revelation is a fascinating book, unique in the New Testament; its place as the final text in the NT canon, its rich symbolism and its apparent concern with the end of the world have made it a favourite text for preachers, prophets of doom, mystics and cultural commentators, who have all offered a range of diverse interpretations, some of which are more fanciful than others. Scholarship has attempted to control some of this variety of opinion, bringing to the text its own particular questions, often concerning historical critical matters, sociopolitical context and the usual issue of authorial intention versus reader response. Nowhere has this scholarly discussion been more interesting or critical than in its treatment of the use of the OT in Revelation. Revelation is particularly dense in allusion to the OT. While it has no clear quotations (though arguments can be made for both Rev. 1.7 and 15.3-4 as citations), the OT stands behind much of its rich symbolism and imagery and informs much of its theology. So, understanding how the Book of Revelation uses OT texts is a critical task, both to aid understanding of the book itself and to give a deeper understanding of early Christian hermeneutics.

By the 1990s, the discussion of the use of scripture in Revelation was energized by the adoption of literary approaches to textual dependence, including intertextuality. While the work of Julia Kristeva and others lies behind this understanding of intertextuality,[1] it was Richard Hays who raised its profile in NT studies[2] and Steve Moyise who subsequently explored its use in the Book of Revelation.[3] This volume is dedicated to Professor Moyise and recognizes his significant contribution to our understanding both of the Book of Revelation and the use of the OT in the NT more generally; this volume especially expresses our appreciation for his insights into the interaction between the contexts of OT texts and NT texts in a process for which he coined the term 'dialogical

---

[1] For example, Julia Kristeva, *Desire in Language: A Semiotic Approach to Literature and Art*, trans. Leon S. Roudiez (Oxford: Blackwell, 1980).
[2] Richard B. Hays, *Echoes of Scripture in the Letters of Paul* (New Haven, CT: Yale University Press, 1989).
[3] Steve Moyise, *The Old Testament in the Book of Revelation*, JSNTSup 115 (Sheffield: Sheffield Academic Press, 1995).

intertextuality'.[4] His clear analyses of interpretative approaches have enriched debate, and his generous collegiality and friendship to many in the subdiscipline mean that we owe him a debt of gratitude. His chairing of the Annual Seminar for the Use of the OT in the NT in Hawarden for many years (most co-chairing with Maarten Menken) was important for shaping a subdiscipline and guiding many through their PhDs. It is with gratitude to him that the contributors of this volume present their essays.

Fittingly then, the focus of this volume is on the use of the OT in the NT apocalyptic material. The first part is on hermeneutical issues. The second is on the Book of Revelation and how it interacts with the OT and how the OT informs its theology. The third considers other passages with apocalyptic features in the NT and more broadly in early Christianity and Judaism. This wider understanding is important for the debate about how Christian apocalyptic texts in general use the OT.

In the first chapter, Frances Young lays an important foundation for the rest of the volume by examining broader hermeneutical concerns in Revelation's use of scripture. In noting that Revelation's use of scripture typically involves acts of interpretation, Young turns to typology to understand that interpretation better and applies it to Revelation in dialogue with Michael Fishbane and Richard Bauckham; she suggests that other early Christian uses of typology may offer helpful illumination which allows an interpreter of Revelation to see the approach taken by the author of Revelation beyond the surface-level allusions which are commonly noted. Her chapter goes on to examine the relationship between the symbolism that Revelation uses, its OT origins and typology, illustrating this through Bauckham's discussion of the lion and the lamb in Revelation 5 (a text on which Steve Moyise has himself written).[5] Young concludes that most typology is focused on the present, but typology in Revelation requires its combination with eschatology: Revelation not only retains a concern for the present but also looks to the future, offering a hope for that future based on what is typologically recognized in the present. In other words, Revelation gives readers the ability to discern, through typology, God's current activity in the light of his previous salvific acts and thereby see the hope for the future.

There follow two chapters discussing aspects of Steve Moyise's thought-provoking debate with Greg Beale on the use of scripture in Revelation. This debate sharpened understanding of different hermeneutical approaches to Revelation's use of the OT and, in particular, drew attention to their presuppositions. Garrick Allen's chapter argues that while both Moyise and Beale were concerned to understand how the author of Revelation used scripture, the interesting aspects of the debate are the deeper issues that it uncovers. Allen adeptly analyses the exchange between Moyise and Beale and argues that at its centre is a conversation about the theological understanding of scripture and its inspiration. Within their exchange, Allen argues, much of subsequent hermeneutical discussion over the next twenty years is encountered, and from their

---

[4] See the recent discussion in Steve Moyise, 'Dialogical Intertextuality', in B. J. Oropeza and Steve Moyise (eds), *Exploring Intertextuality: Diverse Strategies for New Testament Interpretation of Texts* (Eugene: Cascade Books, 2016), 3–15.

[5] Steve Moyise, 'Does the Lion Lie Down with the Lamb?', in Steve Moyise (ed.), *Studies in the Book of Revelation* (Edinburgh: T&T Clark, 2001), 181–94.

debate, much modern research has developed. Allen specifically notes this is the case for the discussion of the Jewish text of scripture and the NT witness to it; the discussions about how Revelation handles scripture, including the texts that it focuses on and how it interprets them; and discussions concerning how Revelation's use of scripture is understood in later literature, including later manuscripts of Revelation.

While agreeing that the Moyise/Beale debate was very illuminating, Benjamin Sargent is concerned to demonstrate the hermeneutical limitations of the positions of both Moyise and Beale. Sargent pitches the conversation between them as arising from the contexts in which they were working and the desire of both to demonstrate that the use of scripture in Revelation is reasonable – with both scholars assuming that Revelation's interpretation of scripture has some concern for the 'original' meaning of the text even if they differ in how this is understood. He questions both whether this assumption is justified and if their desire to show the reasonableness of the interpretation of scripture in Revelation leads them both to a weaker understanding of early Christian hermeneutical approaches. He proceeds to investigate how early Christian texts regarded original meaning, and while many of these texts differ from Revelation in their use of scripture, he detects in the Letter to Ephesus of Ignatius of Antioch some similarity to Revelation. Taking this text into account he concludes that explanations of the use of scripture in Revelation which depend on Revelation's interest in prior meaning (however that is expressed) are not in accordance with the evidence. As such, he concludes Revelation is not written to teach hermeneutics.

The second part focuses on the Book of Revelation itself. David Allen's contribution concerns the OT origins of the Song of Moses and the Lamb in Rev. 15.3-4, a fascinating case study in Revelation's use of the Jewish scriptures and in OT/NT methodology more generally. Noting that the combined title of the song (of Moses and the Lamb) seems to imply that it is some combination of old (Moses) and new (Lamb), Allen proceeds to evaluate what these old/new categories mean and how they interrelate in Revelation's scriptural use. Revelation is often said to have no quotations from the OT, but if the title of the song is regarded as an introductory formula, then the song may be the only quotation in Revelation – if that is the case then its textual origins are not obvious. Allen reviews various options for what the textual origin may be and concludes it is complex, with Exodus 15 and Deuteronomy 32 both clear contenders, but with other texts also proving important. Turning to the song as it is in Revelation, he finds that this is similarly complex and considers it in the light of Michelle Fletcher's description of pastiche.[6] While Allen does not find pastiche adequate on its own to understand this particular instance exhaustively, pastiche does highlight this text as an example of scriptural use in Revelation freed from concerns over a single underlying text. As such, this text is a complex mixture of old and new which raises fascinating hermeneutical questions for Revelation as a whole.

Much focus has been given in prior literature to the reuse of material from the prophets, especially Daniel, but Gert Steyn offers a stimulating chapter on the Psalms. He focuses his study on the hymnic material of Revelation which is typically

---

[6] Michelle Fletcher, *Reading Revelation as Pastiche: Imitating the Past*, LNTS 571 (London: Bloomsbury T&T Clark, 2017).

understood to be the creative compositions of the author of Revelation, drawn from his familiarity with a range of sources, and Steyn looks specifically for echoes of the Psalter. Having identified the relevant hymnic passages in Revelation, he focuses on four key motifs within these worship scenes: worship expressions, divine address, divine nature and divine actions. For each of these, Steyn searches for parallel motifs in the Psalms where there is demonstrable verbal allusion. In doing this he makes a case that the author of Revelation may have had such imagery and phrasing from Psalms in mind when composing his hymns. The result of the study is a persuasive case for the reuse of material from the Psalms throughout Revelation's worship imagery, with many clear echoes identified. As such, one can be confident that the author of Revelation is familiar with the Psalter, using a broad range of material drawn from the Psalms – though excluding the pilgrim songs (LXX 119–33).

Beate Kowalski examines two important motifs in Revelation – sound and silence – and demonstrates that there is a significant background in the OT for both of them. Her chapter begins with the noise which fills the Book of Revelation, seeking out the OT background to voices and sounds, musical instruments and the hymnic elements in the book. She also examines places in Revelation where one would expect noise, but one finds silence, focusing on places where silence represents desolation or the presence of God, with particular attention to the silence that comes as the first plagues reach a climax in 8.1. This contribution clearly highlights the great variety of the use of the OT by the author of Revelation and his oftentimes very creative use of texts. Kowalski's overview makes it clear that the author can use the same OT text with variation in multiple places in Revelation, and that the author also combines multiple OT texts together in places – that latter point being especially clear in the rich textual use of the hymnic portions when this chapter is read alongside Steyn's contribution.

Ian Paul offers a contribution which evaluates Revelation's portrayal of time, especially in relation to its eschatology. Paul reviews the significant temporal markers within the text, where textual reuse, echo or adaptation of language or imagery from the OT forms an important part of the discussion. From the picture this builds he is able to address the question of the time in which Revelation is set. In addition to the discussion of time itself, this chapter makes helpful observations on the use of the OT in Revelation. First, he notes that the relationship of Revelation with the OT is dialogical, with Revelation viewing the OT texts in the light of the Christ event and implicitly inviting readers to reread the canon in the light of this. Second, he notes that Revelation incorporates and develops the scriptural themes of exodus and exile by combining further prophetic and apocalyptic imagery, again offering an integrated reading of the whole canon of scripture. In addition to this, the different ways that Revelation takes temporal imagery and motifs from the OT enable it to create its own temporal map, something that permits Paul to identify the time of the Book of Revelation as being a partially realized eschatology, where the reign of God and the opposition against the reign coexist – something consistent with the rest of the NT canon.

Finally, there are two chapters which take the discussion in a different direction and consider aspects of the reception of Revelation. First, Paul Collins discusses the earliest extant English commentary on the Book of Revelation, the *Expositio Apocalypseos* of the Venerable Bede. Bede's approach to the text was descended from the work of Origen, Augustine and others, and Collins identifies three main concerns of Bede in the text: concerns related to the challenges his church faced; concerns for the salvation of individual believers; and a focus on Easter, a time associated with contemporary expectation of the end. Bede's commentary remained influential for centuries, and reading Collins's chapter it is notable how different its concerns are to those of the modern academy: it is focused on the church of his day, not so much on the hermeneutical questions which are pressed by modern scholarship, nor with the issue of the use of scripture by Revelation. Finally, Clive Marsh writes a contribution which draws the reader into an interesting discussion of how film may inform the reading of biblical apocalyptic literature. He does this by looking at the BBC drama TV series *Years and Years*, a series in which Marsh sees the projection into the future of a set of contemporary concerns about the present. Marsh sees some similarities in function to Revelation and addresses the question of how such contemporary Revelation-like 'texts' can help readers read the Book of Revelation. In doing so he notes how the reading of Revelation is affected by the TV series and in turn how Revelation also speaks to the concerns of the present. This dialogue between modern texts and Revelation is interesting to consider in the light of Moyise's understanding of Revelation as a form of dialogical intertextuality.

Apocalyptic is one of the most enduring forms of religious literature, so the final part of the volume turns to the interpretation of the scriptures within a selection of early Jewish and Christian apocalypses beyond the Book of Revelation. It begins with a study of one of the oldest extant examples of the genre, *1 Enoch*. Susan Docherty explores the reuses of the language, motifs and literary structure of the Psalms within this corpus. Such an investigation presents significant methodological challenges, given the complex composition and transmission history of the Enochic writings and the lack of explicit scriptural citations which characterize them. Docherty begins, therefore, by proposing a set of criteria to distinguish intentional allusions from incidental linguistic and thematic parallels. She emphasizes the importance of specific and unique verbal links and also looks for evidence of exegetical engagement with an underlying scriptural source. On this basis, she is able to identify nine probable allusions to the Psalms across *1 Enoch* and a further nine possible cases. This, together with the contribution of Psalms texts to the development of key metaphors such as the son of man and the Lord of the Sheep, indicates that the extent of their influence on the Enochic composers is often underappreciated. Docherty also uncovers some important features of the hermeneutical practice and axioms of these interpreters, including their understanding of the Psalms as prophetic texts which have been fulfilled in the concrete experiences of the community or are about to be realized in the impending eschaton.

The following three chapters in this part consider apocalyptic passages and imagery within New Testament writings other than Revelation. Wendy North's focus is the Fourth Gospel, a work which has the concept of revelation at its heart and which demonstrates throughout a familiarity with apocalyptic traditions. She offers a detailed investigation of the evangelist's assertion that he and his audience have seen the glory of the Father's 'only one' (Jn 1.14; cf. 3.16). This verse forms part of a dense network of scriptural references and is clearly intended to evoke the account of the Sinai theophany in Exodus 33–34. North makes a compelling case, however, for recognizing that it also intentionally recalls the synoptic transfiguration narratives and the revelatory vision of Jesus's glory as God's beloved son experienced by his first disciples on that occasion. This would fit with the evangelist's wider technique of referring in passing to events known to his readers.

The next two chapters seek to illuminate Paul's thought. B. J. Oropeza analyses the place of Israel in Paul's apocalyptic vision through a detailed exegesis of Romans 9–11 and the scriptural texts underlying this section of the letter. He contends, against commentators such as Tom Wright, that the phrase 'all Israel' (Rom. 11.26) should be understood in a purely ethnic sense, as referring only to Jews, rather than to the gentiles and Jews who now form part of God's people within the Christian communities. On this reading of Romans, 'Israel' is to be understood as constituted for a limited time of two groups, a 'remnant', who believe the gospel about Christ, and the rest who are presently 'hardened'. Paul hopes that some of the latter company will turn to Christ in the present age but is convinced that once the good news has been received by all the nations, in line with prophetic expectations, the other Jews too will have their hardened state removed and so 'all Israel' will be saved at the second coming of Christ. Next, Lionel North investigates the apostle's self-presentation as a 'matchmaker' who is responsible for having 'betrothed' the members of the Corinthian Church to Christ (2 Cor. 11.2), considering in particular how this metaphor relates to his eschatological expectation. Wedding imagery features elsewhere in the New Testament, especially in Revelation 16–19, and has clear scriptural roots. By shining a spotlight specifically on the role and expectations of a matchmaker in the ancient Jewish and Graeco-Roman context in which Paul operated, however, North is able to deepen our understanding of the whole argument of 2 Corinthians. This background helps to explain, for example, Paul's emphasis on his zeal and honesty, and his anticipation of the final eschaton, when the work he has done to bring the Corinthians to their Lord Jesus will be reciprocated as he himself achieves full unity with the Body of Christ.

This section concludes with a new study of a little-known early Christian apocryphal work directly inspired by the Book of Revelation, the first *Apocalypse of John*. Craig Evans sets its reuse of scripture in the context of the widely held early Jewish and early Christian belief in David's prophetic status, since the text cites extensively from the Psalms and presents their words as predictions of the future. Evans offers a careful exegesis of all the passages containing references to the Psalms, highlighting the ways in which they build upon and develop the use of the Psalms in the canonical Apocalypse. Differences as well as similarities emerge from this investigation, such as the marked preference for explicit citations over allusions in the later work. Evans concludes that, for this author, David is the most important figure in Israel's scriptures for understanding Jesus, who, as his descendant, fulfilled all his prophecies about the coming divine judgement and salvation. This chapter makes a significant contribution to the underexplored area of the interpretation of scripture in the first apocryphal *Apocalypse of John*, and it reinforces the importance of the Psalms for early Jewish and early Christian interpreters in the apocalyptic tradition.

The contributors to this volume have all sought to build on the pioneering work of Steve Moyise on the interpretation of Israel's scriptures in early Christian writings. This has resulted in fresh insights into the exegetical techniques of the author of Revelation; into specific passages, metaphors and theological themes within the text; and into its reception from the early church to the present. It has also foregrounded broader methodological and hermeneutical questions about the nature and ongoing validity of the interpretation of scripture across apocalyptic literature. The conclusions reached in these studies have the potential to illuminate a New Testament book which has often bewildered its readers, both ancient and modern, but which also challenges them imaginatively and practically to engage with its call to oppose the forces of oppression in their own societies.

Part 1

Reusing scripture:
Methodological issues

1

Typology and eschatology: The scriptural shaping of imagery in the Book of Revelation

Frances Young

It is a pleasure to acknowledge the success of a former graduate student by writing for a volume celebrating his contribution to a significant aspect of New Testament study – namely, the deep dependence of the earliest Christian texts on the Jewish scriptures. Necessarily specialist research has analysed more and more exactly both quotations and allusions, as well as the implications of their identification for understanding text and context.[1] But here I want to shift discussion to broader hermeneutical concerns: from wording to patterns, parallels and paradigms; from final fulfilment to disclosure and discernment – reading the signs of the times. My perspective on the Book of Revelation comes from reflection on typology and eschatology, neither of which emerges from the last century of scholarship with clear uncontested reference – each demands, therefore, some overview. But the initial inspiration for my approach arose from two key studies, Austin Farrer's book, *A Rebirth of Images* and Richard Bauckham's *The Climax of Prophecy*,[2] neither of which uses the word 'typology', yet underlying typologies often seem presupposed in their treatment of scriptural images in Revelation.

It was decades ago that I picked up Farrer's volume – it proved a memorable moment. The detail of his reconstruction of 'The Making of St. John's Apocalypse' proves unconvincing, with its elaborate schemata in diagrammatic form showing how the Apocalypse unfolds through the Jewish liturgical year and how it draws on supposed synagogue 'lectionaries' while also corresponding to the six-day creation week of Genesis and leading up to the Sabbath/new creation. The problem is not only his frequent need to resort to dubious explanations of hiatuses in his proposed patterns and structures but also the lack of hard evidence: 'Farrer's account of the way John uses the Old Testament is often very speculative and is insufficiently based on comparison with other post-biblical Jewish literature' – as Bauckham puts it.[3] What stayed with me, however, was Farrer's insight into the author's imaginative hermeneutic, as summed up by the following quotations:

---

[1] For example, Steve Moyise, 'The Wilderness Quotation in Mark 1.2-3', in R. S. Sugirtharajah (ed.), *Wilderness: Essays in Honour of Frances Young* (London: Continuum/T&T Clark, 2005), 78–87.
[2] Austin Farrer, *A Rebirth of Images* (Westminster: Dacre Press, 1949); Richard Bauckham, *The Climax of Prophecy* (Edinburgh: T&T Clark, 1993).
[3] Bauckham, *Climax*, 178, n. 9.

- He interpreted: he never copied out 'sources' or used undigested matter or stopped short of the grasp of the ancient scripture which was reborn through his interpretation.[4]
- St. John's images do not mean anything you like; their sense can be determined. But they still have an astonishing multiplicity of reference.[5]
- ... exact prose abstracts from reality, *symbol presents it*. And for that very reason, symbols have some of the many-sidedness of wild nature ... We make no pretence of distinguishing between what was discursively thought and what intuitively conceived in a mind which penetrated its images with intelligence and rooted its intellective acts in imagination.[6]
- For the visions when examined appear to have little to do with the visual imagination, they are 'seen with the mind' ... [in other words] *thought*.[7]
- St. John's, then, is one of those strong minds in which many things meet to be fused and refashioned.[8]

Typology would seem to me to be the heuristic tool which Farrer was implicitly deploying and which could help to uncover the multiple interlocking allusions and overlapping symbols embedded in Revelation; while the insight that 'this is that' roots its message in its present so that its so-called eschatology is in process of realization.

Much more recent has been my acquaintance with Bauckham's work – the corrective which does attend to post-biblical Jewish literature while also noting both the distinctive ways in which John reminds prophetic material from the scriptures and the text's implicit engagement with the then present reality faced by the persecuted churches which it addresses. His identification of allusions to the 'Old Testament' can hardly be bettered, least of all in a brief essay; yet his material has implications for the so-called eschatology of Revelation while also having the potential to be enriched by the tracing of underlying typological assumptions. Before proceeding we need to refine what we mean by those terms: typology and eschatology.

Typology

There are always dangers in reading back from later material, but early Christian exegesis has been my principal research area for more than thirty years, and sometimes it is later more explicit material which illuminates earlier implicit assumptions. Over the course of my career views on typology have shifted substantially. I began with the position current in the mid-twentieth century – promulgated by Daniélou[9] and championed in Anglophone scholarship by Lampe and Woollcombe.[10] Essentially

---

[4] Farrer, *Rebirth*, 19.
[5] Ibid.
[6] Ibid., 20. Italics mine.
[7] Ibid., 304–5.
[8] Ibid., 315.
[9] Jean Daniélou, *Sacramentum Futuri* (Paris: Beauchesne, 1950).
[10] G. W. H. Lampe and K. J. Woollcombe, *Essays on Typology*, SBT 27 (London: SCM Press, 1957).

typology was espoused in contradistinction to allegory, and the claimed difference was that typology, unlike allegory, was grounded in history. Modernity had long since despised allegory as being *eisegesis* not *exegesis*, while at the time both historical research and theological focus were trained on the significance of Christianity as a historical religion. Thus, the claimed link with history meant typology could be treated as respectable, allowing reclamation of some of the symbolic insights of early Christian biblical interpretation.

So that is where I began: with history enabling a clear distinction between typology and allegory. But that distinction soon proved unsustainable in the light of serious research on early Christian exegesis. There were a number of reasons for this:

1. The word 'typology' is a modern coinage with no ancient equivalent: yes, *typoi* were regularly listed along with symbols, parables and other *tropoi* or figures of speech, but to systematize such 'types' as some kind of interpretative 'method' and formally analyse early Christian exegesis in terms of literal, typological and allegorical categories turned out to be a dubious procedure. A 'type' as a figure of speech could simply mean, say, a moral example: Job as a 'type' of patience.
2. No distinction between allegorical interpretation and the discernment of *typoi* can be firmly identified in early Christian practice. They shade into one another and are compounded: they may begin with a basic 'type' – a corresponding pattern – but rapidly all kinds of details get allegorized as the parallel is developed. The point is that a narrative might be treated as prophetic sign, and so, as with any other prophecy, its details could be treated as oracular riddles.
3. Such *typoi* were not always nor straightforwardly events, historical or otherwise. Passover and Passion, Crossing the Red Sea and Baptism, Manna in the desert and Eucharist – all these might at a stretch fit that characterization, but others were surely better treated as mimetic signs: take, for example, Moses anticipating the cross in holding out his arms and as long as he did so his followers were victorious over Amalek. Other types were 'persons' or perhaps 'roles' rather than events: Elijah/John Baptist, Joshua/Jesus, Moses/Christ and so forth. As for the typology of, say, the Epistle to the Hebrews – this interprets the death of Christ as a sacrifice by setting it in parallel with ritual practices prescribed in the written Torah (not as actually practised); this can hardly be justified in terms of events in history.

So the proposed model whereby history differentiates typology from allegory can hardly stand. I concluded at first that typology was not a useful category for the analysis of early Christian exegesis. But that was not the end of the story.[11] The way forward

---

[11] In the first series of Speaker's Lectures in Oxford (1992) I contested typology; in the second series (1993) I reinstated it! The published version, *Biblical Exegesis and the Formation of Christian Culture* (Cambridge: Cambridge University Press, 1997), reached more consistency. A full discussion of these moves is found in Frances Young, 'Typology', in Stanley E. Porter, Paul Joyce and David E. Orton (eds), *Crossing the Boundaries: Essays in Biblical Interpretation in Honour of Michael D. Goulder* (Leiden: Brill, 1994), 29–48.

was signalled by the turn to literary approaches and the reclamation of typology as a heuristic device, a literary trope or a hermeneutical key.[12]

Most significant for the purposes of this immediate discussion is the work of Michael Fishbane.[13] Recognizing that typology belongs to 'classical Christian exegesis' so is potentially 'both anachronistic and methodologically problematic' if used to categorize 'inner-biblical exegesis', he nevertheless suggested that 'the post-biblical phenomena ... help to identify the inner biblical phenomena'.[14] He distinguished various categories, one of which is 'Typologies of a Historical Nature':[15] thus, Joshua 3-5 presents the crossing of the Jordan river in terms of the exodus, while new exodus motifs are found in Isaiah and Jeremiah. 'Typologies of a Biographical Nature'[16] draw parallels with characters, such as Joshua or Moses, in their 'personal traits and personal behaviours': both Noah and Abraham appear in the guise of new Adam, Elijah and Ezekiel in that of new Moses, while Israel is represented by the 'type' of Jacob. This approach was further developed by Walter Moberley, who traces the way in which the Abraham narratives parallel the story of Israel and the exodus.[17] Fishbane also finds 'Typologies of a Spatial Nature',[18] teasing out 'sacred geography' – 2 Chron. 3.1, for example, states that Solomon built the temple on Mount Moriah 'against all historical-geographical likelihood' – that this was where Abraham (almost) sacrificed Isaac is implicit. Eden and Zion in particular provide such spatial typologies, and these are closely associated with Fishbane's primary category, 'Typologies of a Cosmological-Historical Nature':[19] in Isa. 65.17-25 the restoration of Jerusalem appears as 'a recreated world, almost Eden-like', while Isa. 51.9-11 he describes as 'the prophet's *exegetical correlation* between a primordial theomachy and the exodus'. This he treats as eschatological, 'a parallelism ... between the *Urzeit* of origins and the *Endzeit* of hope':

> The mythic prototype ... enables the historical imagination to assess the significance of certain past or present events; and correlatively, it projects a configuration upon future events by which they are anticipated and identified.

This, he suggests, requires a 'reconsideration of the common view that the Israelite apprehension of history is linear only'.

---

[12] See e.g. A. C. Charity, *Events and Their Afterlife* (Cambridge: Cambridge University Press, 1966) – though Charity is still largely wedded to history, as his title suggests; also Tibor Fabiny, *The Lion and the Lamb: Figuralism and Fulfilment in the Bible, Art and Literature* (Basingstoke: Macmillan, 1992), who took up Northrop Frye's interest in typology as explored in *The Great Code: The Bible and Literature* (London: Routledge and Kegan Paul, 1982) – both, in common with then current theological suppositions, treated typology as about 'real or supposedly real historical events' (Fabiny, *Lion and the Lamb*, 2), but they shifted attention from such events to the texts and their import.
[13] Michael Fishbane, *Biblical Interpretation in Ancient Israel* (Oxford: Clarendon, 1985).
[14] Ibid., 350-1.
[15] Ibid., 358-68.
[16] Ibid., 372-9.
[17] R. W. L. Moberley, *The Old Testament of the Old Testament: Patriarchal Narratives and Mosaic Yahwism* (Minneapolis, MN: Fortress, 1992), 142-6.
[18] Fishbane, *Biblical Interpretation*, 368-72.
[19] Ibid., 354-7; the quotations in succeeding sentences are drawn from the discussion in these pages.

Fishbane's discussion implies 'typological composition' – literary shaping to bring out correspondences, making the claim that 'this is that'. It also demonstrates that typology was not necessarily tied to history and 'events' – it might in a variety of ways be symbolic; despite his tendency still to assume that history and eschatology are fundamental to typology (his use of the terms *Urzeit* and *Endzeit* points in that direction), Fishbane uncovers a variety of 'mimetic' possibilities – implicit signs whose discernment generated a sense of disclosure or revelation, keys to the signs of the times. Indeed, as a kind of prophetic genre typology may imply fulfilment but not necessarily finality – its message is for the here and now.

The significance of biblical typology as conveying a contemporary message had already been highlighted by A. C. Charity. It was not just an exegetical tool:

> Its employment is all for the sake of the now, the present situation, the present or coming event the announcement of which it helps to articulate.[20]

It worked with a tension between 'divine initiative' and 'divine steadfastness'.[21] But it also demanded response:

> Prediction, and typological prediction, is not the final object of prophecy or typology. They have existential objectives, they relate to the 'now' of decision … The end-time is made to appear almost present in many passages, in order that the disobedient and complacent nation may realize her situation and, perhaps, take the opportunity of repentance.[22]

It is fundamental to Charity's argument that typology was 'imperative' and not simply 'indicative' – not just 'descriptive of the presented relation between acts of God' or a mere statement of 'correspondences' but rather 'demand' – for the 'signs' may be 'rejected' or acted upon.[23]

What I will dare to suggest, then, is this: that by following these leads, especially Fishbane's, and so reading back certain early Christian typologies into Revelation, we may discover key messages and perspectives underlying its surface allusions.

Two key interlocking typologies in early Christianity

Let me outline a classic early Christian example of typological composition, namely Melito's *Peri Pascha*. A second-century text, rediscovered during the twentieth century and at first understood to be a homily, it has convincingly been shown to be a Christian

---

[20] Charity, *Events and Their Afterlife*, 98.
[21] Ibid., 28.
[22] Ibid., 71–2.
[23] Ibid., 80.

Passover Haggadah – a liturgy to be used on 14th Nisan at the same time as Jews everywhere were sharing their Passover meal.[24]

The text begins by noting that the scriptures describing the Hebrew exodus have been read – how the sheep was sacrificed, the people saved and Pharoah overcome. Then it states that this mystery is both old and new, eternal and provisional – old with respect to the law, new with respect to the Word, provisional with respect to the 'type', yet everlasting through grace. The text ends with an invitation from Christ:

> So come all families of people,
> Adulterated with sin,
> And receive forgiveness of sins.
> For I am your freedom.
> I am the Passover of salvation.
> I am the lamb slaughtered for you.
> I am your ransom,
> I am your life,
> I am your light, I am your salvation.
> I am your resurrection.[25]

This concluding summary presupposes what Melito has throughout made clear – that through Adam humankind had been enslaved in the Egypt of sin and death, subjected to Pharoah = the devil, and that the blood of the lamb enabled escape. The Passover sacrifice had originally nothing to do with the forgiveness of sins. The connection was made by the interlocking of two typologies – the reimagining of Passover/Exodus in terms of Christ's reversal of Adam's Fall, the latter being a typology already found in the Pauline epistles.

Elsewhere[26] I have suggested that the earliest understanding of the cross was through this Passover/exodus typology, with the interlocking of these types implicit, occasionally explicit. I hardly need rehearse in detail the New Testament precursors to the Passover-type, but they include:

- The Johannine saying attributed to John the Baptist – 'Behold the lamb of God that takes away the sin of the world';
- The association of manna, the bread of life and the eucharist in John 6;
- The Johannine dating of the crucifixion, whereby Jesus dies at the time the Passover lambs were slaughtered in the Temple in preparation for the Passover meal: Jn 18.28; 19.14;

---

[24] Alistair Stewart-Sykes, *The Lamb's High Feast: Melito,* Peri Pascha *and the Quartodeciman Paschal Liturgy at Sardis* (Leiden: Brill, 1998).
[25] *Peri Pascha*, 103.
[26] Frances Young, *Construing the Cross: Type, Sign, Symbol, Word, Action*, Didsbury Lecture Series (Eugene, OR: Cascade Books, 2015; London: SPCK, 2016); cf. also Tom Wright, *The Day the Revolution Began: Rethinking the Meaning of Jesus' Crucifixion* (London: SPCK, 2016), though he explains Passover's acquired link with sin through the enhanced consciousness of sin induced by the exile.

- Jn 19.31 – an explicit allusion to the direction not to break the bones of the Passover lamb (Exod. 12.46);
- 1 Cor. 5.7 – Christ our Passover is sacrificed for us;
- 1 Cor. 11.23-34 and the Last Supper narratives in the Synoptic Gospels;
- Hebrews' use of Psalm 95; and
- The lamb slain in the Book of Revelation.

Typology and eschatology

The parallels between the two saving events are drawn out through Melito's text, and in an important digression Melito explains the notion of 'type'. Any creative composition is preceded by a sketch or prototype – a draft or model, which is not the finished work but indicates what is to be: it is a preliminary outline made in wax, clay or wood which represents the completed statue or whatever is planned. That will be much bigger, stronger and better. The type bears the likeness of the reality to come but then becomes obsolete; what was once valuable becomes worthless. So, Melito suggests, the Lord's salvation was prefigured in the people of God, the gospel in the law; but once the church and the gospel arose the type was depleted, the law fulfilled, and they gave up their meaning to the gospel and the church.[27] Surely fulfilment here is not so much eschatological as supersessionary – the claim to a new beginning. It is time we considered our second contested term.

Strictly speaking the word 'eschatology' refers to the 'last things' – the final judgement and the end of the world. It implies finality but became more ambiguous in twentieth-century scholarship, often signifying an ultimacy less time related. The story has, of course, been told many times, but a reminder can open up the issues as they impinge on the current argument. It was Schweitzer's reaction to the nineteenth-century liberal lives of Jesus which put 'throroughgoing eschatology' on the scholarly map.[28] The tendency had been to play down miracles and reduce the teaching of Jesus to 'the Fatherhood of God and the Brotherhood of Man' (as classically stated), with an ethic of love and a notion of God's kingdom as a spiritual realm gradually expanding; against this Schweitzer set Jesus in an apocalyptic context, framing him as an eschatological prophet proclaiming the end of the world, the Day of Judgement, the coming of the Son of Man. When it did not happen his plans were modified: he journeyed to Jerusalem to take on the 'Messianic woes' so that the kingdom of God might break in. The predictions of the Parousia and the apocalyptic material in the gospels were to be taken with the utmost seriousness.

Ensuing debate led to a certain acceptance that Schweitzer was right, and as a consequence the delay of the Parousia was assumed to have had a determinative effect on emerging Christian writings. Yet there was also a sense that such a literal reading of particular gospel texts was neither adequate nor comprehensive. C. H. Dodd pointed to material which suggests the presence of the kingdom already, proposing a 'realised

---

[27] *Peri Pascha*, 36–46.
[28] A. Schweitzer, *The Quest of the Historical Jesus*, 2nd edn (London: A & C Black, 1936).

eschatology';[29] others, pursuing similar lines, refined this to 'inaugurated eschatology', 'now and not yet'.[30] Emphasis was placed on the claims to fulfilment, the immediate crisis: judgement already happening as the people responded to Jesus and his message, eschatology realizing itself. It is hardly surprising that Bultmann could turn this into the immediacy of decision for or against Christ, shifting the emphasis from God's action bringing history to its climax to an existential ultimatum – for 'in early Christianity history is swallowed up in eschatology'.[31]

> According to the New Testament *Jesus Christ is the eschatological event* (original italics), the action of God by which God has set an end to the old world ... The old world has reached its end for the believer, he is 'a new creature in Christ'.
>
> ... the eschatological event, according to Paul and John, is not to be understood as a dramatic cosmic catastrophe but a happening within history ... It becomes an event repeatedly in preaching and faith ... Jesus Christ is the eschatological event not as an established fact of past time but as repeatedly present, as addressing you and me here and now in preaching. Preaching is address, and as address it demands answer, *decision* (original italics).[32]

This divorce between history and eschatology has inevitably encountered sharp rejoinder, not least from Tom Wright. For him, however, the ultimate revolution has already happened on the cross; the New Testament is not about the end of the space-time universe but a new world order.[33]

So does 'eschatology' still have any kind of clear reference? And might we achieve greater clarity by focussing on the notion of 'fulfilment'? Perhaps neither typology nor eschatology need imply finality in an end-of-the-world sense but rather point to the fulfilment of hopes and promises for a new start based on recognition in the present of prophetic words or signs ('this' is 'that'), which provide renewed assurance that God's ultimate purposes are now in the process of being worked out.

Further exploration of the Adam-Christ typology suggests again that typology is not necessarily to be understood in strictly eschatological terms. True, Irenaeus maps out the once for all recapitulation and reversal of Adam's testing in the garden of Eden:

> For it was necessary for Adam to be recapitulated in Christ, that 'mortality might be swallowed up in immortality'; and Eve in Mary, that a virgin ... might undo and destroy the virginal disobedience by virginal obedience. And the transgression which occurred through the tree was undone by the obedience of the tree.[34]

---

[29] C. H. Dodd, *The Parables of the Kingdom* (London: Nisbet, 1935).
[30] Cf. e.g. N. Perrin, *The Kingdom of God in the Teaching of Jesus* (London: SCM Press, 1963).
[31] Rudolf Bultmann, *History and Eschatology: The Gifford Lectures 1955* (Edinburgh: Edinburgh University Press, 1957), 37.
[32] Ibid., 151–2.
[33] Wright, *The Day the Revolution Began*; and N. T. Wright, *History and Eschatology* (London: SPCK, 2019).
[34] *Dem. Evang.* 33.

Certainly this was to be read as a new start for humanity. But Adam was also taken as universal 'type'. In the *Hymns on Paradise* by Ephrem the Syrian, for example, we find 'the king of Babylon resembled Adam king of the universe' and in David 'did God depict Adam' – 'because it was not easy for us to see our fallen state ... He depicted it all together in that king, portraying in his fall our fall, and portraying our return in his repentant return.'[35] In succeeding stanzas Samson, Jonah, Joseph all become 'types' of Fall and Redemption. Likewise in the Pentateuchal exegesis of Cyril of Alexandria, the narratives of descent into Egypt and escape, whether those about Abraham or the children of Israel, become types of universal Fall and Redemption.[36]

The notion, then, of Christ's recapitulation and reversal of Adam's testing in the Garden of Eden was taken to shape the overarching scriptural narrative of Fall and Redemption, and this typological pattern was discerned all over scripture. Furthermore typology thus drew the hearer/reader into this narrative, which was fulfilled as it was replayed in the life of everyone. In what sense if any might this be treated as 'eschatological'? Perhaps only in the somewhat Bultmannian sense that the reader's response would prove ultimate.

Typology in the Book of Revelation

If we were limited to Revelation for our understanding of apocalyptic, we would probably get the impression that symbolism and extravagant imagery were some of the hallmarks of apocalyptic. In this respect at least, the New Testament Apocalypse is not typical of the rest of Jewish apocalyptic literature.[37]

The symbolism which, according to Chris Rowland, is recognizably distinctive of the Book of Revelation surely justifies Farrar's turn to deciphering imagery, and the sources of that imagery are certainly more often than not to be found in the Old Testament. What Richard Bauckham does is further illuminate those sources, and as I read his work, I was struck by the implicit typological relationships.

Let us begin with the most obvious, the Lamb slain. Bauckham's discussion opens by noting the contrast between the Lion and the Lamb in Rev. 5.5-6 and then draws attention to 'the third image in these verses: the Root of David'. The question concerning 'the true Messiah' is at stake. Gen. 49.9 (the Lion) and Isa. 11.1 (the Root) were classic texts for 'Jewish messianic hopes', both implying the conquest of nations, as Bauckham documents. This Revelation appropriated, but here 'the Lion of Judah appears as a lamb'.

---

[35] Ephrem, *Hymns on Paradise* XIII.4, 5–7; translation slightly amended to correspond with the line following 'and portraying our return in his repentant return'.

[36] See my chapter, '*Theotokos*: Mary and the Pattern of Fall and Redemption in the Theology of Cyril of Alexandria', in Thomas G. Weinandy and Daniel A. Keating (eds), *The Theology of Cyril of Alexandria: A Critical Appreciation* (London: T&T Clark, 2003), 55–74. Republished in my collected papers, *Exegesis and Theology in Early Christianity* (Farnham: Ashgate/Variorum, 2012).

[37] Christopher Rowland, *The Open Heaven: A Study of Apocalyptic in Judaism and Early Christianity* (London: SPCK, 1982), 61.

> The notion of messianic conquest is reinterpreted. Jesus Christ *is* the Lion of Judah and the Root of David, but John 'sees' him as the Lamb. Precisely by juxtaposing these contrasting images, John forges a symbol of conquest by sacrificial death which is essentially a new symbol.[38]

Against some previous scholarship Bauckham emphasizes the novelty of 'the notion of a sacrificial lamb as a conqueror'. The Passover lamb is likely to be the primary reference, he suggests, noting how much new exodus motifs are to be found in this work; and he concludes: 'The vision of the Lamb therefore portrays the manner of Christ's victory: through death.'[39]

What, then, was this victory? Bauckham next explores the Dragon.

> John was concerned, in common with contemporary Jewish apocalypses, about the victory of God over the forces of evil as they manifested themselves in his contemporary world. The oppressive power of Rome, the Imperial cult, the corrupt civilization of Rome are all portrayed, in a series of vivid images, as enemies who fall before the conquering Lamb and his people.[40]

But this is now envisaged as 'the conquest of all evil' – 'the fall of Satan himself' effected through the death of Christ, 'the decisive blow at the forces which inspire the Beast'.[41] Gathering Old Testament references to Leviathan, or the dragon, Bauckham builds a picture of the chaos-dragon as an image of the powers opposed to God, which in Revelation is identified as the 'ancient serpent who is called the Devil and Satan, the deceiver of the whole world' (Rev. 12.9). Bauckham has found 'no Jewish precedent for this representation of ultimate evil, the devil, as "the great dragon" '[42] and draws out the implied association between Leviathan and the serpent of Genesis 3. A range of associations give the dragon-symbol power – not only the Eden-narrative but also its pagan associations in the cities of Asia to which the book is addressed.

> Just as in 5:5–6 he showed the crucified Christ as the unexpected fulfilment of Jewish hopes of a messianic conqueror, so he was ready to take up also whatever pagan symbol might embody an aspiration of divine triumph over evil and show the crucified Christ as the Dragon-slayer.[43]

What I would like to suggest is that Bauckham's illuminating discussion and references are all the more telling set in the context of those interrelated typologies already discussed – explicit in Melito, implicit in earlier New Testament material. The blood of Christ, the Passover lamb, enables both victory over the serpent – the embodiment of evil, the Satan – and escape from the Egypt of idolatry and sin

---

[38] Bauckham, *Climax*, 183.
[39] Ibid., 184.
[40] Ibid., 185.
[41] Ibid., 193.
[42] Ibid.
[43] Ibid., 198.

which was initiated in Eden. This suggestion becomes even more compelling when consideration is given not only to the frequent traces of Exodus motifs in Revelation but also to the ultimate vision in chapter 22 of a restored Eden where the tree of life is for the healing of the nations.

For the two basic intertwined typologies tended to take on and integrate further symbolic motifs. Already in Isaiah, as earlier we found Fishbane observing, Zion restored was envisaged in Eden-like terms, a new heaven and earth, a new beginning. Thus it is hardly surprising that Eden restored in Revelation 21–22 takes the form of the heavenly city – an example of Farrer's melding of images with multiple references, all integrated, I suggest, into that basic twofold salvific typology. Similar associations are made in II Esdras:

> For for you
> is opened Paradise,
> planted the Tree of life;
> the future Age prepared,
> plenteousness made ready;
> a City builded,
> a Rest appointed.[44]

In Revelation the city is without a temple; for, as on Sinai, the presence of God, and here also the presence of the Lamb, pervades and illuminates its entirety. Thus, Jerusalem, Eden and Sinai cluster together to provide symbolic focus on the restoration of true worship and the reversal of humankind's idolatrous subservience to the power of evil.

And the mention of Sinai draws us back to those Exodus motifs running through Revelation. Bauckham comments:

> Like the psalmists he thought of the whole Exodus event from the plagues of Egypt to the conquest of Canaan as one great manifestation of God's power to judge the nations and to deliver his people.[45]

Most obvious in Revelation is the series of seven plagues, but the trumpets and bowls may recall the fall of Jericho. Bauckham also draws particular attention to the earthquake motif; linked with theophany it is often

> part of a cosmic quake: the whole universe, firmament, heavenly bodies, earth, sea and the foundations of the world tremble at the coming of God.[46]

This he establishes with references to many texts, particularly focussing on Sinai. If largely absent from Exodus 19–20 and Deuteronomy, 'the theophany imagery of

---

[44] II Esdras (IV Ezra) viii.52; R. H. Charles, *Apocrypha and Pseudepigrapha of the Old Testament* (Oxford: Clarendon Press, 1913), vol. II, 587–8.
[45] Bauckham, *Climax*, 205.
[46] Ibid., 199.

thunderstorm and earthquake' is developed in psalms and prophets and later texts, especially apocalyptic. 'God's redemptive acts in the future are portrayed on the model of his past acts' – in other words, typologically. So, in Revelation, earthquakes allude to the Sinai theophany and herald the coming of God in judgement.[47] In particular, stereotyped phrases, compounded from Exod. 19.16 and Ezekiel's chariot vision (Ezek. 1.13), punctuate the book at Rev. 4.5; 8.5; 11.19 and 16.18-21.[48]

Another link is found in the Song of Moses: Rev. 15.3 echoes Exod. 14.31, though how the Song that follows relates to Moses's Song in Exodus 15 is problematic. But Bauckham makes a good case for reading it in terms of a new exodus:[49] God delivers the people by judging their enemies and leading all nations to acknowledge that God is king; the beast is overcome through the Lamb's victory. One might further rehearse Bauckham's discussion of Elijah and Moses as models for (= types of) the two witnesses in Rev. 11.3-13, with allusions to their confrontations with paganism – Moses and the magicians, Elijah and the prophets of Baal.[50] As Bauckham notes the witnesses move beyond these precedents in being martyrs, and their story follows the pattern of Jesus's crucifixion and resurrection: thus they participate in the victory of the Lamb. But again, I suggest, it is by the melding of typologies that new insights are generated and expectations re-fashioned.

Eschatology in the Book of Revelation

Typological insight is often about the present, discerning that 'this is that', sensing the *kairos*, the moment of *krisis*, the signs that God is now working out the divine purposes, and so suggesting the demand for present repentance, present commitment. It is a way by which people could read themselves into a fresh replaying of scripture. Typology implies fulfilment but, as we have seen, does not necessarily indicate finality; what is termed eschatology turns out to be hope for a new beginning, which may well imply the end of the old corrupt order but, as Tom Wright has argued, not necessarily the end of the space-time universe.

One striking thing about Bauckham's study is his emphasis on the message of this text for the people of John's own day – it is to enable them to 'perceive … their vocation and their destiny'.[51] It is not meant to be prophecy in the sense of prediction but prophecy calling the faithful to perseverance and hope, to assurance that God is at work, that Christ is the one promised, that the victory has been accomplished, though not through holy war but by sacrificial death. What we have called eschatology might actually be discernment of such hope through identifying the signs of God's current activity, signs recognized through typology, through a fresh mimetic replay of God's past acts of deliverance, through the reversal of Adam's failure and the

---

[47] Ibid., 200-2.
[48] Ibid., 202.
[49] Ibid., 296-307.
[50] Ibid., 277-83.
[51] Ibid., 169.

restoration of true worship. It is this hope, fundamental to early Christian re-reading of the scriptures, which Revelation's prophet discovers by perceiving the death and resurrection of Christ as the fulfilment of scripture's promises and then presenting it through the power of resonant images.

2

Smells like teen spirit: Steve Moyise and G. K. Beale on the use of scripture in Revelation in the 1990s

Garrick V. Allen

I grew up in Seattle in the 1990s. When I think about this decade as an era in my childhood I conjure images of the grunge aesthetic: lots of flannel, ill-fitting ripped jeans, hoodless sweatshirts tied around your waist, baseball in the Kingdome and, of course, Nirvana. When I think about this period as a scholar (a much less nostalgic prospect), my thoughts instantly go to the formative debate between Steve Moyise and G. K. Beale surrounding the use of scripture in Revelation, an association created by my own work on this topic.[1] I will not try to argue that Steve Moyise is the Kurt Cobain of 'Old Testament in the New' type studies (although maybe he is the Dave Grohl), but that the 1990s, capsulized in their exchange, were essentially the grunge era for this type of research. It is the period in which something new emerged that set the stage for what followed, something that continues to have resonance today. The breadth of critical approaches to the use of Jewish scripture in the Book of Revelation that have emerged since the 1990s is due in large part to Moyise's adoption of intertextuality as a literary-critical way of understanding the evidence. The proliferation of studies on this topic can be traced to Moyise's stimulating polemical interaction with Beale on methodological and hermeneutical issues.

Moyise's own work and defence of his approach in the face of vociferous pushback from a loquacious interlocutor created a permission structure to explore this question in new ways, inviting further engagement with intertextual and other critical approaches, along with many unforeseen developments.[2] Just as we understand the Foo Fighters

---

[1] For example, Garrick V. Allen, *The Book of Revelation and Early Jewish Textual Culture* (Cambridge: Cambridge University Press, 2017); Garrick V. Allen, 'Scriptural Allusions in the Book of Revelation and the Contours of Textual Research 1900–2014: Retrospect and Prospects', *CBR* 14 (2016): 319–39; Garrick V. Allen, 'Textual Pluriformity and Allusion in the Book of Revelation: The Text of Zechariah 4 in the Apocalypse', *ZNW* 106 (2015): 136–45.

[2] For examples of intertextual and other critical-theoretical approaches see Michelle Fletcher, *Reading Revelation as Pastiche: Imitating the Past* (London: T&T Clark, 2018); David M. Allen, *Deuteronomy and Exhortation in Hebrews: A Study in Narrative Re-presentation* (Tübingen: Mohr Siebeck, 2009); Steve Smith, *The Fate of the Jerusalem Temple in Luke-Acts: An Intertextual Approach to Jesus' Lament over Jerusalem and Stephen's Speech* (London: T&T Clark, 2018).

better by listening to Nirvana, so too do we understand the shape of enquiry into John's use of scripture today by returning to one of the foundational critical discussions that has shaped the field in significant ways. Nirvana's lyrics are notoriously difficult to comprehend; so too are the underlying stakes of the debate between Moyise and Beale. But their discussion remains important because the seeds of the field as we know it today already existed within it.

The main point that I want to make is that the extended debate between Moyise and Beale was not really primarily about understanding the ways that the author of Revelation referenced and made use of literary material from Jewish scripture. Of course Beale, Moyise and others who engaged Revelation in this period were genuinely interested to understand what John was doing,[3] why the Apocalypse is so replete with allusions and what this meant for its interpretation in antiquity and today. And there are multiple places where Beale and Moyise disagree on how to interpret the textual data and the viability of particular proposed references.[4] But these concerns are superficial, representing ways of getting at their underlying critical differences. The substratum of this debate concerns a number of interlocking issues, including the nature of scripture, the value of historical-critical exegesis, the role of canonical ideologies and theological hermeneutics. Modern theological discussions on the nature of scripture stand at the core of the discussion; John's use of these traditions is a vector for this modern debate. These discussions play themselves out within the boundaries of the 'Use of the New Testament in the Old' discourse, but the real areas of contention live in the background, only occasionally coming to the surface in their direct engagement, even if they can now be seen clearly in Beale's subsequent work in particular. Within this framework we learn much about the finer points of John's various allusive practices but only as a by-product of a larger critical discussion.

This observation is not new.[5] Moyise himself makes a similar statement in his introductory book, noting that 'evangelical scholarship is naturally interested in how the New Testament uses the Old Testament since one of its main tenets is the unity of scripture'.[6] And as we will see in more detail, Beale has been very explicit about the

---

[3] For example, J.-P. Ruiz, *Ezekiel in the Apocalypse: The Transformation of Prophetic Language in Revelation 16.17–19.10* (Frankfurt: Peter Lang, 1989); Jan Fekkes, *Isaiah and Prophetic Traditions in the Book of Revelation* (Sheffield: Sheffield Academic Press, 1994); Jon Paulien, *Decoding Revelation's Trumpets: Literary Allusions and the Interpretation of Revelation 8:7–12* (Berrien Springs, MI: Andrews University Press, 1987).

[4] For example, Moyise dismisses Beale's construal of Revelation 1, 4–5, 13, 17 as midrash on Daniel 7 as 'forced'. See Steve Moyise, *The Old Testament in the Book of Revelation* (Sheffield: Sheffield Academic Press, 1995), 60–1, and his critique of G. K. Beale, *The Use of Daniel in Jewish Apocalyptic Literature and in the Revelation of St. John* (Lanham, MD: University of America Press, 1984) (repr. Eugene, OR: Wipf and Stock). Beale stridently responds to Moyise's critiques in *John's Use of the Old Testament in Revelation*, JSNTSup166 (Sheffield: Sheffield Academic Press, 1998), 41–59, a pattern of response to criticism that has continued. See G. K. Beale, 'Questions of Authorial Intent, Epistemology, and Presuppositions and Their Bearing on the Study of the Old Testament in the New: A Rejoinder to Steve Moyise', *IBS* 21 (1999): 152–80; G. K. Beale, 'The Old Testament in Colossians: A Response to Paul Foster', *JSNT* 41 (2018): 261–74.

[5] I am also not the first person to intervene into the debate between Beale and Moyise: see Jon Paulien, 'Dreading the Whirlwind: Intertextuality and the Use of the Old Testament in Revelation', *AUSS* 39 (2001): 5–22.

[6] Steve Moyise, *The Old Testament in the New: An Introduction*, 2nd edn (London: Bloomsbury, 2015), 9. See also Steve Moyise, 'Does the NT Quote the OT out of Context?', *Anvil* 11 (1994): 133–43: OT

apologetic stakes of this conversation, going so far as to suggest that 'if Jesus and the apostles were impoverished in their exegetical and theological method and only divine inspiration salvaged their conclusions, then the intellectual and apologetic foundation of our faith is seriously eroded. What kind of intellectual or apologetic foundation for our faith is this?'[7] This concern for the nature and consistency of scripture is certainly not illegitimate. But I want to advance the idea that, although this focus bracketed off for a time important critical questions that John's use of Jewish scripture might inform, the nascent forms of the next two decades of scholarship are largely contained within this exchange. These new developments include a renewed focus on the textual form of Jewish scripture in antiquity, John's exegetical repertoire and the reception of his allusive compositional practices within subsequent literature, art and media. Before chasing up these developments, however, it is important to summarize the debate that, in part, contributed to the rise of these new critical focal points.

Beale and Moyise on John's use of scripture, or Beale and Moyise on hermeneutics

In 1984, Beale published his 1980 Cambridge doctoral thesis as *The Use of Daniel in Jewish Apocalyptic Literature and in the Revelation of St. John*.[8] Although a handful of studies had appeared on this topic in the mid-twentieth century,[9] Beale's work sparked renewed interest in the way that the New Testament authors engaged Jewish scripture, a trend that continues today. The book is characterized by a number of related concerns, including criteria for identifying allusions and other instances of reuse, questions of authorial intention and, most pointedly, the question of whether ancient authors 'respected' the contexts of the works they reused. Ultimately, Beale concludes that large sections of the Book of Revelation are structured by and modelled upon the Book of Daniel, especially Daniel 7. These sections constitute midrashim on Daniel; Rev. 1.8-20, for example, is 'a "midrash" on these two chapters from Daniel [7 and 10]', and other scriptural material in this section has been used to 'supplement the Daniel midrash'.[10] More significantly, the Book of Revelation, along with other apocalyptic traditions, uses Daniel 'in a manner harmonious with the context of Daniel itself'.[11]

---

in the NT 'presents a particular challenge to the upholders of the inspiration of Scripture' because we cannot now always accept that the 'OT passage [has] the meaning assigned to it by the NT author' (133).

[7] G. K. Beale, 'Positive Answer to the Question Did Jesus and His Followers Preach the Right Doctrine from the Wrong Texts? An Examination of the Presuppositions of Jesus' and Apostles' Exegetical Method', in G. K. Beale (ed.), *The Right Doctrine from the Wrong Text? Essays on the Use of the Old Testament in the New* (Grand Rapids, MI: Baker, 1994), 387–404 (404).

[8] G. K. Beale, *The Use of Daniel in Jewish Apocalyptic Literature and in the Revelation of St. John* (Lanham, MD: University of America Press, 1984).

[9] For example, Adolf Schlatter, *Das alte Testament in der johanneischen Apokalypse* (Gütersloh: Mohn, 1912); and Albert Vanhoye, 'L'utilisation du livre d'Ézéchiel dans l'Apocalypse', *Biblica* 43 (1962): 436–76, among others.

[10] Beale, *Use of Daniel*, 171, 173.

[11] Ibid., 309, see also 327.

This holds true for Daniel in the Qumran material as well due to Daniel's eschatological orientation: 'the Qumran writers did not have to twist its original meaning, as was often the case with their use of other non-eschatological O.T. books.'[12]

Beale's book clearly demonstrates Daniel's influence on the production of apocalyptic literature in early Judaism and Christianity, and it identifies the main points of contention for understanding scriptural reuse, even if the exegetical techniques that he identifies are not unique to apocalypses.[13] And although it is not explicitly confessional in any sense,[14] the book carries with it a number of hints at where the theological aspects of Beale's research were headed. We begin to see these inklings in the fact that Beale draws a strict division between ancient Jewish and Christian exegesis, the former being largely 'atomistic' and the latter entirely 'contextual'. This idea is explicit in places[15] but also seen in the larger structure of the study that begins with his examination of the relevant Danielic passages, using these results as a stick to measure the contextuality of other ancient instances of reuse.[16] By beginning with his own contextualization of Daniel, ancient instances of reuse are automatically set against his historical-critical reading.[17] This approach leads Beale to see the concept of 'context' as a broad phenomenon, even appealing to the idea of an 'ironic use' of Daniel when later texts seem to use Daniel in the exact opposite way it was meant in its original context (according to Beale's reckoning).[18] The overriding importance of context in the study shows that larger theological issues associated with canon and biblical consistency are lingering not too far below the surface.[19]

---

[12] Ibid., 327.

[13] Beale argues for a specific 'apocalyptic method of O.T. usage' (ibid., 3), but as many have argued since, early Jewish and Christian exegesis shared an ambient textual culture predicated on a number of shared literary and interpretive practices. See e.g. Jonathan D. H. Norton, *Contours in the Text: Textual Variation in the Writings of Paul, Josephus and the Yahad*, LNTS 430 (London: T&T Clark, 2011).

[14] Unlike some recent studies that continue in a similar methodological vein, e.g. Bret A. Rogers, *Jesus as the Pierced One: Zechariah 12:10 in John's Gospel and Revelation* (Eugene, OR: Pickwick, 2020).

[15] Beale, *Use of Daniel*, 327.

[16] Ibid., 12–22.

[17] This is a problem that is, at least to my mind, endemic to 'OT in the NT' type studies because it creates a study that is a really a mirror that allows us to test historical-critical exegesis against ancient interpretive practices. It is no wonder that some ancient authors do not share our own interpretive proclivities, but it is unfair to characterize their treatment of scriptural sources as 'atomistic' or lacking in sensitivity to context. Beale's discussion of the use of Daniel in column 1 of 1QM is a good example of this dynamic at play (ibid., 60–6). See further, Allen, *Book of Revelation*, 20–37; William A. Tooman, *Gog of Magog: Reuse of Scripture and Compositional Technique in Ezekiel 38–39* (Tübingen: Mohr Siebeck, 2011), 15–17.

[18] Beale, *Use of Daniel*, 320–3. G. K. Beale, *The Book of Revelation: A Commentary on the Greek Text*, NIGTC (Cambridge: Eerdmans, 1999), 94–6, refers to this phenomenon as 'inverted uses'.

[19] This idea is reinforced further by Beale's appeal to anachronistic canonical language, a problem that stands at the very centre of this discourse. Not only is the collocation 'the use of the Old Testament in the New' anachronistic (neither the Old Testament nor New existed in any concrete sense in the first century), but Beale assumes that Daniel was 'canonized scripture' for the Qumran community (Beale, *Use of Daniel*, 41), referring specifically to the adoption of the '*pesher* method'. His view becomes explicit in Beale, 'Positive Answer', 401: 'if we assume the legitimacy of an inspired canon, the new should seek to interpret any part of that canon within its overall canonical context (given that one divine mind stands behind it all and expresses its thoughts in logical fashion).'

Moyise's monograph *The Old Testament in the Book of Revelation* appeared about a decade later in 1995.[20] Following Julia Kristeva and others, the book introduces the concept of 'intertextuality' into the discussion, arguing for a dialogical, interactive relationship between New Testament texts that reuse the Old Testament and the Old Testament itself. Moyise tests whether 'intertextuality can shed any light on John's allusive use of Scripture',[21] acknowledging that instances of textual reference always recontextualize the reused utterance. The question then becomes not "has the author respected the context" but 'in what ways do the contexts interact? ... has the author chosen a quotation or allusion which leads to "harmonies", or does it simply produce "interference?"'[22] More foundationally, Moyise problematizes the idea of respect for context, noting that what may appear an arbitrary redeployment of scriptural material to us may actually reflect legitimate contextual engagement to someone like John. Conceptions of context are multifaceted, mediated by a number of historical, cultural and textual practices. Overall, Moyise sees the genius of Revelation not in terms of John's ability to create something new out of old language but in his juxtaposition of two contexts through incessant allusion. The interpreter's task, then, 'is to give an account of how these two contexts potentially affect one another'.[23] Moyise is not offering a new method but a way to co-read Revelation next to the traditions it engages, attempting to reframe the discussion: it is not a hermeneutical question about reading inspired texts but a pragmatic question of literary interpretation.[24]

It is no surprise that Moyise's implied critique of theological exegesis also addresses Beale's work directly, focusing primarily on the more indulgent aspects of Beale's descriptions of John's reuse, along with his overemphasis on Daniel as the controlling frame of the work. He rejects Beale's characterization of sections of Revelation as a midrash on Daniel, arguing specifically that this argument for Revelation 4–5 is 'sleight of hand' and that 'it certainly goes well beyond the evidence to conclude that the whole of Revelation is to be "conceived of ultimately within the framework of Daniel"'.[25] This direct engagement, however, is not the most threatening to Beale's project; it is Moyise's fundamental reorientation of 'OT in the NT' studies towards a more literary (and less theological or historical-critical) approach that implicitly calls into question Beale's method and conclusions. The locus of meaning in John's reuse is not found in the original context of the references but in the 'new figuration' that John has created, creations 'whereby the old words are given a new context and principally derive their meaning from that'.[26]

Beale's initial response to Moyise's study appeared as a lengthy section of his collection of reworked essays entitled *John's Use of the Old Testament in Revelation*

---

[20] Moyise, *Old Testament in the Book of Revelation*, JSNTSup 115.
[21] Ibid., 18.
[22] Ibid., 19–20.
[23] Ibid., 135.
[24] See also, Moyise, 'Out of Context', 141.
[25] Moyise, *Old Testament*, 61, 62, the latter quoting Beale, *Use of Daniel*, 277. On his critique of Beale's use of 'midrash', see Moyise, *Old Testament*, 63 n.40.
[26] Moyise, *Old Testament*, 115.

in 1998.[27] His response to Moyise (and others) is unusually strident, suggesting to me that the stakes, at least for Beale, are high. According to Beale, Moyise's goal is 'not to provide a thorough exegetical analysis of any aspect of John's use of the Old Testament, but to focus on the kind of hermeneutical approach one should take toward understanding the allusions'.[28] Moyise's conclusion that John's allusions create a two-way interpretive pathway is ultimately, however, 'somewhat general and vague'.[29] The underlying problem with Moyise's approach, Beale claimed, is not his exegetical issues or hermeneutical frame but his inability to recognize John's four overriding (and unacknowledged) presuppositions:

> (1) Christ corporately represents true Israel of the Old and New Testament; (2) history is unified by a wise and sovereign plan, so that the earlier parts of canonical history are designed to correspond typologically and point to latter parts of inscripturated history; (3) the age of end-time fulfillment has been inaugurated with Christ's first coming; and (4) in the light of points 2 and 3, the later parts of biblical history interpret earlier parts ... so that Christ as the centre of history is the key to interpreting the earlier portions of the Old Testament.[30]

If these presuppositions are granted to John, then he must have treated the Old Testament contextually; if they are mistaken, then John's interpretations must be seen as 'foreign to the original intention of the Old Testament writers', a conclusion that Beale cannot countenance.[31] Even though Beale simply assumes the veracity of these highly specific presuppositions – views that appear to me to stand very close to Beale's own view of scripture as far as I can reckon it from his writings – it is incumbent upon Moyise to have intuited them as well. 'If Moyise had been cognizant of these presuppositions, he might not have been so persuaded to see unresolvable tensions of interpretation within the Apocalypse.'[32] These presuppositions resolve all potential interpretive problems; the puzzle pieces fall into place.

The main issue that Beale has with Moyise's conclusions comes back to the idea of context and Moyise's lack of textual analysis.[33] Although Beale acknowledges that 'there may be times when these contexts yield ambiguous information, it does not mean that John was ambiguous in his own mind' when it comes to his understanding of the Old Testament author's intentions.[34] These instances are best viewed not as

---

[27] G. K. Beale, *John's Use of the Old Testament in the Book of Revelation*, JSNTSup 166 (Sheffield: Sheffield Academic Press, 1998), 41–59.

[28] Ibid., 41. This take is right insofar as Moyise's critical aim was to alter the frame of the discussion towards literary questions, but it is an overstatement because Moyise does engage in exegetical analysis of relevant texts, even if not in such a thoroughgoing way as Beale.

[29] Ibid., 45.

[30] Ibid., see also 100, 127–8; Beale, 'Positive Answer', 391–3.

[31] Beale, *John's Use*, 45.

[32] Ibid., 46.

[33] This latter point is made clear when he notes that 'Moyise needs more detailed interaction with the material on both sides of the argument before his evaluation could be persuasive' (ibid., 92), appealing to his own lucubration as evidence for his conclusions.

[34] Ibid., 47.

evidence for tension and complexity in the Apocalypse's referentiality but as 'part of John's overall Semitic style: it is an expression of Semitic paratactic thinking which allowed the setting in close proximity of two different, and sometimes seemingly contradictory, ideas of a word, without the discomfort experienced by some twentieth century readers.'[35] Setting aside the deeply problematic concept of attributing particular thought patterns to the 'Semitic mind',[36] a fallback that I find troubling for multiple reasons, Beale concludes his critique of Moyise with the accusation that he has taken refuge in reader-response criticism, working to refute the theory as a whole.[37] Instead of intuiting John's surreptitious interpretive approach, which is 'ultimately traceable to Christ's own interpretive approach which he probably passed on to his disciples',[38] Moyise chose to examine the material through 'reader-response criticism'.

Moyise responded in brief in a 1999 article entitled 'The Old Testament in the New: A Reply to Greg Beale' in *Irish Biblical Studies*.[39] He identifies three main points of umbrage that Beale takes with his work: (1) that Old Testament texts cannot receive new meaning, (2) that New Testament authors do not take texts out of context and (3) that meaning derives from author intention, not the work of readers.[40] At the outset it is interesting that none of these points deal with the interpretation of specific texts but with larger hermeneutical positions that undergird particular views of scripture as an inspired canon with an overarching divine authorship. In any case, Moyise critiques Beale's distinction between original meaning and new significance as a 'hermeneutical cover-up'; what Beale means by '"new significance" is what most of us mean by "new meaning"'.[41] This is true too for Beale's construal of context, arguing that New Testament authors retained an awareness of context, even if that context was influenced by new presuppositions. For Moyise, Beale's construal of context makes it a truism that New Testament authors always respected context and, furthermore, Beale's construal of reader-response criticism does not reflect the nuances of this approach.[42] Moyise concludes by suggesting that authorial intention is always a construct and that what Beale is really defending are his own presuppositions.

If it was not already clear at this point, Beale's lengthy response shows that the stakes are not about the Book of Revelation at all but about larger hermeneutical issues and

---

[35] Ibid.
[36] See also ibid., 82–3, 125. The 'Semitic mind' concept is used as a way to acquit apparent faults in John's reasoning vis-à-vis Beale's construal of John's ideal interpretive practices (see also Beale, *Book of Revelation*, 99). Beale also begins to differentiate between meaning and application as a way to maintain the contextuality of John's reuse. He may apply the meaning of an Old Testament text to his new situation, but that does not change the underlying meaning found in the author's original intentions. There are also multiple types of contexts to which a New Testament author can remain faithful (see 71–4), even if 'John does handle the Old Testament in a compatible way with the original author's intention' (81).
[37] Beale, *John's Use*, 50–9.
[38] Ibid., 45.
[39] Steve Moyise, 'The Old Testament in the New: A Reply to Greg Beale', *IBS* 21 (1999): 54–8.
[40] Ibid., 54.
[41] Ibid., 55.
[42] See also Steve Moyise, 'Does the Author of Revelation Misappropriate the Scriptures', *AUSS* 40 (2002): 3–21, where Moyise continues the debate with Beale by taking on the underlying scholars (Vanhoozer especially) who undergird Beale's critical approach.

theological positions.[43] Published two fascicles later in the same journal, Beale clarifies a number of points raised by Moyise. First, he attempts to unravel the difference as he sees it between meaning and significance, drawing upon Hirsch, Vanhoozer and, to a lesser degree, Tom Wright to make the case for maintaining the distinction between 'original meaning and contemporary relevance, meaning and application'.[44] For Beale, the original meaning of an Old Testament passage – something that is coterminous with the original author's intention – remains recoverable, at least proximately, and this means that we must distinguish between that eternal original meaning and any later significance applied to that text by subsequent authors. Moyise is wrong to insist that new meanings can be generated in the process of reading; Beale 'is loath to confuse *original* meaning with anything that is subsequently *derivative* of it'.[45] His approach to interpretation is linear, and meaning is created once and for all; Moyise's approach is multidirectional, and meaning is a negotiation between author(s) and interpreter. This places Moyise into the 'radical' camp of reader-response critics, a group that holds that meaning is unbounded – texts can say whatever a reader wants them to, even if Moyise 'does not want to say it so baldly'.[46] Perhaps if Moyise had done more actual exegesis 'in the publica arena', instead of simply applying theory to other lines of interpretation, he may be more familiar with the '"nuts and bolts" of validation in the exegetical method'.[47] The discussion had begun to feel a bit too personal for my liking.

Beale also takes umbrage with Moyise's analysis of his proposed presuppositions and their role in the discussion regarding respect for context. He offers six defences of his position, taking aim in particular at the 'politically correct fad' of viewing all human thought as the 'mere expression of each reader's "socially constructed world"'.[48] Because John's presuppositions go back to Jesus, then questioning these presuppositions calls into question one's views of Jesus.[49] Moyise's adoption of reader-response criticism makes it impossible to assess the correctness of any given interpretation – no interpretation could ever be wrong. Anything goes. This view leads Beale to posit that their dispute is not exegetical or hermeneutical but epistemological: Moyise 'lines

---

[43] G. K. Beale, 'Questions of Authorial Intent, Epistemology, and Presuppositions and Their Bearing on the Study of the Old Testament in the New: A Rejoinder to Steve Moyise', *IBS* 21 (1999): 152–80.

[44] Ibid., 155. See E. D. Hirsch, *Validity in Interpretation* (New Haven, CT: Yale University Press, 1967); and K. J. Vanhoozer, *Is There a Meaning in This Text?* (Grand Rapids, MI: Zondervan, 1998).

[45] Beale, 'Questions', 158.

[46] Ibid., 162. In this section, Beale also appeals to canonical ideologies and divine authorship as laying the groundwork for assuming consistency in context and meaning between Old Testament and New Testament text (165).

[47] Ibid., 166.

[48] Ibid., 172.

[49] Ibid. 'Can we be bold enough in a scholarly forum to ask the question whether or not Jesus' interpretive perspective was wrong? One's view of who Jesus was should determine decisively the answer to this question.' I am troubled by this line of argument for a number of reasons, including the assumed fact that the compositional and interpretive practices of New Testament authors can be traced back to Jesus in the first instance (I am not confident that the Apostle John is the author of the Apocalypse, and even if he were it does not follow that he learned his entire trade from Jesus himself) and the resulting implication that to question the veracity of these practices is to question Jesus. John's presuppositions as Beale sees them are his constructs based on his own work with the texts, but that does not necessarily mean that they can be used to measure one's faithfulness to Jesus's own perspectives.

up with the more radical side of postmodern "reader-response critics",[50] while Beale views his own epistemological place alongside Wright's construal of critical realism.[51] Again, textual examples are sparse in this exchange; all analytical effort is in meta-critical realm of hermeneutics and epistemology.

The final direct tête-à-tête in this debate was moderated by Jon Paulien in a fascicle of the *Andrews University Seminary Studies* published in 2001. Paulien attempts to assuage the intensity of the debate as it played out in *Irish Biblical Studies*, arguing that Moyise and Beale are really not as far apart from one another as they seem to think.[52] He reiterates the centrality of understanding Old Testament allusions for making sense of the Apocalypse and emphasizes the complexities involved in this area of research, complexities that may naturally lead to misunderstandings. Paulien's primary goal, however, is to lower the temperature: when Moyise and Beale are 'read separately, one can easily get the impression that the issue between them is life and death. Read together, one wonders at times if it is much ado about nothing.'[53] Does anyone, even Beale, think that they can really fully achieve the intentions of any author? Does anyone, even Moyise, really think that all meaning is entirely subjective? This consonance breaks down, Paulien observes, when Beale shifts the question of authorial intent from John or the Old Testament authors to a divine author of all scripture,[54] creating a situation where the two interlocutors' presumed theological suppositions indelibly creates a chasm of understanding. Beale 'accepts the idea of divine superintendence of Scripture; Moyise (by implication) does not',[55] therefore Moyise must be wrong, at least according to Beale. Here I think Paulien has placed his finger on the main artery of the debate and rightly identified why Beale has responded at such length to Moyise's work: a focus on intertextuality (however nuanced) has the potential to undermine a particular view of (inerrantist) inspiration because it shifts the focus of analysis from an internal discussion of a divinely created canon to a literary-critical discussion of ancient texts and their complex relationships.

Moyise's and Beale's responses are typical of the discussion thus far. Moyise offers a terse reflection on whether the phrase 'authorial intention' is useful for this discussion in the first place.[56] He makes a number of observations that problematize Beale's view of intention, including the fact that Jewish scriptural works developed significantly over the life of their transmission and existed in different forms in different languages in antiquity, a point that foreshadows the conversation on textual pluriformity that subsequently developed. This is not even to mention that the governing voices of most Jewish scriptural works are anonymous and that single authorship is hardly a dominant construct in the Second Temple period, some exceptions notwithstanding. Moyise explains that he adopted intertextuality because other schema for understanding John's reuse (typology, midrash, etc.) all seemed inadequate to describe the realities of

---

[50] Ibid., 173.
[51] Ibid., 175–9.
[52] Paulien, 'Dreading the Whirlwind', 5–22.
[53] Ibid., 18–19.
[54] Ibid., 20.
[55] Ibid.
[56] Steve Moyise, 'Authorial Intention and the Book of Revelation', *AUSS* 39 (2001): 35–40.

John's work; so he attempted to open up new horizons for engaging this question. His overarching critique of Beale is that he equates his own scholarly constructs with John's intentions: 'I am suspicious of those who claim that there is but one correct way to read Revelation. Unsurprisingly, that one way is of course their own!'[57]

Beale's response, again, clarifies his own thinking on a number of points, including his distinction between meaning and significance, quoting his own *Irish Biblical Studies* article at length. He also protests against Paulien's assertion that views of divine authorship undergird his differences with Moyise,[58] even though he does note that those who hold to a Hirschian view of authorial intention without also supposing the 'existence of a person God who reveals himself' are inconsistent.[59] He sees an 'inextricable link between a Christian, theistic biblical worldview and epistemology, including how people know that they know anything in reality',[60] collapsing epistemology, hermeneutics and theology into an unassailable Gordian knot. It is this link that Beale seeks to maintain in his response to Moyise's approach to John's use of scripture – a specifically Christian epistemology that allows for access to (non-exhaustive) certainty in terms of all kinds of interpretation, from quotidian aspects of daily life to the details of ancient biblical interpretation.

The contours of this debate are certainly more complex than I have summarized here. But it seems clear, at least on my retrospective reading, that the debate is not really about Revelation at all in the end but about an epistemological stance associated with a particular view of scripture and its ultimate authorship. Of course we learn about Revelation, John's activity and the extent of his allusive networks, but the focus on hermeneutics and modern theologies prioritized critical questions that quickly moved beyond John's exegetical repertoire and composition habits. Even so, the debate carried within itself the embryonic forms of multiple strands of research that have now emerged. And while both Beale and Moyise have been very productive in continuing to publish collaborative and single-author works in this area in the intervening twenty years, they have (more or less) gone their own ways, developing their distinctive approaches forged in the polemics of the 1990s.[61] The ways that they approach this subject have become parallel tracks of engagement that suit different research contexts, each calling often upon the other as a critical foil. Their debate remains important not only on its own merits but because parts of it augured what has since developed, both

---

[57] Ibid., 40.
[58] G. K. Beale, 'A Response to Jon Paulien on the Use of the Old Testament in Revelation', *AUSS* 39 (2001): 23–34.
[59] Ibid., 30.
[60] Ibid.
[61] For example, Moyise's series of co-edited books with M. J. J. Menken published in LNTS by T&T Clark and Beale's co-edited reference work (with D. A. Carson), *Commentary on the New Testament Use of the Old Testament* (Grand Rapids, MI: Baker, 2007). For just one example of each of their single-author works, see Steve Moyise, *Evoking Scripture: Seeing the Old Testament in the New* (London: T&T Clark, 2008); and G. K. Beale, *Handbook on the New Testament Use of the Old Testament* (Grand Rapids, MI: Baker, 2012). Direct engagement between the two fizzled out but references to their debate and their underlying disagreements do appear from time to time. See Moyise, 'Misappropriate', 3–21 (where Moyise returns to detailed textual analysis of Revelation's references to Ezekiel, Daniel and Isaiah); and Moyise, *Evoking*, 132–5, where he notes that behind Beale's approach lies 'a particular theological commitment to the unity of Scripture' (132).

in terms of their own research and in the continued engagement with this area by many other scholars.

Developments since the Debate

Since the direct debate between Beale and Moyise withered on the vine in the early 2000s, the hermeneutical and epistemological aspects of 'Old Testament in the New Testament' studies have largely retreated to the background.[62] But other facets of the discourse have since spun out in different directions. Three examples comes to mind. The first is the question of the text of Jewish scripture in the first century and the status of the New Testament as a witness to this tradition. Although Revelation is more complicated here due to the lack of explicit citations,[63] significant ground has been gained in identifying the form and language of Jewish scripture that John had access to in one form or another (via manuscripts, memory or existing interpretive traditions). Both Beale and Moyise touched on this issue in various ways, Moyise probing the textual possibilities of John's references and Beale working to identify an assumed source text.[64] This substratum of their conversation is now a topic with much wider import; it is now clear that the complexity of John's allusive practices reflects the complexity and pluriformity of the textual culture in which he produced his work. The work of Beate Kowalski, Martin Karrer and Michael Labahn, among others, has been important to show that John's textual practices reflect a deep continuity with other patterns of literary composition in the late Second Temple period.[65] The textual and material aspects of his reuse are foundational for how we understand his literary activity. He is an interpreter of his scriptural traditions, but his interpretation has a deep compositional valence

---

[62] I can only guess, but I suspect that discussion has moved away from these areas because the debate between Moyise and Beale did not reach any consensus or chasten either scholar to seriously consider a new path forward and because the underlying issue is really a theological one that is better got at through different bodies of evidence. Is the 'New Testament's use of the Old' really the best way to adjudicate divine superintendence of the canon, inerrancy or consistency? I doubt it.

[63] See Beate Kowalski, 'Die Ezechielrezeption in der Offenbarung des Johannes und ihre Bedeutung für Textkritik', *SNTU* 35 (2010): 51–77.

[64] For example, G. K. Beale, 'The Origin of the Title "King of Kings and Lord of Lords" in Revelation 17.14', *NTS* 31 (1985): 618–20; G. K. Beale, 'A Reconsideration of the Text of Daniel in the Apocalypse', *Biblica* 67 (1986): 539–43; Steve Moyise, 'The Language of the Old Testament in the Apocalypse', *JSNT* 76 (1999): 97–113. In this article Moyise briefly engages Beale on the question of textual form, challenging his position that John referred to the Old Testament in its Greek proto-Theodontic form and offering a much more nuanced textual discussion. See Beale, *John's Use*, 61–2. See also Steve Moyise, 'The Language of the Psalms in the Book of Revelation', *Neot* 37 (2003): 246–61.

[65] For example Beate Kowalski, *Die Rezeption des Propheten Ezechiel in der Offenbarung des Johannes* (Stuttgart: Katholisches Bibelwerk, 2004); Martin Karrer, 'Von der Apokalypse zu Ezechiel: Der Ezechieltext der Apokalypse', in D. Sänger (ed.), *Das Ezechielbuch in der Johannesoffenbarung* (Neukirchen-Vluyn: Neukirchener, 2004), 84–120; Michael Labahn, 'Griechische Textformenm in der Schriftrezeption der Johannesoffenbarung? Eine Problemanzeige zu Möglichkeiten und Grenzen ihrer Rekonstruktion anhand von Beispielen aus der Rezeption des Ezechielbuchs', in S. Kreuzer, M. Meiser and M. Sigismund (eds), *Die Septuaginta - Entstehung, Sprache, Geschichte* (Tübingen: Mohr Siebeck, 2012), among many others.

and function that aligns with how texts are written and rewritten in this period.[66] The idea that there is a specific 'New Testament' way to interpret 'Old Testament' traditions is problematic to the point that we should refrain from framing our analyses of the ways the early Christian writers engage Jewish scripture as studies in 'the use of the Old Testament in the New'. This retrospective canonical characterization obfuscates the textual and literary realties of John's practices, assuming fixed and final entities for Jewish scripture (authored once and for all by known individuals) and a precise text of Revelation that has been entirely recovered in every detail. In light of this burgeoning consensus, Beale's views in particular seem somewhat naïve.

Moyise began to show that perceptions of John's situation reflect scholarly reliance on critical editions, a situation that obscured the textual realities and contingencies of a culture where texts remains fluid (to a degree) and pluriform.[67] When we mistake critical editions of Jewish scripture and the New Testament for ancient texts, in terms of both their wording and their materiality, we are really building 'castles in the air' to borrow a phrase from David Parker.[68] Scriptural traditions were surely 'authoritative' for John in some sense as a constellation of textual forms, languages and materials, but it is not clear that he preferred one textual form in one medium over another. Beale and Moyise laid a foundation for further research in this area, but it has developed beyond the confines of their debate. This emerging reality vindicates, to my mind, Moyise's approach, calling into question Beale's view of authorial intention and the rhetoric of the 'Old Testament' as a self-evident, fixed entity.

Another area of progress in the past twenty years that had its start as part of the debate is understanding John's exegetical repertoire, both in terms of the features of texts that attract his interpretive interest and the ways he displays these interpretations within his own work. We have mostly moved beyond typology, allegory and midrash as the primary categories for thinking about his reuse, or at least we have a better understanding of what these terms mean in larger literary contexts.[69] We have also successfully lowered the stakes of the terminology used to describe John's reuse and compositional practices. There is no native language in the late Second Temple period to talk about composition and interpretive practices.[70] This reality means not only that no modern terminology used to describe John's activities is sacrosanct but also that we must continue to endeavour to describe John's interpretive activities within the context of Second Temple Jewish literature and the transmission of Jewish scripture in this

---

[66] See Marko Jauhiainen, 'Revelation and Rewritten Prophecies', in A. Laato and J. van Ruiten (eds), *Rewritten Bible Reconsidered: Proceedings of the Conference in Karkku, Finland August 24-26 2006* (Winona Lake, IN: Eisenbrauns, 2008), 177–97.

[67] See Martin Karrer, 'Scriptural Quotations in the Jesus Tradition and Early Christianity: Textual History and Theology', in G. V. Allen and J. A. Dunne (eds), *Ancient Readers and Their Scriptures: Engaging the Hebrew Bible in Early Judaism and Christianity* (Leiden: Brill, 2019), 98–127.

[68] See D. C. Parker, *The Living Text of the Gospels* (Cambridge: Cambridge University Press, 1998), 76. See also Larry W. Hurtado, *The Earliest Christian Artifacts: Manuscripts and Christian Origins* (Grand Rapids, MI: Eerdmans, 2006), 8: 'Scholars ... often treat the text of a printed edition of the Greek New Testament as all they need to consider.'

[69] See Susan E. Docherty, *The Use of the Old Testament in Hebrews: A Case Study in Early Jewish Bible Interpretation* (Tübingen: Mohr Siebeck, 2009).

[70] Allen, *Books of Revelation*, 7–16.

period.⁷¹ The terminology that we use to describe John's activities reflects not a native description of his activity but our own view of what he is doing and how he operated in his particular textual culture.⁷² The impetus to reconsider our critical language can be traced, at least in part, to the discussion of 'intertextuality', 'midrash' and 'intention' that characterized the exchange between Beale and Moyise.

A final issue that has begun to receive attention on a number of fronts is the reception of John's use of scripture embedded within Revelation's manuscripts themselves. Neither Moyise nor Beale addressed this issue directly, but both recognized that John's use of scripture is an act of reception itself and that the expected acknowledgement of the presence of an allusion in subsequent works can help us understand what John was doing. Those with an interest in manuscripts or textual criticism have taken this position to new material. One good example is the ongoing project that explores Revelation's paratexts being carried out in Wuppertal and Munich.⁷³ Some of these paratexts show cognizance of John's embedded allusions, often filtered through Andrew of Caesarea's late antique commentary. For example, one of the multiple marginal glosses extracted from Andrew's commentary that appears in GA 2323 (Athens, Benaki Musem, Μπ. 46, diktyon 8081, thirteenth century, 283r) identifies the keys of David (Rev. 3.7) either as 'the kingdom or the prophecy of the psalms' (την βασιλειαν η την προφητειαν των ψαλμων), connecting this general allusion to a work attributed to David and opening up new interpretive possibilities.⁷⁴ Another example of how Revelation's use of scripture is embedded in its own manuscripts can be found on 15r of Athos, Pantokratoros 44 (GA 051, diktyon 29063), a partially preserved tenth-century copy of the Book of Revelation with Andrew's commentary that begins at Rev. 11.15 (Figure 1).

There is a lot happening on this folio. The first two lines are the end of the Andrew commentary from the previous section; line 3 is the Andrew *titlos* for Rev. 13.18 (περι του ονοματος του αντιχριστου, 'Regarding the Name of the Antichrist'); and lines 4–6 are Rev. 13.18 in a special uncial script (*Auszeichnungsschrift*). The rest of the main text of the page is the Andrew commentary in minuscule script. Even more is going on in the margins, including a later hand's attempt to calculate the number of the name by assigning numerical values to Greek graphemes and the phrase αρνου με ('deny me'), a collocation whose Greek graphemes add to 666 when given their normal numerical

---

71 See Beate Kowalski, 'Selective versus Contextual Allusions: Reconsidering Technical Terms of Intertextuality', in D. Allen and S. Smith (eds), *Methodology in the Use of the Old Testament in the New: Context and Criteria* (London: T&T Clark, 2020), 86–102.

72 See William A. Tooman, 'Scriptural Reuse in Ancient Jewish Literature: Comments and Reflections on the State of the Art', in D. Allen and S. Smith (eds), *Methodology in the Use of the Old Testament in the New: Context and Criteria* (London: T&T Clark, 2020), 23–39, who points out that the terminology used by scholars reflects their own theories of ancient literary practices and their wider contexts.

73 See Darius Müller and Peter Malik, 'Rediscovering Paratexts in the Manuscripts of Revelation', *Early Christianity* 11 (2020): 247–64. See also, previously, Martin Karrer, Siegfried Kreuzer and Marcus Sigismund (eds), *Von der Septuaginta zum Neuen Testament: Textgeschichtlice Erörterungen* (Berlin: de Gruyter, 2010).

74 Even though most view Rev. 3.7 as an allusion to Isa. 22.22. On this manuscript and its glosses, see Peter Malik and Edmund Gerke, 'Marginalglossen in GA 2323: Edition und Übersetzung', in M. Sigismund and D. Müller (eds), *Studien zum Text der Apokalypse III* (Berlin: de Gruyter, 2020), 371–415.

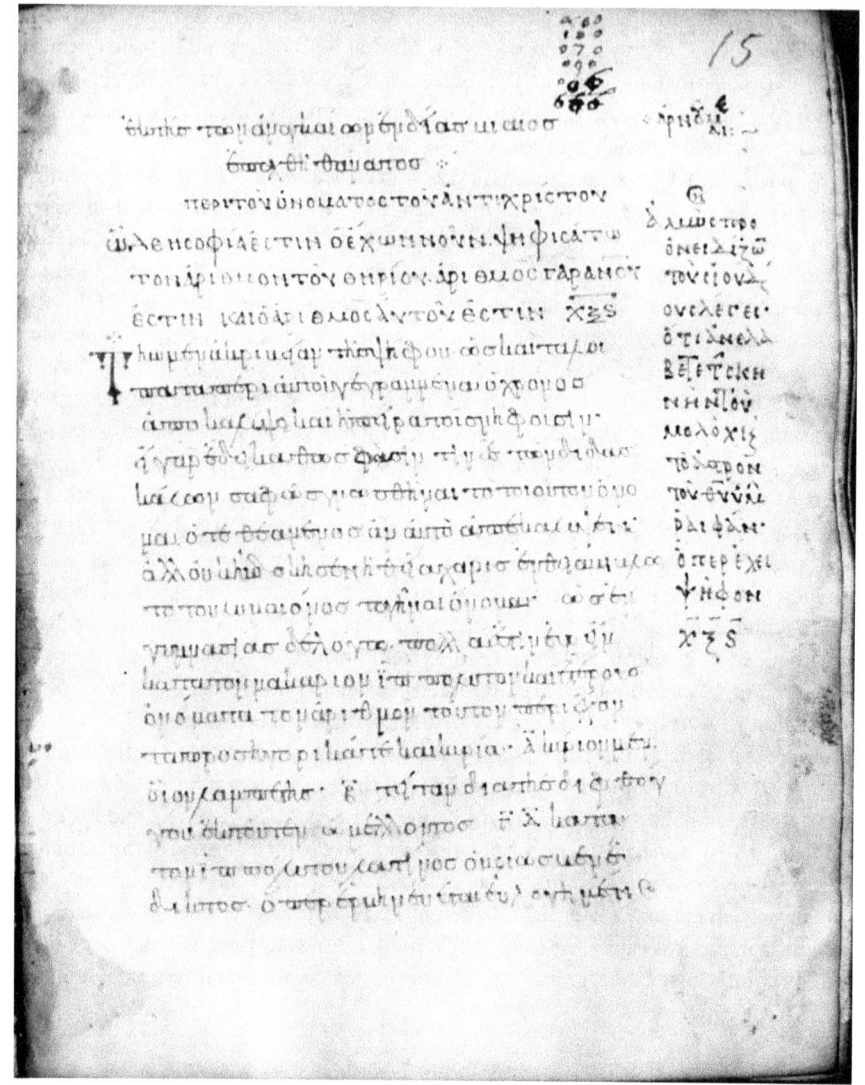

Figure 1 Athos, Pantokratoros 44 (GA 051), tenth century, 15r, Rev. 13.18 with dense paratexts. Public Domain: Library of Congress Collection of Manuscripts from the Monasteries of Mt Athos.

value.[75] But most interesting for this purpose is the lengthy comment in the right margin, which reads:

---

[75] 1 (α) + 100 (ρ) + 50 (ν) + 70 (ο) + 400 (υ) + 40 (μ) + 5 (ε) = 666. The math in the upper corner appears to represent another word beside αρνου με. On marginal notes on Rev. 13.18, see Garrick V. Allen, *Manuscripts of the Book of Revelation: New Philology, Paratexts, Reception* (Oxford: Oxford University Press, 2020), 121–55; and Garrick V. Allen, 'An Anti-Islamic Marginal Comment in the Apocalypse of "Codex Reuchlin" (GA 2814) and Its Tradition', in M. Karrer (ed.), *Der Codex*

Αμως προ(φητης) ονειδιζων τους ιουδαιους λεγει οτι ανελαβετε την σκηνην του μολοχ και το αστρον του θυ υμων ραιφαν οπερ εχει ψηφον χξς.[76]

Reprimanding the Jews, Amos the prophet said that 'you took up the tent of Moloch and the star of your God Raiphan, which has the calculation 666'.

As far as I have been able to ascertain, this is the only marginal note outside of the Andrew, Oecumenius and Arethas commentary traditions that explicitly identifies one of John's references to Jewish scripture, in this case the Greek version of Amos 5.26.[77] The link in this case is not made because the commentor intuits John's use of language from Amos in Rev. 13.18 but because the graphemes in the name of the antagonists in Amos 5.26, Raiphan, add to 666, at least when it is spelled ρειφαν. The coded wordplay in Rev. 13.18, and the call for the reader to actively interpret, offered the space necessary to decode the name of the beast by using names whose graphemes add up to that number. Amos's Raiphan becomes one such option, creating a new link between Revelation and Amos that the John likely never intended but which lived on in Byzantine understandings of John's use of scripture. Revelation's persistent allusions and explicit paronomastic play underwrote continued interpretive engagement between Revelation and what became the Old Testament, reflecting a more expansive hermeneutic towards textual reference.

The marginal note in GA 051 is but one example of ongoing engagement with Revelation's referential horizon from antiquity through to modern scholarship. The debate between Beale and Moyise oriented the field towards particular theological questions pertaining to scripture, canon and divine authorship; but it also opened new opportunities to interpret John's work in a way that informs new questions. Moyise's responses in particular implicitly laid out a road map to take the topics of debate in new directions, giving cover for scholars to experiment and think afresh about old critical (or ideological) orthodoxies. Further discourse on criteria for discerning references, authorial intent, respect for context and the theological consequences of this type of literary composition is ongoing. But the real value in the debate, especially in Moyise's responses, is its ability to pinpoint and to anticipate the issues that need further interrogation. In light of his important body of work, Steve Moyise will remain a key interlocutor in this conversation. Because he was willing to forge new directions in research, undaunted by staunch resistance, he will continue to influence whatever types of scholarship emerge. His trailblazing makes his work enduringly essential for those who seek to understand the Book of Revelation and John's allusive network.

Reuchlins zur Apokalypse: Byzanz – Basler Konzil – Erasmus, MB 5 (Berlin: de Gruyter, 2020), 193-8. αρνου με appears as an options for the name of the Antichrist in pseudo-Hippolytus's *De consummatione mundi* (28) and appears in other manuscripts like GA 2073.

[76] Cf. Amos 5.26^OG: καὶ ἀνελάβετε τὴν σκηνὴν τοῦ Μολοχ καὶ τὸ ἄστρον τοῦ θεοῦ ὑμῶν Ραιφαν, τοὺς τύπους αὐτῶν, οὓς ἐποιήσατε ἑαυτοῖς. Images of GA 051 available for download at https://www.loc.gov/item/00271051554-ma/ (accessed 4 February 2020).

[77] See also the use of Amos 5.25-26 in CD VII and Acts 7.42-43, discussed in brief in Moyise, *Old Testament in the New*, 18–20.

3

Dreaming with scripture: Revisiting the Beale-Moyise debate

Benjamin Sargent

The debate between Steve Moyise and G. K. Beale in the late 1990s to early 2000s (summarized and evaluated by Jon Paulien in 2001) was a fascinating exploration of biblical hermeneutics in relation to the use of scripture in Revelation.[1] At its heart was the question of whether the use of scripture in Revelation was exegetically defensible, given the seeming contrasts between the historically contingent and authorially intended meanings of particular scriptural texts and the meanings ascribed to them in Revelation. This debate was, to some extent, the product of the scholarly contexts in which both Moyise and Beale were working: both were attempting to be faithful both to their evangelical convictions and to the disciplines of biblical criticism, largely shaped by historical criticism. This chapter will offer another summary of the debate, arguing that the desire of both scholars to demonstrate the exegetical and hermeneutical plausibility of the use of scripture in Revelation undermines their analysis of how interpretation takes place in the text. It will be argued, through a comparison of the interpretation of Gen. 37.9 in Rev. 12.1 and Ignatius of Antioch's *Eph.* 19.2, that ideas of *sensus plenior* have no real purchase as a means of understanding early Christian biblical interpretation.

An inner-evangelical debate

Some may now have difficulty in seeing Moyise's diverse and critical scholarly contributions as evangelical, but this is certainly the context of some of his early work as well as the issues with which he was engaging in the 1990s. Having recently completed his substantial doctoral research on the use of scripture in Revelation, Moyise was in a position to respond to an article by Richard N. Longenecker in the evangelical journal *Themelios*.[2] Longenecker had argued that contemporary Christians could

---

[1] J. Paulien, 'Dreading the Whirlwind: Intertextuality and the Use of the Old Testament in Revelation', *AUSS* 39 (2001): 5–22. I also offer my own analysis in Benjamin Sargent, *Written for Our Learning: The Single Meaning of Scripture in Christian Theology* (Eugene, OR: Cascade, 2016), 86–9.
[2] Richard N. Longenecker, '"Who Is the Prophet Talking About?" Some Reflections on the New Testament's Use of the Old', *Themelios* 12 (1987): 4–8.

accept the exegetical conclusions of New Testament writers, without accepting the exegetical means by which those conclusions were reached: that, for example, one does not need to accept the validity of allegorical interpretation to accept the theological claim of Gal. 4.24-25. Moyise offered his response in another (albeit less conservative) evangelical journal: *Anvil*.[3] Longenecker's solution to the problem of New Testament interpretations of scripture was inadequate, Moyise argued, since it is not really possible to separate theological claims from the arguments through which they have been reached. Instead, by introducing the work of Julia Kristeva, Moyise notes that all intertextual interpretation is, in a sense, out of context and that the source text always resists the new meaning being created for it.[4] Drawing upon Thomas Greene's *The Light in Troy*, Moyise suggests that New Testament authors treat scripture 'eclectically', drawing upon a rich inheritance of language and imagery to add depth to writing; 'heuristically', using scriptural style and language to frame writing as the continuation of scripture and finally through 'dialectical imitation', presenting the source text with an interpretation which seeks to add to what readers may understand as its prior meaning.[5] In this argument, Moyise seems to suggest that the New Testament writers were not seeking to exhaust the meaning of scriptural texts but were simply offering, in Gadamerian terminology, new horizons of meaning and significance. Further detail is given to Moyise's application of intertextuality to the use of scripture in Revelation in the sixth chapter of *The Old Testament in the Book of Revelation*, presumably written before the *Anvil* article, though published after it.[6] Here, Moyise also emphasizes the role of the reader's response to the author of Revelation's invitation to enter into an open-ended dialogue with Revelation and the texts used and interpreted within it.

Beale's *John's Use of the Old Testament in Revelation*, published in 1998, was also the fruit of doctoral research concluded many years before at the University of Cambridge.[7] The introduction to this monograph contained a substantial engagement with Moyise's application of intertextuality to Revelation. Beale's response to Moyise was hermeneutically conservative, arguing that John's interpretation of scripture in Revelation is derived from the plain meaning of source texts, and offering a defence of authorial intention (against Moyise's reader-oriented approach), drawing upon E. D. Hirsch and D. A. Carson.[8] Beale does not dispute that the interpretation of scriptural texts in Revelation exceeds the meaning implied in an original context but suggests that new interpretation flows from the will of the author whose intention

---

[3] Steve Moyise, 'Does the NT Quote the OT Out of Context?', *Anvil* 11.2 (1994): 133–43. For a detailed analysis of the history of this journal of relevance to the time in which Moyise chose to publish in it, see Andrew Atherstone, *An Anglican Evangelical Identity Crisis: The Churchman-Anvil Affair of 1981–1984* (London: Latimer Trust, 2008).

[4] Ibid., 138–9.

[5] Ibid., 139–41. Cf. Thomas Greene, *The Light in Troy: Imitation and Discovery in Renaissance Poetry* (New Haven, CT: Yale University Press, 1982).

[6] Steve Moyise, *The Old Testament in the Book of Revelation*, JSNTSup 115 (Sheffield: Sheffield Academic Press, 1995), 108–38.

[7] G. K. Beale, *John's Use of the Old Testament in Revelation*, JSNTSup 166 (Sheffield: Sheffield Academic Press, 1998).

[8] Beale, *John's Use of the Old Testament*, 41–59. Cf. E. D. Hirsch, *The Aims of Interpretation* (Chicago: University of Chicago Press, 1976); and D. A. Carson, *The Gagging of God* (Grand Rapids, MI: Zondervan, 1996).

only limits meaning in certain ways. Beale made a distinction between meaning and significance: that Revelation does not create new meanings for scripture but by placing scriptural texts in new contexts reveals their significance in new ways. These new significances are in continuity with the meaning of the text intended by its author.

The year 1999 saw the publication of a short response by Moyise in *Irish Biblical Studies* (published by the conservative and evangelical Union Theological College, Belfast) and a much longer rejoinder by Beale. Moyise argued that the distinction between meaning and significance is insubstantial: that meaning is not a fixed and determinate property, but that every act of reading and interpretation posits new meaning, even when someone chooses to call that meaning 'significance'.[9] Further to this, Moyise attempted to clarify the main points of disagreement between them: whether Revelation creates new meanings; whether it takes texts out of context; and whether meaning is derived purely from authorial intention. Beale's rejoinder repeated and developed his analysis of Hirsch, arguing for a form of *sensus plenior* derived from authorial intent: that scriptural authors would recognize the use of their words in Revelation, even though they could not have imagined that their words had that significance when they were first used.[10]

In 2001, the Seventh Day Adventist journal *Andrews University Seminary Studies* hosted the next part of the Moyise-Beale debate, introduced by Paulien's summary and analysis of the debate thus far: analysis which seems to have favoured Moyise. Paulien argued that Beale had characterized Moyise (particularly in *John's Use of the Old Testament in Revelation*) as a radical reader-response critic and has responded to this hermeneutic, rather than the actual claims Moyise made about how scripture is used in Revelation.[11] He also suggested that Beale's identification with Hirsch's account of authorial intention could not enable the sort of *sensus plenior* readings Beale saw in Revelation on account of Hirsch's historicism. Instead, Paulien argued that the hermeneutical resolution to the issue of the use of scripture in Revelation lay with canonical criticism: that the author of Revelation understood scriptural texts in their relation to other texts and a broader salvation-historical narrative. These literary contexts, Paulien argued, invite interpretation which sees meaning in texts that goes beyond what an author can reasonably be expected to have intended. Further to this, Paulien concluded that the exegetical fruit of Moyise and Beale's engagement with the use of scripture in Revelation differed very little and that both Moyise and Beale were concerned to demonstrate the reasonableness of the interpretation of scripture in Revelation. It is argued here that this concern is a hindrance to understanding early Christian hermeneutics.

Beale responded to Paulien in the same issue of *AUSS*, arguing that Paulien had misrepresented his view of authorial intent. He argued that the authors of the

---

[9] Steve Moyise, 'The Old Testament in the New: A Reply to Greg Beale', *IBS* (1999): 54–8. Cf. Steve Moyise, 'Intertextuality and the Study of the Old Testament in the New Testament', in Steve Moyise (ed.), *The Old Testament in the New Testament: Essays in Honour of J. L. North*, JSNTSup 189 (Sheffield: Sheffield Academic Press, 2000), 14–41.

[10] G. K. Beale, 'Questions of Authorial Intent, Epistemology, and Presuppositions and Their Bearing on the Study of the Old Testament in the New: A Rejoinder to Steve Moyise', *IBS* 21 (1999): 152–80.

[11] Paulien, 'Whirlwind', 15–19.

scriptures of Israel would see themselves as belonging within an unfolding story of salvation (so, not dissimilar to the hermeneutics of canonical interpretation) and that this gives legitimacy to new interpretations of their words which could be understood as within the spirit of what was first meant.[12] Moyise responded in the next issue of the journal, seeking to demonstrate that the interpretation of some texts in Revelation actually contradicts the likely intended meaning of those texts, so that any idea of new interpretation stemming from authorial intention seems implausible.[13] Moyise noted here that Ezekiel's vision of a restored temple is the opposite of the vision of no temple at all in Rev. 21.22, arguing that it cannot be claimed that the idea of the latter is inherent in the intention of the former. Returning to the work of Greene, Moyise argued again that the use of scripture in Revelation is not arbitrary but follows a trajectory of interpretation which begins with the plain meaning of an original context but is not limited by it. This interpretation can be imaginative, allowing the text to speak to the new contexts in which it is read.

> John is serious about the original context of his allusion, in so far as the trajectories have a starting point. But his focus is not on that starting point. It is on what has happened since, as a clue to what is still to come. John is a seer not a scholar.[14]

Since 2001, Moyise and Beale have not engaged each other in writing on the theme of the use of scripture in Revelation, though their work continues to make reference to the issues their debate raised.[15]

In summary, during the debate both Moyise and Beale were concerned to demonstrate the appropriateness of the use of scripture in Revelation. One wonders if Moyise would still be so concerned to demonstrate the reasonableness of early Christian interpretation of scripture. Moyise argued then that its interpretation is reasonable on the basis of the idea of intertextuality from the field of literary criticism. Though this interpretation may not be that of the modern reader or the biblical scholar, schooled in the disciplines of historical criticism, it demonstrates a certain respect for the intentions of biblical authors whose words are interpreted for a new context with a creativity that does not overwhelm them. Beale argued that interpretation in Revelation is reasonable on the basis of John's interest in authorial intention as a dynamic and developing concept, one through which new significances are seen as the interpretive context changes through time. Both make the assumption that the interpretation of

---

[12] G. K. Beale, 'A Response to John Paulien on the Use of the Old Testament in Revelation', *AUSS* 39 (2001): 23–34.

[13] Steve Moyise, 'Does the Author of Revelation Misappropriate the Scriptures?', *AUSS* 40.1 (2002): 3–21.

[14] Ibid., 21.

[15] As in Steve Moyise, 'Models for Intertextual Interpretation of Revelation', in R. B. Hays and S. Alkier (eds), *Revelation and the Politics of Apocalyptic Interpretation* (Waco, TX: Baylor University Press, 2012), 31–45; and G. K. Beale and D. A. Carson, 'Introduction', in G. K. Beale and D. A. Carson (eds), *Commentary on the New Testament Use of the Old Testament* (Grand Rapids, MI: Baker, 2007), xxiii–xxviii. Indeed, the methodology of the commentary to which the latter is an introduction assumes a relation between original meaning, history of interpretation and use in the New Testament.

scripture in Revelation demonstrates some degree of concern for 'original' meaning. But to what extent is this assumption justified? Moyise and Beale were both determined to show something of the reasonableness of the use of scripture in Revelation, but does this determination lead to a relatively *unreasonable* interpretation of early Christian hermeneutics?

Hermeneutical assumptions in early Christianity: A comparison with Ignatius *Eph*. 19

Authorial intention has been an important element in the way texts have been read in the modern era stemming, in part, from Renaissance, early Modern and Romantic approaches to interpretation.[16] While some early Christian use of scripture demonstrates an interest in using the identity of an author (always David) to establish an interpretation (Mk 12.37; Acts 2.29-31, 34; and Heb. 4.7), this is certainly not widespread, nor does it come close to what one might recognize as authorial intention in a modern sense, as both Moyise and Beale would undoubtedly recognize.[17] The idea of establishing meaning on the basis of an author's identity or intentions is utterly absent from early Jewish exegesis and is only really attested in fairly sophisticated works of Homeric textual criticism in antiquity.[18] Early Christian authors could be said to demonstrate something of an interest in what texts originally meant in their use of typological interpretation, since this necessarily attends to the features of an antetype as a prerequisite for establishing Christological interpretation, for example. However, while the typological interpretation of scriptural people and events is well attested, the typological interpretation of scriptural texts themselves is not.[19] This is an important distinction if one intends to demonstrate that any early Christian writers attended first to 'original' meaning, before developing that meaning in new ways or exploring new ways in which a text may have significance. Instead,

---

[16] John Barton, *The Nature of Biblical Criticism* (Louisville, KY: Westminster John Knox Press, 2007), 117–36; B. H. McLean, *Biblical Interpretation and Philosophical Hermeneutics* (Cambridge: Cambridge University Press, 2012), 35–9; and Joseph A. Fitzmyer, *The Interpretation of Scripture: In Defense of the Historical-Critical Method* (New York: Paulist Press, 2008), 61–3.

[17] For a study of early Christian use of ideas of authorship in interpretation, see Benjamin Sargent, *David Being a Prophet: The Contingency of Scripture upon History in the New Testament*, BZNW 207 (Berlin: de Gruyter, 2014). In the context of this volume, it is certainly appropriate to note that this study was the fruit of my University of Oxford doctoral research for which Moyise was the external examiner. I remain grateful for his expert and gracious feedback.

[18] It was often suggested that the Rabbinic exegetical middah דבר הלמד מעניינו was concerned with elucidating meaning from historical or authorial context, but there are no examples of the rule where context is anything other than literary. See Benjamin Sargent, 'The Exegetical Middah דבר הלמד מעניינו and the New Testament', *NovT* 57.4 (2015): 413–17; and Benjamin Sargent, '"Interpreting Homer from Homer": Aristarchus of Samothrace and the Notion of Scriptural Authorship in the New Testament', *TynBul* 65.1 (2014): 125–39.

[19] Benjamin Sargent, 'The Typological Interpretation of Scriptural Quotations in the New Testament: A Test Case for the Bible in the Academy', in H. Clifford and M. Daffern (eds), *The Exegetical and Ethical: The Bible and the Academy in the Public Square: Essays for the Occasion of Professor John Barton's 70th Birthday*, BIS, 197 (Leiden: Brill, 2022), 162–71.

a concern for previous meanings of scripture appears to be alien to the hermeneutic perspectives of early Christianity that one may be able to establish with any degree of certainty.

Of course, Revelation does not offer anything like the kind of hermeneutically revealing reflection on the nature of scripture or its presumed authors seen in Jn 5.39; Rom. 15.4; 1 Cor. 10.1-11; 2 Cor. 3.12-16; Heb. 4.12-13; 1 Pet. 1.10-12; or 2 Pet. 1.19-21. Such reflections do, however, give the impression that the only interpretive context of interest is that of the interpreter: there is no sense of distinction between what a text meant in the past and what it means in the present, no indication of historical consciousness. Take 1 Pet. 1.10-12 as an example. The prophets of Israel's past searched in vain for the meaning their words might have in their own time. It was revealed to them by the Spirit of Christ, contends Peter, that their words were uttered entirely in the service of the Church and pertain to the sufferings of Christ and the glories that would follow. Christ and the Church stand at the climax of history: everything that came before finds its meaning in this dramatic moment. 1 Peter has an eschatological and ecclesiological hermeneutic, borne out in its actual use of scripture too: scripture is interpreted as though its meaning is solely about the Church or Christ.[20] Similarly, in the case of Rom. 15.4 and 1 Cor. 10.1-11, the value of scripture is limited by the theological assumption that it is 'written for our learning' and 'written down for our instruction'.

> Paul reads Scripture in the conviction that its narratives and prophecies all point to his own time; the church lives in the exhilarating moment in which all of God's past dealings with Israel and the world have come to their climactic point. When Paul says that 'the ends of the ages ... have come', he is referring to the eschatological point of collision between the old age and the new. That point of collision is precisely 'upon us': the church stands in the crucial moment in which a bright new light is shed upon everything past, particularly everything in Scripture.[21]

Of course, these examples are specific and relate to the use of scripture in a very particular form of writing: the early Christian letter. Much of the use of scripture in such texts is paraenetic: directly requesting certain outcomes through reference to sacred texts. It might, then, be unwise to imagine that these hermeneutical positions adequately explain the use of scripture in Revelation. At this point, a comparison with another early Christian exposition of a mysterious and apocalyptic event might prove instructive. Ignatius of Antioch's interpretation of the birth of Jesus Christ in his letter to the Church in Ephesus contains a few notable similarities with Rev. 12.1-6.

---

[20] Benjamin Sargent, *Written to Serve: The Use of Scripture in 1 Peter*, LNTS 547 (London: T&T Clark/Bloomsbury, 2015), 41–50; Benjamin Sargent, 'The Narrative Substructure of 1 Peter', *ET* 124.10 (2013): 485–90; K. H. Schelkle, *Die Petrusbriefe, der Judasbrief*, HThKNT (Freiburg: Herder, 1970), 38; and Lutz Doering, 'Gottes Volk: Die Adressaten als "Israel" im Ersten Petrusbrief', in David S. du Toit (ed.), *Bedrängnis und Identität: Studien zu Situation, Kommunikation und Theologie des 1. Petrusbriefes*, BZNW 200 (Berlin: de Gruyter, 2013), 106–9.

[21] Richard B. Hays, *First Corinthians*, Interpretation (Louisville, KY: John Knox, 1997), 162. Cf. Francis Watson, *Paul and the Hermeneutics of Faith* (London: T&T Clark, 2004), 16–17.

πῶς οὖν ἐφανερώθη τοῖς αἰῶσιν; ἀστὴρ ἐν οὐρανῷ ἔλαμψεν ὑπὲρ πάντας τοὺς ἀστέρας, καὶ τὸ φῶς αὐτοῦ ἀνεκλάλητον ἦν καὶ ξενισμὸν παρεῖχεν ἡ καινότης αὐτοῦ, τὰ δὲ λοιπὰ πάντα ἄστρα ἅμα ἡλίῳ καὶ σελήνῃ χορὸς ἐγένετο τῷ ἀστέρι, αὐτὸς δὲ ἦν ὑπερβάλλων τὸ φῶς αὐτοῦ ὑπὲρ 'πάντα ταραχή τε ἦν, πόθεν ἡ καινότης ἡ ἀνόμοιος αὐτοῖς. ὅθεν ἐλύετο πᾶσα μαγεία καὶ ' πᾶς δεσμὸς ἠφανίζετο κακίας ἄγνοια καθηρεῖτο, παλαιὰ βασιλεία διεφθείρετο θεοῦ ἀνθρωπίνως φανερουμένου εἰς καινότητα ἀϊδίου ζωῆς ἀρχὴν δὲ ἐλάμβανεν τὸ παρὰ θεῷ ἀπηρτισμένον. ἔνθεν τὰ πάντα συνεκινεῖτο διὰ τὸ μελετᾶσθαι θανάτου κατάλυσιν.

How then was this revealed to the ages? A star in heaven shone greater than all stars and its light was indescribable, and its novelty caused amazement. The remainder of all the stars, with the sun and moon became a chorus to the star, and its light surpassed all of them. There was confusion concerning the origins of this novelty. Then every kind of magic was destroyed and every binding spell, wicked ignorance was removed, the old kingdom abolished when God was revealed in human form so as to give newness of life and what had been prepared by God began. Then all things were in disarray because the destruction of death was being carried out.

Ignatius is almost certainly developing a theme he has received from others, possibly including Revelation.[22] There is some degree of similarity in the significance of the 'chorus' of stars with Rev. 12.1:

Καὶ σημεῖον μέγα ὤφθη ἐν τῷ οὐρανῷ, γυνὴ περιβεβλημένη τὸν ἥλιον, καὶ ἡ σελήνη ὑποκάτω τῶν ποδῶν αὐτῆς καὶ ἐπὶ τῆς κεφαλῆς αὐτῆς στέφανος ἀστέρων δώδεκα.

And a great sign appeared in heaven, a woman clothed with the sun, and the moon under her feet and a crown of twelve stars upon her head.

In both cases, the dream of Joseph in Gen. 37.9 is probably an influence, and a heavenly astral vision heralds the coming destruction of the powers of evil. Whereas the number of stars in the crown is the evidence for an allusion to Gen. 37.9 in Rev. 12.1, the relationship between one great star and the lesser stars that surround it indicates the presence of an allusion in *Eph.* 19.1.[23] But Ignatius also draws upon other texts and

---

[22] Gregory Vall, *Learning Christ: Ignatius of Antioch and the Mystery of Redemption* (Washington, DC: Catholic University of America Press, 2013), 130–1. It must be noted that a relationship between Rev. 12.1 and *Eph.* 19.2 is not widely recognized. Early Christian interpretation of the woman of Revelation 12 as Mary and the early second-century witness to Rev. 12.7-9 in Papias *Frag.* 24.2-10 supports Vall's argument. While parallels with Revelation in the letters of Ignatius are not strong, significant evidence is documented in Henning Paulsen, *Studien zur Theologie des Ignatius von Antiochien* (Göttingen: Vandenhoeck & Ruprecht, 1978), 126; C. J. Hemer, *The Letters to the Seven Churches of Asia in Their Local Setting*, JSNTSup 11 (Sheffield: Sheffield Academic Press, 1986), 228; and Christine Trevett, 'The Other Letters to the Churches of Asia: Apocalypse and the Letters of Ignatius of Antioch', *JSNT* 37 (1989): 124–30.

[23] Steve Moyise, 'Genesis in Revelation', in Maarten J. J. Menken and Steve Moyise (eds), *Genesis in the New Testament*, LNTS 466 (London: Bloomsbury, 2012), 166–79, 172 n.18; and R. H. Charles, *The Revelation of St. John*, ICC (Edinburgh: T&T Clark, 1920), 316. Cf. David E. Aune, *Revelation 6–16*, WBC 52B (Nashville, TN: Thomas Nelson, 1998), 681, for the argument that the twelve stars represent the zodiac.

traditions in his interpretation of the stars. The prophecy of Balaam in Num. 24.17 is a likely influence and the passage itself is something of an interpretation of Mt. 2.2.[24] Likewise, Wis. 18.14-19 is undoubtedly an important influence upon *Eph.* 19.[25] This is an imaginative example of the intertextual interpretation Moyise describes in Revelation. Ignatius brings together a number of texts and traditions of interpretation. Aside from the obvious hermeneutical creativity in seeing the dream of Gen. 37.9 as prophetic beyond the events of the Joseph Cycle, Gregory Vall suggests that Ignatius conflates Joseph's two dreams, taking the idea of the stars gathering around the greater star from the dream of the sheaves (Gen. 37.7) and adding it to worship of the greater star from the dream of the stars. One could say that, like the author of Revelation, Ignatius dreams imaginatively with the scriptural texts and traditions known to him. However, unlike Revelation, Ignatius offers something of an account of his scriptural hermeneutic, most famously in *Philad.* 8.2.

> Παρακαλῶ δὲ ὑμᾶς μηδὲν κατ' ἐρίθειαν πράσσειν, ἀλλὰ κατὰ χριτομαθίαν. ἐπεὶ ἤκοθσά τινων λεγόντων ὅτι ἐὰν μὴ ἐν τοῖς ἀρχείοις εὕρω, ἐν τῷ εὐαγγελίῳ οὐ πιστεύω καὶ λέγοντός μου αὐτοῖς ὅτι γέγραπται, ἀπεκρίθησάν μοι ὅτι πρόλειται. ἐμοὶ δὲ ἀρχεῖά ἐστιν Ἰησοῦς Χριστός, τὰ ἄθικτα ἀρχεῖα ὁ σταυρὸς αὐτοῦ καὶ ὁ θάνατος καὶ ἡ ἀνάστασις αὐτοῦ καὶ ἡ πίστις ἡ δι' αὐτοῦ.
>
> But I exhort you to do nothing with contentiousness, but according to the learning of Christ. For I heard some saying, 'if I do not find it in the archives, I do not believe it in the Gospel.'[26] I said to them, 'it is written ...' and they answered, 'that is the issue!' But to me the archives are Jesus Christ: the unchangeable archives are his cross and death and his resurrection and the faith which is through him. (*Philad.* 8.2)

Like *Eph.* 19, this is another of the most debated and best-known parts of Ignatius's letters. The charge against Ignatius appears to be that he often claims scriptural support for his arguments, without being able to substantiate them.[27] This has led many to assume that Ignatius was relatively disinterested in the use of scripture, perhaps representative of where he might be situated on a trajectory towards the 'parting of the ways'.[28] Ignatius's response is to contend that the substance of scripture, the true

---

[24] Jean Daniélou, *Primitive Christian Symbols*, trans. Donald Attwater (Baltimore, MD: Helican Press, 1964), 113; and Jean Daniélou, 'L'Étoile de Jacob et la mission chrétienne à Damas', *VC* 11 (1957): 121–38.

[25] M. D. Goulder and M. L. Sanderson, 'St. Luke's Genesis', *JTS* 8.1 (1957): 26; Alan Cabaniss, 'Wisdom 18.14ff.: An Early Christmas Text', *VC* 10 (1956): 100–1; and Vall, *Learning Christ*, 130–1. Heinrich Schlier, *Religionsgeschichtliche Untersuchungen zu den Ignatiusbriefen*, BZNW 8 (Geißen: Alfred Töpelmann, 1929), 5–81, also argues for the influence of the *Ascension of Isaiah* and the *Odes of Solomon* in his claim that *Eph.* 19 reflects a gnostic hymn.

[26] Not as Theodor Zahn, *Ignatius von Antiochen* (Gotha: Perthes, 1873), 373–9, suggests, 'If I do not find it in the archives, that is, in the Gospel, I do not believe it', implying that the gospel has the status here of written text.

[27] William R. Schoedel, 'Ignatius and the Archives', *HTR* 71 (1978): 97–8.

[28] Manlio Simonetti, *Biblical Interpretation in the Early Church: An Historical Introduction to Patristic Exegesis*, trans. John A. Hughes (Edinburgh: T&T Clark, 1994), 13; Walter Bauer, *Orthodoxy and*

referent of 'the archives', is the work of Jesus Christ.[29] This perspective on the meaning of scripture is substantiated earlier in the letter in a claim Ignatius makes about the prophets of Israel's past.

> Καὶ τοὺς προφήτας δὲ ἀγαπῶμεν, διὰ τὸ καὶ αὐτοὺς εἰς τὸ εὐαγγέλιον κατηγγελκέναι καὶ εἰς αὐτὸν ἐλπίζειν καὶ αὐτὸν ἀναμένειν ἐν ᾧ καὶ πιστεύσαντες ἐσώθησαν, ἐν ἑνότητι Ἰησοῦ Χριστοῦ ὄντες ἀξιαγάπητοι καὶ ἀξιοθαύμαστοι ἅγιοι, ὑπὸ Ἰησοῦ Χριστοῦ μεμαρτυρημένοι καὶ συνηριθμημένοι ἐν τῷ εὐαγγελίῳ τῆς κοινῆς ἐλπίδος.
>
> And we love the prophets because they proclaimed the Gospel beforehand: they hoped in it and waited for it. Because they believed they were saved, being one in Jesus Christ, holy ones worthy of love and worthy of wonder, borne witness to by Jesus Christ and added into the Gospel of common hope. (*Philad.* 5.2)

For Ignatius, the prophets of Israel's past hoped in what is, by Ignatius's time, understood as the substance of the gospel about Jesus Christ. The orientation of their words is towards Christ: they are, in a sense, proto-Christians, playing their part in the economy of salvation.[30] This has much in common with the hermeneutics of 1 Pet. 1.10-12 and Rom. 15.4 discussed earlier. One might imagine, then, that as Ignatius wove together the dreams of Joseph with the prophecy of Balaam and the Wisdom of Solomon, as well as the visit of the Magi, that he understood the gospel to be the true meaning of all of these events and words: that there is no meaning besides this. Ignatius, like other early Christian interpreters of scripture, does not appear to demonstrate any interest in what texts originally meant in order to understand his own interpretation as a supplement to it or expansion of it. The same might be said of the interpretation of scripture in Revelation. As Richard Bauckham contends, the author imaginatively and creatively 'gathered up the prophetic meaning of the Old Testament scriptures' as he wove together a host of scriptural texts and images.[31] Because of the apparent focus of meaning towards the eschatological present and future, interpretive explanations of the use of scripture in Revelation which presuppose an interest in some form of prior meaning, whether seen in ideas of *sensus plenior* or typological interpretation, do not do justice to the evidence available.

Heresy in Earliest Christianity, ed. Robert A. Kraft (London: SCM, 1972), 65-70; Zahn, *Ignatius von Antiochen*, 368-9; and R. M. Grant, 'Scripture and Tradition in St. Ignatius of Antioch', *CBQ* 25 (1963): 322-35.

[29] This possibly generous interpretation of *Philad.* 8.2 is that of Jonathan Lookadoo, 'Ignatius of Antioch and Scripture', *ZAC* 23.2 (2019): 201-27.

[30] Allen Brent, 'History and Eschatological Mysticism in Ignatius of Antioch', *Ephemerides Theologicae Lovanienses* 65.4 (1989): 310-16; and Edward Fudge, 'The Eschatology of Ignatius of Antioch: Christocentric and Historical', *JETS* 15.4 (1972): 231-7.

[31] Richard Bauckham, *The Climax of Prophecy: Studies in the Book of Revelation* (London: T&T Clark, 1993), xi.

Conclusion

This chapter began by arguing that the debate between Moyise and Beale is best understood as a debate shaped by evangelical conviction and the need to demonstrate the plausibility or reasonableness of the use of scripture in Revelation. This concern limited the debate somewhat as it relied upon an early Christian interest in historically contingent or authorial meaning, for which there is very little evidence. The debate was inspired in part by Longenecker's contention that one did not need to see the hermeneutics of Revelation as exemplary. There is, perhaps, still merit in this approach. Many biblical claims are made on the basis of reasoning which may seem untenable to modern audiences. Many evangelicals have found ways of seeing the truth of biblical claims about the created world, without accepting, for example, that the earth has four corners. Just as theological claims do not depend on geographical accuracy, so Revelation was not written to teach hermeneutics.

Part 2

Scriptures and interpretation in the Book of Revelation

4

Something old, something new: The origins of the Song of Moses in Rev. 15.3

David M. Allen

Introduction

It is a famous dictum within Revelation scholarship that although it is wholly embedded in the language and landscapes of Israel's scriptures, the Apocalypse lacks a formal or explicit quotation drawn from those scriptures.[1] While images and motifs from Daniel and Ezekiel abound across Revelation's constitutive acts, they appear to do so without any formal, specific, signalled quotation from those texts (or indeed from any other scriptural source).[2] However, if there is one potential candidate to which one might assign the quotation designation, one citation that might counter the received dictum, then it could well be Rev. 15.3-4 and its presentation of the Song of Moses and the Lamb (SML).

On an initial reading at least, there are good reasons to classify Rev. 15.3-4 as a quotation. The Song is prefaced by λέγοντες, which may qualify as some form of introductory formula, particularly as the word could be said to be otherwise syntactically redundant. The introduction of the hymn as (at least in part) the Song of Moses hints at the perception of a familiar text, one whose Mosaic provenance may be recognized and identified. As such, some scholars have conceded that it may therefore qualify as a genuine quotation[3] and thus be distinctive, unique even, in the Apocalypse on that basis. However, as is equally well recognized within Revelation scholarship, irrespective of how one 'categorizes' the citation – quotation, allusion, composite allusion – it remains the case that the precise origin of the citation's *Vorlage*

---

[1] While one recognizes the fluidity or slipperiness of such terms, I am using here a reasonably standard designation of a quotation, namely a citation, normally marked or introduced by a recognizable 'formulaic expression' that points to the citation's prior existence elsewhere. Cf. Christopher D. Stanley, *Paul and the Language of Scripture: Citation Technique in the Pauline Epistles and Contemporary Literature*, SNTSMS 69 (Cambridge: Cambridge University Press, 1992), 33; E. Earle Ellis, *Paul's Use of the Old Testament* (Grand Rapids, MI: Baker, 1957), 22–5. One recognizes, of course, that 'unmarked quotations' may also exist, but they are not our concern here.

[2] UBS4 specifies no quotation for Revelation in its list of cited OT texts.

[3] Steve Moyise, *Evoking Scripture: Seeing the Old Testament in the New* (London: T&T Clark, 2008), 129, concedes that Rev. 15.2, uniquely for Revelation, may be introducing an explicit quotation.

is contested and/or potentially unavailable to the contemporary reader. Hence Rev. 15.3-4 manifests the irony of being the one apocalyptic text that may be classified as a quotation while almost deliberately refusing to follow the perceived conventions with which quotations generally operate.

Moreover, the scenario is complexified by the apparent dual designation of the introductory formula (15.3). The text is both the Song of Moses *and* the Song of the Lamb. As such, any Mosaic reference, however parsed or defined, does not exhaust the implied, explanatory significance of the Song and/or the search for its prior scriptural origins. Equally, the Song's ovine characterization is similarly solely insufficient; the inclusion of the Lamb may remind the reader of the earlier Song sung to – rather than by – the Lamb (5.9-14),[4] or indeed may relate to the new song chorused in the previous chapter (14.3), but the accompanying Mosaic reference surely points more to some Old Testament association and thereby renders the Song as being not completely *de novo*. Furthermore, these two prior Revelation hymns are explicitly demarked as 'new' (5.9, 14.3),[5] an attribute not accorded to the refrain of 15.3-4. Does the fact that the Song is *not* described as being 'new' therefore have any resulting interpretative significance (particularly as rabbinic tradition does anticipate Moses singing a 'new song' in the age to come)?[6]

One might therefore suggest that Rev. 15.3-4 offers a suitable case study on the Apocalypse's use of the Jewish scriptures. To quote the wedding apophthegm, there is simultaneously 'something old, something new' about Rev. 15.3-4, and such a tagline may offer a potential window onto how the Apocalypse appropriates and represents scriptural material, an example of the fusion of various images, both old and new.[7] Commenting on the SML, Greg Beale captures some of this old/new paradox: 'That the song in 15.3-4 is also a "new song" is evident because the saints sing not only the old "song of Moses" but also the "song of the Lamb", which has hitherto not been sung.'[8] Les Hardin draws similar old/new conclusions:

> Even the 'new song' sung by the multitudes (5:9, 14:3) seems to reflect material of the ancient songs as John recontextualizes themes from Israel's hymnody and Scriptures for his readers. A good example of this 'new couched in old' methodology is 'The Song of Moses the servant of God and the song of the Lamb' (15:3).[9]

---

[4] The genitive ἀρνίου could theoretically be objective (i.e. the Song is sung to the Lamb – so Stephen S. Smalley, *The Revelation to John: A Commentary on the Greek Text of the Apocalypse* (Downers Grove, IL: InterVarsity, 2005), 386); but this would differ from the previous genitive (Μωϋσέως) – Moses would unlikely be the 'recipient' of the Song.

[5] They may, in effect, be the same song – the 'content' of 14.3 is not specified.

[6] So Laszlo Gallus, 'The Exodus Motif in Revelation 15–16: Its Background and Nature', *AUSS* 46 (2008): 21–43, 32 n64: *Qoh. Rab.* 1.9; *Mek. Exod.* 15.1; *Tanh. Exod.* 30b.

[7] For a not dissimilar lens/approach, see Wolfgang Fenske, '"Das Lied des Mose, des Knechtes Gottes, und das Lied des Lammes" (Apokalypse des Johannes 15,3f): Der Text und seine Bedeutung für die Johannes-Apokalypse', *ZNW* 90 (1999): 250–64.

[8] G. K. Beale, *The Book of Revelation: A Commentary on the Greek Text* (Grand Rapids, MI: Eerdmans, 1999), 793.

[9] Les Hardin, 'A Theology of the Hymns in Revelation', *Stone-Campbell Journal* 17 (2014): 233–45 (240).

We will seek to probe the new/old fusion in more detail, moving beyond merely recognizing its existence and on to probing the wider interpretative significance of such temporal fusion.

Interpretative questions

Before we turn to considering the source(s) of the Song, several initial interpretative questions arise, all of which might be seen to impact on the old/new classification. Unlike the two previous hymnic instances (5.9-10, 14.3), the SML does not take place in the divine presence,[10] and this may serve to enforce its particularity and distinctiveness – and/or its performance – even if, as noted earlier, it is not specifically designated as 'new'. But perhaps the key presenting question is how many songs Rev. 15.3 purports to identify, one or two? The most straightforward reading of the Song is to view it as one entity, rather than two, with the two attributive authors/sources responsible for this unity. This would seem to be the present scholarly consensus, or at least the most commonly posited viewpoint,[11] and broadly speaking, the καί of 15.3 would function epexegetically, to denote the unity of the hymn. Assuming that it is one song, other questions then follow. Is it one (new) combination of two (familiar) songs?[12] Or is it one (new) song that is linked with both named figures? Or is it one old song – formerly that of Moses – with which the Lamb subsequently becomes associated? And to what degree is it a 'joint composition', so to speak?[13]

The answers to such questions are more moot and, in effect, cannot be determined convincingly from the text, but as we shall see, the co-existence of old and new characteristics within 15.3-4 may be of relevance. It may be that Song is the (one) fusion (or 'pastiche') of two traditions or sets of material – one old, one new (or less old) – into one unit; the old incorporates a number of scriptural elements, generally associated with Moses, whereas the new embraces their representation or reworking in the light of the work of the Lamb. This would effectively imply the existence of three songs. Alternatively, and for this author, more likely, the one (Mosaic) song is reworked and expanded in the light of the Lamb, thus underscoring its respective old and new elements. We will assume this position and see if/how the old/new categorization might go about corroborating it. Perhaps Macchia and Thomas articulate the tension well, though, without resolving the question concerning one song or three, in that whatever the putative origins, '(t)he songs are ... to be understood in the light of one another and yet are, *at the same time one song*'.[14]

---

[10] John Christopher Thomas and Frank D. Macchia, *Revelation* (Grand Rapids, MI: Eerdmans, 2016), 269.

[11] It is the view taken by Beale, *Revelation*, 792, or Smalley, *Revelation*, 386, for example. See also Brian K. Blount, *Revelation: A Commentary* (Louisville, KY: Westminster John Knox, 2009), 286.

[12] One might term this a three-song solution – cf. Rudolph Scharneck, 'The Song of Moses Which Is Not (Also) the Song of the Lamb: An Investigation into the Number of Songs at Play in Rev. 15', *JECH* 9 (2019): 59–73.

[13] Sigve Tonstad, *Revelation* (Grand Rapids, MI: Baker, 2019), 221. He continues: 'The two sing the same tune, theologically speaking.'

[14] Thomas and Macchia, *Revelation*, 270, emphasis added.

Alternatively, it has been ventured that Revelation has two distinct songs in mind, namely that the Song of Moses (SOM) is 'sung', but not textually cited, and hence the 'lyrics' of 15.3-4 pertain just to the Song of the Lamb (SOL).[15] This solution has the advantage of removing the presenting question of the SOM's source, and in effect, the scriptural (or 'something old') aspect is negated or rendered irrelevant. Viewing the cited hymn as solely the SOL does have some merit, particularly if it has some connection to 14.3, and it is a fair question as to why τὴν ᾠδὴν is repeated if only one Song is portrayed. However, the two-song solution effectively becomes an argument from silence and is thus hard to resolve; and if the SOM is not being sung, then it begs the question as to why reference/mention it at all? Moreover, the argument offered by the advocates of the two-song position only serves to reinforce the presenting question, namely to move the debate on from a 'search for the Historical SOM *Vorlage*' and instead to seek after a different lens by which to assess Rev. 15.3-4's scriptural usage. The suggestion that the SOL may be an existing source, drawing on the Tosefta Targum on 1 Sam. 17.43, is an intriguing one;[16] if it were the case, it would represent a pre-Christian source for the Song of the Lamb upon which Revelation might draw, and it would also necessarily recalibrate how we parse the respective oldness and newness of Revelation's casting of the Song. However, until there is more evidence for the pre-existence of the SOL, we will treat the Tosefta Targum theory as a theoretical parallel, rather than dependent, text.

Second, in terms of who sings the Song, the referent of ᾄδουσιν would seem to be primarily the conquerors referenced in 15.2. Moses's previous actions as the singer of songs attributed to him (Exod. 15.1-18; Deut. 32.1-43) might suggest a similar role in the Revelation 15 example, but equally, that would seem to necessitate the Lamb so doing – and there is nothing in Rev. 15.2-6, or elsewhere in the Apocalypse, to deem that necessary; the Lamb does many things, but being a cantor does not appear to be explicitly one of them.[17] Hence, the reference to Moses is likely more to capture or key into wider traditions that accompanied the act of singing, rather than necessarily to revisit Moses's vocal prowess.

Something(s) old

To what, then, might the Song pertain in terms of prior reference? As noted earlier, there is no specific source for the Song, and this questions its characterization as a quotation or formal citation. Revelation's wider debt to scriptural material does, though, point towards origins from within the scriptures, and the declaration that '(s)carcely a word in the song is not richly informed by its place in the OT'[18] would

---

[15] Scharneck, 'Song of Moses'.

[16] See J. C. de Moor and E. Van Staalduine-Sulman, 'The Aramaic Song of the Lamb', *JSJ* 24 (1993): 266–79.

[17] Ian Boxall, *The Revelation of Saint John*, BNTC (London: Continuum, 2006), 218, places particular emphasis on Moses and the Lamb participating in the choral delivery, but this does not seem to be required by the text/context.

[18] Thomas and Macchia, *Revelation*, 270. Ben Witherington III, *Revelation*, NCBC (Cambridge: Cambridge University Press, 2003), 206, likewise acknowledges that the text manifests a 'patchwork

seem apposite. Likewise, the ascription to Moses points the reader back to 'something old', and to two potential source texts, the preceding examples of Songs of Moses found in Exodus 15 and Deuteronomy 32.

The SOM's Exodus 15 provenance or reference point is affirmed by several commentators,[19] and there are certainly significant echoes of Exodus 15 within the Song and its immediate context.[20] The links tend towards the thematic, however, rather than the explicitly lexical (at least in terms of identifying any *Vorlage*). Rev. 15.5, for example, represents the imagery of the tent of meeting (cf. Exod. 38.26 LXX), while Rev. 15.6 refers to the advent of plagues (the parallels between the bowls of Revelation 16 and Exodus are well mapped elsewhere; cf. also 15.8).[21] Exodus 15 is sung by the Sea, or at least it possesses a 'maritime' disposition, and this is in tandem with the sea of glass location for Revelation 15's delivery (15.2). Likewise, those assembled to sing the hymn of Rev. 15.3-4 are those who have conquered the Beast (15.2), and this may resonate with the deliverance from Egypt within the Red Sea and thereby the implied association of Pharoah and the Beast. However, the actual 'wordage' of the Rev. 15.3-4 hymn differs significantly from the mooted Exodus 15 predecessor. While Exod. 15.11 could be said to capture the ethos or tenor of Rev. 15.3-4 (or vice versa), it is not the precise language of the Song. Likewise, the description of Moses as 'servant of God' (Rev. 15.3) may appear to parallel the same appellation in the verse preceding the Song (Exod. 14.31), but the LXX here renders θεράπον rather than the δοῦλος of Rev. 15.3.[22] And whereas the Exodus SOM recounts and celebrates a victory over the Egyptian enemies, the Revelation 15 equivalent is a song of praise to YHWH. Hence the respective contexts for the Songs vary and suggest therefore a more creative assessment of how the Exodus 15 links might be operative is warranted. That said, Moses is not named elsewhere in the Apocalypse, so his inclusion warrants some comment or justification, perhaps as symbolic of a wider exodus/plagues reference. He may fulfil a more keying role, capturing here a wider discourse than purely the events alluded to in Exodus 15.[23]

---

quilt of OT phrases', though equally affirms that Exodus 15 is the primary text in mind (cf. the Rev. 15.4/Exod. 15.11 parallel). At the same time, he concedes – perhaps testifying to the complexity of the question – 'its content owes more to Deut. 32 than to Exod. 15'.

[19] Smalley, *Revelation*, 386; Beale, *Revelation*, 792; Richard Bauckham, *The Theology of the Book of Revelation* (Cambridge: Cambridge University Press, 1993), 98–101; Elisabeth Schüssler Fiorenza, *Revelation: Vision of a Just World* (Minneapolis, MN: Fortress Press, 1991), 91–2; implicit in Gallus, 'Exodus Motif', 30–2.

[20] Pace Steve Moyise, 'Singing the Song of Moses and the Lamb: John's Dialogical Use of Scripture', *AUSS* 42 (2004): 347–60 (350): 'John seems to have gone out of his way to avoid any connection with this famous OT song, despite deliberately pointing to it by the ascription, "the song of Moses, the servant of God."' The differences notwithstanding, there remain significant points of contact between Exodus 15 and the SML.

[21] Cf. for example, Gallus, 'Exodus Motif', 21–43.

[22] And it is far from the only instance where such a label is ascribed to Moses (cf. Num. 12.7-8; Josh. 1.2, 7; Ps. 105.26 *inter alia*).

[23] Bauckham, *Theology*, 98, for example, opines that a 'new exodus motif' sets the backdrop to Revelation 15-16, and that the church's 'passage through martyrdom to heaven is compared with the passage of the Israelites through the Red Sea'.

The alternative Song of Moses is that found in Deuteronomy 32,[24] and some have made the case that Revelation 15 is attuned to that source rather than to the Exodus 15 predecessor.[25] Again, the parallels are essentially thematic rather than lexical. The Song's witness characterization (Deut. 31.21), and its appeal to divine justice (Deut. 32.4), is commensurate with the SML's tenor, and the declaration of divine judgement on Israel's adversaries (Deut. 32.43) is resonant with the SML's immediate context (15.1-2). The fact that the Deuteronomic Song is also sung by Ἰησοῦς (32.44 LXX) may also be relevant, attesting both to dual singing (the Exodus version is sung by all Israel – cf. Exod. 15.1) and specifically with a Jesus figure. However, the lexical links for Deuteronomy 32 remain even more limited than with Exodus 15. There may be an echo of Deut. 32.4 in Rev. 15.4 – the description of YHWH as ὅσιος – but that remains fairly limited and not restricted to just Deut. 32.4 (cf. e.g. Ps. 144.17 LXX, where the similarity is lexically closer). Hence '(i)t is best to see the second song of Moses playing a supporting role by supplying references to God's name and greatness, and to his just and holy ways'.[26]

One might also mention echoes, or even allusions, of other scriptural texts in this regard. The allusion to Ps. 86.8-10 in Rev. 15.3-4 is arguably stronger – linguistically at least – than the prior Songs of Moses.[27] Appeal is made to YHWH's mighty deeds (Ps. 86.8, 10; Rev. 15.3), and the nations are summoned to worship (Ps. 86.9; Rev. 15.4); the overall tenor of both passages is to stress the incomparability of YHWH. Similarly, Rev. 15.3b-4a would seem to be a close paraphrase – maybe even some form of amended quotation – of Jer. 10.7. The same question (who will not fear you O Lord, king of the nations?) is asked in both texts, and the implied answer is effectively consistent in both texts (Jer. 10.7; Rev. 15.4), namely that no one is like YHWH in terms of wisdom and authority.[28] Rev. 15.4 may also derive in some way from Ps. 97.2 LXX, and the shared emphasis on divine vindication and righteousness, but the lexical similarity is not close. Other echoes and points of similarity may also be operative – the declaration of Rev. 15.3a may reflect Tob. 12.22 or might equally draw on Ps. 111.2 or Dan. 9.24 or Job 42.3. Similarly, Rev. 15.3b's claimed appeal to ὁ θεὸς ὁ παντοκράτωρ might seem to have its origins in Amos's frequent usage of the term (cf. Amos 3.13, 4.13, 5.8,

---

[24] Psalm 89 LXX is a προσευχὴ of Moses but is of a different ilk to Exodus 15 or Deuteronomy 32, so it does not form part of our enquiry. We rule out the notion of another pre-existing Song of Moses.

[25] Cf. Joseph L. Trafton, *Reading Revelation: A Literary and Theological Commentary* (Macon, GA: Smyth & Helwys, 2005), 142–3; Fenske, 'Lied', 264; Eugene H. Peterson, *Reversed Thunder: The Revelation of John and the Praying Imagination* (San Francisco, CA: Harper & Row, 1988), 139. Cf. William Horbury, 'Septuagintal and New Testament Conceptions of Church', in Markus N. A. Bockmuehl and Michael B. Thompson (eds), *A Vision for the Church: Studies in Early Christian Ecclesiology in Honour of J. P. M. Sweet* (Edinburgh: T&T Clark, 1997), 1–17 (2n1): 'the song sung by the victorious martyrs echoes and parallels that of Deut 32.'

[26] Craig R. Koester, *Revelation: A New Translation with Introduction and Commentary*, AB 38A (New Haven, CT: Yale University Press, 2014), 634–5.

[27] Steve Moyise, *The Later New Testament Writers and Scripture* (London: SPCK, 2012), 135, avers that Rev. 15.3-4 is 'based on' Ps. 86.8-10.

[28] Ps. 86.8 and Jer. 10.7 are therefore very similar texts, and it is likely no coincidence that they have been juxtaposed or fused together within Rev. 15.3-4 – cf. Moyise, 'Singing', 351. One might also suggest that such similarity makes them ideal candidates as constituent elements of a pastiche – see later in this chapter.

5.14-16, among others), though it could derive from Revelation's own frequent use of the phrase in hymnic or liturgical settings (cf. Rev. 4.8, 11.17, 16.7).

In sum, therefore, Rev. 15.3-4's 'oldness' is complex; attempts to reduce the mooted source of the SML to just one or two scriptural predecessors fail to take account of the wide array of texts and images that might be said to feed it. That is, it is the essential diversity of 'sources' feeding Rev. 15.3-4 that makes the hymn distinct and opens up wider consideration of how the Apocalypse appropriates and (re)presents scriptural material.

Something(s) new

If the SML's old disposition is intricate, its 'newness' is equally so, and one might make two immediate observations in that regard. First, the very essence or 'reworking' of the Song is, in and of itself, 'new'; that is, however one ends up parsing the sources of the Song, it is no longer the same Mosaic oration found in either of the Exodus or Deuteronomy situations. We have here the creation of a 'new' SOM (now the SML), a new 'scriptural' text, a reworking of old content in new form. Second, one might suggest that Revelation is making such 'old' allusions in a 'new' way; and such 'newness' pertains not just to the novelty of the heavenly, Christ era, or to the new content of the Song itself (the invitation to all nations to worship (15.4),[29] for example, is an additional detail not found in the exodus-related precedents), but also to the techniques by which the old connections are articulated. To put it another way, Revelation's use of the Old Testament, particularly in Rev. 15.2-6, is *different* from that of other New Testament writers; it announces something new (drawing on the old) but does so in a methodologically 'new' fashion.

We turn, now, to consider such methodological novelty but do so recognizing that – to continue the wedding mantra 'something old, something new, something borrowed' – Revelation's methods may not be completely *de novo* but instead may be better described as a 'borrowing'. To generate something 'new' in 15.2-6, Revelation 'borrows' from pre-existing material and recasts and represents it in a fresh way.

One of the most significant recent monographs on Revelation's use of Israel's scriptures has been Michelle Fletcher's *Reading Revelation as Pastiche*.[30] Addressing current debates on the use of the OT within Revelation, and particularly the contextual continuity (or otherwise) of Revelation's intertextual appropriation, Fletcher offers a new lens or framework for categorizing Revelation's borrowing of scriptural material. She adopts the convention or motif of 'pastiche' to describe Revelation's intertextual engagement,[31] a process that recognizes (and celebrates) the plurality of constituent

---

[29] For Bauckham, *Theology*, 101, this is the most distinctive novelty of Rev. 15.3-4: 'The effect is to shift the emphasis in the significance of the new exodus, from an event by which God delivers his people by judging their enemies to an event which brings the nations to acknowledge the true God.'

[30] Michelle Fletcher, *Reading Revelation as Pastiche: Imitating the Past*, LNTS 571 (London: Bloomsbury, 2017).

[31] Fletcher, *Pastiche*, 48: 'Pastiche is a specific practice of imitation and combination that sits somewhere between original and copy, parody and homage, and collage and mosaic.' Cf. also: 'When parody is too harsh and emulation too positive, and when collage is too disparate but mosaic too

material in Revelation and which resists the notion of finding merely one or a primary motif being operative. Whereas, in twenty-first-century discourse, pastiche can assume an essentially pejorative or negative dimension,[32] Fletcher embraces it, considering it a positive appellation or technique, a means by which to bring a multiplicity of voices to the interpretative table. On her construal, pastiche 'describes texts which are highly intertextual, imitative, multivocal, combined and reader involving' and it occupies the 'space between slavish imitation and creative reworking' of the material it utilizes.[33] In particular, she identifies two key characteristic features to pastiche – imitation and combination – arguing that Revelation thereby draws together a variety of images and themes to imitate prior imagery. As such, we might say that, through the pastiche of images, something 'new' is created, something distinct and novel, something *de novo*, but equally something which (knowingly?) alludes to, or imitates, something(s) prior.

Fletcher uses contemporary art forms (particularly cinema) to unpack how the pastiche functions to 'imitate the past' and chooses four case studies against which to apply the pastiche lens (three specific texts – Revelation 1, 17, 18, and then Revelation as an apocalypse). At one level, there is something quite critical or 'destabilizing' as to her assessment of Revelation's approach and particularly in assessing the Apocalypse's appropriation of scriptural material. Fletcher's construal of pastiche is very much reader-orientated (she has little interest in authorial concerns), and she focuses instead on what connections are generated by the reader or audience of the portrayal. The pastiche lens thus subverts (or at least could be seen as so doing) previous or accepted takes on the OT/NT discourse; it moves the debate away – at least in some form – from attending solely to the source(s) of the Old Testament reference (and the relative abundance of that) and instead focuses on the final effect this so engenders.[34] The 'technical' categories of quotation, allusion and echo are not invoked, at least not in the terms customarily utilized within the subdiscipline. But equally, her proposal takes seriously the full 'effect' of the combination of images, and bearing in mind the elusive polyphony of influences impacting on Rev. 15.3-4, pastiche may actually be a useful lens or mode by which to assess the impact of their combination, rather than getting bogged down in trying to discern which are more causative or effective than others.

It is interesting that the SML – seemingly an ideal candidate for the type of analysis for which Fletcher advocates – is not discussed in her monograph, as the lens offers a potential locus for exploration of Rev. 15.2-6's old/new tensions. Its veritable amalgam of scriptural imagery, and the potential blurring of constituent material, constructs the 'same but different' character Fletcher sees as intrinsic to Revelation's

---

harmonized, and when original is too distinct but copy too exact, then pastiche can enter in and fill the gap.'

[32] Cf. David E. Aune, *Word Biblical Commentary. Volume 52b, Revelation 6–16* (Nashville, TN: Thomas Nelson, 1998), 874. Moyise, 'Singing', 353, is cautious about using Aune's term 'pastiche' because of its potentially random overtones and uses the term 'amalgam' instead. Pieter G. R. De Villiers, 'The Composition of Revelation 14:1–15:8: Pastiche or Perfect Pattern?', *Neot* 38 (2004): 209-49, uses the term 'pastiche' for his analysis of Revelation 14–15 but essentially as a qualitative assessment rather than a methodological one.

[33] Fletcher, *Pastiche*, 61.

[34] Such a tendency is present in Moyise, but Fletcher's attempt is avowedly more explicit in this regard.

(re)presentation of previous material.³⁵ Hence rather than seeking to restrict the *Vorlage* or backdrop of Rev. 15.3-4 to Exodus 15 or Deuteronomy 32, the pastiche lens would seem to recognize – celebrate even – such plurality and warrants against a reductionistic approach that limits the 'imitation' to one particular text or occasion. Likewise, the destabilizing tendency that Fletcher suggests pastiche may occasion might well manifest itself in terms of the mistaken familiarity of the song; the Mosaic designation initially leads the reader in one direction (be it Exodus 15 or Deuteronomy 32), but the actual text of the Song leads elsewhere, particularly when coupled with the concurrent association of the Lamb. To use Fletcher's criteria more explicitly, Rev. 15.2-6 is *imitative* (in replaying Moses's prior cantorial performance), is *intertextual* (in terms of wanting to engage with echoes from another text(s)), is *multivocal* (with a polyphony of 'source' material) and (perhaps most distinctively) is *involving of the reader*; as a Song, it is participatory,³⁶ as a picture, it is visual. The reader is implicitly invited to make external connections and equally has 'work' to do when making them.

In her case study of Revelation 18, Fletcher draws on Todd Haynes's 2002 film *Far from Heaven* and specifically its representation (or imitation) of Douglas Sirk's 1955 piece *All That Heaven Allows*. In her analysis, she draws attention to not only the evident similarities between the films but, more significantly, also the key points of difference ('Like but not the Same') and sees such themes likewise outworked in Revelation 18. In particular, the film comparison underscores the fact that 'the world has changed',³⁷ but such changes are mediated or understood through recognizing the differences with the past. With Fletcher, and following her categorization for *Far from Heaven* and Revelation 18, we might suggest that Revelation 15 exhibits similar tendencies or characteristics:

- *Reading the whole text*: As noted earlier, there are multiple points of reference to previous texts, and just as with Revelation 18, 'there are simply too many nods to other texts';³⁸ the whole full 'old' portfolio needs to be embraced. The *Vorlage* text or source ceases to be the driving issue – it becomes more about the new, pastiched situational usage. Rev. 15.3-4 manifests the suggestive pointing to the Song of Moses, the hint at a quotation and the potential keying into a wider e/Exodus framework, but the full effect of the portrayal – or pastiche – only emerges when other texts come to the interpretive fore.
- *Similar is not the same*: The similarities are there, particularly in terms of exodus-related imagery, but their presence and/or reworking actually serves to draw attention to the *novelty* or differences in the situation. The inclusion of the Lamb (15.2), the summons to the nations (15.4), the angelic presence (15.1, 6) or the divine harps (15.2, instead of tambourines – cf. Exod. 15.20) all function as novel additions to the potentially familiar Mosaic landscape.

---

³⁵ Fletcher, *Pastiche*, 136.
³⁶ On this, see Lourdes García Ureña, *Narrative and Drama in the Book of Revelation: A Literary Approach*, SNTSMS 175, trans. Donald Murphy (Cambridge: Cambridge University Press, 2019), 155–8.
³⁷ Fletcher, *Pastiche*, 175.
³⁸ Ibid., 170.

- *The world has changed*: *This is exercised through the past*. This goes to the very heart of our proposal regarding Rev. 15.2-6. The 'new' world portrayed on or by the sea of glass is fundamentally premised or built on 'old', familiar discourse.

Something borrowed? Some implications

What then does the application of the pastiche lens to Rev. 15.2-6 yield? For a start, Fletcher's approach frees the reader from dependence on one voice and/or trying to solve the *Vorlage* of the Rev. 15.3-4 'citation'. It encourages the exploration of the full choir of allusive voices, a recovery of the full extent or range of 'borrowing', and this seems fitting for the multivalent – might one even say multicontextual? – portrayal Revelation engenders. In that sense, it offers a new approach to the OT/NT studies and their practice. Rather than looking backward to see what has 'sourced' the SOM, we may pose an alternative question, namely what 'text' (and arguably what new scripture) is (re)created in this way? Just as pastiche frees the reader from the 'Search for the Historical *Vorlage*', it may also enable the interpreter to give more attention to other features of the alleged citation. The locations of both earlier SOMs are intrinsic to their respective interpretation, and one might similarly note that such locational interest impacts on the overall pastiche found in 15.3-4. Hence, interpretation of the SML becomes far more than just a *textual* affair – its performative context and presentation is integrally germane.

There is perhaps a similarity here to Rewritten Bible processes or at least a resemblance to the way in which 'old' scriptural texts are reworked and recontextualized in a new milieu.[39] Speaking of Rev. 15.3-4, Craig Koester notes, for instance: 'Recasting an older biblical song was not unique to Revelation. For example, Jewish writers created new lyrics for the songs ascribed to Deborah and Hannah (L.A.B. 32:1–18; 51:3–6). Revelation does something similar by reworking the song of victory at the sea.'[40] That said, however, one suggests that the pastiche mode, or its outworking within Revelation, is more than simply a reworking or recasting, or at least its ramifications have more pressing, significant outcomes. Rev. 15.3-4 *qua*-pastiche is about more than just assigning the SOM new lyrics; the (new) SML becomes a new entity in its own right, with a new performer(s), new content and a new authority (while still retaining its old traditions and credentials).

At the same time, one might still want to offer some caveats or nuances in respect of Rev. 15.3-4 as 'pastiche'. For instance, were it indeed to qualify as a quotation in Revelation terms, it would differ generically from the more allusive examples to which Fletcher attends. More significantly perhaps, within the more inclusive approach she advocates, Fletcher is generally reluctant to ascribe any hierarchy within the constituent elements of the pastiche.[41] In terms of Rev. 15.2-8, however, there does

---

[39] On the concept of Rewritten Bible, see for example Sidnie White Crawford, *Rewriting Scripture in Second Temple Times* (Grand Rapids, MI: Eerdmans, 2008).
[40] Koester, *Revelation*, 635.
[41] See Fletcher, *Pastiche*, 71–98, on Revelation 1, for example.

seem to be some implicit prioritization or pecking order, through which the reader appropriates the material. We would suggest, for example, that the Mosaic and/or Exodus imagery is more foregrounded than the other mooted allusions named earlier (and indeed that the Jewish scriptures function as the primary source of Revelation's pastiche creation). The naming of the Song as *of Moses* surely gives a strong steer in that particular intertextual direction. Indeed, the explicit context of Revelation 15 – the specific identification of the Song – gives sustenance for prioritizing or giving extra weight to the Mosaic element(s) and the implied exodus context. The other examples Fletcher analyses lack such signposting, and hence the equality of voices – OT textual or otherwise – has more grounding or justification. Revelation 15 is different (and may indeed be the exception that proves the general 'no hierarchy' rule!), as it does appear to inculcate a pecking order. One can debate whether this is occasioned by one or more of authorial steer, textual direction or reader competency, but some allusions will simply be louder than others to the reader, and Rev. 15.3-4 and its surrounding context seem to exhibit that quite explicitly.

Likewise, whereas the pastiche lens rightly gives space – or permission – for other voices to be recognized or present within the portrayal, their recognition can well necessitate some quite extensive awareness on the part of the reader. While Rev. 15.3-4 demonstrably manifests a reframing or representation, and while it may well derive from a plurality of voices, such reframing is necessarily premised on some form of prior knowledge of the SOM(s) for the full contours or nuances to properly 'work'. While Rev. 15.3-4 may well subvert the perceived Exodus backdrop, such a process requires some awareness or foundation to make the subversion operative or functional.[42]

In some ways, in an earlier article, Steve Moyise asks similar questions of Rev. 15.3-4 and its idiosyncratic merging of various OT texts (but does so without recourse to the pastiche methodology embraced by Fletcher). Moyise's approach is essentially to see a dialogical interplay between Moses and the concept of the Lamb, a fusion together of the two images:

> It is not that lamb replaces Moses any more than lamb replaces lion. John's technique is to force the hearers/readers to wrestle with the tension created by the juxtaposition. In other words, this is not simply exegesis, typology, or midrash, which assumes a unidirectional move from source text to interpretation. It is a dialogical use of Scripture, which brings two or more texts together in order that they might mutually illuminate one another.[43]

---

[42] This may echo some of the hesitation that Steve Moyise has in respect of Fletcher's approach, generally sympathetic as he is to its overall tenor. Moyise proposes that the pastiche lens might take more account of relevance theory in assessing the respective impact of constitutive allusions and echoes. See Steve Moyise, 'Concluding Reflection', in David Allen and Steve Smith (eds), *Methodology in the Use of the Old Testament in the New: Context and Criteria*, LNTS 597 (London: T&T Clark, 2019), 183–5; also Steve Smith, 'The Use of Criteria: A Proposal from Relevance Theory', in David Allen and Steve Smith (eds), *Methodology in the Use of the Old Testament in the New: Context and Criteria*, LNTS 597 (London: T&T Clark, 2019), 142–54.

[43] Moyise, 'Singing', 354.

Moyise's approach, however, and his advocacy of the 'dialogical tension'[44] between Moses and the Lamb effects a reading of the text that ultimately becomes limited or unsatisfactory or which reduces the effect of the intertextual associations. By focusing on the absence of Exodus 15 material in the SML, the SOM is 'barely affecting the interpretation of Rev 15'; it is 'an almost subliminal presence that accompanies a reading of the text. But it is no more than that.'[45] Such a conclusion seems overly – and inappropriately – reductive and does not take account of the potential capacity of 15.3-4 to signal Exodus or Deuteronomic images (along with other 'old' material) and to do so in a new, *qua*-pastiche way. The 'tension' is in some sense resolved, one might suggest. The effect of the amalgam or juxtaposition of the multiple 'echoes' is to generate something essentially hybrid out of the old and new, something that remains essentially de novo, but the 'priorness' of which the hearers are still reminded. Hence Revelation cannot classify the SML as a 'new' song; it can't be, as its roots and heritage are in the variety of similar songs previously sung.

Conclusion

Even if it has its own internal distinctives and particularities, the SML of Rev. 15.3-4 opens up fresh questions when considering how Revelation appropriates OT imagery. Specifically, viewing Rev. 15.3-4 through a pastiche lens recalibrates OT/NT discussion away from merely focusing on questions of OT citational text form(s). Its intricate amalgam of old and new is complex and intricate, its various 'borrowing' thereby generating something which is simultaneously 'old-new', and hence the search for specific textual origins (and related questions, e.g., of original context) becomes only one element of a much wider scope of inquiry. Rev. 15.3-4 *qua*-pastiche encourages consideration of a diversity of textual borrowing but also extends such consideration to the borrowing of sounds, images, context, the performance, even, of the combined material. That is, the interpreter might be freed from solely inter*text*uality – and to a wider engagement by which narratival, thematic connections being made. To put it another way, when considering Rev. 15.3-4, the 'something' of the something old/new (and not just the adjectival comparison) warrants further definition or consideration.

---

[44] Ibid., 350.
[45] Ibid., 360.

5

Echoes from the Septuagint Psalter in the apocalyptic texture of Revelation

Gert J. Steyn

Introduction

Scholarship has identified many hymns in Revelation in the past and debated their origin, nature and function. It was initially thought that the hymns display the remnant of early Christian liturgies but striking similarities with Graeco-Roman hymns were later noted. There is currently a broad consensus that the hymns in Revelation are the author's own compositions, which he composed from many intertextual phrases[1] and imagery, creating a mosaic of numerous small elements.[2] This portrays an author who creatively compiles his apocalyptic tableau from familiarity with a range of apocalyptic, worship and hymnic literature in his Hellenistic setting. The influence of Jewish apocalyptic literature, particularly Daniel and Ezekiel,[3] and other prophetic literature, such as Isaiah and Zechariah, has received extensive attention in the past. The prominent role of hymnic literature, such as the Psalms, has often been noted,[4] but – aside from some important studies – extensive investigations about their identification, occurrence and function within the apocalyptic texture of Revelation are still lacking. In this brief contribution, intending to honour the work of Steve Moyise in this field, we will attempt to show how prominent worship imagery from the Septuagint Psalter resurface as echoes within the hymnic sections of Revelation, as

---

[1] 'That is not to say that discussion of the effect of intertextual echo must be limited to John's conscious intention. There is no reason to assume that John thought out all the possibilities of bringing Psalm 89 into a relationship with the living Christ [in Rev. 1:5]' (Steve Moyise, *The Old Testament in the Book of Revelation*, JSNT Sup 115 (London: Bloomsbury, 2014), 118).

[2] It is no strange phenomenon as certain compositions, such as 4Q381 (a Hebrew collection of psalms from the first century BCE), 'seem to be built around allusions to, and even direct quotation of, biblical psalms' (E. Schuller, 'Psalms, Apocryphal', in J. J. Collins and D. C. Harlow (eds), *The Eerdmans Dictionary of Early Judaism* (Grand Rapids, MI: Eerdmans, 2010), 1105).

[3] Cf. A. J. Kostenberger: 'About half of the references are from the Psalms, Isaiah, Ezekiel, and Daniel' ('The Use of Scripture in the Pastoral and General Epistles and the Book of Revelation', in S. E. Porter (ed.), *Hearing the Old Testament in the New Testament* (Grand Rapids, MI: Eerdmans, 2006), 230–54, here 249).

[4] G. K. Beale, *John's Use of the Old Testament in Revelation*, JSNT Sup 166 (Sheffield: Academic Press, 1998), 60–1, 193.

they unfold there within apocalyptic worship scenes that were composed by the author of the Apocalypse.

Revelation presents its reader with a dense texture of apocalyptic imagery and numerical symbolism, scriptural allusions and echoes, worship motifs, liturgical formulas and hymns – a composition characterized by its striking intertextual nature.[5] It presents its reader with a literary archaeological site, where the strata of scriptural traditions and their receptions lie ready for exploration and interpretation. It holds the treasures of apocalypticism and eschatology, prominent theological themes, tradition and redaction history and literary composition. It opens its doors as a laboratory to exegetes to experiment with a range of diverse methodological approaches – from microscopic, detailed historical-critical tools, through a range of literary-criticism magnifying glasses, to its tropical greenhouses of reception-historical analyses.

To get a hold on the composition and the multifaceted theological dimension of Revelation is no easy task.[6] The point of entry into any study of this unique book is almost as important as the angle and speed with which an extraterrestrial object enters earth's atmosphere. If the coordinates of this entry point are wrong, then the exegetic-hermeneutical tools might disintegrate before they even touch the surface of the text. Then the opportunity to access its treasure trove of information might be missed. Thus, the trajectory that we are setting here for ourselves requires careful coordinates when we intend to descend into Revelation's treasure trove of allusions – particularly allusions from the Psalter. One of these coordinates is the fact that we are not dealing here with explicit quotations but with allusions, echoes and motifs or, at the most, with some possibly intended references.[7] In fact, it is a matter of debate whether there is indeed a single quotation to be found in Revelation at all![8] Introductory formulae that usually mark explicit quotations are strikingly absent. Attempts to determine possible *Textvorlagen* underlying these Psalm-echoes or allusions are therefore virtually impossible. If the pretexts of these intertextual traces from the Psalter could not be determined in this manner, then another angle ought to be explored. Hence, another important coordinate as point of orientation is the fact that the Psalm-echoes in Revelation display the rich colours of worship imagery, especially liturgical, hymnic and poetic formulae. It is at the nexus of these two coordinates, the Psalm-allusions as allusions *per se* and the deployment of worship imagery, where we will focus our point of entry into the apocalyptic texture of Revelation. It is also precisely this point of entry that Steve Moyise used, for instance, in his essay on the Psalms in Revelation.[9]

---

[5] Steve Moyise concludes: 'John does not quote Scripture but his visions allude to numerous biblical passages' and 'usually John weaves together a number of texts to form a richly evocative tableau' (*The Later New Testament Writers and Scripture* (London: SPCK, 2012), 111–12).

[6] 'The non-formal character of OT references in Revelation makes textual identification more difficult' (Kostenberger, 'Use of Scripture', 249). Kostenberger also refers to the many conflations of texts that are merged into one picture and that one deals here with 'a mind saturated with OT Scripture' (249–50).

[7] Cf. D. S. Huffman: 'the book of Revelation is clearly steeped in OT imagery and contains dozens of allusions and verbal parallels to the Old Testament' ('A Two-Dimensional Taxonomy of Forms for the NT Use of the OT', *Themelios* 46.2 (2021): 308).

[8] Huffman, 'Two-Dimensional Taxonomy', 308.

[9] Steve Moyise, 'The Psalms in the Book of Revelation', in S. Moyise and Maarten J. J. Menken (eds), *The Psalms in the New Testament* (London: T&T Clark, 2004), 231–46.

He has shown how the author of Revelation used Psalm 2 to testify to the ultimate victory of Christ, Psalm 89 to point to Jesus as 'the firstborn, faithful witness and ruler of the kings of the earth' and Psalm 86 to describe the eschatological ingathering of the nations.[10]

Apocalyptic worship scenes and the hymnic sections in Revelation

The Apocalypse portrays God Almighty (κύριος ὁ θεὸς ὁ παντοκράτωρ, 4.8), the 'One who is, who was and who is to come' (ὁ ἦν καὶ ὁ ὢν καὶ ὁ ἐρχόμενος, 4.8), as the One who is seated on the throne (ἐπὶ τὸν θρόνον καθήμενος, 4.2) in the heavenly sanctuary. A series of worship scenes unfolds during Revelation with four alternating liturgical elements. Their hymnic contents consist of confessional formulas, praise songs, judgement formulas, acquittal pronouncements and blessings. In particular four liturgical elements are prominent: (1) *proclamation* (λέγοντες), where reciting, uttering, confessing and announcing happen; (2) *veneration* (προσκυνήσουσιν), where bowing down in worship during confessing takes place; (3) *singing* (ᾄδουσιν), during which a new Ode, or the Ode of Moses and the Ode of the Lamb, follows; and (4) *exaltation* or *annunciation* ((κράζουσιν) φωνῇ μεγάλῃ λέγοντες), where proclaiming with a loud voice takes place.

There are four occasions in Revelation where *singing* (ᾄδουσιν) occurs during the unfolding of the apocalyptic vision, namely in Rev. 5.8-10, 14.3 and 15.3-4. At least the first two instances are explicitly connected with a 'new song'[11] being sung by the four creatures and the twenty-four elders around the throne. The last instance implies a similar phenomenon when the conquerors of the beast, its image and the number of its name sang the Song of Moses and the Song of the Lamb.

These occasions are preceded and alternated by liturgical elements being introduced with λέγοντες. Four such acts of *proclaiming*, or *confessing* (λέγοντες), are expressed by the four living creatures as the first scene (4.8), by every creature in the universe (5.13-14), by the angel of the waters (16.5-6) and by the response of the altar (16.7). Two further acts in the same λέγοντες-category are *divine announcements* from the voice of heaven (18.4-8) or from the throne (19.5). Four other such proclamations, or confessions, are combined with acts of worship by bowing down, face on the ground (προσκυνήσουσιν), that is, falling prostrate before God, as expressions of *veneration*: 4.10-11; 7.11-12; 11.16-18; and 19.4. Six further occurrences take place by means of *exaltation* through a loud voice (φωνῇ

---

[10] J. Grant, 'Review of The Psalms in the New Testament edited by Steve Moyise and Maarten J. J. Menken', *Themelios* 32.2 (2006): 93-5.

[11] 'In Greek literature, there is a *topos* that new songs are the best songs' (D. E. Aune, *Revelation 1-5*, WBC 52A (Dallas, TX: Word, 1997), 360). 'The phrase "new song" occurs nine times in scripture: six times in the Psalms, once in Isaiah, and twice in Revelation' (K. H. Easley, *Revelation*, Holman NT Comm. 12 (Nashville, TN: Broadman & Holman, 1998), 100). 'New song' occurs in the Psalter in Pss. 32(33).3; 39(40).4; 96(96).1; 97(98).1; 143(144).9; 149.1 – often dealing with the theme of deliverance.

μεγάλη) – by the angels (5.11-12), the great multitude with white robes and palm branches (7.9-10), unidentified loud voices in heaven after the sounding of the seventh trumpet (11.15), an angel with great authority and splendour (18.1-3) and the great multitude in heaven (19.1-3 and 19.6-8). In two further instances, *divine announcements* also occur by means of a single loud voice from heaven (12.10-12) or from the throne (21.3-4).

The different parties involved in these liturgical acts (or worshiping rituals) consist of seven categories and include (1) the four living creatures (τὰ τέσσαρα ζῷα 4.6-9; 5.8-10; 7.11-12; 19.4), (2) the twenty-four elders (εἴκοσι τέσσαρας πρεσβυτέρους; 4.10-11; 5.8-10; 7.11-12; 11.16-18; 19.4), (3) many angels (ἀγγέλων πολλῶν; 5.11; 7.11-12) or specific angels (16.5-6; 18.1-3), (4) every creature in the universe (πᾶν κτίσμα; 5.13-14), (5) a great multitude (ὄχλος πολύς; 7.9-10; 19.1-3; 19.6-8), (6) the 144,000 (14.3) and (7) 'the altar' (16.7). Each of these categories are specified with descriptive qualifiers as the scenes unfold.

In these worship scenes, the Almighty, that is, the One on the throne, and 'the Lamb' are worshipped by means of alternate, liturgical responsive elements. The hymnic compositions (excluding that of 15.3-4) are arranged into seven such liturgical response (antiphonal) units: 4.8-11; 5.9-14; 7.9-12; 11.15-18; 16.5-7; 19.1-4; 19.5-8.[12] It is against this backdrop where it is no surprise to find numerous echoes, allusions, imagery and motifs from the Psalter.

Psalm echoes in the hymnic worship sections

A range of motifs can be identified from the Psalter that resurface as echoes in the hymnic material of Revelation. Several of these motifs circulated more broadly in the repertoire of available pretexts for the author of Revelation. However, if several such echoes show an evident overlap in terms of a particular motif, as well as verifiable verbal allusion to a particular psalm, then the chances are higher that the author might have had motifs, phraseology and terminology from the Psalter in memory when compiling his hymnic sections in Revelation. It is based on this assumption that we will explore the Septuagint Psalter as a possible pretext of choice for our author, given its hymnic, worship and liturgical character – a *Gattung*, which the author of Revelation surely imitates in his hymnic sections. Furthermore, when the sum total of all the data is being put together, then it becomes clear how these echoes together reveal a picture of some pre-knowledge of *specific* Psalms by the author – as Moyise indicated, for instance, with regard to Psalms 2, 86 (LXX 85) and 89 (LXX 88). Departing from the following broader motifs and the overlap in wording, a range of possible echoes from the Septuagint Psalter might be identified and compared to the hymnic material in Revelation.

In order to trace the different motifs, allusions and echoes from the Greek Psalter in the apocalyptic texture of Revelation, a different route will be followed in structuring

---

[12] Aune, *Revelation 1–5*, 315.

this brief survey. It makes more sense methodologically to identify and classify different motifs (*Leitthemen*) in the worship scenes or hymnic sections and to search for verbal analogy in the Psalter, rather than to follow Revelation's sequence or the numerical sequence of the Psalms. If our author constructed the hymnic sections from memory, based on his familiarity with liturgical formulations and worship imagery from the Psalms, then this route might reveal how imagery, allusions and echoes found their way into the literary texture through familiarity with these liturgical formulations and worship imagery, rather than conscious knowledge and application of specific psalms. For this purpose, and due to space limitations, our investigation will focus only on the following four categories: worship expressions; divine address; divine nature and attributes; and divine actions.

Worship expressions

Rev. 15.2 reports how 'those who had conquered the beast, its image, and the number of its name, are standing beside the sea of glass with harps of God in their hands'. They then sing the Song of Moses (ᾄδουσιν τὴν ᾠδὴν Μωϋσέως) and the Song of the Lamb (τὴν ᾠδὴν τοῦ ἀρνίου). A single hymn follows (15.3b-4), being introduced with λέγοντες.[13] The first epithet of 15.4, which describes the works of God (μεγάλα τὰ ἔργα σου), alludes to LXX Ps. 91.6 (ὡς ἐμεγαλύνθη τὰ ἔργα σου, κύριε) and to LXX Ps. 110.2 (μεγάλα τὰ ἔργα κυρίου), while the second epithet (θαυμαστὰ τὰ ἔργα σου) alludes to LXX Ps. 97.1 (ὅτι θαυμαστὰ ἐποίησεν κύριος) and to LXX Ps. 138.14 (θαυμάσια τὰ ἔργα σου).[14] Three further phrases in 15.5 also evoke Psalm formulations.[15] The first phrase is τίς οὐ μὴ φοβηθῇ, κύριε, which displays a verbal analogy with LXX Ps. 32.8 (φοβηθήτω τὸν κύριον πᾶσα ἡ γῆ)[16] and LXX Ps. 33.10 (φοβήθητε τὸν κύριον, οἱ ἅγιοι αὐτοῦ).[17] Collins pointed out that 'in the vast majority of cases in Hebrew and Aramaic, holy ones are angels' but that 'in Ps 34:10, the holy ones are the community of the faithful.'[18] He refers to

---

[13] Cf. W. J. Harrington: 'The Canticle Itself Is a Mosaic of Old Testament Phrases: Ps 111:2; 139:14; Amos 4:13; Ps 145:17; Deut 32:4; Jer 10:7; Ps 86:9; Mal 1:11; Ps 98:2' (*Revelation*, SP 16 (Collegeville, PA: Liturgical Press, 2008), 159).

[14] R. H. Charles, *The Revelation of St. John, Vol. II*, ICC (Edinburgh: T&T Clark, 1980), 36; J. Roloff, *Die Offenbarung des Johannes*, ZBK 18 (Zürich: Theologischer Verlag, 1984), 158; W. Klaiber, *Die Offenbarung des Johannes*, BNT (Göttingen: Vandenhoeck & Ruprecht, 2019), 213.

[15] 'Inspired by a number of Old Testament passages (Deut. 32:4; Ps. 86:8–10; 111:2; 139:14; 145:17; Jer. 10:6–7), the heavenly singers laud God's power and justice' (C. R. Koester, *Revelation and the End of All Things*, 2nd edn (Grand Rapids, MI: Eerdmans, 2018), 141). R. H. Mounce noted, 'Practically every phrase of the hymn comes from the rich vocabulary of the OT (Ps 11:2; 139:14; Amos 4:13 LXX; Deut 32:4; Ps 86:9; Mal 1:11; Ps 144:17 LXX; 98:2)' (*The Book of Revelation*, NICNT (Grand Rapids, MI: Eerdmans, 1977), 287).

[16] Referring to LXX Ps. 32.2-3, Aune reminds us: 'There is a close association in the OT and early Jewish literature between hymns and the kithara or lyre, a stringed instrument commonly used to accompany songs of praise' (*Revelation 1–5*, 355).

[17] 'The term "saints," or "holy ones" (*hagioi*), was used for God's people in Jewish tradition (Ps 34:10; Dan 7:21) and early Christianity (Acts 9:13; Rom 12:13; 2 Cor 1:1). Revelation uses it for the followers of Jesus (Rev 14:12; 17:6)' (C. R. Koester, *Revelation: A New Translation with Introduction and Commentary*, AB 38A (New Haven, CT: Yale University, 2014), 379).

[18] Similarly, J. R. Davila: 'The title "holy ones" is used mostly of angels or divinities in the H[ebrew] B[ible] (e.g., Deut 33:3; Ps 89:6, 8; Job 5:1; Zech 14:5; Dan 4:14). The only clear exception is Ps

Laato,[19] who 'recognizes that the holy ones are angels, but thinks that the reference indicates that the messiah is a "Son of Man" figure who appears together with angels'.[20] Blenkinsopp understood 'the holy ones' as an unqualified title 'to either Israel as a whole or a particular social entity within Israel' and also reckoned that 'there is clear biblical attestation for this titular usage only in Ps 34:10'[21] 'and in the Danielic vision of the Ancient of Days and the Son of Man (Dan 7)'.[22]

The second phrase is καὶ δοξάσει τὸ ὄνομά σου, which displays a verbal analogy with LXX Ps. 85.9[23] (καὶ δοξάσουσιν τὸ ὄνομά σου). The third phrase is καὶ προσκυνήσουσιν ἐνώπιόν σου, which displays a verbal analogy with LXX Pss. 21.28[24] and 85.9 (καὶ προσκυνήσουσιν ἐνώπιόν σου).[25]

Rev. 19.1 reports the 'loud voice of a great multitude (ὄχλου πολλοῦ) in heaven'. Their praise is expressed in two consecutive exaltations (19.1b-2 and 19.3b), which are introduced by λεγόντων (19.1) and εἴρηκαν (19.3) and starting both times with 'Hallelujah'.[26] The twenty-four elders and four living creatures then fall down and worship God on the throne with the brief liturgical response 'Amen. Hallelujah!', introduced by λέγοντες (19.4). A voice responds from the throne (λέγουσα), which calls to worship (αἰνεῖτε τῷ θεῷ ἡμῶν, 19.5). The response (λεγόντων) by the great multitude follows hereafter for a third time (19.6b-8a), starting again with 'Hallelujah'

34:10, in which the holy ones seem to be human' (*Liturgical Works*, Eerdmans Commentaries on the Dead Sea Scrolls (Grand Rapids, MI: Eerdmans, 2000), 100).

[19] A. Laato, *A Star Is Rising: The Historical Development of the Old Testament Royal Ideology and the Rise of the Jewish Messianic Expectations* (Atlanta, GA: Scholars Press, 1997), 309–10.

[20] J. J. Collins, *The Scepter and the Star: Messianism in Light of the Dead Sea Scrolls*, 2nd edn (Grand Rapids, MI: Eerdmans, 2010), 137.

[21] Cf. Aune: This 'is the only undisputed passage in the Hebrew OT in which the term קְדֹשִׁים qĕdōšîm, "holy ones," is used of Israelites' (*Revelation 1–5*, 359).

[22] J. Blenkinsopp, *Opening the Sealed Book: Interpretations of the Book of Isaiah in Late Antiquity* (Grand Rapids, MI: Eerdmans, 2006), 207.

[23] Steve Moyise has drawn attention to the fact that 'the closest parallel to Rev. 15:3-4 is Ps. 86.8-10' (*Evoking Scripture: Seeing the Old Testament in the New* (Edinburgh: T&T Clark, 2008), 113–14). The connection with Psalm 86(85) was already observed by A. T. Robertson, *Word Pictures in the New Testament* (Nashville, TN: Broadman, 1933), UBS5, 836. Cf. C. S. Keener: 'the addition of "glorify" is from the base text, Ps. 86:9' (*Revelation*, NIV Appl. Comm. (Grand Rapids, MI: Zondervan, 1999), 386). Also Aune: 'There is a likely allusion here and in v 4c to Ps 86:9–10 (LXX 85:9-10)' (D. E. Aune, *Revelation 6–16*, WBC 52B (Dallas, TX: Word, 1998), 875), and 'this verse alludes to Ps 86:9–10 (LXX 85:9-10), where it is said that God is great and does wonderful things' (Aune, *Revelation 6–16*, 876). So, too, R. H. Charles, *Revelation II*, 36; G. E. Ladd, *A Commentary on the Revelation of John* (Grand Rapids, MI: Eerdmans, 1972), 206; J. Roloff, *A Continental Commentary: The Revelation of John* (Minneapolis, MN: Fortress, 1993), 184; M. Wilson, *Charts on the Book of Revelation: Literary, Historical, and Theological Perspectives*, Kregel Charts of the Bible and Theology (Grand Rapids, MI: Kregel Academic & Professional, 2007), 28; and Harrington, *Revelation*, 159.

[24] Also Aland, *Apparatus*, 846; J. H. Smith, *The New Treasury of Scripture Knowledge* (Nashville, TN: Thomas Nelson, 1992), 1528.

[25] Also Charles, *Revelation II*, 36. That the Jews 'will come and bow down before your feet' in Rev. 3.9 is a collective allusion to Ps. 86.9 and Isa. 45.14; 49.23; 60.14, according to Beale, *John's Use of the OT*, 122. A 'strand of tradition expected the Gentiles to participate completely in the worship of Yahweh and in eschatological salvation, though it is rarely clear whether full proselytism is expected' (D. E. Aune, *Revelation 17–22*, WBC 52C (Dallas, TX: Word, 1998), 1172).

[26] 'Hallelujah (wörtlich: lobe Jahwe) ist eigentlich Aufforderung zum Gotteslob (vgl. Ps 104,35)' (Klaiber, *Offenbarung*, 244).

(19.6).[27] The 'Hallelujah' liturgical motif surfaces strongly in LXX Pss. 104-6; 110-18; 134-5 and 145-50.[28] The call to praise God (αἰνεῖτε τῷ θεῷ ἡμῶν, 19.5)[29] displays a verbal analogy with LXX Ps. 99.4[30] (ἐξομολογεῖσθε αὐτῷ, αἰνεῖτε τὸ ὄνομα αὐτοῦ), the Hallel Psalms LXX Pss. 112.1, 3 and 134.1, 3 (Αἰνεῖτε, παῖδες, κύριον, αἰνεῖτε τὸ ὄνομα κυρίου),[31] LXX Ps. 116.1 (Αἰνεῖτε τὸν κύριον,[32] πάντα τὰ ἔθνη),[33] LXX Pss. 146.1 and 148.1-4, 7 (Αἰνεῖτε τὸν κύριον / αὐτόν) as well as LXX Ps. 150.1 (Αἰνεῖτε τὸν θεὸν ἐν τοῖς ἁγίοις αὐτοῦ).[34] The action to 'rejoice, exult and give glory' (Rev. 19.7) recalls verbal analogy with a range of Psalms. Close similarities between the beginning of Rev. 19.6b-7 and the opening lines of LXX Ps. 96.1 are particularly striking:[35]

Rev. 19.6b-7	LXX Ps. 96.1
ὅτι ἐβασίλευσεν κύριος ὁ θεὸς [ἡμῶν] ὁ παντοκράτωρ. χαίρωμεν καὶ ἀγαλλιῶμεν καὶ δώσωμεν τὴν δόξαν αὐτῷ	Ὁ κύριος ἐβασίλευσεν, ἀγαλλιάσθω ἡ γῆ, εὐφρανθήτωσαν νῆσοι πολλαί

The motif echoes several other Psalms as well: LXX Ps. 9.3 (εὐφρανθήσομαι καὶ ἀγαλλιάσομαι ἐν σοί, ψαλῶ τῷ ὀνόματί σου, ὕψιστε), LXX Ps. 13.7 (ἀγαλλιάσθω Ιακωβ καὶ εὐφρανθήτω Ισραηλ), LXX Ps. 20.2 (εὐφρανθήσεται ὁ βασιλεὺς καὶ ἐπὶ τῷ σωτηρίῳ σου ἀγαλλιάσεται σφόδρα), LXX Ps. 31.11 (εὐφράνθητε ἐπὶ κύριον καὶ ἀγαλλιᾶσθε, δίκαιοι),[36]

---

[27] 'Among the distinctive features of this hymnic section is the occurrence of the transliterated Hebrew liturgical formula "hallelujah" four times' (Aune, *Revelation 17-22*, 1022).
[28] 'The term "hallelujah" is used in the Psalms both in the *titles* to individual psalms ... and as *conclusions* to individual psalms ... [where it concludes the fourth book of the Psalter]' (Aune, *Revelation 17-22*, 1024).
[29] 'The introductory hallelujah is not used simply as a liturgical formula but corresponds in meaning to "praise our God" in v 5b' (Aune, *Revelation 17-22*, 1028).
[30] So also G. K. Beale, *The Book of Revelation: A Commentary on the Greek Text*, NIGTC (Grand Rapids, MI: Eerdmans, 1999), 1140.
[31] Cf. also Harrington, *Revelation*, 186.
[32] αἰνεῖτε τὸν κύριον (LXX 116:1) 'suggests that αἰνεῖτε τῷ θεῷ is a relatively close way of rendering "hallelujah"' (Aune, *Revelation 17-22*, 1028).
[33] Cf. especially Rom. 15.11 and the citation of LXX Ps. 116.1. 'The phrase πάντα τὰ ἔθνη, "all the nations," is a fixed phrase that occurs five times in Revelation (12:5; 14:8; 15:4; 18:3, 23) and frequently elsewhere in the NT and early Christian literature' (Aune, *Revelation 6-16*, 688). See also G. W. Grogan, *Psalms*, The Two Horizons OT Commentary (Grand Rapids, MI: Eerdmans, 2008), 301, 305.
[34] So also Koester, *Revelation*, 728. Cf. N. T. Wright: 'The summons of the final psalm, "Praise God in his sanctuary", draws together the entire message of the entire Psalter' (*Paul and the Faithfulness of God*, COQG 4 (Minneapolis, MN: Fortress, 2013), 100).
[35] See Mt. 5.12. 'The verbal parallels that follow suggest that the expression was relatively fixed in Greek-speaking Judaism' (Aune, *Revelation 17-22*, 1029). 'God was often called "Almighty," and the Old Testament frequently celebrates his reign, especially with regard to his rule over creation (Ps 97:1)' (C. S. Keener, *The IVP Bible Background Commentary: New Testament* (Downers Grove, IL: InterVarsity, 1993), Rev. 19.5-6). Cf. Klaiber: 'Hier wird eine Formulierung aus den sog. Jahwe-König-Psalmen aufgegriffen, in denen im Tempel in Jerusalem der Herrschaftsantritt Gottes gefeiert wird (Ps 93,1; 96,10; 97,1; 99,1)' (*Offenbarung*, 245).
[36] The LXX translators of LXX Pss. 31.11; 32.21; 34.9 and 39.17 consistently avoided χαίρω and used either ἀγαλλιάω or εὐφραίνω, whereas Paul, for instance, preferred χαίρω and its cognates. See G. D. Fee, *Paul's Letter to the Philippians*, NICNT (Grand Rapids, MI: Eerdmans, 1995), 291.

LXX Ps. 32.1-2[37] (Ἀγαλλιᾶσθε, δίκαιοι, ἐν τῷ κυρίῳ· τοῖς εὐθέσι πρέπει αἴνεσις. ἐξομολογεῖσθε τῷ κυρίῳ), LXX Ps. 97.4 (ἀλαλάξατε τῷ θεῷ, πᾶσα ἡ γῆ, ᾄσατε καὶ ἀγαλλιᾶσθε καὶ ψάλατε), LXX Ps. 117.24 (ἀγαλλιασώμεθα καὶ εὐφρανθῶμεν ἐν αὐτῇ) and LXX Ps. 144.7 (καὶ τῇ δικαιοσύνῃ σου ἀγαλλιάσονται).

Divine address

The four living creatures around the throne proclaim (λέγοντες) their triple ἅγιος ἅγιος ἅγιος 'day and night without ceasing', addressing the Lord God Almighty (κύριος ὁ θεὸς ὁ παντοκράτωρ, 4.8). The allusion to LXX Isa. 6.3 is clear: Ἅγιος ἅγιος ἅγιος κύριος σαβαωθ. Dependence on Isaiah 6 by LXX Ps. 98 in this regard has been noted before.[38] The author of Revelation refers also elsewhere to the Almighty as **κύριος ὁ θεός**: Rev. 4.11 (ἄξιος εἶ, ὁ κύριος καὶ ὁ θεὸς ἡμῶν); Rev. 11.17 (εὐχαριστοῦμέν σοι, κύριε ὁ θεός); Rev. 15.3 and 16.7 (κύριε ὁ θεός); as well as Rev. 18.8 (ὅτι ἰσχυρὸς κύριος ὁ θεὸς ὁ κρίνας αὐτήν). Being a well-known address or reference to the God of Israel, which continued in early Judaism and Christianity, its use by Revelation could certainly not be limited to knowledge only via the Greek Psalter. However, instances of correspondence in formulation should at least be noted in LXX Pss. 40.14[39] and 105.48 (Εὐλογητὸς κύριος ὁ θεὸς Ισραηλ ἀπὸ τοῦ αἰῶνος καὶ ἕως τοῦ αἰῶνος).[40] In both cases, the latter verse of Psalm 41(40) concludes Book I of the Psalter (LXX Pss. 1–40) and that of Psalm 106(105) concludes Book IV of the Psalter (LXX Pss. 89–105).[41] Especially to be noted is the similarity with LXX Ps. 98.9:

Rev. 4.8	LXX Ps. 98.9
ἅγιος ἅγιος ἅγιος κύριος ὁ θεὸς ὁ παντοκράτωρ ὁ ἦν καὶ ὁ ὢν καὶ ὁ ἐρχόμενος	ὑψοῦτε κύριον τὸν θεὸν ἡμῶν καὶ προσκυνεῖτε εἰς ὄρος ἅγιον αὐτοῦ, ὅτι ἅγιος κύριος ὁ θεὸς ἡμῶν

The same applies to the reference ὁ παντοκράτωρ in the hymnic sections of Revelation (4.8; 11.17; 16.7; 19.6), which is consistently linked with the combination κύριος θεός in all these cases. The term παντοκράτωρ is indeed widely used in the LXX – at least 126 times (including the LXX Odes) but only 20 times with the combination κύριος

---

[37] Ps. 33(32).2 is quoted in 1QM (1Q33) IV,5. (A. Lange and M. Weigold (eds), *Biblical Quotations and Allusions in Second Temple Jewish Literature*, JAJS 5 (Göttingen: Vandenhoeck & Ruprecht, 2011)).

[38] 'The term "holy" occurs three times in Ps 99, in a way that suggests dependence on Isa 6' (Aune, *Revelation 1–5*, 303).

[39] The presence and prominence of 'Amen' attached to this formulation in Ps. 41.14 (MT) should be noted here.

[40] A benediction, or *berakah*, is typically introduced by the term ברוך or εὐλογητός ('blessed'). Cf. Aune, *Revelation 1–5*, 43. Charles, *Revelation II*, 120 also sees an allusion to Ps. 106(105).48 in Rev. 19.4.

[41] 'Blessing God was the classic form of prayer in Second Temple Judaism, as it is in modern Judaism ... Evidence for this can be seen in the benedictions incorporated in the final form of the Psalter (Ps 40:14; 72:18-19; 89:52; 106:48)' (D. H. Johnson, 'Blessing', in R. P. Martin and P. H. Davids (eds), *Dictionary of the Later New Testament and Its Developments* (Downers Grove, IL: InterVarsity, 1997), 129–30).

θεός.[42] The verbal analogies with the *Prayer of Baruch* and the *Prayer of Manasseh* – included as Ode 12 among the LXX Odes – should be noted here. The latter contains allusions to 4 Kgdms 21 and 2 Chron. 33.

Rev. 4.8; 11.17; 16.7; 19.6	Bar. 3.1, 4	Ode 12.1
κύριος ὁ θεὸς ὁ παντοκράτωρ	κύριε παντοκράτωρ ὁ θεὸς Ισραηλ	Κύριε παντοκράτωρ, ὁ θεὸς τῶν πατέρων ἡμῶν

Also, the reference to ὁ ἐρχόμενος (4.8) is not restricted only to the Psalter, and its allusion to the coming of someone like the Son of Man in Dan. 7.13 comes as no surprise: καὶ ἰδοὺ μετὰ τῶν νεφελῶν τοῦ οὐρανοῦ ὡς υἱὸς ἀνθρώπου ἐρχόμενος ἦν. However, the resemblance with LXX Ps. 117.26 should be noted as well: εὐλογημένος ὁ ἐρχόμενος ἐν ὀνόματι κυρίου. Several echoes and allusions to LXX Ps. 117 are present in Revelation.[43] Intertextual connections with the early Christian tradition should certainly not be overlooked – cf. Mk 11.9 (par. Mt. 21.9; Lk. 19.38) and Q (Mt. 23.39; par. Lk. 13.35) as well as Jn 12.13. At the beginning of Jesus's ministry, it is John the Baptist who wanted clarity on Jesus's identity and who had sent his disciples to enquire from Jesus himself whether he is 'the One who is to come' (σὺ εἶ ὁ ἐρχόμενος, Lk. 7.19-20; cf. Mt. 11.3).[44] LXX Ps. 117.26 is alluded to in the Jesus-logion of Mt. 23.39 and Lk. 13.35 (lacking in Mark), where Jesus links this reference to his own appearance as 'the One who comes in the Name of the Lord' (ὁ ἐρχόμενος ἐν ὀνόματι κυρίου). It also includes the explicit quotation from LXX Ps. 117.26 during Jesus's entry into Jerusalem (which takes place prior to Matthew's Jesus-logion). John's Gospel places the reference to ὁ ἐρχόμενος into the mouths of the people who observed Jesus's sign, when they say: 'This is indeed the prophet who is to come into the world' (οὗτός ἐστιν ἀληθῶς ὁ προφήτης ὁ ἐρχόμενος εἰς τὸν κόσμον, Jn 6.14). The author of Hebrews, in turn, takes the reference to ὁ ἐρχόμενος from Hab. 2.3-4[45] in Heb. 10.37 (ὁ ἐρχόμενος ἥξει καὶ οὐ χρονίσει), when he links the same term to the second coming of Christ.

In Rev. 16.5, the *Angel of the Waters* addresses (λέγοντος) the 'One who are and who were' as 'the Holy One' (ὁ ὅσιος). The term surfaces nine times in the LXX. In all cases except one (Prov. 21.15), it occurs in Odes and Psalms – including the Song of Moses (Deut. 32/Ode 2) and the *Psalms of Solomon*. Particularly interesting are the following similarities and a possible combined allusion[46] to both Deut. 32.4[47] and LXX Ps. 144.17:[48]

---

[42] See 2 Kgdms 7.25, 27; 1 Chron. 17.24; Odes 12.1; Hos. 12.6; Amos 3.13; 4.13; 5.8, 14, 15, 16, 27; 9.5, 6, 15; Nah. 3.5; Zech. 10.3; Jer. 39.19; Bar. 3.1, 4.
[43] LXX Ps. 117.25 is alluded to in Rev. 7.10 and LXX Ps. 117.27 in Rev. 9.13.
[44] Especially the trajectories of 'God's Son', 'the Christ' and 'the King of the Jews' seem to be prominent in Luke's Gospel and are linked to 'the one who would come (ὁ ἐρχόμενος) in the name of the κυρίος' (LXX Ps. 117.26).
[45] Cf. F. Bovon, *Luke 1: A Commentary on the Gospel of Luke 1:1–9:50*, Hermeneia (Minneapolis, MN: Fortress, 2002), 282: 'In Hab 2:3, according to the text of Aquila, the expression alludes to a messianic figure (not necessarily and exclusively a royal one).'
[46] So observed by Aune, *Revelation 6–16*, 874.
[47] 'The Jerusalem Targum in its paraphrase of Deut. 32:4 ("God of *faithfulness*") goes on and calls God "a *faithful* God and *true*"' (Beale, *John's Use of the OT*, 289).
[48] Cf. Charles, *Revelation II*, 36. 'When used in connection with God, ὅσιος is found in hymns of praise closely related to OT expressions (Rev 15:4: ὅτι μόνος ὅσιος; 16:5: δίκαιος εἶ, ὁ ὢν καὶ ὁ ἦν,

Rev. 16.5	Deut. 32[Ode 2].4	LXX Ps. 144.17	Pss. Sol. 10.5
δίκαιος εἶ, ὁ ὢν καὶ ὁ ἦν, ὁ ὅσιος, ὅτι ταῦτα ἔκρινας	δίκαιος καὶ ὅσιος κύριος	δίκαιος κύριος ἐν πάσαις ταῖς ὁδοῖς αὐτοῦ καὶ ὅσιος ἐν πᾶσιν τοῖς ἔργοις αὐτοῦ	Δίκαιος καὶ ὅσιος ὁ κύριος ἡμῶν ἐν κρίμασιν αὐτοῦ εἰς τὸν αἰῶνα

Divine nature and attributes

In the hymnic sections lists of attributes are ascribed to express the divine nature of the Lord God Almighty on the throne as well as the divine nature of the Lamb.

- The pair *glory and honour* (ἡ δόξα[49] καὶ ἡ τιμή) is present in Rev. 4.11; 5.12; 5.13; 7.12; and 19.1, 7. Elsewhere in the NT, these qualities are also ascribed to Christ: glory (Jn 1.14) and honour (Phil. 2.11).[50] The combination echoes the same pair in especially LXX Ps. 8.6 (δόξῃ καὶ τιμῇ ἐστεφάνωσας αὐτόν)[51] and LXX Ps. 95.7 (ἐνέγκατε τῷ κυρίῳ δόξαν καὶ τιμήν).[52]
- The attribute of *power*, (ἡ δύναμις)[53] is mentioned in Rev. 4.11; 5.12; 7.12; 11.17; 12.10; 19.1. The quality of power (together with that of wisdom discussed here later) is also ascribed to Christ in 1 Cor. 1.24[54] (Χριστὸν θεοῦ δύναμιν καὶ θεοῦ σοφίαν). Correlation with LXX Pss. 62.3 and 144.4-5 attracts attention here:

Rev. 11.17	Rev. 12.10	LXX Ps. 62.3	LXX Ps. 144.4-5
εἴληφας τὴν δύναμίν σου τὴν μεγάλην	ἡ σωτηρία καὶ ἡ δύναμις	τοῦ ἰδεῖν τὴν δύναμίν σου καὶ τὴν δόξαν σου	καὶ τὴν δύναμίν σου ἀπαγγελοῦσιν. τὴν μεγαλοπρέπειαν τῆς δόξης τῆς ἁγιωσύνης σου λαλήσουσιν

ὁ ὅσιος; cf. on this Deut 32:4; Ps 144:17 LXX)' (H. R. Balz and G. Schneider, *EDNT* (Grand Rapids, MI: Eerdmans, 1990), 536). Similarly, Klaiber, *Offenbarung*, 214.

[49] 'A doxology is a short liturgical formula that usually ascribes to God the attribute of glory (δόξα), which may be amplified through the inclusion of a number of other attributes as well' (Aune, *Revelation 1-5*, 43).

[50] Mounce, *Revelation*, 150.

[51] 'The portrayal of the ideal Adam's reign as "the son of man" from Psalm 8, never completely realized in the Old Testament period, is applied to Christ' (Beale, *John's Use of the OT*, 140). R. H. Charles also noted this allusion but stated that it is not used in the same connection as Rev. 4.9 (*The Revelation of St. John, Vol. 1*, ICC (Edinburgh: T&T Clark, 1985), 127-8).

[52] 'The attributes τιμή and δόξα are frequently paired in the LXX' (Aune, *Revelation 1-5*, 365).

> The combination of τιμή and δόξα, 'honor and glory,' occurs occasionally in the LXX, though probably not yet as an idiomatically fixed hendiadys (for God, e.g.: Ps 8:6; 95:7 LXX; for Aaron: Exod 28:2; or for human beings in general: Ps 8:6). It does function as such a phrase, however, in the NT, particularly in doxological and hymnic texts praising God (1 Tim 1:17; cf. 6:16 with κράτος αἰώνιον instead of δόξα; Rev 4:11 [see also v. 9]; 5:13; 7:12) or the 'Lamb' (Rev 5:12f.). (Balz and Schneider, *EDNT*, 358)

[53] 'The attributes of glory, honor, and might (τὴν δόξαν καὶ τὴν τιμὴν καὶ τὴν δύναμιν) are all arthrous because they denote that which is due or requisite' (Aune, *Revelation 1-5*, 273).

[54] Mounce, *Revelation*, 150.

- Another divine attribute included in some of the hymnic sections of Revelation is that of *wisdom*: ἡ σοφία (Rev. 5.12; 7.12). As might be expected, references to σοφία abound in the LXX, especially in the Wisdom literature. Particularly interesting is also the overlap with Esdras A:

Rev. 5.12	Rev. 7.12	1 Ezra (Esd. A) 4.59-60
τὴν δύναμιν καὶ πλοῦτον καὶ <u>σοφίαν</u> καὶ ἰσχὺν καὶ τιμὴν καὶ <u>δόξαν</u> καὶ εὐλογίαν	<u>ἡ εὐλογία</u> καὶ <u>ἡ δόξα</u> καὶ <u>ἡ σοφία</u> καὶ ἡ εὐχαριστία καὶ ἡ τιμὴ καὶ ἡ δύναμις καὶ ἡ ἰσχύς	Παρὰ σοῦ ἡ νίκη, καὶ παρὰ σοῦ <u>ἡ σοφία</u>, καὶ σὴ <u>ἡ δόξα</u>, καὶ ἐγὼ σὸς οἰκέτης. <u>εὐλογητὸς</u> εἶ

The combination πλοῦτον καὶ σοφίαν (Rev. 5.14) is also to be seen in 2 Chron. 9.22 (πλούτῳ καὶ σοφίᾳ). The term σοφία itself occurs only nine times in the Psalter[55] but is used only in LXX Ps. 89.12 (ἐν σοφίᾳ), LXX Ps. 50.8 (τὰ ἄδηλα καὶ τὰ κρύφια τῆς σοφίας σου ἐδήλωσάς μοι) and LXX Ps. 103.24 in terms of the Lord's wisdom (πάντα ἐν σοφίᾳ ἐποίησας).

- A further divine attribute is that of *strength*: ἡ ἰσχύς (Rev. 5.12; 7.12), which is slightly more expanded in Rev. 18.8 (ὅτι ἰσχυρὸς κύριος ὁ θεὸς ὁ κρίνας αὐτήν). The quality of strength is also ascribed to Christ in Lk. 11.22.[56] The same motif can be traced in LXX Ps. 17.2 (κύριε ἡ ἰσχύς μου),[57] LXX Ps. 117.14 (ἰσχύς μου καὶ ὕμνησίς μου ὁ κύριος) and LXX Ps. 146.5 (μέγας ὁ κύριος ἡμῶν, καὶ μεγάλη ἡ ἰσχὺς αὐτοῦ).

- Another divine attribute in some of the hymnic sections is *praise* or *blessing* (ἡ εὐλογία), which is mentioned in Rev. 5.12 (δόξαν καὶ εὐλογίαν). Blessing as a quality is also applied to Christ in Rom. 15.29 (ἐν πληρώματι εὐλογίας Χριστοῦ).[58] Note LXX Ps. 3.9 (ἡ εὐλογία σου). Particularly interesting are the verbal parallels between Rev. 5.13 and Rev. 7.12[59] on the one hand and LXX Ps. 20.6-7 on the other hand.

---

[55] LXX Pss. 18.8; 36.30; 48.4; 50.8; 89.12; 103.24; 104.22; 106.27; 110.10.
[56] Mounce, *Revelation*, 150.
[57] Intertextual connections with LXX Ps. 17.3 in Heb. 2.13 have also been noted before. See G. J. Steyn, *A Quest for the Assumed Septuagint Vorlage of the Explicit Quotations in Hebrews*, FRLANT 235 (Göttingen: Vandenhoeck & Ruprecht, 2011), 158, 160, 164–5, 168, 379.
[58] Mounce, *Revelation*, 150.
[59] This is the longest doxology in Revelation with a list of seven attributes.

Rev. 5.13	Rev. 7.12	LXX Ps. 20.6-7
ἡ εὐλογία ... καὶ ἡ δόξα ... εἰς τοὺς αἰῶνας τῶν αἰώνων	ἡ εὐλογία καὶ ἡ δόξα ... εἰς τοὺς αἰῶνας τῶν αἰώνων	μεγάλη ἡ δόξα αὐτοῦ ... δώσεις αὐτῷ εὐλογίαν εἰς αἰῶνα αἰῶνος

- Among the attributes listed in Rev. 5.13 is the quality of *might*: καὶ τὸ κράτος εἰς τοὺς αἰῶνας τῶν αἰώνων. The same quality, also connected to God, is found in LXX Ps. 61.13[60] (ὅτι τὸ κράτος τοῦ θεοῦ) and LXX Ps. 85.16 (δὸς τὸ κράτος σου). Moyise has drawn attention to the fact that God's just judgement is elaborated in the refrain from Ps. 62(61).13 – which is also quoted in Rom. 2.6.
- *Salvation* (ἡ σωτηρία) is mentioned in Rev. 7.10 (ἡ σωτηρία τῷ θεῷ[61] ἡμῶν τῷ καθημένῳ ἐπὶ τῷ θρόνῳ). The motif of the Lord's salvation surfaces furthermore in LXX Ps. 3.9 (τοῦ κυρίου ἡ σωτηρία).[62] Some identify a Hebraism in the three places in Revelation where σωτηρία appears as part of a doxology (Rev. 7.10; 12.10; 19.1). The construction is, however, not necessarily a Hebraism, 'for it can be construed simply as a dative of possession, which can best be translated "deliverance belongs to God".'[63] Especially striking are the similarities between Rev. 12.10 and LXX Ps. 27.8 on the one hand and those of Rev. 19.1 and LXX Ps. 95.2-3[64] on the other hand:

Rev. 12.10	LXX Ps. 27.8
ἄρτι ἐγένετο <u>ἡ σωτηρία</u> καὶ ἡ δύναμις καὶ ἡ βασιλεία τοῦ θεοῦ ἡμῶν καὶ ἡ ἐξουσία <u>τοῦ χριστοῦ αὐτοῦ</u>	καὶ ὑπερασπιστὴς <u>τῶν σωτηρίων τοῦ χριστοῦ αὐτοῦ</u> ἐστιν

Rev. 19.1	LXX Ps. 95.2-3
<u>ἡ σωτηρία</u> καὶ <u>ἡ δόξα</u> καὶ ἡ δύναμις <u>τοῦ θεοῦ</u> ἡμῶν	εὐαγγελίζεσθε ἡμέραν ἐξ ἡμέρας <u>τὸ σωτήριον αὐτοῦ</u> ἀναγγείλατε ἐν τοῖς ἔθνεσιν <u>τὴν δόξαν αὐτοῦ</u>

---

[60] LXX Ps. 61.13 is also alluded to in Rev. 2.23, where it is connected to the principle of *lex talionis*. Similarly, Moyise, on V.13b 'since Jer. 17:10 speaks of "ways" rather than "works"' (Moyise, 'Psalms in Revelation', 242).

[61] 'The same construction occurs in doxologies when various attributes are ascribed to God or Christ in the dative' (Aune, *Revelation 6-16*, 429).

[62] So also H. B. Swete, *The Apocalypse of St. John*, 2nd edn, Classic Commentaries on the Greek NT (New York: Macmillan, 1906), 99. Roloff has drawn attention to the fact that Rev. 7.10 'nimmt fast wörtlich eine alttestamentliche Formel auf, in der die gottesdienstliche Gemeinde ihrer Zuversicht Ausdruck gab, daß Gott der einzige Helfer und Retter sei (Ps. 3,9; 38,23; 42,12; 43,5; Jon. 2,10)' (*Offenbarung*, 91).

[63] Aune, *Revelation 6-16*, 429.

[64] Another possible allusion to LXX Ps. 95.3 is found in Rev. 14.6 and possibly also in Mt. 28.19; Mk 16.15; Jn 20.21 and Acts 1.8. 'The good news of God's salvation was to be proclaimed from day to day, calling all nations to true worship' (Koester, *Revelation*, 612).

- The *Kingdom of God* (ἡ βασιλεία τοῦ θεοῦ) belongs to the very nature of the Almighty on the throne according to Rev. 11.15 and 12.10.[65] This royal motif runs through several Psalms, including LXX Pss. 21.29 (τοῦ κυρίου ἡ βασιλεία). Especially noteworthy are the verbal analogies between Rev. 11.15 and LXX Pss. 44.7,[66] 102.19[67] and 144.11, 12[68] – where kingship and eternal reign (βασιλεύσει εἰς τοὺς αἰῶνας τῶν αἰώνων) are combined with this motif.

Rev. 11.15	LXX Ps. 44.7	LXX Ps. 102.19	LXX Ps. 144.11, 12
ἐγένετο ἡ βασιλεία τοῦ κόσμου τοῦ κυρίου ἡμῶν … καὶ βασιλεύσει εἰς τοὺς αἰῶνας τῶν αἰώνων	ὁ θρόνος σου, ὁ θεός, εἰς τὸν αἰῶνα τοῦ αἰῶνος, ῥάβδος εὐθύτητος ἡ ῥάβδος τῆς βασιλείας σου	κύριος ἐν τῷ οὐρανῷ ἡτοίμασεν τὸν θρόνον αὐτοῦ, καὶ ἡ βασιλεία αὐτοῦ πάντων δεσπόζει	δόξαν τῆς βασιλείας σου ἐροῦσιν … καὶ τὴν δόξαν τῆς μεγαλοπρεπείας τῆς βασιλείας σου

- The attribute of ἡ ἐξουσία (*dominion*) occurs in the hymnic sections only in Rev. 12.10 and is directly linked to the Christ (ἡ ἐξουσία τοῦ χριστοῦ αὐτοῦ). The term is not unknown in the LXX and surfaces mainly in the historical and wisdom literature, as well as in Daniel. It is rare in the Psalms with only three occurrences – the closest being LXX Ps. 113.2 (Ισραηλ ἐξουσία αὐτοῦ). However, the similarities with 1 Esdras 4 and its connections there with royal rulership are especially interesting:

Rev. 12.10	1 Ezra (Esd. A) 4.40
ἄρτι ἐγένετο ἡ σωτηρία καὶ ἡ δύναμις καὶ ἡ βασιλεία τοῦ θεοῦ ἡμῶν καὶ ἡ ἐξουσία τοῦ χριστοῦ αὐτοῦ	καὶ αὐτῇ ἡ ἰσχὺς καὶ τὸ βασίλειον καὶ ἡ ἐξουσία καὶ ἡ μεγαλειότης τῶν πάντων αἰώνων. εὐλογητὸς ὁ θεὸς τῆς ἀληθείας

Note the presence of ἡ ἰσχύς, εὐλογητός, ὁ θεὸς τῆς ἀληθείας and τῶν πάντων αἰώνων, which all occur in the same breath in 1 Esd. 4.40 – attributes that are also spread over the hymnic sections of Rev. 5.13; 7.12; 11.15 and 12.10.

---

[65] Charles saw also an allusion to Ps. 2.2, 6 in Rev. 12.10 (*Revelation I*, 326).
[66] Heb. 1.8-9 also quotes LXX Ps. 44.7-8 and interprets it Christologically. Cf. Balz and Schneider, *EDNT*, 157; Steyn, *Quest Septuagint Vorlage*, 82–102. 'The scepter is primarily associated with the royal role of meting out justice (Isa 11:4; Ps 45:7) and is frequently used in a context of punishment' (Aune, *Revelation 1–5*, 210).
[67] 'All creation (the largest choir possible) blesses the Father and the Son (cf. v. 14; Ps. 103:19–20; Phil. 2:8–11)' (R. J. Utley, *Hope in Hard Times – the Final Curtain: Revelation*, Study Guide Commentary Series 12 (Marshall: Bible Lessons International, 2001), 57).
[68] 'A "kingdom" normally meant a ruler's right to reign (Ps. 145:11–14)' (Keener, *Revelation*, 71).

- The *Angel of the Waters* proclaims that the Holy One is *just* (δίκαιος εἶ) in Rev. 16.5 - a quality that is frequently mentioned in the Psalter. Five specific Psalms emphasize the same thought: LXX Ps. 9.5 (ἐκάθισας ἐπὶ θρόνου, ὁ κρίνων δικαιοσύνην), LXX Ps. 10.7 (ὅτι δίκαιος κύριος καὶ δικαιοσύνας ἠγάπησεν),[69] LXX Ps. 96.6 (ἀνήγγειλαν οἱ οὐρανοὶ τὴν δικαιοσύνην αὐτοῦ), LXX Ps. 118.137 (Δίκαιος εἶ, κύριε)[70] and LXX Ps. 144.17 (δίκαιος κύριος).[71] Related to this attribute is the fact that the Lord's 'ways' (αἱ ὁδοί σου, Rev. 15.3) and his 'judgements' (αἱ κρίσεις σου, Rev. 16.7; 19.2) are *'just and true'* (δίκαιαι καὶ ἀληθιναί, Rev. 15.3; 16.7; 19.2). A similar motif is also present in LXX Ps. 44.5: ἕνεκεν ἀληθείας καὶ πραΰτητος καὶ δικαιοσύνης. Still in the same vein and within the context of Rev. 15.3-4, the hymn there ends on a similar note: 'your judgements have been revealed' (τὰ δικαιώματά σου ἐφανερώθησαν). The motif closely resembles LXX Ps. 17.23 (τὰ δικαιώματα αὐτοῦ οὐκ ἀπέστησα ἀπ' ἐμοῦ), LXX Ps. 118.12 (δίδαξόν με τὰ δικαιώματά σου), Ps. 118.64 (τὰ δικαιώματά σου δίδαξόν με) and 118.68 (δίδαξόν με τὰ δικαιώματά σου).
- That the Holy One is just presupposes his attribute as *Judge*. The One on the Throne is the ultimate Judge, who executes his *judgement*. Hence, 'his judgements are true and just' (ἀληθιναὶ καὶ δίκαιαι αἱ κρίσεις σου, Rev. 16.7; 19.2). The motif surfaces in several Psalms,[72] with verbal analogies in LXX Pss. 88.15 and 96.2;[73] 95.13;[74] 97.9;[75] 118.121; and 118.160. In all these cases, however, δικαιοσύνη (rather than δίκαιαι) is closely linked with κρινεῖ.

Divine actions

The divine actions, referred to in the hymnic sections, reiterate the royal rulership, judgement and omnipresence of the Holy One. The worship hymns picture him sitting on the throne, ruling in eternity, executing his wrath and judgement, performing great and amazing deeds, leaving a trail of smoke with the enemies, yet dwelling with his people. These actions confirm the eschatological hope of Israel's restoration, and the

---

[69] 'The promise that the righteous might one day see the Lord comes to its fulfillment (Ps. 11:7; Matt. 5:8; 1 John 3:2)' (Koester, *End of All Things*, 197).

[70] Cf. Moyise: 'If we are looking for a source for the specific statement that God's "judgements" (κρίσεις) are just, it is probably Ps. 119:137 (along with Ps. 19:9) that is in mind' (Moyise, 'Psalms in Revelation', 244). He also lists Ps. 119(118).137 (his judgements are just and true) among the attributes of God and his Anointed (245). See Mounce, *Revelation*, 295; Aland, *Apparatus*, 837.

[71] 'Those who have conquered the beast - with its traits of imperial Rome - use traditional biblical language to acclaim God's justice (Deut 32:4; Ps 145:17 …)' (Koester, *Revelation*, 632).

[72] Mounce saw similarities with Ps. 19.9 (*Revelation*, 296).

[73] Pss. 89(88).15 and 97(96).2 are alluded to in 11QPs[a] (11Q5) XXVI,10-11 (Hymn to the Creator).

[74] Moyise lists Ps. 96(95).13 (he judges in righteousness) among the attributes of God and his Anointed (Moyise, 'Psalms in Revelation', 245). Cf. B. J. Eastman: 'In Revelation 19:11-16 we see a typical NT phenomenon: what the OT applies to God, the NT unabashedly applies to Christ. Christ, appearing in apocalyptic glory, is called "faithful and true" (cf. Ps 96:13)' ('Name', in Martin and Davids, *Dictionary*, 785). An allusion to Ps. 96(95).13 occurs in 2 Thess. 1.10.

[75] 'The references to the exodus in the psalm form part of the basis for a final statement that God "will judge the world in righteousness, and the nations in uprightness" (Ps. 98:9). The same transition of thought is present in Revelation 15, where the "song" of the first exodus serves as a broad model for the end-time exodus' (Beale, *Book of Revelation*, 799).

motifs are all present in the Septuagint Psalter with the overlap in formulation being clear from the following table:

τῷ καθημένῳ ἐπὶ τῷ θρόνῳ (Rev. 5.13; 7.10; 15.13-14)	ὁ θεὸς κάθηται ἐπὶ θρόνου ἁγίου αὐτοῦ (LXX Ps. 46.9)[76]
καὶ βασιλεύσει εἰς τοὺς αἰῶνας τῶν αἰώνων (Rev. 11.15); καὶ ἐβασίλευσας (Rev. 11.17);[77] ἐβασίλευσεν κύριος / ὁ βασιλεὺς τῶν ἐθνῶν (Rev. 15.3)	βασιλεύσει κύριος εἰς τὸν αἰῶνα καὶ εἰς τὸν αἰῶνα τοῦ αἰῶνος (LXX Ps. 9.37);[78] ἐβασίλευσεν ὁ θεὸς ἐπὶ τὰ ἔθνη (LXX Ps. 46.9); Ὁ κύριος ἐβασίλευσεν (LXX Ps. 96.1);[79] βασιλεύσει κύριος εἰς τὸν αἰῶνα (LXX Ps. 145.10)[80]
καὶ τὰ ἔθνη ὠργίσθησαν, καὶ ἦλθεν ἡ ὀργή σου (Rev. 11.18)	Ὁ κύριος ἐβασίλευσεν, ὀργιζέσθωσαν λαοί (LXX Ps. 98.1);[81] τότε λαλήσει πρὸς αὐτοὺς ἐν ὀργῇ αὐτοῦ (LXX Ps. 2.5);[82] ἀνάστηθι, κύριε, ἐν ὀργῇ σου, ὑψώθητι ἐν τοῖς πέρασι τῶν ἐχθρῶν μου (LXX Ps. 7.7); ὅτι ὠργίσθη αὐτοῖς ὁ θεός (LXX Ps. 17.8)

[76] Ps. 47(46).9 was identified as an allusion to Rev. 4.2-3, 9-10 by Moyise, 'Psalms in Revelation', 243.
[77] Charles identified allusions to Ps. 93.1 in Rev. 11.17 and to Ps. 98 in Rev. 11.18. He suspects, furthermore, that Ps. 2.1, 5 'was also in the mind of the writer as it was in (verse) 15' (*Revelation I*, 295–6). Klaiber, too, states, 'Dass Gott die Herrschaft angetreten hat und auch über die Völker als König regiert, war schon in den Psalmen als Realität proklamiert.' He refers to Pss. 47.8-9; 93.1; 97.1; 99.1 (*Offenbarung*, 170).
[78] Cf. G. D. Fee: 'Although this sentiment can be found throughout the OT, the present language is a close echo of the LXX of Ps 9:37' (*Revelation*, NCCS (Eugene, OR: Cascade, 2011), 157). Aune also identified an allusion to LXX Ps. 9.37 in Rev. 11.15 (*Revelation 6–16*, 639).
[79] Keener identifies an allusion to Ps. 97(96).1 in Rev. 19.5-6 (*IVP Background Commentary*, Rev. 19.4-6).
[80] Aune identified an allusion to Ps. 145.10 in Rev. 11.15 (*Revelation 6–16*, 639). 'The name "Mount Zion" has positive connotations as the place where the faithful gather in safety (Isa. 24:23; Joel 3:21) to worship the God who creates and delivers them (Ps. 146:10)' (Koester, *End of All Things*, 135).
[81] 'The hostile nations of the world are enraged (v 18a), a motif paired with the kingly rule of God in Ps 99:1 (LXX 98:1)' (Aune, *Revelation 6–16*, 636). Ps. 99(98).1 was also identified as an allusion to Rev. 11.17-8 by Roloff, *Offenbarung*, 120, and by Moyise, 'Psalms in Revelation', 240, 244.
[82] 'The language may be reminiscent of Ps 2:5' (Koester, *Revelation*, 515). 'The same way in which the enemy would try to subdue God's people would be used by God to subdue his enemy, even to the extent of resembling the enemy's likeness. This mimicking figuratively emphasizes divine justice, which often mocks those who attempt to thwart God's purposes (e. g. Ps. 2:1–5)' (Beale, *John's Use of the OT*, 348). Similarly, Roloff, *Offenbarung*, 170. 'Various passages from Ps 2 are frequently alluded to in Revelation (Ps 2:1 in Rev 11:18; Ps 2:2 in Rev 6:15; 11:15; 17:18; 19:19; Ps 2:5 in Rev 11:18; Ps 2:8 in Rev 2:26; Ps 2:9 in Rev 12:5; 19:15; Ps 2:12 in Rev 11:18)' (Aune, *Revelation 17–22*, 1061). An allusion to Ps. 2.2 in Rev. 11.15 and to Ps. 2.5 in Rev. 11.18 was also noted by Charles, *Revelation I*, 294; Mounce, *Revelation*, 231.

τῷ καθημένῳ ἐπὶ τῷ θρόνῳ (Rev. 5.13; 7.10; 15.13-14)	ὁ θεὸς κάθηται ἐπὶ θρόνου ἁγίου αὐτοῦ (LXX Ps. 46.9)[76]
καὶ ὁ καιρὸς τῶν νεκρῶν κριθῆναι (Rev. 11.18); ὅτι ταῦτα ἔκρινας (Rev. 16.5); κύριος ὁ θεὸς ὁ κρίνας αὐτήν (Rev. 18.8); ὅτι ἀληθιναὶ καὶ δίκαιαι αἱ κρίσεις αὐτοῦ (Rev. 19.2)	ὅτι ἐποίησας τὴν κρίσιν μου καὶ τὴν δίκην μου, ἐκάθισας ἐπὶ θρόνου, ὁ κρίνων δικαιοσύνην (LXX Ps. 9.5); καὶ αὐτὸς κρινεῖ τὴν οἰκουμένην ἐν δικαιοσύνῃ, κρινεῖ λαοὺς ἐν εὐθύτητι (LXX Ps. 9.9); κρίνειν τὸν λαόν σου ἐν δικαιοσύνῃ καὶ τοὺς πτωχούς σου ἐν κρίσει (LXX Ps. 71.2); ὅτι ἔρχεται κρῖναι τὴν γῆν· κρινεῖ τὴν οἰκουμένην ἐν δικαιοσύνῃ καὶ λαοὺς ἐν τῇ ἀληθείᾳ αὐτοῦ[83] (LXX Ps. 95.13); ὅτι ἥκει κρῖναι τὴν γῆν· κρινεῖ τὴν οἰκουμένην ἐν δικαιοσύνῃ καὶ λαοὺς ἐν εὐθύτητι (LXX Ps. 97.9)
καὶ τοῖς φοβουμένοις τὸ ὄνομά σου, τοὺς μικροὺς καὶ τοὺς μεγάλους (Rev. 11.18)	τοὺς φοβουμένους τὸν κύριον, τοὺς μικροὺς μετὰ τῶν μεγάλων (LXX Ps. 113.21)[84]
μεγάλα καὶ θαυμαστὰ τὰ ἔργα σου (Rev. 15.3)	τῷ ποιοῦντι θαυμάσια μεγάλα μόνῳ (LXX Ps. 135.4); μεγάλα τὰ ἔργα κυρίου (LXX Ps. 110.2)
ὁ καπνὸς αὐτῆς ἀναβαίνει (Rev. 19.3)	ἀνέβη καπνὸς ἐν ὀργῇ αὐτοῦ (LXX Ps. 17.9)
ἡ σκηνὴ τοῦ θεοῦ μετὰ τῶν ἀνθρώπων, καὶ σκηνώσει μετ' αὐτῶν (Rev. 21.3-4)	τόπον σκηνώματος δόξης σου (LXX Ps. 25.8); καὶ ἀπώσατο τὴν σκηνὴν Σηλωμ, σκήνωμα αὐτοῦ, οὗ κατεσκήνωσεν ἐν ἀνθρώποις (LXX Ps. 77.60); Ὡς ἀγαπητὰ τὰ σκηνώματά σου, κύριε τῶν δυνάμεων (LXX Ps. 83.2)

Conclusion

Some interesting observations became clear from our brief survey on echoes from the Septuagint Psalter in the hymnic sections of Revelation. First, the fact that echoes from the Psalter are present, often with clear verbal analogy (and in some cases even as clear

---

[83] 'The love of God and the justice of God converge by bringing the beast's reign to an end (compare Ps. 9:8; 72:2; Isa. 11:4)' (Koester, *End of All Things*, 176).

[84] LXX Ps. 113.21 = MT Ps. 115.13. The allusion is also noted by Charles, *Revelation I*, 297; Mounce, *Revelation*, 232; Klaiber, *Offenbarung*, 172. See Rev. 19.5.

allusions), has been confirmed. The author of Revelation is familiar with the Psalter. Echoes from a range of Psalms were intertextually integrated during the composition of the hymnic sections of the worship scenes. Some of these Psalms clearly played a more prominent role than others. In addition to Psalms 2, 86(85) and 89(88) that were highlighted by Moyise, traces from particularly Book I (LXX Pss. 3; 9, 17; 20–21; 32–33; 40), Book IV (LXX Pss. 89; 95–98; 103–104) and Book V (LXX Pss. 106; 110; 113; 116–118; 134–135; 144–146; 148; 150) surfaced often in the hymnic sections. These include acrostic Psalms (LXX Pss. 9; 33; 110; 118; 144), Festival Psalms (LXX Pss. 112–117) and the Hallelujah-Psalms (LXX Pss. 145–150). The absence of the Pilgrim Songs (LXX Pss. 119–133) in the apocalyptic hymnic compositions is striking.

Second, the author of Revelation intentionally formulates some of the expressions from the Psalter in the exact opposite manner. Examples are, for instance, Rev. 12.10 where the accuser accuses the 'brothers' before God – in contrast to LXX Ps. 67.4 where the call is to praise and sing to God and to be exultant before him or Rev. 12.12 where woe is expressed regarding the land and sea – in contrast to LXX Ps. 95.11[85] where the earth should rejoice and the sea should shake.

Third, some of the phrases and echoes in the hymnic sections of Revelation surface again in the Septuagint Odes, a collection of existing songs and prayers that were selected from the Greek scriptures and attached as an appendix to the Greek Psalter in Codex Alexandrinus[86] (early fifth century CE) – probably for liturgical purposes. Similarities in wording are particularly noticeable in Ode 12 (*The Prayer of Manasseh*) and Ode 14 (*The Morning Song*). The latter contains allusions to LXX Pss. 118.12; 144.2 and Lk. 2.14. It originated mainly from a Christian tradition. The similarities between Revelation and Ode 14 point to the same phenomenon of reception, where the Psalter served as a collection of liturgical and worship pretexts during the composition of early Christian hymnic and worship material.[87]

---

[85] The allusion to Ps. 95.11 in Rev. 12.12 was also noted by Charles, *Revelation I*, 329; Mounce, *Revelation*, 244; Roloff, *Offenbarung*, 131.

[86] The collection is completely absent in the earlier codices Sinaiticus and Vaticanus from the fourth century CE. There is also no attestation of the collection of Odes in the extant corpus of Hebrew witnesses and it is lacking as a collection in the Latin Vulgate.

[87] Cf. Kostenberger: 'Christ serves as the hermeneutical key, and the OT provides the salvation-historical backdrop against which the apocalyptic visions in the book are to be understood' ('Use of Scripture', 251).

6

The Old Testament background of sound and silence in the Book of Revelation

Beate Kowalski

Exegetes are specialists in ancient and modern languages which are spoken and written in various cultural contexts. Their world is different from that of the ancient biblical texts, their authors and addressees. To grasp the meaning of biblical words, they need the silence and solitude of libraries and working spaces. Steve Moyise, to whom this volume is dedicated, is such a specialist of words and languages. Gratefully I think of many annual OT/NT seminars in Hawarden that Steve Moyise led and regularly attended for many years. They have always been a place of sharing, encouragement and inspiration. The atmosphere of solitude at Gladstone's Library and the picturesque backdrop of Hawarden helped attendees to listen carefully to the enriching paper presentations and motivating discussions. It is precisely the mixture of sound and silence in Hawarden that contributes to a good, constructive atmosphere, which is appreciated in particular by young researchers.

Sound and silence are also two central motifs in the Revelation of John. The last book of the New Testament and the Bible as a whole is not only characterized by a flood of images but also by smells and sounds, and by silence. In addition to auditions, (liturgical) dialogues,[1] heavenly and earthly voices (that cannot be assigned to a certain speaker),[2] noises and the sound of musical instruments, numerous hymnal elements weave a net over the dramatic developments of Revelation from chapter 1 to 19. Moments of absolute silence at the end of the three series of plagues are surprising, as is the great final vision of the heavenly Jerusalem. The praise of God falls silent in the seven epistles (2.1–3.22), at the fall of the dragon to earth (13.1-18) – the dramatic climax of Revelation – and in the final vision of the heavenly Jerusalem (21.1–22.7). Silence is an ambivalent sign: it is an expression of God's presence (a sign of theophany), and also an indication of the dead silence, the silencing of all human voices in the face of the doomsday scenario (18.22-23).

In the last two decades, exegetical research has paid more and more attention to the fact that John consistently draws on OT pretexts, and therefore Revelation is described

---

[1] Ugo Vanni, 'Liturgical Dialogue as a Literary Form in the Book of Revelation', *NTS* 37 (1991): 348–72.
[2] Cf. Maynard Eugene Boring, 'The Voice of Jesus in the Apocalypse of John', *NovT* 34 (1992): 334–59; Giancarlo Biguzzi, 'The Chaos of Rev 22,6–21 and Prophecy in Asia', *Biblica* 83.2 (2002): 193–210.

as a text mosaic by some scholars.[3] Steve Moyise has also dealt with this issue in many ways.[4] The OT background is also important for the two motifs of sounds and silence, which are shown in more detail in this chapter.

1: Sound in the Book of Revelation of John

We will explore first the numerous sounds and voices which permeate the last book of the Bible, the Revelation to the prophet John, which is noisy, sometimes loud, filled with voices with tremendous power, disturbing sounds and melodious vocals and instrumental music.

Voices and sounds

John's production plays with voices and acoustic sounds from different directions (14.15, 18), which call out to each other in the form of alternating choruses. The soundscape reaches the spectator of the event mostly from above, from or around the throne (4.5; 5.11-12; 19.5-6; 21.3), in the heavenly throne room (5.2; 6.1, 6, 7), in front of, from, out of or under the altar (6.9; 7.10; 8.5; 9.13; 14.18), in or out of heaven (4.1; 8.13; 10.1, 4, 8, 12; 11.15; 12.10; 14.2, 6, 9, 13; 18.2, 4; 19.1), from or clothed in a cloud (10.2), from the east (7.2), in or outside the temple of God (11.19; 14.15, 18; 16.1, 17-18), in the sun (19.17). But it also resounds on earth, though less frequently. With this mode of presentation, which reveals God's message of salvation and disaster, John remains faithful to the prophetic-epistolary genre,[5] which also contains apocalyptic elements like OT prophecy.

Voices are compared to the loud sound of a trumpet (1.10; 4.1; 8.13), to the sound of water, to the roar of a lion or to the sound of a harp, or are accompanied by thunder (4.5; 6.1; 14.2; 19.6). The confusion of voices is often difficult to classify and has caused even exegetes headaches. In many cases, there is the same number of voices sounding polyphonically and from different directions at the same time (5.11).

---

[3] The characterization of Revelation as a mosaic of texts is stated by Fred W. Jenkins, *The Old Testament in the Book of Revelation* (Grand Rapids, MI: Baker Book House, 1972), 21; A. van Schaik, 'De Apocalyps als Tekstmozaïek', *Schrift* 114 (1987): 231–4.

[4] Cf. the fundamental study of Steve Moyise, *The Old Testament in the Book of Revelation*, JSNTSup 115 (Sheffield: Sheffield Academic Press, 1995). In addition, he published further articles on individual aspects of the OT in Revelation: Steve Moyise, 'Ezekiel and the Book of Revelation', in Andrew Mein and Paul M. Joyce (eds), *After Ezekiel, Essays on the Reception of a Difficult Prophet*, LHBOTS 535 (New York: T&T Clark 2011), 45–57; Steve Moyise, 'Models for Intertextual Interpretation of Revelation', in Richard B. Hays and Stefan Alkier (eds), *Revelation and the Politics of Apocalyptic Interpretation* (Waco, TX: Baylor University Press 2012), 31–45; Steve Moyise, 'Genesis in Revelation', in Maarten J. J. Menken and Steve Moyise (eds), *Genesis in the New Testament*, LNTS 466 (London: Bloomsbury 2012), 166–79.

[5] Cf. Beate Kowalski, 'Prophetie und die Offenbarung des Johannes? Offb 22,6-21 als Testfall', in Joseph Verheyden and Korinna Zamfir (eds), *Prophets and Prophecy in Jewish and Early Christian Literature*, WUNT II/286 (Tübingen: Mohr Siebeck, 2010), 253–93; Martin Karrer, *Die Johannesoffenbarung als Brief*, Studien zu ihrem literarischen, historischen und theologischen Ort (FRLANT 140) (Göttingen: Vandenhoeck & Ruprecht 1986).

OT Background of Sound and Silence 85

In two places in Revelation, the voice can be identified with Christ as the speaker: 1.12 (Καὶ ἐπέστρεψα βλέπειν τὴν φωνὴν ἥτις ἐλάλει μετ' ἐμοῦ); and 3.20 (ἐάν τις ἀκούσῃ τῆς φωνῆς μου καὶ ἀνοίξῃ τὴν θύραν). It is noticeable that in both verses the voice is not described as loud but is simply named as a voice that enters into a relationship with John or the Christians in Laodicea. Sounds of natural events such as thunder, lightning, earthquakes and hail (8.5; 10.3; 11.19; 16.18) make theophany audible. The rustling of the wings of various creatures (9.9: locusts) as well as the throwing down of a censer (8.5: λιβανωτός) complement the auditory event (8.5); and John underlines the drama through exaggerations (e.g. seven thunders: 10:3-4; great earthquake: 6.12; 11.13; 16.18).

The following table gives an overview of all the voices and sounds that appear in Revelation. The first column contains comparisons, introduced by ὡς/ὥσπερ and followed by a metaphor. The second column gives the location of the voice; the third column lists all references that speak of a loud voice. The fourth column lists the sounds produced by theophanies. Finally, the last column lists all references in which music or sounds are mentioned.

Metaphorical comparison of the voice(s) with metaphors	Place of the voice(s)	Loud voice(s)	Theophanic signs	Music, noises
1.10: καὶ ἤκουσα ὀπίσω μου φωνὴν μεγάλην **ὡς σάλπιγγος**	4.5: Καὶ ἐκ τοῦ θρόνου ἐκπορεύονται ἀστραπαὶ καὶ φωναὶ καὶ βρονταί	5.2: καὶ εἶδον ἄγγελον ἰσχυρὸν κηρύσσοντα ἐν **φωνῇ μεγάλῃ**	4.5: Καὶ ἐκ τοῦ θρόνου ἐκπορεύονται **ἀστραπαὶ καὶ φωναὶ καὶ βρονταί**	18.22: καὶ **φωνὴ κιθαρῳδῶν** καὶ **μουσικῶν** καὶ **αὐλητῶν** καὶ **σαλπιστῶν** οὐ μὴ ἀκουσθῇ ἐν σοὶ ἔτι
1.15: καὶ ἡ φωνὴ αὐτοῦ **ὡς φωνὴ ὑδάτων πολλῶν**	5.11: καὶ ἤκουσα φωνὴν ἀγγέλων πολλῶν κύκλῳ τοῦ θρόνου καὶ τῶν ζῴων καὶ τῶν πρεσβυτέρων	5.12: λέγοντες **φωνῇ μεγάλῃ**	8.5: καὶ ἐγένοντο **βρονταὶ καὶ φωναὶ καὶ ἀστραπαὶ καὶ σεισμός**	18.22: καὶ **φωνὴ μύλου** οὐ μὴ ἀκουσθῇ ἐν σοὶ ἔτι

Metaphorical comparison of the voice(s) with metaphors	Place of the voice(s)	Loud voice(s)	Theophanic signs	Music, noises
4.1: καὶ ἡ φωνὴ ἡ πρώτη ἣν ἤκουσα ὡς σάλπιγγος λαλούσης μετ' ἐμοῦ λέγων	6.7: ἤκουσα φωνὴν τοῦ τετάρτου ζῴου λέγοντος	6.10: καὶ ἔκραξαν φωνῇ μεγάλῃ λέγοντες	11.19: καὶ ἐγένοντο ἀστραπαὶ καὶ φωναὶ καὶ βρονταὶ καὶ σεισμὸς καὶ χάλαζα μεγάλη	18.23: καὶ φωνὴ νυμφίου καὶ νύμφης οὐ μὴ ἀκουσθῇ ἐν σοὶ ἔτι
6.1: λέγοντος ὡς φωνὴ βροντῆς	9.13: καὶ ἤκουσα φωνὴν μίαν ἐκ τῶν [τεσσάρων] κεράτων τοῦ θυσιαστηρίου τοῦ χρυσοῦ τοῦ ἐνώπιον τοῦ θεοῦ	7.2: καὶ ἔκραξεν φωνῇ μεγάλῃ	16.18: καὶ ἐγένοντο ἀστραπαὶ καὶ φωναὶ καὶ βρονταὶ καὶ σεισμὸς ἐγένετο μέγας	
6.6: καὶ ἤκουσα ὡς φωνὴν ἐν μέσῳ τῶν τεσσάρων ζῴων λέγουσαν	10.4: καὶ ἤκουσα φωνὴν ἐκ τοῦ οὐρανοῦ λέγουσαν	7.10: καὶ κράζουσιν φωνῇ μεγάλῃ λέγοντες		
9.9: καὶ ἡ φωνὴ τῶν πτερύγων αὐτῶν ὡς φωνὴ ἁρμάτων ἵππων πολλῶν τρεχόντων εἰς πόλεμον	10.7: ἀλλ' ἐν ταῖς ἡμέραις τῆς φωνῆς τοῦ ἑβδόμου ἀγγέλου	8.13: καὶ ἤκουσα ἑνὸς ἀετοῦ πετομένου ἐν μεσουρανήματι λέγοντος φωνῇ μεγάλῃ		

Metaphorical comparison of the voice(s) with metaphors	Place of the voice(s)	Loud voice(s)	Theophanic signs	Music, noises
10.3: καὶ ἔκραξεν φωνῇ μεγάλῃ **ὥσπερ λέων μυκᾶται**	10.8: Καὶ ἡ φωνὴ ἣν ἤκουσα **ἐκ τοῦ οὐρανοῦ** πάλιν λαλοῦσαν μετ' ἐμοῦ καὶ λέγουσαν	14.7: λέγων **ἐν φωνῇ μεγάλῃ**		
14.2: καὶ ἤκουσα φωνὴν ἐκ τοῦ οὐρανοῦ **ὡς φωνὴν ὑδάτων πολλῶν** καὶ **ὡς φωνὴν βροντῆς μεγάλης**, καὶ ἡ φωνὴ ἣν ἤκουσα **ὡς κιθαρῳδῶν κιθαριζόντων ἐν ταῖς κιθάραις αὐτῶν**	11.12: καὶ ἤκουσαν φωνῆς μεγάλης **ἐκ τοῦ οὐρανοῦ** λεγούσης αὐτοῖς	14.9: Καὶ ἄλλος ἄγγελος τρίτος ἠκολούθησεν αὐτοῖς λέγων **ἐν φωνῇ μεγάλῃ**		
19.1: ἤκουσα **ὡς φωνὴν μεγάλην ὄχλου πολλοῦ** ἐν τῷ οὐρανῷ λεγόντων	11.15: καὶ ἐγένοντο φωναὶ μεγάλαι **ἐν τῷ οὐρανῷ** λέγοντες	14.15 κράζων ἐν **φωνῇ μεγάλῃ** τῷ καθημένῳ ἐπὶ τῆς νεφέλης		

Metaphorical comparison of the voice(s) with metaphors	Place of the voice(s)	Loud voice(s)	Theophanic signs	Music, noises
19.6: Καὶ ἤκουσα ὡς φωνὴν ὄχλου πολλοῦ καὶ **ὡς φωνὴν ὑδάτων πολλῶν** καὶ **ὡς φωνὴν βροντῶν ἰσχυρῶν λεγόντων**	12.10: καὶ ἤκουσα φωνὴν μεγάλην **ἐν τῷ οὐρανῷ** λέγουσαν	14.18: καὶ ἐφώνησεν **φωνῇ μεγάλῃ** τῷ ἔχοντι τὸ δρέπανον τὸ ὀξὺ λέγων		
	14.2: καὶ ἤκουσα φωνὴν **ἐκ τοῦ οὐρανοῦ**	16.1: Καὶ ἤκουσα **μεγάλης φωνῆς** ἐκ τοῦ ναοῦ λεγούσης τοῖς ἑπτὰ ἀγγέλοις		
	14.13: Καὶ ἤκουσα φωνῆς **ἐκ τοῦ οὐρανοῦ** λεγούσης	16.17: καὶ ἐξῆλθεν **φωνὴ μεγάλη** ἐκ τοῦ ναοῦ ἀπὸ τοῦ θρόνου λέγουσα		
	14.15: καὶ ἄλλος ἄγγελος ἐξῆλθεν **ἐκ τοῦ ναοῦ**	18.2: καὶ ἔκραξεν **ἐν ἰσχυρᾷ φωνῇ** λέγων		
	16.1: Καὶ ἤκουσα μεγάλης φωνῆς **ἐκ τοῦ ναοῦ** λεγούσης τοῖς ἑπτὰ ἀγγέλοις	19.17: Καὶ εἶδον ἕνα ἄγγελον ἑστῶτα ἐν τῷ ἡλίῳ καὶ ἔκραξεν [ἐν] **φωνῇ μεγάλῃ** λέγων		

Metaphorical comparison of the voice(s) with metaphors	Place of the voice(s)	Loud voice(s)	Theophanic signs	Music, noises
	16.17: καὶ ἐξῆλθεν φωνὴ μεγάλη **ἐκ τοῦ ναοῦ** ἀπὸ τοῦ θρόνου λέγουσα	21.3: καὶ ἤκουσα **φωνῆς μεγάλης ἐκ τοῦ θρόνου** λεγούσης		
	18.4: Καὶ ἤκουσα ἄλλην φωνὴν **ἐκ τοῦ οὐρανοῦ** λέγουσαν			
	19.5: Καὶ φωνὴ **ἀπὸ τοῦ θρόνου** ἐξῆλθεν λέγουσα			
	21.3: καὶ ἤκουσα φωνῆς μεγάλης **ἐκ τοῦ θρόνου** λεγούσης			

Let us have a close look at the first column. The comparisons are made with a trumpet (σάλπιγγος: 1.10; 4.1), many waters (ὑδάτων πολλῶν: 1.15; 14.2; 19.6), thunder (βροντῆς: 6.1; 14.2; βροντῶν ἰσχυρῶν: 19.6), a roaring lion (λέων μυκᾶται: 10.3), harpists playing on their harps (κιθαρῳδῶν κιθαριζόντων ἐν ταῖς κιθάραις αὐτῶν: 14.2) and a great multitude (μεγάλην ὄχλου πολλοῦ: 19.1). Three of the metaphorical descriptions of the voice are also found in the OT (trumpet, many waters, thunder), while the remaining three (roaring lion, harpist, great, multitude) are originally formulated by John. The greatest correspondence with an OT pretext can be found for the metaphor 'many waters' in Ezek. 1.24. For the description of the voice with thunder, three different OT pretexts come into question (LXX Pss. 76.19; 103.7; Sir. 43.17). With these examples, one can clearly observe how John uses the OT. With breathtaking ability, he juggles with the OT, combines different pretexts and uses them to create new metaphorical comparisons (roaring lion, harpist, great multitude) with biblical echoes.

trumpet (σάλπιγγος: 1.10; 4.1)	Isa. 58.1 Ἀναβόησον ἐν ἰσχύι καὶ μὴ φείσῃ, ὡς σάλπιγγα ὕψωσον τὴν φωνήν σου καὶ ἀνάγγειλον τῷ λαῷ μου τὰ ἁμαρτήματα αὐτῶν καὶ τῷ οἴκῳ Ιακωβ τὰς ἀνομίας αὐτῶν.
many waters (ὑδάτων πολλῶν: 1.15; 14.2; 19.6)	Ezek. 1.24 καὶ ἤκουον τὴν φωνὴν τῶν πτερύγων αὐτῶν ἐν τῷ πορεύεσθαι αὐτὰ ὡς φωνὴν ὕδατος πολλοῦ, καὶ ἐν τῷ ἑστάναι αὐτὰ κατέπαυον αἱ πτέρυγες αὐτῶν
thunder (βροντῆς: 6.1; 14.2; βροντῶν ἰσχυρῶν: 19.6)	Ps. 76.19 LXX φωνὴ τῆς βροντῆς σου ἐν τῷ τροχῷ, ἔφαναν αἱ ἀστραπαί σου τῇ οἰκουμένῃ, ἐσαλεύθη καὶ ἔντρομος ἐγενήθη ἡ γῆ.
	Ps. 103.7 LXX ἀπὸ ἐπιτιμήσεώς σου φεύξονται, ἀπὸ φωνῆς βροντῆς σου δειλιάσουσιν
	Sir. 43.17 φωνὴ βροντῆς αὐτοῦ ὠνείδισεν γῆν καὶ καταιγὶς βορέου καὶ συστροφὴ πνεύματος.
a roaring lion (λέων μυκᾶται: 10.3)	[NA[28] refers to Hos. 11.10 and Amos 3.8]
harpists playing on their harps (κιθαρῳδῶν κιθαριζόντων ἐν ταῖς κιθάραις αὐτῶν: 14.2)	
a great multitude (μεγάλην ὄχλου πολλοῦ: 19.1)	[NA[28] refers to Dan. 10.6: ὡσεὶ φωνὴ θορύβου]

In the following, we will deal especially with the OT background of the theophany signs in 8.5; 11.19; 16.18.

In addition to the individual theophanic signs, John also combines different signs to form a series of three or five items, in which the various natural events are lined up as signs of God's presence. In Rev. 4.5; 11.19; 16.18 the three theophany signs ἀστραπαὶ καὶ φωναὶ καὶ βρονταί are mentioned. They only occur in Ps. 76.19 LXX which can therefore be regarded as the main OT pretext for this section.

The combination of thunder (βροντή), sound (φωνή), lightning (ἀστραπή) and earthquake (σεισμός) is used in all four verses of Revelation; only in 11.19 hailstorm (χάλαζα) is added as the fifth item. This combination of theophanic signs is unique in the entire Greek Bible. Similar to the metaphorical transcription of the voice(s), John deals very freely and creatively with the OT in the various theophany signs. We can only assume a pretext for the series of φωνή – βροντή – ἀστραπή (Ps. 76.19 LXX). The OT pretexts mentioned in the text-critical editions cannot be correct.

OT Background of Sound and Silence

Theophany signs	Rev.	OT
Three signs • Lightning (ἀστραπή) • Sound (φωνή) • Thunder (βροντή)	4.5 Καὶ ἐκ τοῦ θρόνου ἐκπορεύονται *ἀστραπαὶ καὶ φωναὶ καὶ βρονταί*	Ps. 76.19 LXX *φωνὴ τῆς βροντῆς σου ἐν τῷ τροχῷ, ἔφαναν αἱ ἀστραπαί σου* τῇ οἰκουμένῃ, ἐσαλεύθη καὶ ἔντρομος ἐγενήθη ἡ γῆ.
Four signs • Thunder (βροντή) • Sound (φωνή) • Lightning (ἀστραπή) • Earthquake (σεισμός)	8.5 καὶ εἴληφεν ὁ ἄγγελος τὸν λιβανωτὸν καὶ ἐγέμισεν αὐτὸν ἐκ τοῦ πυρὸς τοῦ θυσιαστηρίου καὶ ἔβαλεν εἰς τὴν γῆν, καὶ ἐγένοντο *βρονταὶ καὶ φωναὶ καὶ ἀστραπαὶ καὶ σεισμός.*	Ezek. 1.13 καὶ ἐν μέσῳ τῶν ζῴων ὅρασις ὡς ἀνθράκων πυρὸς καιομένων, ὡς ὄψις λαμπάδων συστρεφομένων ἀνὰ μέσον τῶν ζῴων καὶ φέγγος τοῦ πυρός, καὶ ἐκ τοῦ πυρὸς ἐξεπορεύετο *ἀστραπή.* Dan. 10.6: καὶ τὸ σῶμα αὐτοῦ ὡσεὶ θαρσις, καὶ τὸ πρόσωπον αὐτοῦ ὡσεὶ ὅρασις ἀστραπῆς, καὶ οἱ ὀφθαλμοὶ αὐτοῦ ὡσεὶ λαμπάδες πυρός, καὶ οἱ βραχίονες αὐτοῦ καὶ οἱ πόδες ὡσεὶ χαλκὸς ἐξαστράπτων, καὶ φωνὴ λαλιᾶς αὐτοῦ ὡσεὶ φωνὴ θορύβου. Est. 1.1 καὶ τοῦτο αὐτοῦ τὸ ἐνύπνιον, καὶ ἰδοὺ *φωναὶ* καὶ *θόρυβος, βρονταὶ* καὶ *σεισμός, τάραχος* ἐπὶ τῆς γῆς Exod. 19.16 καὶ ἐγίνοντο *φωναὶ καὶ ἀστραπαὶ*

Theophany signs	Rev.	OT
Five signs • Lightning (ἀστραπή) • Sound (φωνή) • Thunder (βροντή) • Earthquake (σεισμός) • Hailstorm (χάλαζα)	11.19 Καὶ ἠνοίγη ὁ ναὸς τοῦ θεοῦ ὁ ἐν τῷ οὐρανῷ καὶ ὤφθη ἡ κιβωτὸς τῆς διαθήκης αὐτοῦ ἐν τῷ ναῷ αὐτοῦ, καὶ **ἐγένοντο ἀστραπαὶ καὶ φωναὶ καὶ βρονταὶ καὶ σεισμὸς καὶ χάλαζα μεγάλη**.	• χάλαζα: twenty times (13x in Exod., 1x in Esd., 2x in Pss., 3x in Isa., 1x in Sir.) • σεισμός: six times (1x in Est., 1x in Isa., 2x in Jer., 2 in Ezek.) • ἀστραπή: four times (1x in Ezek., 1x in Zech., 1x in Sir., 1x in Ep. Jer.) • βροντή: 1x in Sir. 40.13 • φωνή: 214x (24x in Pss., 22x in Isa., 23x in Jer.)
Four signs • Lightning (ἀστραπή) • Sound (φωνή) • Thunder (βροντή) • Earthquake (σεισμός)	16.18: καὶ **ἐγένοντο ἀστραπαὶ καὶ φωναὶ καὶ βρονταὶ καὶ σεισμὸς** ἐγένετο μέγας, οἷος οὐκ ἐγένετο ἀφ᾽ οὗ ἄνθρωπος **ἐγένετο ἐπὶ τῆς γῆς τηλικοῦτος σεισμὸς οὕτως μέγας**.	Ezek. 3.12: καὶ ἀνέλαβέν με πνεῦμα, καὶ ἤκουσα κατόπισθέν μου **φωνὴν σεισμοῦ μεγάλου** Εὐλογημένη ἡ δόξα κυρίου ἐκ τοῦ τόπου αὐτοῦ. Ezek. 38.19: καὶ ὁ ζῆλός μου. ἐν πυρὶ τῆς ὀργῆς μου ἐλάλησα Εἰ μὴν ἐν τῇ ἡμέρᾳ ἐκείνῃ ἔσται **σεισμὸς μέγας** ἐπὶ γῆς Ισραηλ, Jer. 10.22 φωνὴ ἀκοῆς ἰδοὺ ἔρχεται καὶ σεισμὸς μέγας ἐκ γῆς βορρᾶ τοῦ τάξαι τὰς πόλεις Ιουδα εἰς ἀφανισμὸν καὶ κοίτην στρουθῶν.

Musical instruments

John names four musical instruments in his writing: κιθάρα (lyre, harp – 5.8; 14.1; 15.2; 18.22), αὐλητής (player of the wood flute – 18.22), σαλπιστής (trumpeter – 18.22), σάλπιγξ (trumpet – 1.10; 4.1; 8.2, 6, 13; 9.14),[6] two of which (κιθάρα, σάλπιγξ) are also

---

[6] Cf. Thomas Staubli, 'Musikinstrumente und musikalische Ausdrucksformen', *WuB* 46 (2007): 7–39; Ulrich Konrad, 'Apocalypsis cum figuris musices. Musikalische Annäherungen an die Offenbarung

known in the Old Testament. κιθάρα is an accompanying instrument for vocal singing of the Psalms (11x); σάλπιγξ occurs frequently (95x), particularly in the context of the temple liturgy (2 Chr. 3.2-6.42; 1 Macc. 4.36-61). Music and musical instruments were media of communication and contact with God in the Ancient Near East and the OT,[7] and this use and function can also be seen in Revelation. Besides the Book of Revelation, αὐλητής is used by Mt. 9.23, while σαλπιστής is an *hapax legomenon* which only occurs in Rev. 18.22.

They are played by the victors over the beast (15.2), by angels and by the worshippers of God in the heavenly throne room (5.8). The voice of God himself also resounds like the sound of a trumpet (1.10). Except for the side instrument (lyre, harp - κιθάρα), mainly wind instruments are mentioned which produce a large volume of sound.

Twice (1.10; 4.10) John describes a loud voice of revelation by comparing it to the sound of a trumpet (σάλπιγξ). Both verses are related to each other as their contexts describe John being moved by the Spirit (1.10: ἐγενόμην ἐν πνεύματι; 4.2: ἐγενόμην ἐν πνεύματι; cf. also the reference verses, each of which introduces a vision journey: 17.3: καὶ ἀπήνεγκέν με εἰς ἔρημον ἐν πνεύματι; 21.10: καὶ ἀπήνεγκέν με ἐν πνεύματι).

σάλπιγξ in combination with φωνή as a description of a voice

Rev. 1.10 ἐγενόμην ἐν πνεύματι ἐν τῇ κυριακῇ ἡμέρᾳ καὶ ἤκουσα ὀπίσω μου **φωνὴν μεγάλην ὡς σάλπιγγος**	Exod. 19.19: ἐγίνοντο δὲ **αἱ φωναὶ τῆς σάλπιγγος** προβαίνουσαι ἰσχυρότεραι σφόδρα, Μωυσῆς ἐλάλει, ὁ δὲ θεὸς ἀπεκρίνατο αὐτῷ φωνῇ.
Rev. 4.1 Μετὰ ταῦτα εἶδον, καὶ ἰδοὺ θύρα ἠνεῳγμένη ἐν τῷ οὐρανῷ, καὶ **ἡ φωνὴ ἡ πρώτη** ἣν ἤκουσα **ὡς σάλπιγγος** λαλούσης μετ' ἐμοῦ λέγων· ἀνάβα ὧδε, καὶ δείξω σοι ἃ δεῖ γενέσθαι· μετὰ ταῦτα·	Isa. 18.3 πάντες ὡς χώρα κατοικουμένη, κατοικηθήσεται ἡ χώρα αὐτῶν ὡσεὶ σημεῖον ἀπὸ ὄρους ἀρθῇ, **ὡς σάλπιγγος φωνὴ** ἀκουστὸν ἔσται.

Exod. 19.19 and – less convincingly – Isa. 18.3 are the most likely OT pretexts not only because of the literal correspondence but also their respective context is comparable to the two verses in Revelation. Both texts deal with a theophany to a single figure (Moses, John) and describe the voice of revelation with the sound of a trumpet.

des Johannes', in Erich Garhammer (ed.), *Bildmontagen. Die Apokalypse in der Bibel und in den Künsten* (Regensburg: Schnell & Steiner, 2013), 33-71, 39-45.

[7] Cf. Friedhelm Hartenstein, '"Wach auf, Harfe und Leier, ich will wecken das Morgenrot" (Psalm 57,9). Musikinstrumente als Medien des Gotteskontakts im Alten Orient und im Alten Testament', in Michaela Geiger and Rainer Kessler (eds), *Musik, Tanz und Gott. Tonspuren durch das Alte Testament*, SBS 207 (Stuttgart: Verlag Katholisches Bibelwerk, 2007), 101-27.

Hymnal elements

Not only musical instruments but also voices and songs permeate the text. Singing (ᾄδω) is practised on earth and in the heavens (5.9; 15.3) and before the throne of God (14.3). It is mainly new songs that are heard (5.9; 14.3: ᾠδὴν καινήν); but there is also an allusion to the Song of Moses (15.3)[8] – even if intertextual analyses hardly reveal any connections. Depending on how it is counted, one can recognize twenty hymns or hymnal elements in the Book of Revelation (1.(4), 6, 7; 4.8, 9-11; 5.9-10, 11-12, 13, 14; 7.9-10, 11-12; 11.15, 16-17; 12.10-12; 15.2-4; 16.5, 7; 19.1-2, 3, 4, 6-8). Two songs are particularly emphasized by the addition of their classification as ᾠδή (5.9-10; 15.3-4), to which either is added the adjective καινή (5.9; 14.3), or the phrase Μωϋσέως τοῦ δούλου τοῦ θεοῦ (15.3). According to 14.3 this new song can only be learned (μανθάνω) by the 144,000 redeemed. Single elements and longer expressions have an OT background (ἀλληλουϊά in the Book of Psalms, the Dreizeitenformel[9] in the Book of Exodus, the Trisagion in Isa. 6:3; Ps. 98.9 LXX). The history of research is particularly devoted to the following four topics: (1) genre of a hymn in the context of the synagogue liturgy or Roman court ceremonies; (2) liturgical dimension of the hymns; (3) theological and Christological significance of the praises; and (4) function of the hymns within the compositional structure. In addition, intertextual references to the longer hymnic elements or songs (such as to the Song of Moses) have been comprehensively explored elsewhere. The history of research shows that music and musical elements play a central role in the drama of the Revelation of John. The embedded hymns and musical elements allow the reader to breathe a sigh of relief in the midst of gloomy doomsday scenarios. At the same time, they are an expression of praise to God, celebrating God's presence in this turmoil of the world. Music thus has a bridging function that is also able to express moments of speechlessness.

---

[8] Cf. Mira Stare, 'Das neu gesungene Lied des Mose (Offb 15,3b-4)', in Simone Paganini and Claudia Paganini (eds), *Führe mein Volk heraus. Zur innerbiblischen Rezeption der Exodusthematik (FS Georg Fischer)* (Frankfurt: Lang, 2004), 121–38; Rüdiger Bartelmus, '"Schriftprophetie" außerhalb des corpus propheticum – eine unmögliche Möglichkeit? Das Mose-Lied (Ex 15,1–21) als deuterojesajanisch geprägtes "eschatologisches Loblied"', in Friedhelm Hartenstein and Jutta Krispenz (eds), *Schriftprophetie* (Festschrift Jörg Jeremias) (Neukirchen-Vluyn: Neukirchener Verlag, 2004), 55–82; Michael Sommer, 'Von politischen Räumen … Das Lied des Mose und die Apokalypsen des frühen Judentums und frühen Christentums', in Erik Eynikel and Elisabeth Hernitscheck (eds), *Mosebilder. Gedanken zur Rezeption einer literarischen Figur im Frühjudentum, frühen Christentum und der römisch-hellenistischen Literatur*, WUNT 390 (Tübingen: Mohr Siebeck, 2017), 299–317; Rita Müller-Fieberg, 'Song of Moses, Song of the Lamb: The Reception of Exodus in the Revelation of John', in Beate Kowalski and Susan E. Dochety (eds), *Reception of Exodus Motifs in Jewish and Christian Literature: 'Let My People Go!'*, TBN 30 (Leiden: Brill, 2021), 334–49.

[9] Cf. Beate Kowalski, '"Let my people go, that they may serve me." (Ex 10:3). Exodus Motifs of Liberation as Key to Understanding Worship in Revelation of John', *Henoch* 38 (2016): 32–53.

2: Silence in Revelation

Silence can speak more eloquently than any words possibly could.[10]

There are different forms of silence: silence can be the exterior absence of sounds but also the interior silence of thoughts, desires and judgements. Silence can be a destructive refusal to communicate but also a de-escalating refrain from verbal expression. Silence can be as small and light as a dewdrop but also heavy as the sound of a millstone when necessary words remain unspoken or people fall silent in the face of hardship and suffering. Both forms of silence can be found in Revelation.

Exterior silence as an expression of desolation

The exterior absence of sounds is verbalized in five parallel sentences in 18.22-23, each of which begins with οὐ μή and ends with ἐν σοὶ ἔτι. The respective odd parallelisms vv.22a, c, 23b use the same verb ἀκουσθῇ. The second parallelism (v.22b) uses the verb εὑρεθῇ, the fourth one has φάνῃ (v.23a). Paradoxically, the dead silence is hammered in linguistically. John plays with the repetition and variation of words to express the finality of the destruction of the city of Babylon – even the absence of any sound. Besides the disturbing silence, it is also dark: the light no longer shines. This means that the two central senses of the human being, hearing and sight, with which communication with the outside world is established, no longer have a task. The destruction of the city of Babylon also destroys the livelihood and future of all its inhabitants.

22a καὶ φωνὴ κιθαρῳδῶν καὶ μουσικῶν καὶ αὐλητῶν καὶ σαλπιστῶν
    οὐ μὴ **ἀκουσθῇ** ἐν σοὶ ἔτι,
22b καὶ πᾶς τεχνίτης πάσης τέχνης
    οὐ μὴ εὑρεθῇ ἐν σοὶ ἔτι
22c καὶ φωνὴ μύλου
    οὐ μὴ **ἀκουσθῇ** ἐν σοὶ ἔτι,
23a καὶ φῶς λύχνου
    οὐ μὴ φάνῃ ἐν σοὶ ἔτι,
23b καὶ φωνὴ νυμφίου καὶ νύμφης
    οὐ μὴ **ἀκουσθῇ** ἐν σοὶ ἔτι

Neither the melodious music of the artists (κιθαρῳδός, μουσικός, αὐλητής, σαλπιστής), who nourish the soul, nor craftsmen of any craft, nor the sounds of the mills, which provide food for physical well-being, can still be heard. This leads to the silencing of all life and joy: bride and groom, who secure the future of a society, are no longer heard either. It is a particular stylistic feature of John, with which he manifests three times the finality of the fall of Babylon. Apart from μουσικός, the other nouns do not occur

[10] Thomas Merton, *The Seven Storey Mountain* (New York: Harcourt Brace 1968), 321.

anywhere in the LXX. For this drastic description, John refers to two pretexts from the Old Testament, specifically the prophecy of Ezekiel against Tyre (Ezekiel 26-27) and the apocalyptic text from Isaiah which deals with earthly judgement and God's reign on Mount Zion (Isaiah 24).[11] Thus, we can discern a composite allusion of Ezekiel and Isaiah in Rev. 18.22.[12] While Isaiah proclaims an apocalyptic doomsday scenario, a kind of anti-creation, in the form of prophetic speech, Ezekiel dramatizes it in the form of a speech of God in prophetic language. John processes both texts in a visionary narrative in which an audition is integrated and which is introduced with 18.1. The particular context of the three texts is thus comparable. Let's take a closer look at the pretexts and how John reuses them:

Isa. 24.8	Ezek. 26.13	Rev. 18.22-23
πέπαυται εὐφροσύνη τυμπάνων, πέπαυται αὐθάδεια καὶ πλοῦτος ἀσεβῶν, πέπαυται **φωνὴ κιθάρας**.	καὶ καταλύσει τὸ πλῆθος τῶν μουσικῶν σου, καὶ ἡ φωνὴ τῶν ψαλτηρίων σου **οὐ μὴ ἀκουσθῇ ἔτι**.	καὶ **φωνὴ κιθαρῳδῶν** καὶ μουσικῶν καὶ αὐλητῶν καὶ σαλπιστῶν **οὐ μὴ ἀκουσθῇ ἐν σοὶ ἔτι** καὶ πᾶς τεχνίτης πάσης τέχνης οὐ μὴ εὑρεθῇ ἐν σοὶ ἔτι καὶ φωνὴ μύλου **οὐ μὴ ἀκουσθῇ ἐν σοὶ ἔτι** 23 καὶ φῶς λύχνου οὐ μὴ φάνῃ ἐν σοὶ ἔτι, καὶ φωνὴ νυμφίου καὶ νύμφης **οὐ μὴ ἀκουσθῇ ἐν σοὶ ἔτι**

The phrase φωνὴ κιθάρας is singular in the OT and only occurs in Isa. 24.8 to express the end of the festivities and joy of life in the face of the destruction of the earth. John uses this expression and adds three more nouns from the semantic field of musicians (μουσικῶν, αὐλητῶν, σαλπιστῶν) to it to strengthen the statement.

The second OT pretext (Ezek. 26.13) comes from the prophet Ezekiel who deals with the judgement on the nations (e.g. Tyre; cf. Ezekiel 26). The text leads to the funeral lament in Ezekiel 27. Both chapters are the background foil of Revelation 18 which have a long product list (Rev. 18.11-13; Ezek. 37.11-24) in common, though the particular items are not identical. John prefers *hapax legomena*, which partially also occur elsewhere in the LXX. Furthermore, Revelation 18 uses eight *hapax legomena*

---

[11] Isa. 24.8 is mentioned by GNT[5].
[12] Benito Marconcini, 'L'utilizzazione del T.M. nelle citazioni Isaeiane dell'Apocalisse', in *RivBib* 24 (1976): 113-36, lists fourteen verses from Isaiah which are combined with Ezekiel.

in the product list: ἄμωμον, διπλόω, θύϊνος, κιθαρῳδός, μύλινος, ῥέδη, σαλπιστής, τιμιότης.[13]

The expression οὐ μὴ ἀκουσθῇ which is used three times in vv.22f reuses the OT pretext Ezek. 26.13. While the expression in Ezek. 26.22 refers to only one item (the sound of the harp: ἡ φωνὴ τῶν ψαλτηρίων σου), John uses it three times, referring to harpist, singer, flute player, trumpeter (v.22a), the sound of the millstone (v.22c) and the voice of the bride and bridegroom (v.23b). This multiple usages of the same OT pretext are typical for Revelation.[14] These multiple usages of a pretext are always accompanied by variations due to the respective new context. In the specific case of Rev. 18.22-23, an intensification of the statement can be seen through the varying repetition.

Exterior silence as an expression of the presence of God

As already mentioned, hymnal elements interrupt the drama of the non-continuous plot of Revelation 1–19 – if one can speak of a plot at all. Such praising elements are unsurprisingly absent from the seven letters to the churches in Asia Minor (Rev. 2.1–3.22) and at the fall of the dragon to earth (13.1-18). But why did John not include a hymn in the great final vision of the heavenly Jerusalem (21.1–22.7)? Would not a hymn be the appropriate response to God's redemption and self-assertion at the end? Although Rev. 22.6 explicitly mentions that God's servants serve him and the Lamb who both sit on the throne, a hymn as well as the temple (21.22: καὶ ναὸν οὐκ εἶδον ἐν αὐτῇ) as a place of praise are strangely missing.

John may be referring here to the final verse from Ezekiel (48.35). The measure of the city of Jerusalem described by the prophet serves John as a model for the description of the Holy Jerusalem (κύκλωμα δέκα καὶ ὀκτὼ χιλιάδες.). The prophet's closing words emphasize the presence of God (ἔσται τὸ ὄνομα αὐτῆς). Here, too, a human reaction to the presence of God in the form of praise is missing. Normally, an omission cannot be identified as a pretext; however, since the Book of Ezekiel has a significant influence on both the structure and the content of Revelation, one could well consider the omission of a hymn as a model for Rev. 22.5.

Interior silence as a theophany sign

The interior silence is a sign of theophany that interrupts the first series of plagues as a climax (Rev. 8.1).[15] Three series of plagues, each with seven plagues, characterize the macro text of Revelation: the seven seals (6.1–8.1), the seven trumpets (8.6–11.19) and

---

[13] Cf. Beate Kowalski, 'Die Ezechielrezeption in der Offenbarung des Johannes und ihre Bedeutung für die Textkritik', *SNTU.A* 35 (2010): 51–77, 54–6.

[14] Cf. Albert Vanhoye, 'L'utilisation du livre d'Ézéchiel dans l'Apocalypse', *Biblica* 43 (1962): 436–76, 461. Besides the double use of Ezekielian motifs in the Revelation, Vanhoye identifies the simplification and compression of OT pretexts.

[15] Silence (8.1) can also be regarded as a theophanic sign. It is an attitude of reverence of God. It is only found in the OT in Hab. 2.20; Zeph. 1.7; Zech. 2.13. Gregory K. Beale, *Revelation* 447, sees the silence in Hab. 2.20; Zech. 2.13; and Zeph. 1.11 in connection with announcements of divine judgement which, however, does not apply to Hab. 2.20. Nevertheless, it is clear that the seventh of the three series of plagues stands out from the previous ones in that it contains statements of

the seven bowls (16.1-21). They are modelled on the Egyptian plagues in the Book of Exodus. All three series of plagues consist of seven interventions of which the last is different from the previous six. The seventh plague has the function of a retarding element: the silence (8.1), the opening of God's heavenly temple (11.15-19) and the mighty destructive theophany signs from the temple (17.17-21). These last plagues interpret each other. The silence is followed by the opening of the temple and the devastating catastrophes that come from it. They are all theophanies, expressing the self-assertion of God.

In the following, we search for the OT pretext of silence for which John uses the term ἐγένετο σιγή, which is unique in the entire Greek Bible as is the idea that this silence occurs in heaven – for half an hour at that. N-A[28] lists Zech. 2.17, Hab. 2.20 and Wis. 18.14 as possible allusions. It is necessary to check these reference verses since the criteria used in N-A[28] for the identification of allusions notoriously lack precision. Are there other OT pretexts, if applicable?

Both Zech. 2.17 and Hab. 2.20 use the verb εὐλαβέομαι but neither a verb nor a noun of the semantic field of silence is employed at all. It is therefore highly unlikely that these two OT verses can be considered as pretexts, even if the idea of silence in the face of God's presence is addressed. Most probably Wis. 18.14 can be assumed as the pretext:

OT pretexts	Rev. 8.1
Zech. 2.17 εὐλαβείσθω πᾶσα σὰρξ ἀπὸ προσώπου κυρίου, διότι ἐξεγήγερται ἐκ νεφελῶν ἁγίων αὐτοῦ.	
Hab. 2.20 ὁ δὲ κύριος ἐν ναῷ ἁγίῳ αὐτοῦ, εὐλαβείσθω ἀπὸ προσώπου αὐτοῦ πᾶσα ἡ γῆ.	
Wis. 18.14 ἡσύχου γὰρ <u>σιγῆς</u> περιεχούσης τὰ πάντα καὶ νυκτὸς ἐν ἰδίῳ τάχει μεσαζούσης 15 ὁ παντοδύναμός σου λόγος ἀπ' οὐρανῶν ἐκ θρόνων βασιλείων ἀπότομος πολεμιστὴς εἰς μέσον τῆς ὀλεθρίας ἥλατο γῆς ξίφος ὀξὺ τὴν ἀνυπόκριτον ἐπιταγήν σου φέρων	Καὶ ὅταν ἤνοιξεν τὴν σφραγῖδα τὴν ἑβδόμην, ἐγένετο <u>σιγὴ</u> ἐν τῷ οὐρανῷ ὡς ἡμιώριον.
For while gentle silence enveloped all things, and night in its swift course was now half gone.	When the Lamb opened the seventh seal, there was silence in heaven for about half an hour.

Rev. 8.1 uses the word σιγή, which only occurs twice in the NT (Acts 21.14; Rev. 8.1) and twice in the LXX (3 Macc. 3.23; Wis. 18.14). Even though Rev. 8.1 has only one word in common with Wis. 18.14 and the respective contexts are substantially different, it seems to be possible to regard this pretext as a possible allusion. Yet, there are other texts in the OT in which silence is a motif of God's presence, such as 1 Kgs 6.7, 19.12 and so on: during the construction of the Jerusalem Temple and on Mount Horeb. However, these OT passages differ from Rev. 8.1 in that there is never any mention of silence in heaven. Rather, the praise of God seems to make the presence of God in heaven audible.[16] The expression contrasts with the prophetic word event formula ('Wortereignisformel' – Καὶ ἐγένετο λόγος κυρίου πρός με λέγων). John uses the formula with a negative sign.

Conclusion

The study of the OT pretexts on the themes of sound and silence has shown, as have many other studies on the OT background of Revelation, that John's reusage is unique within the OT. First, John uses the pretexts very creatively. Second, the pretexts cannot always be identified. Third, mixed allusions are part of John's common practice. Fourth, the same pretexts are used several times and with variations. In the use of OT scriptures, the Book of Exodus, the Psalter and prophetic books (such as Ezekiel and Daniel) stand out particularly in their foregrounding of the thematic complex of sound and silence. The embedding of hymns or hymnic elements within narrative texts also has models in the OT (e.g. Exodus; Judges; 1 Samuel; Judith). Like the use of silence as a motif, these have the function of interrupting the drama of the plot, taking a different perspective, commenting on the events and anticipating central theological statements in a condensed form that go beyond the scope of the scripture as a whole.[17]

A contrast to the many noises and powerful voices, which primarily give expression to the struggle between good and evil, are the musical elements and praises, which are anticipatory expressions of joy over God who conquers evil. Language, sounds and silence point to a larger and more reliable reality that is more than coping with existence or escaping the world.

---

salvation. Cf. further Beate Kowalski, *Die Rezeption des Propheten Ezechiel in der Offenbarung des Johannes*, SBB 52 (Stuttgart: Verlag Katholisches Bibelwerk, 2004) (see II. Teil, esp. 4.3).

[16] Cf. Rüdiger Lux, '"Man lobt dich in der Stille" Ps 65,2. Ein biblisches Essay über Gott und das Schweigen in den Psalmen', *Leqach* 9 (2009): 7–19.

[17] Cf. James W. Watts, *Psalm and Story: Inset Hymns in Hebrew Narrative*, LHBOTS 139 (Sheffield: JSOT Press 1992); James W. Watts, 'Biblical Psalms Outside the Psalter', in Peter W. Flint and Patrick D. Jr Miller (eds), *The Book of Psalms: Composition and Reception*, VTSup 99 (Leiden: Brill, 2005), 288–309. With regard to hymns in Revelation cf. Justin Jeffcoat Schedtler, *A Heavenly Chorus: The Dramatic Function of Revelation's Hymns*, WUNT II/381 (Tübingen: Mohr Siebeck, 2014); Sean Michael Ryan, 'Animate Praise: The Heavenly Temple Liturgy of the Apocalypse and the Songs of the Sabbath Sacrifice', *ScrB* 42.1 (2012): 13–25.

7

The reimagining of theological time: Revelation's use of the OT in defining its temporality

Ian Paul

Issues around time and temporality are central to the interpretation of the Book of Revelation. Inasmuch as Revelation should be read as an 'apocalypse' in terms of its genre, it shares this question with other contemporary and near-contemporary apocalypses. John J. Collins notes the prevalence of 'periodization' in what he calls the 'historical' apocalypses and speculates whether this tendency arose from the influence of Persian Zoroastrianism during the Babylonian exile – though questions of dating make that uncertain.[1]

What we can see from the New Testament's development of its inherited Jewish eschatology is that the theological dimension of hope and fulfilment is expressed in temporal terms from the very beginning. Mark's summary of Jesus's early preaching ministry is announced as the 'fulfilment' of καιρός as the kingdom of God has drawn near, combining both temporal and spatial metaphors. Although καιρός has more of a sense of 'moment' or 'opportunity' (and in modern Greek has pushed further to mean the season or the weather) than χρόνος, there is an overlap in their semantic ranges, and καιρός has an irreducible temporal sense.[2] If Revelation fits at all within the main thought lines of the eschatology in the rest of the canon, then we should expect its message of hope, expectation and endurance to have a significant temporal element.

Yet, by any estimation, Revelation is saturated with allusions to the Old Testament.[3] We might therefore also expect that its temporality will be shaped by this. In fact, as we shall see, not only does Revelation make use of Old Testament ideas and language to express its temporality, it does so precisely in its adaption of and 'dialectical relationship' with key Old Testament material.[4] And the theological meaning of

---

[1] John J. Collins, *The Apocalyptic Imagination*, 3rd edn (Grand Rapids, MI: Eerdmans, 2016), 15–16, 40–1.
[2] This is illustrated by any standard lexicon entry for the two terms; see, for example, BDAG.
[3] One edition of the Bible Society's Greek New Testament, UBS 3, estimates that there are 676 allusions to the Old Testament in Revelation's 405 verses. For an overview, see Ian Paul, *Revelation*, TNTC (London: IVP, 2017), 39–41. For a more detailed analysis, see Ian Paul, 'The Use of the Old Testament in Rev 12', in Steve Moyise (ed.), *The Old Testament in the New Testament*, JSNTSup 189 (Sheffield: Sheffield Academic Press, 2000), 256–78.
[4] Steve Moyise, *The Old Testament in the Book of Revelation*, JSNTSup 115 (London: T&T Clark, 1995), 58.

Revelation's temporality is deeply dependent on the theological meaning of the Old Testament language that it uses.

Thus we find that the key textual markers, 'Do not seal up' and the triple reference to 'time, times, and half a time', '1,260 days' and '42 months', are not only drawn from the Old Testament but are also adapted from it, and that their theological significance in construing Revelation's sense of temporality depends on a Christological reinterpretation of their theological meaning.

Textual markers of time and temporality

'Do not seal up'

There are also some specific textual reasons for exploring the temporality of this text. One of the most striking contrasts between Revelation and other Jewish apocalypses is the absence of pseudonymity. Rather than write in the name of an ancient prophetic or worthy figure, John writes in his own name to people whom he appears to know. The contemporary reality with which he engages is therefore not portrayed as final events as viewed from long ago but in a simpler sense as present reality. This does not underplay, however, their significance as climactic within God's plan.[5]

The importance of the present moment for John is expressed in striking terms in the conclusion of this prophetic apocalyptic letter.[6] After the final elements of the description of the New Jerusalem in Rev. 22.6, there is a double epistolary postscript, from John as the human author of the text but also signed off by Jesus as the originator, much in the same way that both Paul and his amanuensis sign off Paul's letters.[7] Within the first part of this, John is for a second time tempted to fall and worship the angel who had guided him around the city, one of those holding the seven bowls (Rev. 21.9). He is rebuked and then instructed:

> Do not seal up the words of the prophecy of this book, for the time is near.

This command must be read intertextually with its antecedents in Dan 12.4 and 9:[8]

> But you, Daniel, shut up the words and seal the book, until the time of the end (Dan 12.4)
>
> Go your way, Daniel, for the words are shut up and sealed until the time of the end (Dan 12.9)

---

[5] This is expressed nicely in the title of Richard Bauckham's collection of essays, *The Climax of Prophecy* (Edinburgh: T&T Clark, 1993).

[6] For a clear expression of the consensus view that the three main genre types within Revelation are prophecy, apocalyptic and letter form, see Mitchell Reddish, 'The Genre of the Book of Revelation', in Craig R. Koester (ed.), *The Oxford Handbook to the Book of Revelation* (Oxford: Oxford University Press, 2020), 21–36.

[7] Craig Koester, *Revelation*, Anchor Yale Bible (New Haven, CT: Yale University Press, 2014), 843; Paul, *Revelation*, 367.

[8] As noted in Moyise, *Old Testament in the Book of Revelation*, 55.

As John Sweet notes, the angel's instruction is 'exactly the reverse of that which is given to Daniel'.[9]

Steve Moyise also notes this modification of Daniel's temporality in relation to the substitutions of the phrase 'what must happen at the end of days' (ἃ δεῖ γενέσθαι ἐπ' ἐσχάτων τῶν ἡμερῶν) in Dan 2.28 with 'what must happen soon' (ἃ δεῖ γενέσθαι ἐν τάχει) as an *inclusio* in Rev 1.1 and 22.6.[10]

The contrast with Daniel has three effects on the temporality of Revelation. First, it locates both John and his readers in the time period of his vision, rather than separating them as Daniel does; the nature of *vaticinium ex eventu* prophecy is that it portrays the prophet at a time and place remote from the contemporary readers whose context is the subject of the prophecies.

> As contrasted with Jewish apocalypses, such as Daniel ... 1 Enoch ... 2 Enoch etc, which were not to be divulged till distant generations, our Apocalypse is to be made known by the Seer to his contemporaries.[11]

Second, it closes the distance between John as author and the 'time of the end'. Where Daniel has visions of things which, in narrative time, are remotely future to him, John's visions are portrayed as being immediately relevant to him. As readers at a temporal distance from John and the writing of this text, we therefore need to conclude either that John was mistaken in believing that 'the time is near' or that we need to interpret the temporal language of 'the end' in something other than a strictly chronological sense.[12]

Finally, given that the words of this book should not be 'sealed up' for the distant future, the visions John sees must have been understood by both John and his first readers as relating to their own world and time and not some distant future (such as ours) which was temporally remote from them.[13]

> What Daniel expected to occur in the distant future – the defeat of cosmic evil and ushering in of the kingdom – John expects to begin in his own generation, and perhaps has already been inaugurated.[14]

---

[9] John Sweet, *Revelation* (London: SCM, 1979), 304.
[10] Moyise, *Old Testament*, 46–7.
[11] R. H. Charles, *Revelation*, ICC (Edinburgh: T&T Clark, 1920), 221.
[12] See the discussion at 'Will Jesus come "soon" like a taxi?' at www.psephizo.com.
[13] For an excellent survey of the way that Revelation and other eschatological texts have repeatedly been interpreted as referring to a temporally distant time, contemporaneous with the later interpreter, see Martyn Whittock, *The End Times, Again?* (Eugene, OR: Wifi and Stock, 2021).
[14] Greg Beale, 'Revelation', in D. A. Carson and H. G. M. Williamson (eds), *It Is Written: Scripture Citing Scripture* (Cambridge: Cambridge University Press, 1998) 318–36, 329. Interestingly, this supports Moyise's conviction that Revelation *reinterprets* and quite freely adapts Daniel's language, in contrast to Beale's own position expressed later in a series of exchanges with Moyise in subsequent articles.

καιρός and χρόνος

The importance of time and temporal issues is indicated by other features of the text.

The term καιρός occurs seven times in the text (1.3, 11.18, 12.12, 12.14 (three times) and 22.10).[15] The first and last of these form an *inclusio* 'the time is near', though as is characteristic of John, the repetition of the phrase incorporates a variation in word order and structure (ὁ γὰρ καιρὸς ἐγγύς/ὁ καιρὸς γὰρ ἐγγύς ἐστιν). The occurrences in 11.8 and 12.12 both have an eschatological sense of imminent judgement, the first in the proleptic anticipation of the end with the blowing of the seventh trumpet, the second in relation to the defeat of the devil through the death and resurrection of the lamb narrated by adaptation of the Python/Leto myth in 12.1-6 and explained epexegetically in the hymnic material in 12.10-12. The other three occurrences form the Danielic phrase in 12.14 usually translated 'time, times and half a time' or 'three and a half years' which we will explore later in this chapter. Together, the uses of this phrase connect urgency, eschatological judgement effected through the death of Christ and patient endurance through tribulation or suffering.[16]

The closely related term χρόνος occurs four times (2.21; 6.11; 10.6 and 20.3) and is also associated with judgement, endurance and hope of The End. In 2.21, a limited period of 'time' has been given to 'Jezebel', the false prophetess who is leading God's people in Thyatira into 'sexual immorality', most likely a metaphor for idolatry.[17] In 6.11, the 'souls' of the martyrs who are beneath the heavenly altar must wait a little more 'time' before God's just judgement vindicates them. In the interlude between the sixth and seventh trumpets in chapters 10 and 11 (which parallels the interlude in chapter 7 between the sixth and seventh seals) the 'mighty angel' who straddles the sea and the land declares that there will be 'no more delay [time]' (10.6).[18] And in 20.3, the dragon = ancient serpent = devil = Satan is released 'for a little while' before final destruction in the lake of fire.[19]

---

[15] It continues to be surprising that commentators pay insufficient attention to the frequency with which key terms occur, given the wide recognition of the importance of numerology in the text. See Bauckham, *Climax*, chapter 11; Paul, 'Revelation's Use of Numbers', in *Revelation*, 34–9; and Ian Paul, 'Source, Structure, and Composition in the Book of Revelation', in G. V. Allen, I. Paul and S. P. Woodman (eds), *The Book of Revelation* (Tübingen: Mohr Siebeck, 2015), 41–54, including a response by Moyise in the afterword.

[16] The term ὑπομονή commonly translated 'patient endurance' occurs seven times in Revelation, at 1.9; 2.2, 3, 19; 3.10; 13.10 and 14.12.

[17] For a discussion of the reasons for this reading, see Paul, *Revelation*, 94.

[18] Following the translation of the AV of 1611, 'there should be time no longer', some have interpreted this as a suggestion that the new creation will be a place of timeless existence. This occurs at a popular level as the inscription on the clock which strikes 13 and allows 'time slip' in the classic children's novel *Tom's Midnight Garden* by Philippa Pearce (Oxford: Oxford University Press, 1958) but in context this cannot be what Rev. 10.6 means.

[19] Note the parallel of the fourfold naming of the evil one with the same four terms in the same order in 12.9 and the parallelism between ὀλίγον καιρόν in 12.14 and μικρὸν χρόνον in 20.3, both accusatives of duration.

Visionary and narrative sequences

The basic narrative structure of Revelation is expressed in terms of temporal succession by the repetition of the phrase 'καί εἶδον' 'and I saw' which occurs in this exact form thirty-two times and with variation on six other occasions.[20] This is complemented by the eighteen occurrences of 'καὶ ἤκουσα' 'and I heard', though without any variations. Most contemporary English translations interpret most of the first and some of the second in temporal terms by translating as '[And] *then* I saw' and '*then* I heard', though this is avoided by the Authorized Version which consistently translates καὶ with 'and'.

This raises a key question for interpretation: how does the apparent temporal sequence of John's visions and their succession in his vision report relate to any kind of temporal relationship between the things that his visions relate to? Michael Gorman offers a helpful two-dimensional chart which describes the different ways in which the interpretative approach to Revelation determines the relationship between succession of events in the text and a perceived temporality in the events described by the text.[21] It has been common to map the approaches to Revelation's interpretation based on questions of temporality using the four categories of idealist, futurist, church historical and contemporary historical ('preterist'), each of which offers some important insight into the text.[22] Gorman revises these categories as follows:

Gorman	Paul	Temporality
Predictive	Church historical	Revelation predicts all of human history.
	Futurist	Revelation relates to a limited 'end times' epoch.
Preterist	Contemporary historical	Revelation relates to the historical time period in which it was written.
Theo-poetic	Idealist	Revelation sets out timeless truths, so it is atemporal.
Theo-political	(Idealist?)	Revelation gives insights into questions of justice and politics in all ages.
Pastoral-prophetic	(Idealist?)	Revelation gives insights into the challenge of faithful discipleship in all ages.

---

[20] There are three notable sections where language of 'and I saw' is missing: the aural report of the angel in the future tense in 11.1-10; the vision of the woman, child and dragon in chapter 12; and the tour of the New Jerusalem in 21.9–22.5, where the angel 'shows' John rather than John 'seeing'.
[21] Michael Gorman, *Reading Revelation Responsibly* (Eugene, OR: Cascade/Wipf and Stock, 2011), 64.
[22] Paul, *Revelation*, 48–51.

Gorman concludes:

> Without ignoring the past or the future (in a general sense), the focus of this book [Gorman's] is on Revelation as a word to the church in the present ... We will do [this] by grounding our contemporary interpretation of Revelation in its message for the first century church, looking for contemporary analogies to first century realities.[23]

The question of narrative sequence, temporality and the implications for chronology is most clearly seen in discussions of the relationship between three main sequences of seven seals being opened, seven trumpets being trumpeted[24] and seven bowls being poured out in chapters 6, 8–9 and 15–16, since these form a kind of backbone for considerations of the structure and temporality of the whole narrative.

The three main approaches to these sequences are to see them as following on from one another chronologically, being chronologically nested or each recapitulating the chronology of the other.[25] But much discussion here is hampered by failure to question why narrative succession should imply chronological sequence, as though the temporality of Revelation's narrative was simple, direct and linear.[26]

A better approach was articulated some time ago by G. B. Caird:

> Simple chronology does not explain the structure of John's work, and even Charles, the most ardent advocate of this theory, was compelled to resort to exclusions and rearrangement which other editors have found quite unconvincing ... The unity of John's book, then, is neither chronological nor arithmetical, but artistic, like that of a musical theme with variations, each variation adding something new to the significance of the whole composition.[27]

Koester traces such a non-linear approach back to the third-century commentary of Victorinus and represents the structure of the text as a series of loops in a progressive spiral.[28]

The other major section of text which is affected by assumptions about the relation between narrative sequence and referent chronology is 19.9–21.1, which includes the battle (anticipated in 16.16 as 'Armaggedon'?) led by the rider on the white horse, the

---

[23] Gorman, *Revelation*, 68.
[24] Most ETs use words with different roots for what the seven angels have and what they do with them, usually 'trumpets' which they 'blow'. But the terms in Greek are cognates, σάλπιγγες and σαλπίζω, creating a sense of repetition and emphasis which is lost in translation.
[25] See the helpful diagrams expressing each of these views in Greg Beale, *The Book of Revelation*, NIGTC (Grand Rapids, MI: Eerdmans, 1999), 117–19, 128.
[26] A good example is the influential essay of Dale Ralph Davis, 'The Relationship between the Seals, Trumpets and Bowls in the Book of Revelation', *JETS* 16.3 (1973): 149–58. His chronology is forced by the elements mentioned in the interlude between sixth and seventh seals in chapter 7, since he does not consider that this sequence of visions might not actually suggest a chronological order (153).
[27] G. B. Caird, *The Revelation of St John the Divine* (London: A & C Black, 1966), 104, 106.
[28] Craig Koester, *Revelation and the End of All Things* (Grand Rapids, MI: Eerdmans, 2001). He also structures his Anchor Bible commentary in this way.

thousand years in which Satan is chained and the saints rule, his release, the judgement before the great white throne and the descent of the New Jerusalem from heaven to earth. Any attempt to read these as a simple chronology leads to multiple problems, as does the attempt to add these as a chronological sequence to linear chronologies from earlier in the book. A better way, following the principles of Caird and Koester, is to see this section as comprised of seven unnumbered visions of The End, each of which portrays a different theological aspect of the *eschaton*.[29]

What time is it for John and his readers?

Given all these issues around temporality, is it possible to locate the text of Revelation, that is, John and his readers, within a particular moment in theological time? Key information is provided for us within the epistolary introduction which sets the spatial and temporal scene; in the disruptive intrusion of the sequence of woes within the seven trumpets; and in the critical temporal phrases '42 months', '1,260 days' and 'time, times and half a time' in which John adapts key ideas from the Old Testament. It is particularly these latter terms which provide confirmation of John's construal of theological time, and he does so precisely in his Christological adaptation of the theological meaning of these terms.

Epistolary introduction

In his epistolary opening, following his initial threefold greeting, John is careful to locate himself spatially, temporally and spirituality through a succession of prepositional phrases each beginning ἐν (1.9-10; the repetition is obscured by colloquial English translation):

ἐν τῇ θλίψει καὶ βασιλείᾳ καί ὑπομονῇ	in tribulation and kingdom and patient endurance
ἐν Ἰησοῦ ...	in Jesus
ἐν τῇ νήσῳ τῇ καλουμένῃ Πάτμῳ ...	in the island called Patmos
ἐν πνεύματι	in the Spirit
ἐν τῇ κυριακῇ ἡμέρᾳ	in the Lord's day

Each of these have significance in shaping John's message.[30] Though he is in a place of restriction and separation (or exile? we cannot be sure) from those to whom he writes,

---

[29] Paul, *Revelation*, 313–36. In this I follow Austin Farrer, Adela Yarbro Collins and Ian Boxall, *The Revelation of St John* (London: A & C Black, 2006), 271–2. Richard Bauckham (*Climax of Prophecy*, 5) rejects the sevenfold structure but does see this section as offering a series of theological perspectives on The End, and Koester identifies the structure under four headings (*End of All Things*, chapter 7; and *Revelation*, 'The Sixth Cycle', 750–2).

[30] Paul, *Revelation*, 70–1.

on the island, he is nevertheless connected to them spiritually and has his first vision on the day when the people of God gather together to worship God – so it is no wonder that his visions are peppered by communal liturgical choruses.

Of particular interest is the opening triad. John locates himself in both the 'tribulation' and 'kingdom' in Jesus and in doing so is deploying language found in Paul and in the gospels regarding theological time.[31] In Acts 14.22, Luke summarizes Paul's message on his 'first missionary journey' joining the same two terms: 'Through many tribulations (διὰ πολλῶν θλίψεων) we must enter the kingdom of God.' The reason that those entering the kingdom experience 'tribulation' is because of the fundamental clash of two domains, kingdoms or systems of rule: 'this age' and the kingdom of God or the 'age to come'.[32] We find this contrast between the two realms in Jesus's farewell discourse: 'In the world you will have tribulation; but take heart, I have overcome the world' (Jn 16.33).

This clash of domains is expressed in both spatial and temporal terms, both in the gospels and in Paul.

> The two realms exist as a result of Paul's inaugurated eschatology. With the death, resurrection and ascension of Christ, a new realm has been established. In an important sense, this realm properly belongs to the future. But since Paul's eschatology is inaugurated, the realm has already broken into the present. Thus, two realms exist side by side, one naturally belonging to this present age, and the other belonging to the age to come, but both existing at once.[33]

John's language in Revelation, and the both spatial and temporal nature of his visions, fits precisely into the Pauline understanding of inaugurated (or partially realized) reconfiguration of Jewish apocalyptic eschatology of 'this age' and 'the age to come'. In terms of theological time, then, John and his readers sit in that period of the overlap of these two ages.

The three woes

Moyise notes the allusions to Amos 1 and 2 in the trumpets sequence, particularly in the sixth trumpet/second woe.[34] Despite the themes of judgement in Amos, the word 'woe' only appears later, in Amos 5.16, 18 and 6.1, so is unlikely to have influenced John's usage here. The three sequences of seven seals, trumpets and bowls each have

---

[31] The term θλῖψις might well be derived by John from its occurrence in Dan. 12.1. The term occurs only in this place in Daniel in the LXX, but it is repeated for emphasis in Theodotion, and the surrounding language of the rising of Michael and the salvation of all those whose 'names are written in the book of life' make it something of a programmatic text.

[32] The idea of two kingdoms, one under the rule of God, the other rejecting the rule of God, and the two domains in (spiritual) conflict is itself developed and adapted from Old Testament ideas of God as king. See Ian Paul, *Kingdom, Hope and the End of the World* (Cambridge: Grove Books, 2016), 3–6.

[33] Constantine Campbell, *Paul and the Hope of Glory* (Grand Rapids, MI: Zondervan, 2020), 65, 101. The pages in between offer an exegetical survey of all the pertinent texts in Paul.

[34] Moyise, *Old Testament*, 80.

a bipartite structure of 4 + 3, though this is less pronounced in the bowls sequence.[35] Despite this, the sudden narrative intrusion of an 'eagle flying in mid-heaven' comes as a surprise, not least because in a sequence saturated with Old Testament allusions, this is a prominent image that belongs to the register of Greco-Roman symbolism, where the eagle is a harbinger of divine warning.[36]

The narrative structure and emphatic repetition related to the first two woes set up a powerful sense of expectation in the reader for the announcement of the third woe:

> The first woe has passed; behold, two woes are still to come (9.12).
> The second woe has passed; behold, the third woe is soon to come (11.14).

The expectation is heightened by the near word-for-word repetition, the inclusion of the emphatic 'behold' (ἰδού) and the use of the key temporal marker ταχύ, meaning 'soon'. This makes the *lack* of reference to the third woe, when the seventh trumpet is trumpeted, both striking and disruptive.

Koester believes that we should read the third woe as associated with the seventh trumpet, on the basis that judgement is coming on 'the destroyers of the earth' – even though John actually avoids using the language of woe at this point.[37] Aune believes this is hardly possible and so attributes the discontinuity here to clumsy editorial error.[38] Maier argues that the oral nature of textual performance links the three woes to the three double woes of 18.10, 16 and 19.[39] Beale notes the use of 'woe' in 12.12 but rejects any connection on the grounds of the temporal proximity of the third woe stated found in the use of 'soon' in 11.14.[40]

Sweet appears to be alone among previous commentators in connecting the third woe with 12.12, but what he and others miss is the numerical structure of woes that John gives us. The introduction of the term in 8.13 gives three occurrences of 'woe'; the reminders in 9.12 and 11.14 provide four more, making seven; the three sets of double 'woes' (where we might otherwise expect triple woes) in 18.10, 16 and 19 provide six more; and the single occurrence in 12.12 makes fourteen 'woes' altogether. Given the significance of this number (as 2 × 7, with 2 the number of witness and 7 the number of completeness),[41] this is unlikely to be accidental.

This locates John and his readers, very precisely, in theological time: they are in the time of 'rejoicing' for heaven dwellers – a way of describing the followers of the lamb against whom the beast from the sea blasphemes in 13.6 and who reside spiritually on Mount Zion in 14.1 – but also of 'woe' for the earth and sea, for Satan in his rage knows

---

[35] See the diagrammatic comparison of the three in Koester, *Revelation*, 44; and Paul, *Revelation*, 142.
[36] Koester, *Revelation*, 454. A speaking eagle occurs in *4 Ezra* 11.7-8, but in the Old Testament eagles are more obviously associated with divine deliverance and renewal (Exod. 19.4, Deut. 32.11, Ps. 103.5, Isa. 40.31) as picked up in Rev. 12.14.
[37] Koester, *Revelation*, 504. Given the evidence of John's extremely careful and deliberate use of language, this seems unpersuasive.
[38] Aune, *Revelation 6–16*, 630.
[39] Harry Maier, *Apocalypse Recalled* (Minneapolis, MN: Fortress Press, 2002), 101.
[40] Beale, *Book of Revelation*, 610.
[41] Paul, 'Revelation's Use of Numbers', in *Revelation*, 34–9.

his time is short. In terms of the sequence of trumpets, this locates John and his readers in the 'end times' immediately preceding the final triumph of God.

Even if this does not make much sense chronologically, it makes perfect sense in terms of theological temporality, not only in Revelation but also within the temporality of the New Testament with its inaugurated eschatology. Jesus has begun his ministry by proclaiming that the 'time is fulfilled' and the long-awaited kingdom of God is now at hand (Mk 1.15). Since the resurrection of the dead was expected at the end of this age and to mark the beginning of the age to come, Jesus's resurrection in some sense marked this transition. Pentecost is explained by Peter in terms of Joel's anticipation of the 'last days' (ἐν ταῖς ἐσχάταις ἡμέραις) in Acts 2.17, and in this time 'everyone who calls on the name of the Lord will be saved', a slogan that Paul repeats in Rom. 10.13.

Moreover, the coincidence of joy and woe matches the nature of the time John and his readers live in as experiencing 'tribulation' (since Satan is enraged) as well as 'kingdom' (since Jesus has won the decisive victory by his blood, 12.11) and living with both of these calls for 'patient endurance' since those who 'hold to the testimony of Jesus' (12.17) are both pursued by the dragon and protected by God.

This implies that we should read the sequences of seals, trumpets and bowls as general descriptions of the way the world has been, experiencing catastrophe while estranged from God but now on the brink of seeing the final victory of God which is anticipated in the lives of those who follow the lamb. This also explains why the interludes in the first two series, in chapter 7 between the sixth and seventh seal and in chapters 10 and 11 between the sixth and seventh trumpets, offer visionary and auditory descriptions of the people of God who have been redeemed by the lamb from every tribe, language, people and nation (1.5, 6; 7.9; 14.3). By means of this narrative structure, John is depicting the new multi-ethnic Israel of God as the 'end times' answer to the judgement of the world.

1,260 days, 42 months, 'time, times and half a time'

Among the temporal markers within the Book of Revelation, perhaps the most striking is the triple reference to this time period in three different ways, all adapted from the time of crisis in the Book of Daniel but also read through the hermeneutical lens of a time period from exodus.[42] These terms occur only in chapters 11 to 13 and in a modified chiastic pattern:

> 11.2 The nations will trample the holy city for forty-two months
> > 11.3 my two witnesses will prophesy for 1,260 days
> > > 12.6 the woman is nourished for 1,260 days
> > 12.14 the woman is nourished for a time, and times, and half a time
> 13.5 the beast exercises authority for forty-two months.

---

[42] We should note that this practice of collating similar terms from the Torah and the haftarah and allowing them to mutually interpret one another, creating a new sense of meaning, was common practice in Second Temple Judaism. We find Jesus doing precisely this when he reads from the scroll in the synagogue in Lk. 4.16-19. See Kenneth Bailey, *Jesus through Middle Eastern Eyes* (London: SPCK, 2008), 149.

Moyise notes:

> The duration is clearly meant to link these episodes together, though it is hard to explain the variation in expression (months, days, days, times, months).[43]

The equivalence of the periods arises from assuming an idealized religious calendar in which each year has twelve months without intercalation, and each month has an unvarying thirty days.[44] Thus 3.5 years comprises 3.5 × 12 = 42 months, and this comprises 42 × 30 = 1,260 days.[45] This equivalence has an interesting and important narrative function, offering a structural connection between two sections of the text, which has not been previously noted.

The narration in 11.1-10 is the only section in the book which is in the future tense and therefore should be taken as the continued speech of the unnamed angelic figure that John hears.[46] The primary narrative imagery in chapter 11 is drawn from the Old Testament, but in chapter 12 the primary narrative framework is drawn from the Python-Leto myth.[47] Chapter 12 is introduced by the new vision formula 'And a great sign appeared', and the chapter is the only narrative section lacking the repeated vision marker 'and I saw' until chapter 21. There is, thus, universal agreement among commentators that 12.1 marks the most significant narrative disjunction in the book.[48] Yet, across this disjunction, the threefold temporal expression links chapters 11 and 12, suggesting an unexpected equivalence between these very different symbolic-narrative accounts.

The phrase 'time, times and half a time' is a word-for-word translation of the phrase in Dan. 7.25 and 12.7 in which the Aramaic dual עִדָּנִין has become a simple Greek plural καιρούς (an accusative of duration). As a *half* week of years, it symbolizes a time where it *appears* as though the forces of evil have the upper hand but where in fact God in his sovereignty has strictly limited their power and is thus equivalent to the description of the devil having real power in the world but knowing 'his time is short' (Rev. 12.12).

John has revised Daniel's calculation of the three and a half years from 1,290 days (Dan. 12.11) to 1,260 by omitting an intercalated month (one added to keep the monthly lunar calendar in line with the annual solar calendar) in order to fit a significant numerological pattern. He has previously used square and cubed numbers (144, 1000) to signify the people of God in chapter 7 and will do so again in the vision of the New Jerusalem, based on the theological notion of the people of God as his temple and the Holy of Holies being a cube (1 Kgs 6.20). He will use a 'triangular' number – one that

---

[43] Moyise, *Old Testament*, 52.
[44] Bauckham, *Climax*, 401.
[45] Beale, *Book of Revelation*, 565–6, agrees with Moyise on the equivalence of the time periods but also agrees that the variation in forms is hard to explain.
[46] My own calculations suggest that 43 per cent of the text of Revelation comprises things that John *hears* rather than things he sees; Revelation is therefore as much an audition report as it is a vision report.
[47] Paul, *Revelation*, 216.
[48] Ibid., 213.

can be represented by objects arranged in a triangle of equal sides – to signify the arch enemy of God's people in the number of the beast (666, the thirty-sixth triangular number).

If the priestly kingdom of God and his people (1.6) is signified by *square* numbers, and the suffering arising from opposition by the forces of evil is signified by *triangular* numbers, it would fit if John is using *rectangular* numbers to signify the overlap of the two – numbers formed by multiplying not the same number by itself but a number by its successor.[49] Both 42 (= 6 × 7) and 1,260 (= 35 × 36) are rectangles; rectangles look very much like squares but are also closely related to triangles since each rectangle is double the corresponding triangle (42 is twice the sixth triangle 21, and 1,260 is twice the thirty-fifth triangle 630).[50] John is doing his theological painting by numbers.

Just as he has adapted the Danielic time period, John has also adapted the other significant equivalent, 42 months, from the Old Testament. As Beale notes:

> The exact number 'forty-two' here and in 13.5 is probably intended to recall Elijah's ministry of judgement which is expressed in the same way,[51] and Israel's wilderness wandering, which included forty-two encampments (so Num 33.5–49), and which might have been reckoned as forty-two years, since it appears that two years passed before Israel incurred the penalty of remaining in the wilderness for forty years.[52]

Adjusting *both* the Danielic time period *and* the time period of the exodus wanderings, and making them equivalent, has a striking effect on the temporality of Revelation. Whereas, in the history of the people of God, the exodus and the exile follow in a temporal sequence, in John's reuse of the Old Testament he folds the second back on the first and equates them both with the theological time that he and his readers are in.

On the one hand, Jesus has been sacrificed as our Passover lamb (1 Cor. 5.17; cf. Jn 1.36), so his followers have been set free from slavery but have not yet entered the 'promised land' of the new creation, so are in the in-between time of the desert wanderings, being tested and yet trusting in God for their protection as they journey in hope.

On the other hand, the 'one like a Son of Man' has now come on the clouds to the Ancient of Days,[53] having 'thrown down' the Satan 'by his blood', that is, his death

---

[49] There are many interesting mathematical connections between square, triangular and rectangular numbers which were well known in the ancient world; see any edition of Nichomachus, *Introduction to Arithmetic*. Squares are the sum of successive odd integers; rectangles are the sums of successive even integers; and triangles are the sums of successive integers.

[50] For detailed study of square, triangular and rectangular numbers, their significance in John's world and their use in Revelation, see Bauckham, *Climax*, chapter 11, 'Nero and the Beast,' 384–452.

[51] Beale, *The Book of Revelation*, notes later (585) that the duration of Elijah's drought is only noted in general terms in 1 Kgs 17.1 (and it appears to be less than three years in 1 Kgs 18.1) but this time period is revised in Lk. 4.25 and Jas 5.17 to be three and a half years. This itself could be through a hermeneutical tradition of identifying Elijah's judgement with the period of tribulation in Dan. 7.25; it therefore points us once more to Daniel rather than Elijah per se, though it fits with Elijah imagery elsewhere in Revelation 11.

[52] Beale, *Book of Revelation*, 656.

[53] Against the majority of commentators, I argue that Rev. 1.7 along with Mt. 24.30 make use of Dan. 7.13 which they parallel to refer to Jesus's ascension to the Father and not to his *parousia* at the end. See Paul, *Revelation*, 63; and 'When Is God "Coming on the Clouds"?' at www.psephizo.com.

(Rev. 12.10; cf. Jn 12.31). Yet the final realization of that defeat is still to come so that the followers of the lamb, in fellowship with John, experience 'tribulation' as well as 'kingdom' as they wait with 'patient endurance' (Rev. 1.9).

So for John, he and his readers are both living in a time of exile and tribulation, awaiting the deliverance of God but also a time of exodus, having been set free from slavery but yet to enter the Promised Land. In connecting these two periods of the history of God's people, John is in fact following a pattern already established in the Old Testament where, particularly in Isaiah, exodus language is used to describe the restoration and return from exile.[54] They follow, worship and stand with the one expressed in the central, paradoxical image of the slaughtered Passover lamb who now stands on the throne of God.

This then points us to the different implications of living in this theological time period and the reason for the three different expressions for it.

1. There are numerological connections between 42 and 666, in that 42 is the sixth triangular number and 36 is the sixth square (so 36 + 6 = 42) of which 666 is the triangle.[55] In the exodus, the 42 years of wandering arise from Israel's being led astray and is a time of testing. In Revelation, the 42 months signify this time as one when the nations trample the holy city and the beast exercises authority and blasphemes. It is thus a *negative* construal of the theological time period, pointing to spiritual opposition and suffering.
2. The equivalent of the 1,260 days in Daniel (the variants 1,290 and 1,335) is linked to the ending of suffering, blessing to those who endure and Daniel 'resting' and 'standing' at the end of days. In Revelation, this expression of the time period is associated with the authority, testimony and powerful prophetic ministry of the two witnesses in 11.3 and the nourishing of the woman in 12.6. The two witnesses and the woman are narrative-symbolic metaphors for the people of God living life under the reign of God. This expression is thus a *positive* construal of the theological time period, pointing to the blessings of the kingdom.
3. In both Dan. 7.25 and 12.7, the period of 'time, times and half a time' depicts a period of suffering which is intense but limited and must be endured. This construal combines both negative and positive aspects of this theological time.

We might therefore read this threefold description, of 42 months, 1,260 days and time, times and half a time, as corresponding respectively to the three realities of tribulation, kingdom and patient endurance in Jesus which we first met in John's epistolary opening at Rev. 1.9.

---

[54] For an exploration of this, see 'Isaiah's Rhapsody', in Bryan Estelle, *Echoes of Exodus* (Downers Grove, IL: IVP, 2018), 149–81. Estelle also notes exodus themes in Jeremiah and some parts of Ezekiel but finds none in Daniel. So John's identification of Daniel's tribulation with the exodus wanderings is genuinely new and unexpected.
[55] Bauckham, *Climax*, 393, 401–2.

Conclusion

Our exploration of the way that John makes use of Old Testament ideas, images and phrases in his depiction of theological time in Revelation points to four concluding observations.

First, Moyise is quite right when he talks of a 'dialectical relationship' between the text of Revelation and the text of Daniel,[56] and the same is true of John's use of other Old Testament texts. On the one hand, John feels free to adapt and revise Old Testament temporal language, though in a way which retains the clear connections with it, in order to make his own theological points.[57] He reinterprets the significance of key elements of the Old Testament narrative in the light of the death, resurrection and exaltation of Jesus as the slaughtered lamb who now reigns with the One on the throne. On the other hand, this also means that John invites us to read these Old Testament texts afresh in the light of Jesus; the placement of Revelation at the end of the Christian canon is highly appropriate, since we now look back and read the whole story in a new light knowing how it ends. Although this is not the way that Jews who were not followers of Jesus would read the Old Testament texts, John is following the approach of other New Testament writers in reading Christologically and indeed is bringing that to its appropriate completion.

Second, in developing the connections between the theological motifs of exodus and exile more fully, building on the connections already found in the Old Testament, but pushing them further to integrate apocalyptic texts as well as prophetic, Revelation presents us with a more fully integrated theological reading of the whole of the canon.

> The reader needs to hear not only how John completes his own literary work, but also listen for the ways in which John's book ties together the canon as a whole ... Revelation is dependent on the rest of the canon; ... it reveals the full meaning of the canon; ... it mirrors the beginning of the canon; ... it resolves the crises of canon narrative; ... and it provides closure whilst also challenging the reader into action.[58]

Third, John's use of very different parts of the Old Testament, and his integration of its varied temporal signifiers, serves to bind together the narrative of Revelation itself. The language of 'not sealing up', the terms καιρός and χρόνος, the repeated vision markers 'and I saw', the sequence of woes and the threefold temporal marker all appear to be expressed in very different registers of language, genre and form. Yet it transpires that they all point to a coherent theological claim that John and his readers are living in the

---

[56] Moyise, *Old Testament*, 58.
[57] We might change the metaphor here to say that John paints his own picture using a palette of colours from the Old Testament – but this is perhaps too imprecise a way of describing it, since it is clear that John is constrained by the texts he is making use of; the meaning of source texts is not abandoned but adapted.
[58] Külle Toniste, *The Ending of the Canon: A Canonical and Intertextual Reading of Revelation 21–22*, LNTS 526 (London: T&T Clark, 2016), 201.

partially realized, or inaugurated, eschatology of experiencing the reign of God, the opposition of the world and the patient endurance that these together demand.

Finally, this understanding of inaugurated eschatology matches what we find in the gospels and in Paul and thus locates Revelation's theological construal of time firmly within the theological outlook of the rest of the New Testament canon. In other parts of the New Testament, its inaugurated eschatology also arises from an adaptation and Christological re-reading of the Old Testament so that it is Jesus who is God's 'last days' word to us (Heb. 1.1). Revelation brings this re-reading of New Testament temporality to a fitting climax and is the text which deploys the Old Testament in this way *par excellence*.

8

The *Expositio Apocalypseos* of the Venerable Bede: An example of early medieval preoccupation with construing time and its end

Paul M. Collins

Introduction

By the end of the seventh century a belief that the earth would exist for Six Ages of one thousand years each was widely accepted among Christians in the West.[1] There is evidence of such belief in Irish and Anglo-Saxon writings.[2] So, we may assume that literate monks and priests would know of it, while the illiterate may have had some understanding of the Six Ages. By 700 CE it was widely held that the end of the world was only one hundred years distant.[3] Christ had been born during the Sixth Age, the date of his birth indicated the amount of time left before the End. Belief in the Six Ages also raised questions about how to establish timescales. With the collapse of the Roman Empire in the West the means of knowing when events occurred, for example in relation to the terms of office of Consuls, disappeared. Various schemes were developed: *Annus Mundi* drew on timescales found in the Old Testament and dated events from the first day of the Creation. Later *Annus Domini*, which Bede himself espoused, dated events from the birth of Christ. In popular understanding, the Six Ages placed Christ's birth at AM 5199, which by 701 CE left only ninety-eight years until the End.[4]

In addition to these beliefs, the Book of Revelation held out a promise of a thousand-year reign of Christ and the saints (Rev. 20.4, 5), which some believed would be an

---

[1] For example, Augustine, *De Genesi Contra Manichaeos* 1.23.40 (J.-P. Migne, *Patrologiae cursus completus, Series latina* (Paris, 1844–64) (hereafter PL), 34.190–3).
[2] For Irish texts see: Marina Smyth, 'Monastic Culture in Seventh-Century Ireland', *JASIMS* 12 (2019): 64–101. For Anglo-Saxon texts see G. T. Dempsey, 'Aldhelm of Malmesbury and the Irish', *PRIA* 99C.1 (1999): 1–22; and '*Aldhelm, Epistola ad Acircium*', in Michael Lapidge and Michael Herren (eds), *Aldhelm: The Prose Works* (Woodbridge: D. S. Brewer, 1979, 2009), 35.
[3] Faith Wallis (ed.), *Bede: Commentary on Revelation* (Liverpool: Liverpool University Press, 2013), 49–51. See for example: Hilarianus, *On the Duration of the World (c. AD 397)*; Julian of Toledo, *Affirmation of the Sixth Age (AD 686)*.
[4] In Eusebius Ecclesiastical History Christ's ministry is dated AM 5228. His birth is 5197 or 5198. But Jerome settled on 5199. See Faith Wallis (ed.), *Bede: The Reckoning of Time* (Liverpool: Liverpool University Press, 1999 republished 2004), 356.

earthly paradise. Conflicting interpretations of this thousand years had developed over the centuries. Chiliasts held a literal understanding,[5] while those who followed an Origenist allegorizing tradition interpreted Christ's reign spiritually.[6] Speculation about Christ's thousand-year reign probably added to uncertainty about the future at the turn of the eighth century.

In this essay we encounter the first commentary by an Englishman on the Apocalypse, a commentary which was widely read in the Middle Ages. Bede's hermeneutical approach to the Apocalypse and understandings of the End sits in the tradition of Origen and Augustine as well as of Gregory the Great. His reception of the eschatological dimensions of faith can still inform and form Christian expectations about the End today.

Belief in the Six Ages of the World, and the speculation and controversy which it produced, shaped the broader context in which Bede wrote his early works *On Times*, *On the Nature of Things* and *John's Apocalypse*. It is beyond the scope of this essay to discuss in detail how these beliefs became so influential among recently Christianized Anglo-Saxons. Rather, I will examine how these concerns relate to Bede's decision to write his commentary *Expositio Apocalypseos*.

It is widely accepted that *Expositio Apocalypseos* was Bede's first biblical commentary.[7] Why did he make this choice? Bede wrote in the context of a monastic community, and his commentary was copied and shared with other monasteries and episcopal households.[8] His audience was an elite literate group of mainly monks and clerics. But even those who could read enough to participate in or celebrate the Church's liturgies did not necessarily have sufficient literacy or the intellectual skills or curiosity to read and understand a biblical commentary.[9] How did monks, nuns, clerics and the wider population discover an interest in the End?

---

[5] Hans Bietenhard, 'The Millennial Hope in the Early Church', *SJT* 6.1 (1953): 12–30.
[6] Henri de Lubac, *Medieval Exegesis, Volume 2: The Four Senses of Scripture* (Grand Rapids, MI: Eerdmans; Edinburgh: T&T Clark, 2000), 114–55.
[7] On the dating of *Expositio Apocalypseos* see: Gerald Bonner, *Saint Bede in the Tradition of Western Apocalyptic Commentary* (Newcastle upon Tyne: Jarrow Lecture, 1966), 703–709 CE; George Hardin Brown, *A Companion to Bede* (Woodbridge: Boydell Press, 2009) (following Charles Plummer (ed.), *Venerabilis Baedae opera historica*, 2 vols (Oxford: Clarendon Press, 1896)): between 703 and 709 CE; George Hardin Brown and Frederick M. Biggs, *Bede, Part 2. Bible: Commentaries. Fascicles 1–4* (Amsterdam: Amsterdam University Press, 2016), 40, soon after 703 CE; Michael Lapidge and Paolo Chiesa (eds), *Beda: Storia degli Inglesi*, vol. 1 (Rome: Fondazione Lorenzo Valla, 2008), xlix, before 716 CE; Faith Wallis, 'Why Did Bede Write a Commentary on Revelation?', in Peter Darby and Faith Wallis (eds), *Bede and the Future* (Farnham: Ashgate, 2014), 23–45, well before 709 CE; Benedicta Ward, *The Venerable Bede* (London: Geoffrey Chapman, [1990] 1998); and Charles Kannengiesser, *Handbook of Patristic Exegesis: The Bible in Ancient Christianity* (Leiden: Brill, 2006), 1479, between 710 and 716 CE.
[8] L. T. Martin (ed.) and Bede, *The Venerable Bede, Commentary on the Acts of the Apostles* (Kalamazoo: Cistercian Studies, 1989), 3; Wallis, *Revelation*, 86–92; Sarah Van der Pas and John Litteral (eds), *Alcuin of York: On Revelation, Commentary and the Questions and Answers Manual* (West Monore, LA: Consolamini, 2016), 1.
[9] See Wallis, *Revelation*, 106; cf. Alcuin, Letter 196, PL 100, 740 C-D. Gisela, Charlemagne's sister (abbess of Chelles), and Rotrud, daughter of Charlemagne, requested Alcuin to write a commentary on John's Gospel 'suited to their level of understanding'. Henning Graf Reventlow, *History of Biblical Interpretation Volume 1: From the Old Testament to Origen* (Atlanta, GA: Society of Biblical Literature, 2009), 123.

Bede's purposes were not only aimed at an elite audience. By teaching and writing he sought to equip monks and priests to minister to the wider population. In his letter to Bishop Ecgbert, Bede indicated that he produced Old English versions of the Lord's Prayer and Apostles' Creed for the clergy to teach to the laity, with the intention that a devout person would memorize the texts and be able to recite them regularly.[10] In these two texts are key elements of a Christian's understanding of 'the End': that is, 'Thy Kingdom come', 'lead us not into temptation; but deliver us from evil', 'he descended into hell', 'and sitteth on the right hand of God the Father almighty, from thence he shall come to judge the quick and the dead', 'the resurrection of the body, and the life everlasting'. These beliefs about Judgement and the Afterlife do not of themselves necessarily produce controversy; rather, they encourage the faithful to consider the outcome of their lives and their ultimate destiny. It is the combination of the awareness of the End which arises from these texts with a belief in the Six Ages which, some have argued,[11] gave rise to anxious anticipation of the End of the World.

By the late seventh and early eighth centuries nonverbal expressions of the End were evident as well as memorized texts. In the church at Wearmouth, Benedict Biscop installed images of scenes from the Book of Revelation.[12] In Northumbria, images relating to the End were also produced in sculpture, for example, on the standing crosses at Bewcastle, Easby, Rothbury and Ruthwell.[13] Such monuments and depictions fed the imagination in the wider population with visual representations of the End.

From this overview of the context in which Bede wrote, we can see that his *Expositio Apocalypseos* was published at a moment of a heightened awareness of the construal of Time and its End.

Why did Bede choose the Apocalypse as the subject of his first commentary?

An explanation of Bede's choice of the Apocalypse of John as the subject for his first commentary is often framed around the expectation that by 701 CE there were less than one hundred years left before the End.[14] The choice of the Apocalypse is understood to complement Bede's work *On Times* c. 703. Some scholars argue that *Expositio Apocalypseos* should itself be dated c. 703.[15] In his work *On Times* Bede had set out a radical readjustment

---

[10] Christopher Grocock and I. N. Wood (eds), *Abbots of Wearmouth and Jarrow* (Oxford: Clarendon Press, 2013), 130–3; cf. Council of Clofesho 747; A. W. Haddan and W. Stubbs (eds), *Councils and Ecclesiastical Documents Relating to Great Britain and Ireland*, 3 vols (Oxford: Clarendon Press, 1869–78), III: 366.

[11] Wallis, *Revelation*, 44, 49.

[12] Grocock and Wood, *Abbots*, 36–7.

[13] See Jane Hawkes, 'The Rothbury Cross: An Iconographic Bricolage', *Gesta* 35.1 (1996): 77–94; Catherine E. Karkov, *The Art of Anglo-Saxon England* (Woodbridge: Boydell Press, 2011), 69–79, 136–45; David M. Wilson, *Anglo-Saxon Art: From the Seventh Century to the Norman Conquest* (London: Thames and Hudson, 1984), 70–7, 105; Eamonn Ó Carragáin, 'Conversion, Justice, and Mercy at the Parousia: Liturgical Apocalypses from Eighth-Century Northumbria, on the Ruthwell and Bewcastle Crosses', *Literature and Theology* 26.4 (2012): 367–83.

[14] Wallis, *Revelation*, 39–57; Wallis, *Why Did Bede Write?*, 23–45.

[15] Brown and Biggs, *Bede*, 40.

of the Six Ages of the World by re-calculating the periods of the Ages based on the *hebraica veritas* of the Vulgate, rather than the timescales found in the Septuagint.[16] Bede's re-calculation of the dates of the Six Ages extended the period until the End by approximately 1,200 years.[17] But such was the hold of the accepted scheme on the popular imagination that Bede was accused of heresy, in the presence of his Bishop, Wilfrid. On hearing of this accusation, Bede responded within days, writing his *Letter to Plegwine* refuting the charge of heresy and labelling his critics as 'rustics'.[18] When Bede wrote a second work on Time, *On the Reckoning of Time* c. 725, the preface still expressed his disquiet regarding the charge of heresy and the inability of some to accept his re-calculation of the Six Ages of the World.[19] However, did Bede's reframing of the Six Ages and its consequences influence his decision to write a commentary on John's Apocalypse?

In *Expositio Apocalypseos* Bede avoids feeding speculation about the End. His approach clearly sits in a tradition of interpretation which rejects a literal understanding of the Millennial Reign.[20] Where he mentions the Six Ages of the World in the commentary, he does not refer to his readjustment of the timescale of the Ages.[21] Bede's reworking of the Six Ages caused the controversy which evoked the writing of his *Letter to Plegwine*. The *Expositio Apocalypseos* was probably published prior to this controversy. It seems that Bede was concerned to reshape popular perceptions of the timescale of the End, but what led him to write his first commentary on the Apocalypse?

The Apocalypse and Easter

Bede's choice of the Apocalypse may relate to the celebration of the Christian calendar at Wearmouth/Jarrow. As a monk, Bede's life was dedicated to the *opus dei* of prayer and worship. His works on Time and *computus* demonstrate a profound commitment to the correct celebration of Easter.[22] He was formed in this tradition by his guides in the monastery as well as by the yearly cycle of worship. The well-spring of the Christian Calendar is the celebration of the Passion and Resurrection of Christ. The night before Easter Day was spent in prayer and reading passages from the Old Testament considered to be prophecies of the Paschal Mystery. In the writings of Jerome, Augustine of Hippo and Isidore of Seville we find evidence of a belief that Christ's second coming would most likely happen at Easter (Jerome *Commentary on the Gospel of Matthew* 4 (Mt. 25.6); Augustine of Hippo, Sermon, Wilmart 4, 3; Sermon, Morin-Guelferbytanus 4, 2[23]

---

[16] Calvin B. Kendall and Faith Wallis, *Bede: On the Nature of Things and on Times* (Liverpool: Liverpool University Press, 2010), 117–26.
[17] Wallis, *Reckoning of Time*, 361.
[18] Ibid., 405.
[19] Ibid., 3–4.
[20] Wallis, *Revelation*, 253–4.
[21] Rev. 9.5 (ibid., 169); Rev. 11.15 (ibid., 187); Rev. 20.2 (ibid., 252); Rev. 21.20 (ibid., 271).
[22] For example, *On Times*, chapters 11–15; *The Reckoning of Time*, chapters 44–65; *Letter to Nechtan* (Bertram Colgrave and R. A. B. Mynors (eds), *Bede's Ecclesiastical History of the English People* (Oxford: Clarendon Press, 1969) (hereafter HE), V.21), Synod of Whitby (HE III.25).
[23] Augustine of Hippo, Germain Morin and Antonio Casamassa (eds), *Miscellanea Agostiniana: Testi E Studi, Pubblicati a Cura Del-l'Ordine Eremitano Di S. Agostino Nel XV Centenario Dalla Morte Del Santo Dottore* (Rome: Tipografia Poliglotta Vaticana, 1930).

and 6; Isidore *Etymologies* VI. xvii (11)[24]. If by cock crow during the Vigil the Parousia had not occurred, the Church proceeded to baptize and confirm the catechumens and to celebrate the Mass of Easter, a sacramental Parousia, 'until his coming again' (1 Cor. 11.26). In his writings on Time Bede provides his detailed understanding of Easter (*On Times*, chapters 11-15; *On the Reckoning of Time*, chapters 61-5). In each work he draws out a connection between the celebration of Easter and the End[25] and cites II Peter and the Apocalypse.[26] He concludes his Homily for the Easter Vigil (*Homily* II.7):[27]

> We do not know the time of our own resurrection, although we are in no way uncertain that it will come to pass; and so at all times let us keep careful watch while we wait for it, and particularly on this special night.
> ... let us take care to conduct our lives, with actions by which we may merit to behold joyfully the outcome of our own resurrection too. Thus when the last trumpet arouses the entire human race, and summons it before the tribunal of the just Judge, the sign of our Judge with which we were made holy may separate us from the lot of the condemned, and the vigil in which we have awaited his coming may separate us from the punishment due to those who are negligent.

His understanding of the Easter Vigil in relation to the End echoes Isidore of Seville's thoughts on the Easter Vigil (Isidore *Etymologies* VI. xvii (11)):[28]

> Easter Eve is held as a continuous vigil because of the coming of our king and God, so that the time of his resurrection might find us not sleeping but vigilant. The reason for this night's vigil is twofold: it is because on that night he then received life, although he suffered death, or because at the same hour at which he was resurrected he will afterwards come for the Judgment.

The sources upon which Bede drew knew a tradition in which there was a clear connection between the celebration of Easter and the expectation of Christ's Second Coming and the End. This tradition can be seen in his homily for the Easter Vigil. In his commentary on the Apocalypse no direct connections are made with such a tradition. His appeal to Christ as 'the Morning Star' (Rev. 2.28)[29] 'who, when the night of this world is past promises and flings open to the saints the eternal light of life', finds resonance with texts of the *Exsultet*, the blessing of the Paschal Candle, sung at the Easter Vigil.[30] This resonance together with the singular reference to Eastertide at Rev.

---

[24] S. Barney, W. Lewis, J. Beach and O. Berghof (eds), *The Etymologies of Isidore of Seville* (Cambridge: Cambridge University Press, 2006).
[25] Kendall and Wallis, *On the Nature of Things*, 117; Wallis, *Reckoning of Time*, 151-2.
[26] Wallis, *Reckoning of Time*, 152.
[27] L. Martin and D. Hurst (eds), *Bede the Venerable: Homilies on the Gospels*, 2 vols (Kalamazoo: Cistercian Studies, 1991), vol. 2, 67-8.
[28] Barney et al., *Etymologies*, 144.
[29] Wallis, *Revelation*, 124.
[30] There is no conclusive evidence for liturgy of the Easter Vigil at Wearmouth/Jarrow in Bede's time, but texts of the Exsultet in Gallican and Frankish sacramentaries from the late seventh or

19.4[31] may suggest that in Bede's mind there were connections between the celebration of Easter and John's Apocalypse.

Wearmouth/Jarrow and Rome

Monastic life at Wearmouth/Jarrow was formed by the vision of Benedict Biscop, whom Bede tells us had experienced the life and rules of seventeen different monasteries.[32] Benedict Biscop had lived in monasteries in Rome, on the island of Lérins, and had been acting Prior of the monastic house in Canterbury c. 669–70.[33] At Lérins Biscop was tonsured and took his vows.[34] These experiences formed Biscop's understanding of monastic life and in turn shaped the life at Wearmouth/Jarrow.

In 680 Biscop returned from one of his visits to Rome accompanied by Abbot John *archicantore* (Precentor) of St Peter's Rome.[35] Pope Agatho sent John to Northumbria to teach the monks how to celebrate the liturgy and chant the texts of the Office and Mass in the tradition of the Roman basilicas.[36] John's work had a formative effect not only in Northumbria but more widely across Anglo-Saxon monasteries. Bede records that John's instructions were written down and kept for future reference. In the seventh century there was no system of musical notation. Musical chants had to be memorized with the texts of psalms, antiphons and responsories, which they accompanied. A responsory would be sung after a reading in an office. At the Night Office a responsory would usually be sung after each of the several readings;[37] the text of the responsory might repeat or echo the reading it followed.[38] There is almost no evidence of what these texts were in seventh- and eighth-century Anglo-Saxon liturgical use.[39] But there is evidence of what the readings at the Night Office were in the mid-seventh century at St Peter's Rome and in relation to their use at Lérins.

---

eighth century refer to *lucifer matutinus*. For example, *Missale Gothicum* Vat Reg 317 (Henry Marriott Bannister (ed.), *Missale Gothicum I, a Gallican Sacramentary*, MS. Vatican. Regin. Lat. 317 (London: Henry Bradshaw Society, 1917), 69) and The Sacramentary of St Gall 348 (L. C. Mohlberg, *Das fränkische Sacramentarium Gelasianum in alamannischer Überlieferung (Codex Sangall. no. 348). St. Galler Sakramentar-Forschungen I* (Münster: Aschendorff, 1918), 83). See also Guido Fuchs and Hans Martin Weikmann, *Das Exsultet: Geschichte, Theologie und Gastaltung der österlichen Lichtdanksagung* (Regensburg: Verlag Friedrich Pustet, 1992), 96–101; Ian Boxall, *Revelation: Vision and Insight* (London: SPCK, 2002), 157.

[31] Wallis, *Revelation*, 244.
[32] Grocock and Wood, *History of Abbots*, 48–9.
[33] Ibid., 28–31.
[34] Ibid., 26–7.
[35] Ibid., 34–7; Colgrave and Mynors, *Ecclesiastical History*, 388–91.
[36] Benedicta Ward, *Bede and the Psalter* (Oxford: SLG Press, 2002), 7.
[37] Robert Taft, *The Liturgy of the Hours in East and West: The Origins of the Divine Office and Its Meaning for Today* (Collegeville, PA: Liturgical Press, 1986), 94; Jesse D. Billett, *The Divine Office in Anglo-Saxon England 597 – c.1000* (Woodbridge: Boydell Press, 2014), 44–5.
[38] Brad Maiani, 'Readings and Responsories: The Eighth-Century Night Office Lectionary and the Responsoria Prolixa', *Journal of Musicology* 16.2 (1998): 254–82.
[39] A. I. Doyle, 'A Fragment of an Eighth-Century Northumbrian Office Book', in Michael Korhammer, Karl Reichl and Hans Sauer (eds), *Words, Texts and Manuscripts: Studies in Anglo-Saxon Culture. Presented to Helmut Gneuss on the Occasion of his Sixty-Fifth Birthday* (Cambridge: D. S. Brewer, 1992), 11–27.

Ordo Romanus XIV,[40] which details the lectionary used at the Night Office at St Peter's Rome, is understood to relate to the period of the second half of the seventh century, the time during which John was precentor. *Ordo Romanus XIII*[41] from a later date provides similar evidence. The monastic rules written by Caesarius, bishop of Arles, who had been a monk on Lérins and Aurelian of Arles indicate similar usage, from the sixth century.[42] The text of *Ordo Romanus XIV* indicates:

[Ordo lectionum in ecclesia sancti Petri]
 <in> diebus autem paschae epistula apostolorum et actus apostolorum atque apocalypsin usque pentecosten.[43]

In the period from Easter Day until Pentecost, at the Night Office at St Peter's basilica the Catholic Epistles, the Acts of the Apostles and the Apocalypse of John were prescribed to be read. The precise lections are not detailed. This usage, also evidenced in the practice of Arles/Lérins, may well have been known to Benedict Biscop from his time at Lérins. It seems highly likely that this lectionary was the usage which informed the work of John the Archcantor and Bede's experience of worship. For monastic communities such as Wearmouth/Jarrow and Hexham, which sought a close affinity with the church in Rome, it seems that from *c.* 680 (if not before) they were exposed during Eastertide to the public reading of at least extracts from John's Apocalypse as well as the Acts of the Apostles and the Catholic Epistles. This liturgical encounter with John's text in the context of the Night Office was perhaps supplemented with private reading and meditation on the text.[44] Benedicta Ward reminds us that it is 'in this structure of the Divine Office [Bede] had what must be called the primary source of his scholarship'.[45] I suggest it is this annual exposure to the Apocalypse in the monastic houses which embraced Abbot John's instruction, which provided an imperative to Bede to write his commentary – along with those on Acts and the Catholic Epistles.[46] An annual encounter with the Apocalypse would provide familiarity with John's visions, which no doubt evoked questions and fears.

---

[40] Michel, Les Andrieu, *Ordines Romani du Haut Moyen Age, Vol. 3, Les Textes (Ordines XIV–XXXIV)* (Leuven: Peeters, 2006), 23–41.

[41] Michel Andrieu, *Les Ordines Romani du Haut Moyen Age, Vol. 2, Les Textes (Ordines I–XIII)* (Louvain: Spicilegium, 1971), 467–526.

[42] Taft, *Liturgy of the Hours*, 97–108. Aurelian of Arles Rule for Monks [Regula ad monachos]: PL 68, 393B: 'In primo dei Paschae ad tertiam ter Kyrie eleison, psalmi duocedim: id est, quatuor fratres binos psalmos et alleluiaticum tertium dicant: perdictis psalmis, Kyrie eleison et antiphonas sex, lectiones tres: una de Actibus apostolorum, alia de Apocalypsi, tertia de Evangelio.'

[43] Andrieu, *Ordines Romani*, vol. 3, 40.

[44] Ward, *Venerable Bede*, 42–3; Scott DeGregorio, 'Bede, the Monk, as Exegete: Evidence from the Commentary on Ezra-Nehemiah', *Revue Bénédictine* 115.2 (2005): 357–9.

[45] Ward, *Venerable Bede*, 41.

[46] Caesarius of Arles's Commentary (or Homilies) on the *Apocalypse* (PL 35, 2423–60) (one of Bede's sources) may have had a similar purpose, if the tradition of Lérins/Arles was to read the Apocalypse in the Night Office during Eastertide. *Commentarius in Apocalypsin* (PL 68, 793–936) of Primasius, Bishop of Hadrumetum (the source which Bede drew upon most of all) was published as an indisputably Catholic exegesis of the Apocalypse (Prologue PL 68, 793C–796B].

A focus on the Apocalypse as well as Acts and the Catholic Epistles is witnessed in Bede's correspondence with Acca bishop of Hexham (*c.* 710–31). Acca commissioned Bede to write a commentary on Acts and the Catholic Epistles.[47] There are examples of Bede's commentaries on these three texts bound together as a single codex.[48] There are nineteen surviving manuscripts, two of which date to the early eighth century.[49] In the illustration of Ezra the Scribe in the *Codex Amiatinus* (716 CE) (fol.5r) the final volume in the cupboard is (the New Testament texts) Acts and the Apocalypse bound together, preceded by the Catholic Epistles.[50] The collection of the commentaries on the three texts in a single codex suggests that the reception and ongoing use of *Expositio Apocalypseos* in the Early and Later Middle Ages may have had some relationship with the Lectionary used at the Night Office in Eastertide.[51]

Bede's commentary and his wider concerns

Thus far I have sought to examine the context in which Bede produced his commentary. What does the text itself tell us about Bede's concerns in commenting on the Apocalypse? Bede's purposes were focused not only on his monastic brothers but also on the life of the Church generally. I will examine three areas of concern which relate to Bede's engagement with the life of Christians beyond the monastery: First, Bede's focus on the challenges which the Church faced, which fashioned his perception for the need for the reform of its practices and ministry.[52] Second, his concern for the salvation of individual believers.[53] Finally, his focus on Easter.[54] In relation to the commentary, I have chosen three topics which relate to these concerns and suggest something of what Bede sought to achieve by producing this text: war, fire and worship.

John's Apocalypse presents the reader with many instances of violent struggle and war. Bede's approach to John's vivid pictures of conflict sits within a tradition of interpretation crafted by Tyconius and embraced by Augustine of Hippo.[55] In the opening poem Bede tells us:

---

[47] Martin and Bede, *Commentary on the Acts*, 3–6; W. F. Bolton, *A History of Anglo-Latin Literature* (Princeton: Princeton University Press, 1967), vol. 1, 597–1066, 110.
[48] Wallis, *Revelation*, 42, 87.
[49] Ibid., 88–91.
[50] Perette Michelli, 'What's in the Cupboard? Ezra and Matthew Reconsidered', in Jane Hawkes and Susan Mills (eds), *Northumbria's Golden Age* (Stroud: Sutton, 1999), 345–58.
[51] See below evidence of Anglo-Saxon and Carolingian Night Office lectionary in Amalarius and Aelfric.
[52] Alan Thacker, 'Bede's Ideal of Reform', in Patrick Wormald, Donald Bullough and Roger Collins (eds), *Ideal and Reality in Frankish and Anglo-Saxon Society: Studies Presented to J. M. Wallace-Hadrill* (Oxford: Basil Blackwell, 1983), 130–53; Scott DeGregorio, 'Bede's In Ezram et Neemiam and the Reform of the Northumbrian Church', *Speculum* 79 (2004): 1–25.
[53] Catherine Cubitt, 'Apocalyptic and Eschatological Thought in England around the Year 1000', *TRHS* 25 (2015): 30; Peter Darby, 'Apocalypse and Reform in Bede's De die iudicii', in M. Gabriele and J. T. Palmer (eds), *Apocalypse and Reform from Late Antiquity to the Middle Ages* (London: Routledge, 2018), 39–40.
[54] Wallis, *Reckoning of Time*; Kendall and Wallis, *On the Nature of Things*.
[55] F. C. Burkitt (ed.), *The Book of Rules of Tyconius* (Cambridge: Cambridge University Press, 1894); J. F. Shaw (trans.), *St Augustine: On Christian Doctrine* (Buffalo: The Christian Literature Co., 1887; Mineola, NY: Dover, 2009).

This conflict's form, its passion, its array,
The strategy, the soldiery, the weapons and the prizes,
I longed to tell:[56]

He begins the preface of the commentary:

> The Revelation of St John, in which God has deigned to reveal in words and symbolic imagery [*figuris*] the wars and inward conflagrations of his Church. ...[57]
> Apocalypsis sancti Iohannis, in qua bella et incendia intestina ecclesiae suae deus uerbis figurisque reuelare dignatus est.[58]

The words *bella ... intestina* suggest that Bede is from the outset situating his text, and his understanding of the conflicts portrayed in the Apocalypse, within the hermeneutics crafted by Tyconius, who wrote a work, now lost, *De bello intestino*.[59] The title refers to the intrauterine struggle of Esau and Jacob and symbolizes the struggles and conflicts of the Church. For Bede, as for Tyconius and other commentators who drew on his work, the conflicts portrayed in the Apocalypse are about the ongoing story of the Church, rather than the End.[60] An instance of this approach to John's text may be seen in Bede's comments on the Seven Seals in chapters 6–8. The openings of the second, third and fourth seals (Rev. 6:3-8) are understood in terms of *bello intestino*:[61]

> Therefore he opened the book then, and he breaks its seals now. In the first seal is seen the glory of the primitive Church; in the next three, the threefold war waged against her.[62]

This approach is also found in the *Capitula Lectionum* which some have ascribed to Bede.

> [The first five seals: the Four Horsemen and the souls beneath the altar]
> VII. The victorious Church is attacked in a threefold war, namely by pagans, by false brethren, and by heretics.[63]

---

[56] Wallis, *Revelation*, 99.
[57] Ibid., 101.
[58] Roger Gryson (ed.), *Bedae Presbyteri, Expositio Apocalypseos ad fidem codicum manuscriptorum edidit adnotationibus criticis instruxit prolegomenis munivit* (Turnhout: Brepols, 2001). *Bedae Opera Pars* II, 5: 221.
[59] Paula Fredriksen, 'Apocalypse and Redemption in Early Christianity: From John of Patmos to Augustine of Hippo', *VC* 45.2 (1991): 151–83.
[60] Ian Boxall and Richard Tresley (eds), *The Book of Revelation and Its Interpreters* (Lanham, MD: Rowman and Littlefield, 2016), 76.
[61] Kenneth B. Steinhauser, *The Apocalypse Commentary of Tyconius: A History of Its Reception and Influence* (Frankfurt am Main: Peter Lang, 1987), 129–30.
[62] Wallis, *Revelation*, 140.
[63] Ibid., 288.

Bede comments on these three seals as follows: On Rev. 6.4 Bede cites Tyconius and the assault on the Church by 'a sinister people'. On Rev. 6.5, we find, 'The black horse is the troop of false brothers.' On Rev. 6.7, 'Worthy to be ridden by Death, heretics who dress themselves up as Catholics carry off in their train the host of those who are lost.'[64] This approach to the interpretation of conflict in the Apocalypse demonstrates that Bede had researched the available commentaries on the text and chose a hermeneutical stance to mitigate speculation about the End, which focused his readers' attention on the present problems of the Church. For Bede, the Christianization of the population was still ongoing, he himself would be a victim of 'false brethren' and the pursuit of Catholic truth and practice was his constant goal.

The imagery of fire is repeatedly used in the Apocalypse.[65] Fire is used to describe the End itself and some of the places which exist after Judgement, and the process of individuals being judged or saved. In Bede's *Ecclesiastical History*, there are descriptions of the post-mortem fate of individuals which employ the imagery of fire. Is there any evidence of such an understanding in *Expositio Apocalypseos*?

The visions of the layman Dryhthelm[66] and an Irish monk, Fursa,[67] refer to post-mortem punishment of sinners. While these descriptions do not constitute a developed doctrine of Purgatory,[68] they do suggest that a sinner might by purified after death by suffering torment by fire. An Irish text *Liber de ordine creaturarum* composed between 655 and 675 CE articulates the understanding that at judgement, an individual who is not so good as to join Christ immediately,[69] nor so bad as to be consigned to Hell, waits for a decision at the Final Judgement. These 'moderate sinners' must be 'subjected in their bodies to the *iudicii ignis* or *ignis purgatorius*, that is, to the purgatorial fire of judgement, before they can join the elect'.[70] Bede cites this work several times in *De natura rerum* c. 703.[71] In *Expositio Apocalypseos* Bede deals circumspectly with John's imagery of fire, akin to the oblique ways in which he interprets conflict. At Rev. 8.7, 8 Tyconius refers to fire refining silver and gold.[72] Bede does not follow his exposition which implies that the good are refined in fire. But at Rev. 11.5 in relation to the Two Witnesses, Bede writes:

> If anyone harm the Church, he is condemned by retributive justice to the very same punishment which he has inflicted and is consumed by fire.

---

[64] Ibid., 142–3.
[65] For example, Rev. 1.14; 2.18 eyes like flames of fire; 3.18 gold refined by fire; 8.5 censer filled with fire; 8.7, 8 fire burns up a third of the earth; 14.10 torment by fire; 19.20; 20.10, 14, 15; 21.8 lake of fire.
[66] Colgrave and Mynors, *Ecclesiastical History*, 488–99.
[67] Ibid., 268–75.
[68] Sarah Foot, 'Anglo-Saxon "Purgatory"', *Studies in Church History* 45 (2009): 87–96.
[69] Marina Smyth, 'The Seventh-Century Hiberno-Latin Treatise *Liber de ordine creaturarum*. A Translation', *JML* 21 (2011): 137–222.
[70] Ibid.
[71] Ibid., 146.
[72] David C. Robinson and Francis X. Gumerlock (eds), *Tyconius, Exposition of the Apocalypse. Fathers of the Church: A New Translation* (Washington, DC: Catholic University of America Press, 2017), 92–3.

Hence the Babylonian fire, directed against the children of God, consumed the agents of wickedness themselves. Or else he is to be consumed in a good fire through the prayers of the mouth of the Church and transformed into something better. He says, You shall heap coals of fire upon his head.[73]

In this single instance in *Expositio Apocalypseos* Bede demonstrates awareness of and interest in the concept of the purification of a sinner through fire and associates it with the prayers of the Church. This exposition is partly dependent on Tyconius, but Bede is more positive about the possibility of transformation. At Rev. 6.16-17 Bede articulates an understanding parallel with 11.5, without reference to fire:

> So that when he comes, he shall find us not worthy of condemnation, but steadfast in our faith, with our sins covered up by the intercession of the saints and the mercy of God.[74]

Bede understood the need for the forgiveness of post-baptismal sin. In *The Reckoning of Time* c. 725 when dealing with the Day of Judgement Bede refers to Rev. 21.1 in conjunction with 1 Thess. 4.15-16. Bede makes a tentative comment about the possibility of sinners being purified in fire, explicitly citing Augustine's *City of God* Book 20 and Gregory the Great's *Homilies on the Gospels* as the authorities for a concept of the transformation of sinners through purifying fire.[75] The fate of individual souls forms part of Bede's construal of the End. Perhaps the first instance of such concern is to be found in *Expositio Apocalypseos*.

In *Expositio Apocalypseos* Bede refers explicitly to the season of Easter[76] in relation to the singing of 'Alleluia' Rev. 19.1-4.[77] He associates the song of the heavenly multitude with the worship offered by the Church on earth. Reference to the Church is made in the comments of Tyconius, Caesarius and Primasius.[78] But Bede iterates his interpretation four times and makes clear connections with liturgical practices on Sundays and in Eastertide.[79] This is the most explicit reference to the liturgy and the Church's calendar in the whole of the commentary. It is perhaps an indication not only of Bede's interest in Easter but also of a connection between liturgical practice and the commentary itself.

It is evident from these three areas that Bede espouses an ecclesial hermeneutic. His exposition of John's Apocalypse helps the faithful to understand the trials and joys of the Church in the time before the Day of Judgement and relates to his ongoing concerns for the renewal of the Church, the salvation of souls and the celebration of Easter.

---

[73] Wallis, *Revelation*, 181–2.
[74] Ibid., 147.
[75] Wallis, *Reckoning of Time*, 245–6.
[76] Nam et alleluia Dominiciis diebus totoque Quinquagesimo tempore propter spem resurrectionis (PL 93, 188B).
[77] Wallis, *Revelation*, 243–4.
[78] Robinson and Gumberlock, *Tyconius*, 171–2; Caesarius (Homily 18) PL 35, 2455; Primasius PL 68, 908D.
[79] Cf. Thomas L. Knoebel (ed.), *Isidore of Seville De Ecclesiasticus Officiis* (New York: Newman Press, 2008), 38.

The reception of Bede's commentary

Bede's works were copied and sent to monasteries in Northumbria and elsewhere during his own lifetime. After Bede's death, c. 746, writing in Germany, Boniface requested copies of Bede's exegetical works from Ecgbert bishop of York and Abbot Hwætberht of Wearmouth/Jarrow.[80] Lullus, archbishop of Mainz, used the list of works at the end of Book V of Bede's *Ecclesiastical History* to request copies from England.[81]

An example of the reception of *Expositio Apocalypseos* may be seen in the explicit reference to the work in Alcuin's own commentary on the Apocalypse.[82] The influence of Bede's exegetical works and homilies was assured over many centuries through their extensive use in the Homiliary of Paul the Deacon, which was commissioned by Charlemagne.[83] This Homiliary became a primary source for lections at the Night Office in many editions of the Breviary in the Middle Ages. Homiletic and exegetic works were probably used to assist public and private reading of scripture in Bede's own time.[84] There is a natural synergy between liturgical reading and the production of homilies and commentaries.

There is evidence that the Roman tradition of reading Acts, the Catholic Epistles and the Apocalypse during Eastertide witnessed in the *Ordines* XIV and XIII was practised in England and the Frankish Kingdom in the Anglo-Saxon period. The prologue of *Liber de ordine antiphonarii* of Amalarius of Metz[85] provides detailed evidence of the use of the Roman lectionary at the Night Office.[86] This usage is also witnessed in Aelfric's *Letter to the Monks at Eynsham c.* 1005. Aelfric knew the work of Amalarius and assured his readers that 'he is drawing on well-established liturgical tradition'.[87] There is evidence from the texts of the responsories which Aelfric uses that he is citing *Ordo Romanus XIIIA*.[88] His description of the lectionary for the Night Office during Eastertide is more detailed than the *Ordo* and 'specifies the canonical Epistles for the Easter Octave, the Apocalypse for the Sunday after the Octave to the Ascension ... and Acts for the period from Ascension to Pentecost'.[89]

Witnesses to the liturgical reading of scripture in Eastertide in the Anglo-Saxon period (and beyond)[90] suggest that Bede's commentary on John's Apocalypse was one element in a keen interest in the End which was in part fuelled by the reading of the Apocalypse in the hours of the night in monastic houses across Western Europe in the

---

[80] Michael Tangl (ed.), *Die Briefe des heiligen Bonifatius und Lullus* (Berlin: Ficker, Gerhard, 1916 [1919]), 158–9, 207.
[81] Ibid., Letters 116, 125, 126.
[82] PL 100, 1087A.
[83] PL 95, 1159–1584.
[84] DeGregorio, *Bede, the Monk, as Exegete*, 359; Ward, *The Venerable Bede*, 62–5.
[85] PL 105, 1243A.
[86] Andrieu, *Ordines Romani*, vol. 2, 469, 471, 474–6.
[87] J. R. Hall, 'Some Liturgical Notes on Aelfric's *Letter to the Monks at Eynsham*', DR 93 (1975): 297–303.
[88] Ibid., 299.
[89] Ibid.
[90] Acts, the Catholic Epistles and the Apocalypse of John were prescribed to be read in the Night Office in the Roman Breviary throughout the Middle Ages and continue to be read in the Office of Readings of the Breviary following Vatican II; George Guiver, *Company of Voices: Daily Prayer and the People of God* (London: SPCK, 1988), 164–5.

early Middle Ages. We can only speculate about Bede's motivation. But the manuscript evidence suggests that his commentary continued to be read and appreciated for many centuries. Bede's approach to the End remains a testimony to the faith of early Anglo-Saxon Church while his use of patristic hermeneutics can still contribute to present-day construal of the Apocalypse and the End.

9

Apocalyptic on screen – can the hermeneutical flow really be reversed? The TV drama series *Years and Years* and the Book of Revelation

Clive Marsh

The Book of Revelation is a baffling read. Even for seasoned Christians it is a tough challenge. Whether a 'book of torment' or 'book of bliss' (or both), to use Stephen D. Moore's recent characterization of the work,[1] or 'a sick text', containing 'vile obscurantism' and constituting 'a guignol of tedium', to adopt Will Self's less sympathetic response to the book in the Pocket Bible Series,[2] it is a vexing set of writings. As the source of the wild and the wacky – Christian or otherwise – and an invitation to deciphering and decoding because of its vivid imagery, it is open to a range of interpretations. Perhaps the nearest thing the New Testament contains to the verbal equivalent of a graphic novel, the book is both the product of and stimulus to the religious imagination. At once elusive in its meanings and sharp in its warnings – both of what now is and what is to come – Revelation continues to invite contemporary citizens, whether Christian believers or not, at the very least to consider deeply how they articulate what it is that they hope for and why and how the distractions and structures of destruction which pervade society are to be identified and opposed.

In this chapter I invite readers to engage less with the detail of the text of Revelation itself, or even its reception in any direct sense, than to consider how cultural resources which parallel the function of Revelation might in turn influence the process of reading the biblical text. In doing so I link with the practice popularized by Larry Kreitzer of 'reversing the hermeneutical flow', the intertextual approach adopted by the biblical scholar in a number of works to the way in which later texts (including films) might prove informative for the practice of reading biblical texts.[3] Unlike Kreitzer, however, my intention is less to focus on specific texts in Revelation, new interpretations of which can be offered as a result of attending to later cultural products or works of art. Rather, my purpose is to explore the 'Revelation-likeness' of an example of popular culture as

---

[1] Stephen Moore, *Revelation: Book of Torment, Book of Bliss* (London: T&T Clark, 2021).
[2] Will Self, *Revelation: The Canon Pocket Bible Series* (Edinburgh: Canongate 1998), xii–xiii.
[3] See e.g. Larry Kreitzer, *The New Testament in Fiction and Film: On Reversing the Hermeneutical Flow* (Sheffield: Sheffield Academic Press, 1993); and *Pauline Images in Fiction and Film: On Reversing the Hermeneutical Flow* (Sheffield: Sheffield Academic Press, 1999).

a means to explore why such cultural resources ('texts' in the widest sense of the term) are necessary, are popular and prove both informative and instructive in life. In so doing, I examine the function of such materials within a largely secular sociopolitical setting, while also positing the possibility that they are serving a religion-like, and potentially even religious, purpose whether or not they may also be deemed implicitly theological works. Then, in turn, I ask how such Revelation-like texts, narratives and artistic products help us see what the Book of Revelation as a whole might look like. How, in the light of this process, is the Book of Revelation to be received and what insights about how it is to be read may be gleaned from such readings in the present, about the present, but 'from the future'? What role, in short, do politically informed, imaginatively prophetic works of art play in religion and society?

Finding an appropriate lens: What 'apocalyptic' is and is not

Revelation is apocalyptic literature. That near-tautologous statement still needs making, though, in order to distinguish apocalyptic from dystopian art (visual or written) or horror. Revelation has elements of both of those forms too. It nevertheless needs rescuing from lazy assumptions that as apocalyptic literature it is only interested in phantasmagorical portrayals of horror scenarios. Future-oriented it certainly is. Radically focussed on and critical of elements of its then (first century CE) present it is too. But how we are to understand the interplay between the imagined and hoped-for future and the allegorical and symbolic evocation of the present is the hermeneutical task required of the book's interpreters.

There have been many important correctives in recent years to the notion of apocalyptic meaning cataclysmic. Christopher Rowland's reorientation of apocalyptic as a concept, so that it focuses more on revelation than disaster, was a major stimulus here.[4] N. T. Wright's work developed, consolidated and almost popularized this approach.[5] As a result, the ways in which apocalyptic writings are received have shifted much more towards attention to how *this world* is being commented on and critiqued, in the hope of its being redirected, than on explaining or predicting how the world will end. The end time remains in view in the sense that current paths are found wanting and seen to be heading for destruction. And the refocussing of apocalyptic literature does not collapse all sense of the future into the present. Attention to this present world does not mean care *only* for this world. But the reorientation exercise nevertheless sharpens the question of what apocalyptic as a genre is *for* and what it is trying to achieve.

If DiTomasso is right, then apocalyptic writings are accompanied by a world view offering clear convictions and assumptions about space, time and the goal of humanity.

---

[4] Christopher Rowland, *The Open Heaven: A Study of Apocalyptic in Judaism and Early Christianity* (London: SPCK, 1982).
[5] N. T. Wright, *The New Testament and the People of God* (London: SPCK, 1992), 280–99, and in many subsequent writings.

Far from being inevitably religious in character or content, apocalyptic insights will, however, offer a reading of what is wrong with the present and how current patterns of living will, if not readjusted, lead to the demise of the present world. Within a linear view of time there will be an inevitability to this demise unless the destructive patterns of living are disrupted. And whether viewed in secular or religious/theological/biblical forms, 'the message that the last days have come and the end is near constitutes the existential dimension of the [apocalyptic] worldview'.[6] The purpose of apocalyptic writing, then, is the disclosure of the truth of the present. When understood in a theological key, this means that such disclosure is none other than God's self-revelation in the present of a vision both of what is possible and what would result without attendance to respect for God's agency in the world.

Granted, however, that secular and theological apocalyptic accounts coexist and jostle for our attention, the question arises of what is to be done with the various contemporary forms of apocalyptic communication and art. Then, in turn, it must be asked how biblical insights into apocalyptic are to be viewed and even contribute (if they can) to the adjudication of the merit of contemporary forms.

Years and Years: A mapping of contemporary anxieties, aspirations and concerns

The six-part drama series *Years and Years*, first shown on BBC TV in 2019, offers a rich, multilayered drama which projects into the future a range of concerns about the present through a series of compelling plotlines.[7] Set mostly between 2022 and 2030, the series mixes sometimes controversial or emergent aspects of life in the present which have become everyday features of life within the drama. Hence, virtual assistant technology has become commonplace, and easy connections between multiple family members have become possible. The use of computer technology as part of, and not just outside, the body has reached new levels. One character, Bethany, is on a quest to transcend her body and become virtual herself, by being translated into data. There is a fluidity of gender identity, evident in the non-binary dress sense of a great grandson, Lincoln.

Alongside these more personal and relational aspects of living, a broader canvas of international political and economic concerns is painted. There is a banking collapse, widespread migration leading to difficulties for refugees seeking asylum, a wave of populist politics including the election of a narrowly nationalistic prime minister and an ongoing health crisis resulting from the use of nuclear weapons by the United States in the Far East.

All plot strands are interwoven through the experience of a single Manchester-based family, the Lyons family, and it is in and through their lived, intergenerational

---

[6] Lorenzo DiTomasso, 'Apocalypticism in the Contemporary World', in Colin McAllister (ed.), *The Cambridge Companion to Apocalyptic Literature* (Cambridge: Cambridge University Press, 2020), 316–42, 318.
[7] *Years and Years* (StudioCanal, 2019).

experience that the various sociopolitical concerns and developments are grounded and explored. They are presented as a typical family, for the 2020s, being multiethnic, with strong characters, diverse political opinions, varying degrees of health and illness, different sexual orientations, mixed levels of success in employment and personal relationships and with some members living with disability.

Rather than catalogue the full range of plotlines I wish simply to focus on four narrative threads which demonstrate how such a drama functions *now* in UK society. I suggest that these threads enable the series to function as an example of contemporary apocalyptic literature in that they expose crucial fault lines in the present while pressing contemporary society to ask how these challenges are to be confronted. The four threads are nationalism and its consequences; economic collapse; the prospects and problems of technological advance; and developing patterns of what constitutes normative sexuality. None of these four themes can be said to dominate within the plotlines of *Years and Years*. They are simply interwoven as aspects of contemporary life which are sharpened in their futuristic, dystopian form. But while simultaneously entertaining and at times shocking TV watchers, the plotlines provide rich material to enable viewers to 'feel' the issues as well as inviting them then to reflect upon them. I shall consider each in turn.

Written and shown in an immediate post-Brexit situation, *Years and Years* maps the rise of populist politician Vivienne Rook (Emma Thompson) until she becomes prime minister in the British government. Showing how she skilfully rides on the back of what (some of) the people 'want to hear', she taps into a deeply introverted, nationalist vein of desired independence. Britain can 'go it alone', needs to be interdependent with no other nation, should shut its borders and should even find ways of quietly allowing citizens it does not particularly want to be allowed to die. By corralling together large numbers of people it wishes to deport into what Rook recognizes are 'concentration camps' (and which she acknowledges were a Boer War British invention), the hope is that diseases become rife enabling mass-scale death by natural causes to take effect.

This introverted nationalism amounts to a refusal to accept human diversity and has, as its consequence, a profound hostility to migration and the welcoming of migrants. As a political approach to life, however, it is challenged and undermined by the de facto make-up of the Lyons family which is humanity in microcosm. While screenplay-writer Russell T. Davies may be accused of creating a fictional cliché – an ethnically diverse family with a member with a physical disability, a range of sexual orientations, marital infidelity, a non-binary child, political difference and family members with differing levels of material wealth – he at least shows how a narrow nationalism is being undermined in practice by the types of family which already exist in Britain today.

Economic collapse is the second thread which runs through the work. Stephen Lyons, an initially wealthy employee in the banking industry, becomes 'the man who lost a million pounds' due to a combination of financial collapse (echoing the 2008 financial crisis) and his own risk-taking, in leaving the proceeds of a house sale in one bank account overnight. His wife, Celeste, had already lost her job due to increased computerization of accounting processes. Harrowing scenes of people from different walks of life seeking to withdraw their savings pounding on the windows of closed banks graphically portray the significance of such loss and the sense of urgency, betrayal and helplessness. This narrative thread reveals the importance of material wealth for everyone, poor and rich alike – it is what provides food and shelter even if the quality and scale of basic human needs differs across socio-economic groups. These basic needs are contextualized in the TV drama within a fragile, global framework where the certainties and securities of personal wealth are revealed to be less certain and secure than was thought. The failure of one American investment bank has global implications.

The third thread to explore is that of digital technological advance. This theme manifests itself in many different ways throughout the series: in breath identity recognition practices to gain entry to buildings; in the ease of communication between family members, where Alexa (b.2014) has become the fictional Señor, producing situations when family members are listening in to conversations without others sometimes realizing; and, above all, in the experimental developments undertaken by great granddaughter Bethany to seek, with mixed results, disembodied existence.

The risks of such development are starkly mapped when an operation undertaken on the eye of Bethany's friend Lizzie goes badly wrong. Far from enabling Lizzie to take steps towards being transhuman, an eye implant fails to function as it should. This element within the plot is a sobering reminder of the risks entailed in digital technological developments. More generally, however, the mood through the series is of the sheer speed and intensity of such developments. This is how things are (and will be), and that we should 'get used to it' is presented as the norm, leaving us to question whether caution and necessary constraint may be able to play any role.

Fourth, and finally in my selection of key plotlines, is the exploration of developing patterns of what constitutes normative sexuality. In simple terms, and as is common in Russell T. Davies's work, there is no 'normative sexuality'. While it may remain statistically true in most societies that the majority of people prove to be of, or have, in practice heterosexual persuasion, the experience of homosexual orientation and practice is incorporated into everyday life so seamlessly that Davies's dramas challenge viewers to be accepting of a range of sexual orientations and gender identities. Davies presents us with interwoven plotlines which invite viewers to recognize that this is how things are and will be, with the messiness and complexity which accompany *all* human relationships in all their diversity, within and outside of family life and friendships.

Placing the emphasis on the complexity of personal relationships within the life of one extended family perhaps implies that it is in relation to blood family ties and immediate kinships that the joys and tensions of intimate relations will be most keenly felt, and this may well remain true. It is also helpful for such a drama to be presented in this way, inviting families who watch the series together to respond to its plotlines openly with each other in frank conversation. In this respect, Davies will have been able to build on his popularity with a younger family audience as a scriptwriter for *Doctor Who* (2005–10), some of whose viewers might now be well into their twenties and be thinking differently both about their own identities and their relationships to their families. Be that as it may, the viewing experience presents a version of British society 'as it is' in relation to sexuality and gender identity and invites viewers to examine how they respond to the way things are.

These four themes, then, are prominent in *Years and Years*. Other viewers may find others more compelling or important. I cannot deny that my own lens may well be directly influenced by the thought and task of writing something about the Book of Revelation for the worthy recipient of this collection of essays! But that merely accentuates much of what I shall go on to explore in the next two sections: all readings are partial and have backgrounds to them and serve interests (whether explicit or implicit). I shall do my best not to make *Years and Years* 'say' what it is not trying to say. It is entertainment first and foremost, even if there are commitments and ethical and political stances implied within it. I have tried, in so far as it is possible, to 'let it speak for itself'. But my purpose in doing so is to acknowledge that as a contemporary piece of secular apocalyptic, it locates itself in a pool of resource material within which the Book of Revelation also sits. It will have been, and continues to be, watched by a range of viewers, religious and not, in the process being located within a wide range of world views. Christians are, then, reading the Book of Revelation, and some will also have viewed *Years and Years*. What difference, though, might this make to how Revelation is read? And what might a reading of Revelation in the light of the concerns of *Years and Years* do to our thinking about both the present and future of Western societies? To these questions I now turn.

Receiving the Book of Revelation through the lens of *Years and Years*

Detecting what may be going on in the interplay between a viewing of *Years and Years* and the contemporary practice of reading/receiving/responding to the Book of Revelation is a two-stage process. First, what does a viewing of *Years and Years* make us especially sensitive to as we read the Book of Revelation? Then we shall need to ask: what might the Book of Revelation want to 'speak back' to the present in the light of the concerns drawn to our attention? I shall take up the first question in this section.

Again, I want to highlight four themes. These are not to be matched directly to the four threads of the previous section, though they do interweave with them. I wish the two sets of observations simply to produce a creative friction between what the drama series evokes and how a reading lens is shaped. The four themes which emerge and seem germane to the task of reading Revelation are: the question of what kind of communities churches are; the extent and scope of human agency (just what is it that human beings can actually do and achieve?); the role that is being played by the exercise of imagination here; and the question of who has the responsibility for whether and how the story continues (and in what form/s). I shall map the ways in which each of these concerns is provoked by *Years and Years* and therefore how a questioning by, or contribution from, the Book of Revelation is being invited by the viewing experience.

The Lyons family is an intergenerational community. At their best, so are churches. But the points of similarity and contrast between the Lyons family and a church are worth pressing, as a backdrop against which to consider Rev. 2.1–3.22 (the messages to the seven churches). The Lyonses are a wonderfully rich and diverse assortment of people. As a family they carry tensions and disagreements, members who profoundly dislike each other, while recognizing they are nevertheless bound together. Equally, there is love, support (overt and quiet), deep solidarity and practical help shown between members. Muriel the grandmother and great grandmother is both the matriarch and the property owner who ends up having to provide for the whole family more than she expects to have to so late in her life. There is, then, an interesting theme of a direct dependence – of all members – on the matriarch.

To switch to talk of a mother Church is too neat, though compelling. But nearly all of what I have just said of the Lyons family is true of churches and not only at their best. As is often said, what differentiates churches significantly from families is that they are communities of people without blood ties who are brought together not primarily by a political or ethical purpose (though such things flow from their life) but because of their common relationship to One who is both inside and outside their life (the one God, known in Christ). This means that their relationships with each other, and their belonging together and accountability to each other, cut across blood ties. Family members may be present but they are there within a more significant sense of what it means to be communal. In Christian understanding, 'church' overrides 'family' and as a social form certainly seeks to undermine any tendency for blood relations between people to control what churches – as communities of followers of Jesus – are attempting to be (Mk 3.31-33; 10.29-30; Lk. 14.26-27).[8]

This has multiple consequences, complex though they are to assert and maintain. At the very least it means that churches must strive to be intergenerational even if it proves difficult to achieve this. Many congregations in historic denominations in the West are ageing. Those who attract younger members (in their twenties to forties, say) may do so because of particular worship styles, because they attract people from a similar socio-economic or ethnic background, or present a particular ethical, political or theological stance. A desired diversity is sometimes very hard to achieve. Furthermore, while it may be true in theory that 'church overrides family', churches often seek to attract families in seeking to be seen as families themselves. They also think they are more likely to perpetuate their own lives as congregations by their family friendliness. Further still, generations of specific families may well have been active and prominent in particular congregational histories, and buildings may sometimes have taken on a significance out of all proportion to living communities ('my grandfather built this church'). The radical nature of what it means to be 'in Christ', as opposed to being 'part of a church family', can thus be undermined all too easily.

We are left, then, at least with a question here: what kind of communities need to be formed and function well to begin to address creatively in the future the issues which come to light for viewers of *Years and Years*? The Lyons family are an example and a symbol of the relationship frameworks (communities) within which all manner of pressing social, political, ethical and economic issues have to be faced and worked

---

[8] The writings of Stanley Hauerwas have been especially significant in recent decades in accentuating both the significance and limitations of the family in the cultivation of Christian virtues and character. See e.g. Stanley Hauerwas, *A Community of Character: Toward a Constructive Christian Social Ethic* (Notre Dame, IN: University of Notre Dame Press, 1981), esp. chapters 8 and 9.

through. But what other communities might there be? And what – as a Christian must ask – is the role of churches to be in the midst of all this?

In a memorable scene in the final episode of the series, great grandmother Muriel declares that it is 'all your fault ... all of you'! This characterizes the second theme from the series which proves instructive for our reading of Revelation. Muriel holds her entire family responsible for being insufficiently active in resisting the trends and practices which have led to the various crises now overshadowing their collective life. While rather harsh, and qualified somewhat when she acknowledges her own complicity in what has happened, it is also a clear statement both of humankind's collective guilt and, ironically, a strong and hopeful assertion of the potency of human agency. If human activity and inactivity have produced the mess then it should presumably be possible for better human activity to rectify matters.

In encouraging attention on the part of viewers to their own ethical and political responsibilities Muriel's words are striking and present, in stark form, one of the lingering, even haunting, challenges of the series. It is worthy of note that it had been the populist prime minister, Vivienne Rook, who explored the possibility of controlling who would be permitted to vote. Viewers are thus left reflecting on not only the privilege of democracy but also the responsibility of making use both of the capacity to vote and what actions to take beyond the freedom of the ballot box. Muriel's castigating of her family members is thus indeed a summons to respect the value of human activity. As such it is a rallying cry against passivity. But the implication, of course, is that human agency really is all that is available. In this case, a theologically inclined viewer, and a reader of Revelation, would have to ask – while respecting the challenge to passivity – what the limits of human agency might be and what an exploration to discern divine agency might disclose.

This takes us to a third theme: the role of imagination. *Years and Years* is fiction. It is futuristic, dystopian fiction. It is a work of the imagination designed to entertain and also stimulate the imagination. The Book of Revelation is likewise a work of the imagination, wrapping up a vast array of complex imagery within a coded account of then contemporary challenges and fears, while also seeking to support and galvanize existing and emergent Christian communities in their responses to dominant and dangerous political developments practised by an imperial power (here, Rome). As an apocalyptic work it maps the present and the future figuratively within a braided narrative. Those 'in the know' can hear what is being said about the present, even as the symbolic language offers insights as to how a hoped-for future is 'read back' into the present. First-century theism would have had more opportunity to be confident of the reality of the God expected to act in and from the future. Twenty-first-century secular readers have less confidence and some would not wish to speak of God at all, which is why the emphasis on human agency is so marked in *Years and Years*. (There is, for many, no God to help.) Non-realist theists too, a somewhat specialist group, admittedly, would have a similar approach to human agency. While recognizing the need for God language, non-realists would claim God to be a necessary fiction: essential but made-up, but crucial in the shaping of human action nonetheless. Few religious readers of Revelation would be thus inclined, of course. Even so, the challenge to the theological reader is how to compute the theological language in the present (what is being, and to be, said of God – the God who *is*?) in a way which neither leaves everything to God nor turns human activity into a collection of good deeds deemed to be God's action by virtue of their being combined. If God's action is not merely a compilation of human actions, then what does it mean for the 'new heaven and a new earth' (Rev. 21.1) to come into being?

These questions lead us to a fourth consideration: what it means for the story (of the world, of humanity, of existence) to continue or to end. The Book of Revelation, and its very position within the Christian canon of scripture, indicates that it is dealing with weighty matters about ultimacy. As an apocalyptic text it is concerned about endings. It wrestles with the possibility that the world may be heading for destruction, even as it voices its conviction that God has something new in store and will include within that future all who take the trouble to attend to what God has done, is doing and will do. *Years and Years* does interesting things with endings too. The 'coda' within which we see that we are looking back through the perspective of Edith's death at all of the action which in fact took place earlier invites us to think of how visions of the future are already shaping the present. What are the pictures of the future we are creating in order to steer our actions in the present not merely in a sense of having a strategy and planning but so that we envision what is to come in a hopeful way?

Christian interpreters of Revelation are, inevitably, not at one even with each other in their conclusions about whether the story mapped out in the book remains open or will come to an end. Consider these two examples taken from the wide range of literature available. First, and tellingly given one of the plotlines of *Years and Years*, from the end of a chapter on Christian responses to the migrant crisis:

> We know how God's story ends. The new heavens and new earth will one day be revealed in their full glory. This is the time and place where suffering will be no more, and the nations will receive their healing from the leaves of the tree of life (Revelation 22:1-2). Eden will be restored, displaced no more, and 'home' will have found its ultimate meaning and resting-place. However, for many this remains an illusory image. Until then the struggle must go on.[9]

Rather differently, and again at the end of a chapter, David L. Barr writes:

> The ending of the Apocalypse allows us, indeed requires us, to re-experience the work, both as story and as continuing experience. While the Apocalypse has most often been read as a story about the end of the world, reflection on the ending of the story calls that reading into question. For in this story the awaited end never quite comes. Faced with this ending, the reader must reconsider the story's meaning, must reread the story.[10]

---

[9] Andy Kingston-Smith, 'Migrants, Justice and Border Lives' in Marijke Hoek et al. (eds), *Carnival Kingdom: Biblical Justice for Global Communities* (Gloucester: Wide Margin, 2013), 101–24, here 122.

[10] David L. Barr, 'Waiting for the End That Never Comes: The Narrative Logic of John's Story', in Steve Moyise (ed.), *Studies in the Book of Revelation* (Edinburgh: T&T Clark, 2001), 101–12, here 112.

There is common ground, of course, between these two senses of Revelation's ending and what they deem, as story, it is meant to do to and for us. Both are acknowledging that there is still much work to be done and that religiously committed readers of Revelation will be committed to it (as God's work enacted in their own activity). But the different approaches to how the story is to be inhabited arguably produce quite different theologies. The former could be seen as more convinced: 'this really will happen, whatever we do'. The latter could be suggesting that we dare not think so conclusively, otherwise we may well slip into passivity. It could, then, be that it is precisely through an open-endedness to, rather than a closure of, the story (and despite mention of the new heaven and the new earth) that Christians would satisfy Muriel Lyons: it may well be 'our fault' but Christians seek the help of God in their efforts to do something themselves about continuing the story of the created order.

This first stage of interaction, then, between *Years and Years* and the Book of Revelation has moved us from watching and receiving (and enjoying) the TV series and its multiple, interweaving plotlines through taking note of things that leap out and take us towards themes with which Revelation deals. Next, we must press the 'so what?' question further. How, if at all, is the hermeneutical flow being reversed such that we gain some insights into how the Book of Revelation is to be understood now?

From *Revelation* forwards: The Bible fights back (without necessarily winning)

Revelation is far from an accessible book. Perhaps it was never meant to be. Though its imagery would have been more resonant to first-century hearers than to twenty-first-century readers, it remains an evocative, stunning and shocking book. In this final section, I shall make no claim to be offering fresh exegetical insights on specific passages. *Years and Years* is not, after all, pretending to contribute directly and intentionally to a religious reading of one of Christianity's own apocalyptic texts. All I am doing is asking how the context in which Christians *now* read Revelation informs reading of selected texts, or the book as a whole, given that that context is in part influenced by a wide range of apocalyptic material which drinks from the same reservoir of imagery drawn upon by Revelation itself.

The name 'Jesus' appears sparingly in Revelation, twice as 'Lord Jesus' (22.20, 21), three times as 'Jesus Christ' (1.1, 2, 5) and nine times by itself (1.9 (twice); 12.17; 14.12; 17.6; 19.10 (twice); 20.4; 22.6). More dominant throughout the work is the interpretation of Jesus Christ as the Lamb, often in extended well-known passages (e.g. 5.11-14 – 'worthy is the Lamb that was slaughtered': 5.12; 7.9-17 – 'from every nation, from all tribes and peoples and languages, standing before the throne and before the Lamb': 7.9; 17.1-18 – 'the Lamb will conquer them, for he is Lord of lords and King of kings, and those with him are called and chosen and faithful': 17.14). At stake here is what may be called 'association' with Jesus/the Lamb. It is clearly a risky business to be so associated. The Lamb himself was slaughtered and followers may be too. But the vision of association is radical, diverse togetherness (7.9). If this association is risky, it is also a glimpse of the new heaven and the new earth.

Such an observation is, of course, possible without any recourse to watching six hours of a TV drama beforehand. But a surprise from episode 2 of *Years and Years* is the rationale provided by Muriel Lyons for her acceptance of Daniel's new Ukrainian boyfriend Victor. Victor's Christian parents had reported him to the authorities because of his homosexuality, thus endangering his life and causing him to flee. Muriel is scathing of his parents' behaviour and uses a Christological argument for why they are wrong: 'in the eyes of Christ you're beautiful.' Here, then, in the midst of a secular (TV) text we encounter the use of a hermeneutical strategy similar to one which has been worked out through painful Christian experience: the Spirit of Christ challenges the stifling letter of tradition. Expressed differently: the word of God in Christ must be attended to not only from within the text (of Bible or tradition) but also alongside it, as the Spirit continues to speak in the act of reception and interpretation of Bible and tradition. The Word of the Spirit of God, as known in Christ, is discernible through many different channels in the process of text and tradition being received, read and acted upon. While it is clear that not all Christians across the world would agree with Muriel's judgement, her words can serve as a reminder to Christians (and to all viewers) to attend to what the Spirit of God in Christ is saying to the churches.

That the Spirit of God needs to be listened to is clear. Assistance from beyond human understanding and human activity will prove vital for the new heaven and earth to have a chance of coming to be. This is far from explicit in *Years and Years*, in which, as we have seen, confidence in human agency is considerable despite the crises at hand. But perhaps here is a point at which the dystopian fable trips itself up. In DiTomasso's words, commenting on most recent developments in the apocalyptic genre: 'the conviction that such systemic problems can be solved through human industry, intellection, or ingenuity has steadily eroded.'[11] This can be heard as a recognition that all apocalyptic literature will therefore seek salvation 'from outside'. Indeed, as DiTomasso also acknowledges, and as we shall probe further shortly: 'Salvation in the apocalyptic mindset ... is always imagined as salvation *out of* this world.'[12]

These observations do not lead to a wholly satisfying framework for understanding how Revelation is now to be received as a text. Christians are likely to assume that God will help, that Jesus/Christ/the Lamb is the one to be followed and looked to and that they are to be among those who are part of the Lamb's community. Names need to be recorded in the book of life (Rev. 13.8; 17.8; 20.12). But what this means in more concrete terms is not the Book of Revelation's main concern. *Years and Years* might be lacking in any sense that salvation must, in some sense, come from beyond. But despite its own futurism and fantasy it at least invites us to think more concretely about the choices we must make, the people we are to link up with, the groups we belong to and the political convictions we need to hold for the future to be hopeful. Revelation runs alongside *Years and Years*, then, as a text to receive and work with, and critiques the anthropocentrism of the TV series, but remains an open work as far as the question of

[11] DiTomasso, 'Apocalypticism', 321.
[12] Ibid., 318.

what, in detail, it means to live in light of the vision of the new heaven and new earth. 'Attach yourself to a church' would of itself sound a tame response, though Christians will always assume it is part of the answer.

And what of the concept of 'the world'? It is not a prominent term in Revelation. There are no sharp Pauline-type concerns about being conformed to this world (Rom. 12.2). There is no satirizing of the wisdom of this world (1 Cor. 1.20; 3.19) or binary resistance to its spirit. Like Paul, Revelation shares an awareness of this world's transience (1 Cor. 7.31) and is clearly concerned about the need to be released from the ways in which this world enslaves us (Gal. 4.3). But whether, somewhat ironically, Revelation is quite as negative about this present world (Gal. 6.14), compared to Paul, is a moot point. Unlike Paul, references to 'flesh' in Revelation carry no symbolic connotations, being brutally raw (Rev. 17.16; 19.18, 21). And the word 'body' does not appear at all in Revelation. There are no careful theological discussions to be had about Revelation's subtle uses of 'soma' and 'sarx'. Rather, Revelation's references are mostly to the 'whole world' (3.10; 12.19; 16.14) in the sense of 'all that is' or 'all that we know' or to 'the foundation of the world' (13.8; 17.8) in the sense of 'since all that we know began'. The only exception to this is Rev. 11.15: 'Then the seventh angel blew his trumpet, and there were loud voices in heaven', saying, 'The kingdom of the world has become the kingdom of our Lord and of his Messiah, and he will reign for ever and ever'.

The concern here, then, is the transformation of all that we know, something which has already been (more than?) anticipated, for it 'has become', already, 'the kingdom of our Lord and his Messiah'. Again, what this means in practice needs more unpacking. But that people should seek to live as if the new heaven and new earth have already come about seems clear. *Years and Years* is, in practice, more pessimistic than the Book of Revelation. In Muriel Lyons's words, as she agrees to pay for fast-tracked medical treatment to improve her eyesight: 'It's a terrible, terrible world, but I want to see every second of it.' This will not do for those who receive Revelation and want to do something with its content. Beyond all its wild and coded imagery it wants its hearers/readers to do something in response in a way which will change the world or, more accurately, contribute to the task of letting God change the world.

And finally, are we to look beyond this world? I have already anticipated Revelation's twofold answer to this question: 'no', for it is the kingdom of this world which has become (and will go on becoming) the kingdom of our Lord and of his Messiah; 'yes', in the sense that salvation comes from God, through Jesus/the Lamb, and we are advised not to rely on human agency alone to transform the world from its present state. Once more, what it means in practice to welcome and inhabit that path of salvation needs further exploration and explanation. It is, however, an important corrective to the 'it's all your fault' (and therefore your responsibility alone) motif from *Years and Years*. By contrast, God wants us to turn to God.

Does this qualify DiTomasso's claim – cited already – that 'Salvation in the apocalyptic mindset … is always imagined as salvation *out of* this world'?[13] It does so

---

[13] Ibid.

only in the sense that we must clarify what it means for a God who is 'out of this world' to be engaged in *this* world. Christians will go on differing from each other in the ways in which they understand God to be intervening (or not) in this world. In truth, all theists should have some notion of intervention or else they have become deists. Non-realists will have no notion of intervention other than in the form of a recognition that God language will help shape human action. Most theists in the West (even if not globally) are likely to believe that God really does influence people's actions and that their actions are more significant, and more required, than they may wish to be the case. They may even be tempted to ask 'why doesn't God *do* more?' while accepting their responsibility is so great because a risk-taking God grants considerable freedom to God's creatures.

The theological irony of *Years and Years* is that the dabbling with the quest to become pure data (explored through the characters of Edith and Bethany) and the wondering of what lies beyond physical death sharpen the scale of respect for embodied existence. Incarnation – being in flesh – is brutally real but also seems to need a sense of what is *not* flesh in order to be made sense of. God (as reality) and God (as image/concept) are both essential to enable the hopeful, future steering of what human bodies are to be and do. This is not the view of *Years and Years* but *is* the view of the Book of Revelation, which is able to see – through and beyond all its own rich and sometimes gruesome imagery – a new heaven and a new earth. Viewing the one brings this out all the more in the contemporary reading of the text of the other.

Conclusion

The simple purpose of this chapter has been to show that it is not weird or misplaced to bring the viewing of a recent piece of popular cultural entertainment alongside the reading of a biblical book. This is because many texts have similar purposes and share similar genres whether or not they may also share similar theological or philosophical outlooks. Some of my earlier work in theology and popular culture worked with the theme of 'religion-likeness'.[14] Such an approach has its limits, and I am not trying to argue here that *Years and Years* is, deep down, a religious text. I am, though, claiming five things in conclusion:

1. Without vision (and without constructing hopeful pictures of the future) the people will perish.
2. Without words of warning (including sometimes some scary pictures of the future), and even though prophecy is not simply prediction, we may be less urgent in thinking about our actions.
3. We shall struggle without communities (both as ideally conceived and existing in real, concrete forms) which work actively towards the hopeful visions we seek to live by.

---

[14] Clive Marsh, *Cinema and Sentiment: Film's Challenge to Theology* (Paternoster: Carlisle, 2004).

4. Without a sense of the limits of human capability (and why that is) we will be unable to face the truth about ourselves and about the world we live in.
5. We need saving (sometimes from ourselves – our own overambitious arrogance as a human race), but quite what shape a 'saviour' figure must take remains a work in progress, despite all that God has shown, has done and is doing in Christ.

All of these claims could be presented in a different (theological) key: we need, for example, understandings of Kingdom of God, prophecy, church, Holy Spirit, anthropology, Christology and soteriology to address the five points just raised. The Book of Revelation has elements of all these things, and an adequate theology for today must have all of these and more. *Years and Years* does not, but it is a reminder to Christian thought and practice of what it does need, and how it needs to be communicated, in the twenty-first century.

Part 3

Scripture in early Jewish and early Christian apocalyptic writings

10

The Psalms in *1 Enoch*

Susan E. Docherty

Introduction: Rationale and methodology

The central place of the Psalms in the liturgy and theology of Second Temple Judaism is well attested in the extant literature. Their ongoing significance for Jewish life, from Qumran to the Diaspora, prompted their selection as the subject of the first volume of Steve Moyise and Maarten Menken's groundbreaking series 'Israel's Scriptures in the New Testament'.[1] Moyise himself contributed a chapter on 'The Psalms in the Book of Revelation' to that collection, so it seems fitting to offer in tribute to him an investigation of their reuse within another early Jewish apocalyptic writing, *1 Enoch*. The appeal to the Psalms within this work has not received extensive scholarly attention to date, no doubt because of the greater prominence within it of other sections of the scriptures, especially the flood narratives of Genesis (e.g. 6–11; 65–68; 86–88; 106–107) and the oracles of major prophets such as Isaiah and Daniel (e.g. 39–40; 45–49; 56.5-8; 62–63). This chapter sets out to offer a focused exploration of the various kinds of intertextual connections between the Psalms and *1 Enoch*, therefore, with the aim of attaining a fuller picture of the extent of the influence of these hymns on the Enochic composers.

The analysis of the interpretation of scripture in early Jewish writings always presents considerable methodological challenges, several of which are magnified in the case of *1 Enoch*. The first particular difficulty arises from the composite nature of this work and its gradual development over approximately three centuries.[2] Later parts of the current text (e.g. the Similitudes or Parables, chapters 37–71) intentionally rework older material (especially the Book of the Watchers, chapters 1–36) so that any scriptural references detected there may have been mediated indirectly via this earlier tradition. Second, the term 'scripture' always has to be nuanced in relation to Second Temple literature, all of which was composed before the establishment of a definitive 'bible', with a stable text and a fixed list of contents. Its use is,

---

[1] Steve Moyise and Maarten J. J. Menken (eds.), *The Psalms in the New Testament* (London: Continuum, 2004).

[2] A convenient recent summary of the consensus positions on the date and provenance of the various sections of *1 Enoch* can be found in Daniel M. Gurtner, *Introducing the Pseudepigrapha of Second Temple Judaism* (Grand Rapids, MI: Baker Academic, 2020), 21–34.

however, even more anachronistic in the case of *1 Enoch*, which in part predates some scriptural books and which may well itself have been considered authoritative divine revelation by its authors and early readers.³ In some passages (e.g. 6.1-7.6; cf. Gen. 6.1-2, 4), therefore, it may reflect a knowledge of the Pentateuchal narratives in a different form. Third, the work is extant in full only in an Ethiopic (Geʻez) translation, based on a partially surviving Greek version, making it difficult to evaluate the degree to which scriptural language was reproduced verbatim in the Semitic original.

Perhaps the greatest challenge, however, is presented by the allusive way in which scripture is generally reappropriated in apocalyptic writings.⁴ Explicit citations are very rare in this genre, but scriptural phrases and motifs are extensively reused and are often combined to create a new text in a kind of mosaic or pastiche style.⁵ This method of intertextual engagement does not lend itself readily to the application of the criteria in common use for the identification of allusions, such as the 'volume' of verbal similarity or their 'thematic coherence' with the surrounding argument.⁶ This may have contributed to an underappreciation of the level of reuse of the Psalms within *1 Enoch*. Two of the standard reference works, Delamarter and Lange and Weigold, each highlight only ten definite Psalms allusions across the entire work, for instance, and just three of these are common to both lists (at 11.2; 51.4; 81.5).⁷ On the other hand, some commentaries on *1 Enoch* demonstrate an opposite tendency and record every linguistic or topical similarity with a psalm verse, however general or faint, without seeking to determine whether an intertextual reference is intended or is essential to the author's purpose.⁸ In this chapter, I will attempt first to distinguish more rigorously between a deliberate scriptural allusion and an incidental verbal correspondence or affinity in thought on the basis of three main criteria:

---

³ See especially George W. E. Nickelsburg, 'Scripture in *1 Enoch* and *1 Enoch* as Scripture', in Tord Fornberg and David Hellholm (eds), *Texts and Contexts: Biblical Texts in Their Textual and Situational Contexts. Essays in Honour of Lars Hartman* (Oslo: Scandinavian University Press, 1995), 333–54.
⁴ This is fully explored by Steve Moyise in his *The Old Testament in the Book of Revelation*, JSNTSup 115 (Sheffield: Sheffield Academic, 1995), 108–38. More recently, see Garrick V. Allen, *The Book of Revelation and Early Jewish Textual Culture*, SNTSMS 168 (Cambridge: Cambridge University Press, 2017). See also the contribution by Gert Steyn elsewhere in this volume.
⁵ The term 'pastiche' is increasingly being used to describe the reuse of scripture in apocalyptic literature; see e.g. William A. Tooman, *Gog of Magog: Reuse of Scripture and Compositional Technique in Ezekiel 38–39*, FAT 2/52 (Tübingen: Mohr Siebeck, 2011); and Michelle Fletcher, *Reading Revelation as Pastiche: Imitating the Past*, LNTS 571 (London: Bloomsbury/T&T Clark, 2017).
⁶ Almost all subsequent studies of scriptural allusions in later texts engage with the seven criteria identified in the seminal work of Richard B. Hays, *Echoes of Scripture in the Letters of Paul* (New Haven, CT: Yale University Press, 1989).
⁷ Steve Delamarter, *A Scripture Index to Charlesworth's The Old Testament Pseudepigrapha* (Sheffield: Sheffield Academic, 2002); Armin Lange and Matthias Weigold, *Biblical Quotations and Allusions in Second Temple Jewish Literature*, JAJS 5 (Göttingen: Vandenhoeck & Ruprecht, 2011), 250–1, 276–9.
⁸ For example, Matthew Black, *The Book of Enoch or 1 Enoch: A New English Edition with Commentary and Textual Notes in Consultation with James C. VanderKam*, SVTP 7 (Leiden: Brill, 1985); and R. H. Charles, *The Book of Enoch or 1 Enoch* (Oxford: Clarendon, 1912).

1. Distinctiveness – whether the phrase in question is unique to and/or particularly closely associated with one or more psalms;
2. Context – whether there are any overlaps between the wider scriptural context of the proposed allusion and its new location in *1 Enoch*;
3. Exegetical engagement – whether there is any indication that the phrase is being interpreted rather than merely reproduced.

The second part of the chapter will explore the influence of the Psalms across *1 Enoch* beyond allusions, considering, for example, their contribution to imagery and literary forms. This should provide a broad base of evidence from which some conclusions can be drawn about the place of the Psalms within the work as a whole.

Incidental echoes: General idioms and tropes

Throughout *1 Enoch*, a number of phrases or concepts appear which are paralleled in various psalms but which, on the basis of the three criteria set out earlier, are unlikely to be directly derived from them. These include theological ideas which were evidently widely held in late Second Temple Judaism and which cannot, therefore, be firmly linked to any one now-scriptural text.[9] Examples of such common tropes include the underlying cosmology of the text (17.2; 18.1-2; 41.4-5; 60.12-21; 69.17, 23; 72.1-5; cf. Pss. 7.12-13; 18.14-15; 24.2; 77.17-18; 104.9; 135.7; 136.6; cf. Gen. 1.9-10; Deut. 28.12; 2 Sam. 22.16; Job 38.22; Prov. 8.23-29; Sir. 43.14) and the references to the 'books of the living',[10] in which the names and/or deeds of the righteous are recorded in heaven (47.3; 69.17; 103.2; 104.1; 108.3, 7; cf. Pss. 24.2; 56.8; 69.28; 104.9; 136.6; 139.16; cf. Gen. 1.9-10; Exod. 32.32-33; Prov. 8.23-39; Dan. 12.1; *Jub.* 30.20; Phil. 4.3; Rev. 3.5; 13.8; 17.8; 20.12, 15; 21.7); cf. the understanding of gentile gods as demons (19.1; cf. Ps. 106.36-37; cf. Deut. 32.17; Bar. 4.7; 1 Cor. 10.20); repayment 'according to your deeds' (95.5; 110.7; cf. Ps. 62.12; cf. Prov. 24.12; *Pss. Sol.* 2.16, 34; Rom. 2.6; 2 Cor. 5.10; Rev. 20.13); and the rejoicing of the wicked over the troubles of the righteous (98.13; cf. Pss. 25.2; 35.26; 38.16; cf. Prov. 24.17; Mic. 7.8; Sir. 23.3). Similarly, some figures of speech, such as the expectation that the son of man 'will crush the teeth of the sinners' when he comes in judgement (46.4; cf. Pss. 3.7; 58.6; cf. 'the finest of the wheat', 96.5; cf. Pss. 81.17; 147.14; cf. Deut. 32.14), do not appear to represent intentional allusions to the Psalms but rather to belong to a category of 'incidental echo' of familiar or stereotyped phrases. The investigation later in the text will, therefore, concentrate only on instances of apparently more deliberate engagement with material from the Psalms.

---

[9] On this point more broadly, see Paul Foster, 'Echoes without Resonance: Critiquing Certain Aspects of Recent Scholarly Trends in the Study of the Jewish Scriptures in the New Testament', *JSNT* 38 (2015): 96–111.

[10] All quotations from *1 Enoch* are taken from George W. E. Nickelsburg and James C. VanderKam, *1 Enoch: The Hermeneia Translation* (Minneapolis, MN: Fortress, 2012); all scriptural citations follow the NRSV.

Significant allusions to the Psalms

Probable allusions

5.6-7

The Book of the Watchers opens with a series of strongly worded pronouncements of divine judgement. The final lines in this section (5.5-9) contrast the impending destruction of the sinners with the joyous salvation which will flow to the chosen faithful. These verses are clearly inspired primarily by an Isaianic oracle (Isa. 65.15-16), and they also evoke the stark choice between blessing and curse offered in Deuteronomy (Deut. 11.8-32; 27.15-28.35; 30.1-20). However, the promise that the righteous 'will inherit the earth' (5.7; cf. 38.4; 63.12) recalls also the repeated refrain of Psalm 37 (vv. 9, 11, 22, 29).[11] This allusion is likely to have been generated by the verbal and thematic correspondences between this hymn and the wider context of the underlying passage from Isaiah (esp. Isa. 65.9, 'my chosen shall inherit it'), thereby illustrating the common Jewish exegetical method of associating texts on the basis of a common word. It may also indicate that the Enochic community read this psalm as relating directly to them, identifying themselves with 'those who wait for the Lord' and with 'the meek' (Ps. 37.9, 11) who will receive the promises of future reward. A similar eschatological and applied interpretation of Psalm 37 among other early Jewish groups is attested both at Qumran (4Q171) and in the New Testament (Mt. 5.5).

17.1

The description of angels as being 'like a flaming fire' is frequently understood as an allusion to Ps. 104.4: 'you make the winds your messengers, fire and flame your ministers' (cf. *Jub.* 2.2; *4 Ezra* 8.22; Heb. 1.7).[12] There is no exact verbal agreement, and the phrase may simply reflect a general view about the non-human form of angels. However, the claim that the appeal to this verse is intentional is strengthened by the repetition of this association between angels and winds a few lines later (18.5). Employing specifically scriptural language here would also serve the author's purpose in adding legitimacy and authenticity to this account of Enoch's visionary journey.

38.1

Within the Similitudes, those who will be saved are called 'the congregation of the righteous' (38.1; cf. 45.1 in some mss.; for related terms, cf. 46.8; 53.6; 62.8). This phrase reflects the language of Ps. 1.5 (cf. Pss. 74.2; 149.1) and seems to offer a further

---

[11] As recognized in Lars Hartman, *Asking for Meaning: A Study of 1 Enoch 1-5*, ConBNT 12 (Lund: Gleerup, 1979), 32-3; and George W. E. Nickelsburg, *1 Enoch: A Commentary on the Book of 1 Enoch*, 2 vols, Hermeneia (Minneapolis, MN: Augsburg Fortress, 2001), I: 162.

[12] Delamarter, *Scripture Index*, 25; Nickelsburg, *Commentary*, I: 281.

example of the concrete reapplication of scriptural phrases within Enochic circles. Other sectarian groups in the Second Temple period also appropriated this term as a self-designation, referring to themselves as, for example, the assembly of the pious (*Pss. Sol.* 17.16), the assembly of holiness (1QS 5.20) or the congregation of the chosen ones (4Q171 ii.5).[13]

39.4-8; cf. 38.2

The eternal resting place of the righteous with God is described throughout the first of the Enochic parables in terms which echo several psalms. The Chosen One and the angels are pictured sheltering 'beneath the wings of the Lord of Spirits' (39.7; cf. Pss. 17.8; 36.7; 57.1; 61.4; 63.7; 91.4; cf. Ruth. 2.12), for example. The seer also voices the same longing to dwell with God as the Psalmist expresses for the temple (39.8; cf. Ps. 89.1-4). Although an allusion to one specific psalm cannot be detected here, the combination of these motifs does appear to be inspired by the imagery of the Psalter. Its language is, therefore, once again transferred or reapplied to the eschatological future anticipated by this interpreter and his community.

41.6

An allusion to Ps. 72.17 is seen here by some commentators in the clause 'and his name endures forever and ever'.[14] This might be considered simply a general expression of prayerful hope, but a deliberate engagement with the psalm seems plausible, given the wider contextual links between the two texts. Both verses are concerned with the praise of God, for example, and connect God's constancy with that of the sun.

48.10

The opposition of the wicked to 'the Lord of Spirits and his anointed one' appears to be an allusion to Ps. 2.2, a text which has a long history of messianic interpretation in Judaism.[15] The possible wider influence of this psalm on the construction of the Enochic son of man figure is discussed further later in the chapter.

51.4

This verse contains a verbal link to the Psalms in the reference to the mountains and hills skipping (Ps. 114.4, 6). Imagery originally used to describe the events of the exodus is applied here to the eschatological age, which will soon be inaugurated by the

---

[13] For further discussion, see Black, *1 Enoch*, 194; and Nickelsburg, *Commentary*, I: 96–97.

[14] Lange and Weigold, *Biblical Quotations and Allusions*, 250; Black, *1 Enoch*, 202. Nickelsburg (*Commentary*, II: 144) suggests a possible allusion to Ps. 19.4-5 in this verse. I consider that it reflects a general understanding of the movement of the sun through the heavens, however, rather than a specific reference to Psalm 19.

[15] This allusion is identified in Black, *1 Enoch*, 212; Charles, *Book of Enoch*, 95; Lange and Weigold, *Biblical Quotations and Allusions*, 250.

Chosen One. This interpretation rests on the assumption that God's past actions on behalf of Israel provide a template for future salvation.[16]

69.12

Among the lethal knowledge said to have been communicated to humans by the rebel angels is 'the blow that comes in the noonday heat, the son of the serpent'. Magical practices, as well as threats to life, seem to be in view in this section of *1 Enoch*. Both of these specific dangers are referred to in Psalm 91 (vv. 6, 13), a hymn which was widely understood within early Judaism as an apotropaic text (see e.g. 11Q11; *b.Sheb. 15b*; *y.Erub* 10.11).[17] This verse may provide, therefore, a further illustration of the early roots of this interpretative tradition.

71.12

Following a vision of God and the angels, the seer is depicted as prostrating himself before the divine throne and uttering blessings which were 'acceptable in the presence of the Head of Days'. This appears to be an allusion to the plea of the Psalmist: 'Let the words of my mouth and the meditation of my heart be acceptable to you, O Lord, my rock and my redeemer' (Ps. 19.14).[18] In their new context here, these words are no longer an expression of hope that God *will be* pleased with the prayers offered by the faithful but a firm declaration that Enoch's praises *have been* favourably received. This is another example, then, of a psalm text being exegeted as concretely fulfilled by the seer.

Possible but less certain allusions

1.2-3

The opening lines of the Book of the Watchers have some correspondences with Ps. 78.2-3. Like the psalm, they depict a wise man addressing the community in a parable, speaking words which were previously hidden but are now being revealed for future generations.[19] This is a literary topos not unique to the Psalms, however, and a closer verbal parallel to this section is to be found in the Balaam narrative (Num. 23.7-24.24).[20] Like the visionary in *1 Enoch*, Balaam is described specifically as having had his eyes uncovered (Num. 24.2-4, 15-16), for instance. The case for regarding these verses as an allusion to Psalm 78 is not, therefore, strong.

---

[16] This implies to me a level of underpinning exegetical activity, not simply literary artistry, *contra* Nickelsburg, *Commentary*, II: 186.
[17] For a full discussion of Psalm 91 and its early reception, see Gerrit C. Vreugdenhil, *Psalm 91 and Demonic Menace*, OtSt 77 (Leiden: Brill, 2020).
[18] So Nickelsburg, *Commentary*, 2: 327.
[19] For further supporting argument, see Hartman, *Asking for Meaning*, 23-6.
[20] This is also the conclusion of Nickelsburg, *Commentary*, I: 139.

14.8

An allusion is detected by a number of commentators here, in the reference to the seer riding on the wings of the wind during his ascent to heaven (Pss. 18.10-11; 104.3).[21] In the psalms, it is God who travels in this way, so the reapplication of this imagery to Enoch indicates the exalted status which he enjoyed in certain circles. It is not certain that this is an example of intentional exegesis, however, as the language may have been considered generally appropriate for describing how the heavenly journeys undertaken by apocalyptic visionaries were facilitated.

14.20

There is a second possible allusion to Psalm 104 (v. 2) later in this section, in the detail that God's 'apparel was like the appearance of the sun and whiter than much snow'.[22] Although other scriptural throne visions appear to have exerted a stronger influence over this passage as a whole (esp. Isa. 6.1-3; Ezek. 1.4-28; Dan. 7.9-10), this psalm does provide a further possible intertext, especially if it is echoed also at 14.8.

43.1 (cf. 69.21)

Among the many astronomical 'secrets' revealed to the seer is the naming of the stars by God (cf. Ps. 147.4).[23] This idea cannot be definitely linked to the psalm verse, however, since it is reflected elsewhere in the scriptures (Isa. 40.26; cf. Gen. 1.5) and was apparently widely held.

48.5

A possible allusion to Ps. 18.49 occurs in the expectation that 'all who dwell on earth ... will glorify and bless and sing hymns to the name of the Lord of Spirits'.[24] Nevertheless, a strong case for purposeful reuse of scripture cannot be made here, since the idea of praising God is very general and does not derive specifically or only from the Book of Psalms. The motif occurs elsewhere in *1 Enoch* (10.21), for instance, without any clear verbal connection with this psalm.

53.1

In a vision of the end times, Enoch sees the inhabitants of every nation making their way with gifts to a deep valley, the place at which divine punishment will be enacted

---

[21] Charles, *Book of Enoch*, 33; Delamarter, *Scripture Index*, 23, 25; and Nickelsburg, *Commentary*, 1: 261–2, 285.
[22] For a more detailed discussion, see Nickelsburg, *Commentary*, I: 254–6, 264; the allusion is highlighted also in Delamarter, *Scripture Index*, 25.
[23] An allusion is suggested by Black, *1 Enoch*, 203; Charles, *Book of Enoch*, 82; and Nickelsburg, *Commentary*, II: 146.
[24] Black, *1 Enoch*, 210; cf. Nickelsburg, *Commentary*, II: 172.

on the sinners. Several commentators regard this as an allusion to Ps. 72.10, in which Israel's king receives tribute from all the peoples of the world.[25] The psalm reflects traditional narratives about the wealth acquired by King Solomon from Egypt and beyond (1 Kgs 10.1-29), and the expectation that this scenario will be repeated in the future is expressed in some prophetic oracles (e.g. Isa. 45.14; Zech. 14.14). It is not a motif unique to Psalm 72, therefore, but it seems plausible that its imagery is being attached in *1 Enoch* to the figure of the Chosen One, who is named in the previous verse (52.9). This royal psalm is interpreted here, therefore, as about to receive its eschatological fulfilment in the coming of the son of man.

62.16

The motif of garments enduring or wearing out echoes the language of Ps. 102.26. The verbal parallels are not exact, and these potential correspondences are not often highlighted in commentaries. An intentional engagement with this psalm does seem possible, however, given that both texts are concerned to reassure the righteous about their continuing preservation: 'The children of your servants shall live secure; their offspring shall be established in your presence' (Ps. 102.28). The Enochic community perhaps identified themselves with these 'children of God's servants', confidently awaiting their glorious future with God and sure that their own 'garments of glory and life' will not fade.

82.3

Enoch instructs his son to pass on his wisdom to future generations, advising him that 'it will be more pleasing to them than fine food to those who eat'. This is regarded by some commentators as an allusion to those psalms which describe God's commandments as being sweeter than honey (Pss. 19.10; 119.103).[26] This idea may well have influenced the composer of *1 Enoch*, but similar language is applied to different 'goods' in other scriptural writings (Prov. 16.24; 24.13-14; Isa. 55.1-3). This appears, therefore, to be another case of an appeal to a general motif rather than a specific allusion to the Psalter.

94.10 (cf. 89.58)

The view that God rejoices at the impending downfall of the wicked is found also in Ps. 37.13 and elsewhere in the scriptures (cf. Ps. 2.4; cf. Deut. 28.63). This may not, then, reflect the influence of a specific psalm but, rather, a prevailing theological trope. Nevertheless, an allusion is possible if this verse is understood as an exegetical reading of Ps. 37.13, interpreting it eschatologically as about to reach its fulfilment in the destruction of the community's oppressors.

---

[25] Black, *1 Enoch*, 217; Lange and Weigold, *Biblical Quotations and Allusions*, 250; Nickelsburg, *Commentary*, II: 195.
[26] Black, *1 Enoch*, 254; Charles, *Book of Enoch*, 175; Delamarter, *Scripture Index*, 25.

96.8

The expectation that 'many good days will come for the righteous' is a possible allusion to Ps. 34.12.[27] Although the verbal parallels are slight, and the idea rather general, there are wider contextual links between the psalm and this section of *1 Enoch*, in the theme of future reward and judgement. This may, then, be a further example of the words of a psalm being interpreted as a promise which will be realized imminently in the concrete experience of the Enochic community.

100.5

This verse expresses the hope that the holy and righteous ones will be guarded by angels like 'the apple of the eye'. This language echoes the Psalmist's plea to God to 'Guard me as the apple of the eye' (Ps. 17.8), but the same idiom is used elsewhere in scripture to describe God's protection (Deut. 32.10; Zech. 2.8) or for the attention due to the Torah or good deeds (Prov. 7.2; Sir. 17.22) so that it may have attained a proverbial-like status.[28] On the other hand, however, it possibly does result from a more deliberate exegetical reading of the psalm, identifying the Enochic community with its pious speaker and assuming that his prayer will be fulfilled in their experience in the final judgement.

101.4-9

Similarities have been proposed between this passage and Ps. 107.23-30 in their description of the power of God over the sea and of the experience of mariners in a storm.[29] However, since these ideas occur frequently in the scriptural wisdom literature (e.g. Job 26.10-12; 38.8-11; Pss. 89.9; 104.5-9; Prov. 8.29) and were also rooted in lived experience (see Jonah 1.4-5; Acts 27.14-20), a specific allusion to the psalm seems unlikely. The influence of Jer. 5.22-24 on this section of *1 Enoch* is actually clearer,[30] because both texts rebuke the sinners who 'do not fear the Most High', despite the manifestation of divine power in creation. Nevertheless, there may be background echoes of Psalm 107 and perhaps also of the exodus psalms in the reference to the extinction of the fish: 'At his rebuke they [the waters] fear and dry up, and the fish die and all that is in it' (101.7; cf. Pss. 105.29; 106.9; cf. Isa. 50.2).

106.3, 11

According to this account of the birth of Noah, as soon as he is delivered by the midwife, 'he opened his mouth and praised the Lord'. This may simply be a stereotypical phrase

---

[27] See especially Loren T. Stuckenbruck, *1 Enoch 91-108*, CEJL (Berlin: de Gruyter, 2007), 302.
[28] This is the view of Nickelsburg (*Commentary*, I: 501); cf. Stuckenbruck, *1 Enoch 91-108*, 441; Charles (*Book of Enoch*, 361), however, appears to regard the phrase as an allusion to Ps. 17.8 and/or Deut. 32.1.
[29] Black, *1 Enoch*, 309-10; Charles, *Book of Enoch*, 252; Stuckenbruck, *1 Enoch 91-108*, 477-80.
[30] This is recognized also by Nickelsburg, *Commentary*, I: 508.

(cf. e.g. Lk. 1.64) but is possibly an allusion to Ps. 51.15, designed to present Noah in terms which emphasize his parallelism with David, the presumed speaker of all the psalms. Its use here may also have been intended to surround him with the priestly overtones present within the wider context of Psalm 51 (Ps. 51.16, 19),[31] thus further strengthening the composer's claims for a special and angel-like status for Noah (106.5-6). Drawing out connections between the leading figures in Israel's history is a technique regularly employed within early Jewish interpretation, reflecting the underlying hermeneutical axiom of scriptural coherence.

Other uses of the Psalms

Psalms as a literary or liturgical model

The extensive use of the Psalms as models for prayers and other liturgical texts within early Judaism is exemplified most clearly by the *Psalms of Solomon* and the Qumran *Hodayot*. There is some evidence of this practice within *1 Enoch*, too. Large parts of the text are composed in verse, for instance, and there is the occasional occurrence of a repeated refrain (e.g. 'from of old and forever', 69.16-21; cf. Pss. 42–43; 46; 56; 57; 67; 80; 99). The prayer of intercession in 9.4-11 displays some particular correspondences with the forms and language of the Psalter. For example, the list of sufferings that are being inflicted on humanity by the rebellious Watchers, and the appeal to God to intervene to ease them, follows a pattern common in the scriptural psalms of lament (e.g. Pss. 22; 31; 44; 56; 60; 74; 79; 80; 86; 142). Other phrases familiar from the scriptural Book of Psalms include the address 'God of gods and lord of lords' (9.4; cf. Ps. 136.2-3) and the call to bless God's name (9.4; cf. 39.9; 108.9; cf. e.g. Pss. 103.1; 113.2-3. This same prayer is reworked and attributed to Enoch later in the text (84.2-6), at which point it concludes with a specific petition that God will 'hide not your face from the prayer of your servant, O Lord' (84.6), a motif present in several psalms (Pss. 13.1; 27.8-9; 69.17; 102.2; 143.7). Direct influence of the Psalms on these passages of *1 Enoch* cannot be assumed, however, since similar themes and language are also characteristic of later Jewish petitionary prayers (e.g. Tob. 3.1-6, 11-15; Jdt. 9.1-14; Pr. Azar.; 3 Macc. 2.1-20, 6.1-15).[32] The Enochic composers may, then, have been interacting with prayer forms which had become stereotypical and which were themselves influenced by the style and language of the scriptural Psalms as well as, or rather than, these hymns themselves.[33]

---

[31] This argument is made most strongly by Stuckenbruck, *1 Enoch 91–108*, 629.
[32] For a detailed treatment of these texts, see Judith H. Newman, *Praying by the Book: The Scripturalization of Prayer in Second Temple Judaism*, EJL 14 (Atlanta, GA: SBL, 1999).
[33] For a fuller discussion of *1 En.* 9.4-11 and its relationship to other extant early Jewish prayers, see Nickelsburg, *Commentary*, I: 205–14.

Contribution of the Psalms to larger imagery

Divine theophany in the Book of the Watchers 1.4-9

As has already been observed, much of the imagery of *1 Enoch* is created through the careful interweaving of motifs and phrases drawn from a range of now-scriptural sources. This method amplifies the intertextual connections between different writings, a feature of other forms of early Jewish exegesis. A particularly intricate example of this kind of scripturally inspired pastiche is found in the vision of the divine theophany which opens the Book of the Watchers (1.4-9).[34] This section is primarily indebted to the descriptions of God's appearance from Sinai in Deut. 33.2 and Judg. 5.4-5 but contains some possible allusions to the Psalms, too. God is seen 'coming forth' from heaven (1.4) in Ps. 68.7, 17 (cf. Isa. 26.21; Mic. 1.3), for instance, and as causing the mountains to quake (1.6) in Ps. 18.7 (cf. Exod. 19.18; 1 Kgs 19.11; Isa. 40.4; Nah. 1.5; Hab. 3.6). The Psalms appear to have contributed two aspects of the imagery in *1 Enoch* in particular: first, the emphasis on God's role as a judge (1.9; cf. Pss. 96.13; 98.9; cf. Isa. 66.15-16; Jer. 25.31), and second, the motif of the mountains 'melting like wax' (1.6; cf. 52.6; Pss. 68.2; 97.5; cf. Mic. 1.4; Nah 1.5).

The 'son of man' in the Parables (chapters 37–71)

The 'son of man' who plays a central role in the eschatology of the Parables of Enoch has attracted considerable scholarly attention, not least because of the ascription of this same title to Jesus in the synoptic gospels.[35] The major scriptural inspiration for this figure is undoubtedly the account of Daniel's visions (cf. e.g. Dan. 7.9-14 and *1 En.* 46.1-5), combined with the hopes expressed within Isaianic circles for a future righteous ruler (cf. Isa. 11.1-5 and *1 En.* 49.3 and 62.2) who will be a true servant of the Lord (cf. e.g. Isa. 42.1 and *1 En.* 49.3-4; Isa. 49.1-7; and *1 En.* 48.2-7; cf. also the idea of wisdom's pre-existence, Prov. 8.22-31). The influence of Psalm 2 should not be overlooked among these more prominent intertexts, however, since the 'kings of the earth' are specifically singled out in the Parables as the opponents of 'the Lord of the Spirits and his anointed one' (48.8, 10; cf. 52.4; 53.5; cf. Ps. 2.2).[36] This allusion to the psalm serves to reinforce the royal associations of the son of man (as emphasized also in Isa. 11.1) and to offer an interpretation of it as awaiting its concrete fulfilment in the near future. The explicit identification of the son of man with Enoch at the end of the Parables (71.13-14) is also recounted in terms reminiscent of the installation of the Lord's anointed as God's son in Ps. 2.7, with its formula of direct address. The closely

---

[34] The scriptural influences on this passage are treated at length in James C. VanderKam, 'The Theophany of 1 Enoch 1:3b-7, 9', *VT* 23 (1973): 129–50; see also Hartman, *Asking for Meaning*, 22–6.

[35] For some recent studies and further bibliography, see the contributions in Gabriele Boccaccini (ed.), *Enoch and the Messiah Son of Man: Revisiting the Book of Parables* (Grand Rapids, MI: Eerdmans, 2007).

[36] Nickelsburg is particularly alert to the range of scriptural allusions underlying the Enochic 'son of man' passages; see his article 'Son of Man', in David N. Freedman (ed.), *The Anchor Bible Dictionary* (New York: Doubleday, 1992), 6: 137–50.

connected Ps. 110.1 also contributes, together with Daniel 7, to the presentation of this Chosen One as enthroned by God on a heavenly seat (45.3; 55.4; 61.8; 62.2; 69.29).[37]

Imagery of the Animal Apocalypse (chapters 85–90)

Similarly, the metaphors employed throughout this review of Israel's history derive from a complex interweaving of scriptural texts and exegetical traditions. Among the many sources of this imagery, the Psalms has its place. The enemies of the righteous are depicted zoomorphically in the Psalms, as, for instance, 'strong bulls of Bashan' (Ps. 22.12). The identification of Esau with a predatory boar (89.12) associates the Edomites with the uncleanness of swine (Lev. 11.7; Deut. 14.8), but this specific term may also have been chosen to echo the description of God's vine Israel being ravaged by 'the boar from the forest' in Ps. 80.5-13 (cf. *Jub.* 37.20).[38] This appellation reflects the view that the people of Edom played a particular role in the destruction of Jerusalem (Ps. 137.7; cf. 1 Esd. 4.45). The characterization of Israel as 'sheep' (89.12–90.38) is also widespread throughout the scriptures. That prophetic passages, especially Ezekiel 34 (cf. Isa. 53.6; Jer. 12.10; 23.1-4; 50.6; Zech. 10.3; 11.3-17; 13.7), are the strongest influences on this author's thought is demonstrated by his emphasis on the theme of the people's straying from the right way under the leadership of negligent shepherds. However, the use of this metaphor in the Psalms (Pss. 74.1; 77.20; 79.13; 95.7; 100.3; cf. 119.176), too, may be significant. The model for the 'Lord of the sheep' in particular possibly draws on the Psalmist's image of God as the 'good shepherd', as he is said to have been 'pasturing them and giving them water and grass' (89.28; cf. Ps. 23.1-2).

Conclusions

This chapter set out first to distinguish between probable allusions to the Psalms within *1 Enoch* and incidental echoes of them on the basis of the three criteria outlined in the introduction: distinctiveness, context and exegetical activity. On these grounds, nine firm allusions have been identified, and a further nine out of thirteen other possible cases also seem to warrant this classification. These eighteen allusions are clustered especially in the Parables (chapters 37–71) but are present also in the Book of the Watchers (chapters 1–36) and the Epistle of Enoch (chapters 92–105). This distribution reflects both general patterns of scriptural reuse within the corpus and the different types of writing contained with it. The Astronomical Book (chapters 72–82) draws on the scriptures more rarely than other parts of *1 Enoch*, for example, and the use of Psalms texts fits better in poetic and visionary sections than in those detailing natural phenomena. In addition to these allusions, the broader influence of the language and literary models of the Psalms can be detected across the text, in the formulation of prayers and in the development of key metaphors such as the son of man and the Lord

---

[37] On these connections, see further Nickelsburg, *Commentary*, II: 261–2, 328.
[38] On this suggestion, see further Patrick A. Tiller, *A Commentary on the Animal Apocalypse of 1 Enoch*, SBLEJL 4 (Atlanta, GA: Scholars, 1993), 274.

of the Sheep. The specific contribution of the Psalms to the creation of this imagery has sometimes been overlooked, due to the presence of more dominant intertexts, especially from the prophetic literature. This finding fits with the conclusions of Moyise, who likewise highlights several passages in the Book of Revelation in which the Psalms provide one strand within a mosaic of scripturally inspired motifs.[39]

This study also aimed to highlight some aspects of the exegetical practice of the Enochic composers. It is evident, for instance, that they eschew formal citations of scripture, a common feature of the apocalyptic genre. Although some or all of the allusions discussed here may have been intended to function as unmarked quotations, this cannot be established with certainty, given the long and complex transmission history of the text. These authors also seem to have regarded the Psalms as containing prophecies, like many of their contemporaries. Indeed, one of the features of their scriptural interpretation to have emerged most strongly from this investigation is the frequent reapplication of Psalms verses to concrete situations in the experience of the community or to the impending eschaton. This hermeneutical attitude underpins other early Jewish writings, such as the Qumran *Hodayot* and the New Testament, so would seem to merit further investigation. This chapter has hopefully, therefore, served to underscore the benefits of following the approach pioneered by Moyise and Menken of attending closely and holistically to the reception of a single scriptural source across one early Jewish text.

---

[39] Steve Moyise, 'The Psalms in the Book of Revelation', in Moyise and Menken, *Psalms in the New Testament*, 231–46 (239–45).

11

Revelation in Johannine perspective: On seeing the glory in Jn 1.14

Wendy E. S. North

Introduction

John's Gospel is a story about revelation, specifically about the revelation of God in the human life of Jesus of Nazareth. As John Ashton has reminded us, revelation was identified as the Gospel's *Grundkonzeption* by Rudolph Bultmann and, as Ashton himself observes, 'in apocalyptic, as in the Fourth Gospel, the *concept* of revelation is everywhere in evidence'.[1] Seen in these terms, Ashton's argument for John's acquaintance with one or more apocalyptic writings and with apocalyptic thinking in general has much to recommend it, especially given his point that the futuristic eschatology that is largely abandoned in John has too often been regarded as definitive of the genre.[2]

Ashton's comment on the general thrust of eschatology in John touches on an important aspect of his Gospel, which is his tendency to signal the tradition he knew while at the same time he moves to interpret it. As regards eschatology, for example, it is noticeable that while Jesus's lengthy monologue in chapter 5 begins with his claim to give life and to judge in the present (5.21-24), the argument then broadens to accommodate the eschatological future in familiar terms, in which Jesus as Son of Man will preside over the general resurrection of the dead (5.25-29). Thus, while his emphasis may rest with the present, it appears that John is well aware of conventional expectation. Indeed, in 5.27, he specifically reproduces the anarthrous form of the title 'Son of Man' (υἱὸς ἀνθρώπου), which relates directly to the apocalyptic vision in Dan. 7.13 and, moreover, is unique to John and to Revelation in the New Testament (cf.

---

[1] John Ashton, 'Intimations of Apocalyptic: Looking Back and Looking Forward', in Catrin H. Williams and Christopher Rowland (eds), *John's Gospel and Intimations of Apocalyptic* (London: Bloomsbury T&T Clark, 2013), 3–35 (7, 11); see earlier John Ashton, *Understanding the Fourth Gospel*, 2nd edn (Oxford: Oxford University Press, 2007), 2–11, 491–529; Rudolf Bultmann, *The Gospel of John: A Commentary*, trans. G. R. Beasley-Murray (Oxford: Basil Blackwell, 1971). See also, more recently, the argument that John wrote an 'apocalyptic' gospel in Benjamin E. Reynolds, *John among the Apocalypses: Jewish Apocalyptic Tradition and the 'Apocalyptic' Gospel* (Oxford: Oxford University Press, 2020).

[2] Ashton, 'Intimations', 8–9.

Rev. 1.13; 14.14).³ Note further his several references to resurrection 'at the last day' in subsequent texts (6.39, 40, 44, 54; 11.24; cf. 12.48).⁴

While his references to the eschaton may constitute a particularly notable example of this tendency, they belong together with other indicators that John knew more than he chose to foreground in his Gospel, a feature he acknowledges in his closing remarks in 20.30-31. These include occasions where John refers to events familiar from the Synoptic record but not from his own. Note, for example, his mention of the Baptist's imprisonment (3.24), Jesus's choice of 'the Twelve' (6.67, 70-71; cf. 20.24) and the agonized prayer in Gethsemane (12.27; cf. 18.11).⁵ These signals can prove to be inordinately telling in that they function to alert the reader to the tradition that undergirds John's text. His depiction of the eschaton in chapter 5, for example, has clearly been formative in his description of the raising of Lazarus in 11.43-44.⁶ Indeed, it is noticeable that his reference to Jesus's voice as a φωνὴ μεγάλη in 11.43 is a development of that imagery that again finds its equivalent in Revelation (1.10, cf. 1.12-13; 21.3). Similarly, the reference to 'the Twelve' in chapter 6 (6.66-71) is taken up again in the last supper scene, in which Jesus's choice of the betrayer is explicated in terms of his foreknowledge of events and fulfilment of scripture (13.11, 18-19; cf. v. 21). Finally also, John's passing reference to Jesus's Gethsemane prayer in 12.27 proves to be verbally linked with the profound emotional turmoil John has already attributed to Jesus in the Lazarus episode (11.33; cf. v. 38).⁷ In sum, there is much in John's story about revelation in Jesus's life to persuade us that he knew – and expected his readers to know – more than he wrote.

In view of these observations, the aim of this study is to investigate whether John's claim in 1.14 that 'we' have beheld the glory of the Father's 'only one' (μονογενής) can be identified as a passing reference to an event familiar from the Synoptic record. The argument will proceed on the assumption that John's prologue, for all its arresting qualities, remains a highly condensed introductory piece that was designed to relate to the story about to be told and so to elucidate, and be elucidated by, that story.⁸ Accordingly, while the focus of our investigation will remain on John's claim in 1.14,

---

³ Elsewhere only at Heb. 2.6, quoting Ps. 8.4. Further on Revelation's links with Daniel 7, including 7.13, see Steve Moyise, *The Old Testament in the Book of Revelation*, JSNTSup 115 (Sheffield: Sheffield Academic Press, 1995), 51-4, 56-61. On John, Daniel and Revelation, see Reynolds, *John among the Apocalypses*, 60-1; see also 167-80 on John and Revelation. For the suggestion that John was influenced by Palestinian Jewish apocalypticism, see Cornelis Bennema, 'The Sword of the Messiah and the Concept of Liberation in the Fourth Gospel', *Biblica* 86 (2005): 35-58.
⁴ For these and further indications of future eschatological expectation in John, see Reynolds, *John among the Apocalypses*, 78-9.
⁵ Note also, for example, John's general remarks about Jesus's miracle-working activity (2.23; 3.2; 6.2), his reference to Jesus's eucharistic words at the Last Supper (6.53-58), his familiarity with expectations about the Messiah (7.37, 41) and his tell-tale awareness that there was more than one woman at the empty tomb (20.2).
⁶ See further, Wendy E. Sproston North, *The Lazarus Story within the Johannine Tradition*, JSNTSup, 212 (Sheffield: Sheffield Academic Press, 2001), 99-101; Reynolds, *John among the Apocalypses*, 77.
⁷ See North, *The Lazarus Story*, 152-3.
⁸ As Jörg Frey puts it, the prologue 'provides major clues for the interpretation of the subsequent Gospel story'; see Jörg Frey, 'God's Dwelling on Earth: "Shekhina-Theology" in Revelation 21 and in the Gospel of John', in Catrin H. Williams and Christopher Rowland (eds), *John's Gospel and Intimations of Apocalyptic*, 79-103 (93).

our approach will also take account of complementary evidence available in his narrative.

Jn 1.14 and the Sinai theophany

The opening words of 1.14 are regarded by many as the climax of John's prologue.[9] Here, he declares that the Word of God from before time and the world's creation became flesh and blood and thus entered the finite human cycle of living and dying. John does not pause at this point to clarify the Christological implications of this statement, and I do not propose to add to that debate; rather, I shall adopt what Jörg Frey identifies as 'the angle of vision' here, which is John's concern to link Jesus's story in the closest possible terms with the primordial purposes of the creator God.[10] This is an important consideration, for it highlights the evidence earlier in his prologue that John has already contemplated the impact of the Word in the world. This is evident in verse 5 in his description of the light that continues to shine and also, more extensively, in verses 9–13 in which he describes the reception of the Word among humankind.[11] In this later section, John begins with a general statement about the light coming into the world and remaining unrecognized (vv. 9–10). He then specifies that he came to his own home (εἰς τὰ ἴδια) and was not received by his own people (οἱ ἴδιοι) (v. 11) before, finally, he turns his attention to those who did receive him and believe, who thereby became the children of God (vv. 12–13).

These verses are essential reading for the narrative to come, in which the Word become flesh does indeed come to his own home and his own people.[12] They are equally essential in introducing 1.14 where, with his reference to 'flesh' in all its perishable mortality (cf. Isa. 40.6-7; Sir. 14.17-18),[13] John punches home the reality that the eternal Word has arrived into history and time and then turns to situate its meaning in scripture.

Scripture in this case is a series of allusions to the Sinai theophany in Exodus 33–34 and related texts.[14] Accordingly, in 1.14b, we are informed that the Word

---

[9] So e.g. Rudolf Schnackenburg, *The Gospel According to St John*, vol. 1, trans. Kevin Smyth (Tunbridge Wells: Burns & Oates, 1990), 266.

[10] See Jörg Frey, *The Glory of the Crucified One: Christology and Theology in the Gospel of John*, trans. Wayne Coppins and Christoph Heilig (Waco, TX: Baylor University Press, 2018), 280.

[11] See the discussion on this aspect of the prologue by Ruth Sheridan in 'John's Prologue as Exegetical Narrative', in Kasper Bro Larsen (ed.), *The Gospel of John as Genre Mosaic*, SAN, 3 (Göttingen: Vandenhoeck & Ruprecht, 2015), 171–90 (177–8, 184–6). See further, Frey's comment on the structure of the prologue in 'God's Dwelling on Earth', 93–4.

[12] In fact, according to John, Jesus never treads on Gentile soil nor meets with a Gentile before Pilate. Note that John makes nothing of the identity of the official in 4.46-53 (contrast the centurion in Mt. 8.5-13; Lk. 7.2-10), nor, despite speculation (7.35), do the Greeks in 12.20 actually get to meet Jesus, who instead responds to their request by announcing the arrival of the hour of his 'glorification' (Jn 12.23).

[13] See Frey, *Glory*, 280–1.

[14] See especially the analysis in Frey, *Glory*, 282–3. On this transition in the prologue from Genesis to Exodus, see Sheridan, 'John's Prologue as Exegetical Narrative', 183–6.

'dwelt' among us, where the verb σκηνόω is deliberately evocative of the concept of God's 'tabernacling' or dwelling with his people in the Exodus narrative, and also as represented in later texts, most notably in the Wisdom tradition (Exod. 25.8; 29.45-46; Ezek. 43.7, 9; Sir. 24.8).[15] Equally evocative is his claim that 'we' – in which he allies himself with believers – 'saw his glory' (δόξα), which is consistent with Exodus references to God's glory in the 'tabernacle', where its presence was denoted by the cloud from which God spoke to Moses (24.15-18; 33.9-11; 34.5; cf. 40.34-35).[16] More specifically, however, this reference relates to Moses's request on Sinai to *see* God's glory in Exod. 33.18 and which, while direct sight was denied him, would subsequently irradiate his appearance (33.18-23; 34.29-35). Thus far, then, John's language is designed to convey to the informed reader that in the 'tabernacling' of the word 'among us' God has come home to dwell with his people Israel, and thus that the 'glory' beheld in Jesus's life by the witnessing 'we' was the glory of God as experienced in the archetypal Sinai theophany. Here also we find John drawing on concepts appropriate to the apocalyptic genre; as Frey points out, the concept of the *Shekhinah*, God's 'tabernacling' with his people, is shared by Jn 1.14 and Rev. 21.3, in which the author envisages the new Jerusalem descending from heaven. Note in particular that the verb σκηνόω is found in John and Revelation only in the New Testament (Rev. 21.3; cf. also 7.15; 12.12; 13.6).[17]

This brings us to the final and, for our purposes, key step in Jn 1.14. Here, having declared that the witnessing 'we' beheld the glory, John repeats the term δόξα and proceeds to clarify what he means by it: first, he specifies that the glory was 'proper to the Father's only one' and, second, he describes its content as 'full of grace and truth'. This second reference is again related to the Sinai theophany: John's πλήρης χάριτος καὶ ἀληθείας is a recognizable rendering of God's description of his glory as he passes Moses by in Exod. 34.6. Moreover, John will expound that phrase with specific reference to Moses and the Law in 1.16-17.[18] This leaves us with his first clarification, namely that the glory 'we' beheld was 'proper to the Father's only one' (ὡς μονογενοῦς παρὰ πατρός), which will now be the focus of our investigation.

---

[15] For detail, see John F. McHugh, *John 1-4: A Critical and Exegetical Commentary* (London: Bloomsbury T&T Clark, 2014), 54–6; also Francis J. Moloney, *The Gospel of John*, SP 4 (Collegeville, MN: Michael Glazier, 1998), 39; Frey, 'God's Dwelling on Earth', 91, 94–5; *The Glory of the Crucified One*, 275–6.

[16] See Schnackenburg, *Gospel*, 269; Frey, *Glory*, 283; Reynolds, *John among the Apocalypses*, 49.

[17] See Frey, 'God's Dwelling on Earth', 85–6, who also notes the occurrence of σκηνή in Rev. 21.3 (cf. 13.6 and 15.5).

[18] On John's expression πλήρης χάριτος καὶ ἀληθείας as a more literal translation of the Hebrew of Exod. 34.6 than the Greek of the LXX, see Barnabas Lindars, *The Gospel of John*, NCB (London: Marshall, Morgan and Scott, 1972), 95. See further, Catrin H. Williams's comment on the scriptural allusions to the Sinai theophany in this passage as a strategy of 'keying', where the Sinai event functions as the 'archetypal-theophanic model for articulating the significance of the revelation of the incarnate Word'; see 'Patriarchs and Prophets Remembered: Framing Israel's Past in the Gospel of John', in Alicia D. Myers and Bruce G. Schuchard (eds), *Abiding Words: The Use of Scripture in the Gospel of John*, SBLRBS, 81 (Atlanta, GA: SBL Press, 2015), 187–212 (194).

God's 'only' son in Jn 3.16

John's description of the Father's μονογενής in connection with glory can only be a reference to Jesus.[19] While on the one hand, he has already affirmed in 1.13 that those who believe become children of God (1.13; cf. 11.52; cf. also 1 Jn 3.1), on the other, as his Gospel proceeds John will consistently distinguish Jesus as the Son, God's special child in whom alone God's glory may be seen.[20] Significantly, also, he will take pains in what follows to develop what it means to 'see' God's glory in Jesus. In 1.14, however, John simply states the claim that believers saw the glory proper to the Father's 'only one' (μονογενής).

What is the status of this claim? Is this an anticipation of post-resurrection insight, a Spirit-inspired disclosure to the believing 'we' beyond Jesus's lifetime? Or has John referred in passing to an event that is known but not narrated in his Gospel as his point of departure – a nod to the familiar, perhaps, before his exegesis gets underway? If, as I have proposed, we explore the second option and contend that this is another of John's references to events offstage, then we shall need to begin with a closer look at μονογενής in John.

Our first example is in 1.18, where John has balanced his introduction of μονογενής in verse 14 with a further use. Having begun the verse by stating, 'No one has ever seen God' – again an echo of Moses's Sinai experience (cf. Exod. 33.20)[21] – John then refers to Jesus as 'the only one' (μονογενής) who is 'in the lap of the Father' (εἰς τὸν κόλπον τοῦ πατρός) before finally he reinforces the theophanic thrust of his argument in declaring that Jesus has made God known (ἐκεῖνος ἐξηγήσατο).[22] Note again how intimately John relates Jesus as μονογενής to God as Father.

For the remaining instances of μονογενής in John, our enquiry will move on to 3.16-21, a passage that is programmatic for the Gospel as a whole. In one respect, the reappearance of μονογενής at this point is not surprising. As John McHugh points out, the passage is thematically linked with the prologue through the concentration of vocabulary not seen since that point. He notes this with reference to 'light', 'darkness', 'world' (except for a single use in 1.29) and, in particular, μονογενής, which is common to these two passages only (3.16, 18).[23]

---

[19] Pace Lincoln, who takes John's Greek here to indicate a human comparison rather than a direct reference to Jesus as the Son; see Andrew T. Lincoln, *The Gospel According to St John*, BNTC, 4 (London: Hendrickson, 2005), 105.

[20] See Craig S. Keener, *The Gospel of John: A Commentary*, vol. 1 (Peabody, MA: Hendrickson, 2003), 416.

[21] John does not concern himself here with other references to God speaking with Moses face-to-face (see Exod. 33.11; Deut. 34.10); see Wendy E. S. North, *What John Knew and What John Wrote: A Study in John and the Synoptics*, Interpreting Johannine Literature (Lanham, MD: Lexington Books, 2020), 46; see further, Catrin H. Williams's comment on this banishment of alternatives as a function of social memory ('Patriarchs and Prophets Remembered', 195).

[22] If θεός is included in 1.18b (so NA28) it must be taken in apposition to μονογενής, so Lindars, *Gospel*, 98-9. For suggestions that θεός may not be original, see North, *What John Knew*, 65 n. 25. On John's concluding ἐκεῖνος ἐξηγήσατο, see Daniel Boyarin's point that the incarnation supplements the Torah in that the Logos become flesh is 'a better teacher, a better exegete', in 'The Gospel of the *Memra*: Jewish Binitarianism and the Prologue to John', *HTR* 94 (2001): 243-84 (284, cf. 280-1).

[23] See McHugh, *John 1-4*, 238-9, for this and further detail.

The key text for our purposes is 3.16. Generally regarded as the 'Johannine kerygma',[24] it is here that John famously describes God's gift of his 'only Son' (τὸν υἱὸν τὸν μονογενῆ) for love of the world. Note that here John brings μονογενής together with υἱός, just as he also does in his final use of the term in 3.18 (τοῦ μονογενοῦς υἱοῦ τοῦ θεοῦ). Further support for the kerygmatic status of Jn 3.16 is to be seen in the text of 1 John, whose author, regardless of any familiarity he may have with the Gospel, introduces himself to his readers as a bearer of Johannine tradition 'from the beginning' (ἀπ' ἀρχῆς) (cf. 1.1-3). In the context of the love command he has already described as ἀπ' ἀρχῆς (3.11), the author applies the same material to believers, referring to God's love revealed among them in that he sent 'his only son' – τὸν υἱὸν αὐτοῦ τὸν μονογενῆ – into the world (4.9). Note again how μονογενής and υἱός are brought together.[25]

As for the statement in Jn 3.16, this clearly has its roots in Gen. 22.2. In this text, God puts Abraham's faith to the test by instructing him to offer up Isaac as a sacrifice and underlines the magnitude of the request by describing Isaac as 'your son, your only son, whom you love'. Here, the Hebrew for 'only' is *yaḥid* יָחִיד, which the Septuagint translates with ἀγαπητός, 'beloved'.

As the story unfolds, Abraham is prevented from killing Isaac by an angel, who conveys God's word in 22.12 that Abraham has demonstrated his devotion, seeing that 'you have not withheld your son, your only son, from me', a reason repeated by God himself in 22.16. Here again, the Hebrew for 'only' is *yaḥid* (יָחִיד), which the Septuagint translates with ἀγαπητός.[26]

The influence of this Genesis text on early Christian credal formulations is not confined to the Johannine tradition. In Rom. 8.32, for example, Paul refers to God who did not 'withhold his own son' (τοῦ ἰδίου υἱοῦ οὐκ ἐφείσατο) but gave him up (παρέδωκεν αὐτόν) for the sake of believers. In this case, the reference has been influenced by the reason in Gen. 22.12, 16, but it is equally clear that Paul and John are in agreement on the relevance of the Genesis text as a means of underlining the enormity of God's sacrifice for believers and as an expression of God's unmerited love (Rom. 8.35-39; cf. also 5.8).[27]

When it comes to the version in Jn 3.16 in relation to the Septuagint, the key difference consists in the fact that when John refers to Jesus as God's 'only' son, he uses μονογενής to represent *yaḥid*, not ἀγαπητός. From an etymological point of view, μονογενής means 'one of a kind', as it combines μόνος and γένος. Nevertheless, given the context of love in 3.16a and given the scriptural backdrop of the depth of Abraham's regard for Isaac, there can be little doubt that John's use of μονογενής here is intended

---

[24] For the expression, see Frey, *Glory*, 195.
[25] For the view that both Jn 3.16 and 1 Jn 4.9 reflect tradition familiar to the Johannine community, see Frey, *Glory*, 331 with n. 88.
[26] For these and further instances where the Septuagint translates *yaḥid*, referring to a child, with ἀγαπητός, see McHugh, *John 1-4*, 99.
[27] Note also that in Col. 1.13, Paul describes Jesus as the son loved by God (τοῦ υἱοῦ τῆς ἀγάπης αὐτοῦ). On the significance of Jesus's death as coloured by the Jewish interpretative tradition that grew up around the events of the *aqedah*, or binding of Isaac, see Susan Docherty, 'New Testament Scriptural Interpretation in its Early Jewish Context', *NovT* 57 (2015): 1-19 (4).

to connote God's special affection for this particular child.[28] This compares well with Luke's use of the term to describe a parent's special regard for a child who is his or her μονογενής, where the child can be 'one of a kind' in the sense of an only child (Lk. 9.38) but can also qualify in the sense of being an only son or an only daughter who is cherished for that reason (Lk. 7.12; 8.42). This Lukan evidence also adds support to the relevance of μονογενής to Isaac in Jn 3.16, as Isaac was not Abraham's only child but was unique in that he was Sarah's son and the bearer of God's promises to Abraham and hence especially precious to his father.[29] Indeed, it seems that John was not alone in his preference for μονογενής to refer to the Genesis text. Later Greek translations by Aquila and Symmachus, for example, translate *yaḥid* with μονογενής in Gen. 22.2 and 22.12, respectively.[30] Similarly, when Josephus refers to Gen. 22.2, he describes Isaac as Abraham's μονογενής who was 'passionately beloved' – ὑπερηγάπα – of his father.[31] Finally, even closer to home, in Heb. 11.17 the author refers to Gen. 22.2 as the measure of Abraham's faith, who was ready when tested to offer up Isaac his μονογενής, who was the child of the promise.[32] These examples, largely contemporary with John, strongly suggest that there was sufficient semantic overlap for μονογενής, in the sense of a child uniquely precious to a parent, to become a translation variant for ἀγαπητός.

In sum, when John declares that God so loved the world that he gave his 'only' son (τὸν υἱὸν τὸν μονογενῆ) in 3.16, his use of μονογενής not only relates his text recognizably with Gen. 22.2 but also, by the same token, it functions to connote that Jesus, as μονογενής, was God's specially loved child. Taken in this sense, John's μονογενής is consistent with the context of God's love at the beginning of this verse (ἠγάπησεν ὁ θεὸς τὸν κόσμον), its presence here all the more telling given that it marks the first reference to love in the entire Gospel.[33] Finally, it is worth adding in this connection that while John's copious references to love will now include more instances of ἀγαπάω than in the rest of the New Testament, he *never* uses the adjective ἀγαπητός.[34] With these observations in view, we shall now return to consider John's use of μονογενής in his prologue.

---

[28] For a comprehensive discussion of the use and meaning of μονογενής with specific reference to this connotation in Johannine usage, see Keener, *Gospel*, I, 414–16. As he notes, 'In John, as in Jewish usage, the "special" son is the "beloved" son' (415).

[29] See Schnackenburg, *Gospel*, vol. 1, 270–1, on the use of μονογενής to translate *yaḥid* to mean both 'unique, only-begotten' and 'beloved'; see also J. Zumstein, *L'Évangile selon Saint Jean (1–12)*, CNT, Deuxième Série IVa (Genève: Labor et Fides, 2014), 121 n. 69, who comments on the 'lien étroit' between 'unique' and 'loved' in this verse.

[30] See Keener, *Gospel*, 415 n. 492; Schnackenburg, *Gospel*, vol. 1, 271 n. 183. For a further example of this phenomenon in John, see his use of ἐκκεντέω in his quotation of Zech. 12.10 (19.37; cf. also Rev. 1.7); see C. K. Barrett, *The Gospel According to St John: An Introduction with Commentary and Notes on the Greek Text*, 2nd edn (London: SPCK, 1978), 558–9; Lindars, *Gospel*, 590–1.

[31] See Keener, *Gospel*, 415; also McHugh, *John 1–4*, 100.

[32] See Keener, *Gospel*, 415, who describes this as 'the only theologically significant use' outside John.

[33] See McHugh, *John 1–4*, 239, who notes that this verse is also John's first statement about God since the prologue.

[34] John's text includes thirty-six instances of ἀγαπάω and seven of ἀγάπη. The same lack of the adjective is evident in 1–3 John, except in the authorial address to the readers (ἀγαπητοί in 1 Jn 2.7; 3.2, 21; 4.1, 7, 11; also ἀγαπητῷ in 3 John 1 and ἀγαπητέ in 3 John 2, 5, 11). This epistolary feature also accounts for the single instance of ἀγαπητός in Hebrews (6.9). See further, R. Morgenthaler, *Statistik des Neutestamentlichen Wortschatzes*, 3rd edn (Zürich: Gotthelf-Verlag, 1982), 67.

Seeing the glory in Jn 1.14 and the Synoptic transfiguration accounts

As we have seen, having established the fleshly reality of the Word in the world in 1.14, John's aim is to affirm that God was definitively revealed in that human life and, accordingly, he describes the presence of the Word in language that evokes the archetypal Sinai theophany. This includes the claim, 'we beheld his glory', which John then elaborates by describing the glory as appropriate to the Father's μονογενής. What we have observed of John's use of μονογενής in chapter 3, and of the status of 3.16 in particular, strongly suggests that the kerygmatic formulation in that verse, already familiar to author and audience, holds the key to interpreting his usage at this point.[35] If so, then his reference to the μονογενής παρὰ πατρός can be taken to apply to Jesus who, as the Son, was God's specially loved child.[36] Furthermore, even though it is not explicit in 1.18, this same relationship is certainly conveyed by John's description of Jesus as the μονογενής 'in the bosom of the Father' (εἰς τὸν κόλπον τοῦ πατρός),[37] as is evident from the fact that he attributes precisely the same posture towards Jesus on the part of the disciple 'whom Jesus loved' in 13.23 (ἐν τῷ κόλπῳ τοῦ Ἰησοῦ, ὃν ἠγάπα ὁ Ἰησοῦς).

If, then, John's reference in 1.14 to seeing the glory of the μονογενής, who is beloved of the Father, is a nod to an event offstage in his Gospel, the occasion in question must relate to Jesus's earthly life and also to the Sinai frame of reference established in this verse. And it follows, I suggest, that the most appropriate event, narrated in all three Synoptics but not in John, is the disciples' witness to Jesus's transfiguration (Mt. 17.1-8; Mk 9.2-8; Lk. 9.28-36; cf. also 2 Pet. 1.17-18). According to Mark, this takes place on 'a high mountain' (9.2). On seeing Moses and Elijah talking with Jesus, Peter suggests that they build three 'tents' (σκηνάς) in their honour (9.4-5) and, at the close and climax of the narrative, a cloud overshadows the disciples and God's voice from the cloud identifies Jesus as 'my beloved son' (ὁ υἱός μου ὁ ἀγαπητός) (9.7; cf. 1.11).[38] When it comes to the versions in Matthew and Luke, it quickly becomes clear that in both cases the Exodus influence in Mark has been taken up and enhanced. Thus, for example, both emphasize the radiance of Jesus's appearance with particular reference to his face (Mt. 17.2; Lk. 9.29), a reminiscence of Moses's post-Sinai appearance (Exod. 34.29-30). Meanwhile, Luke, who has followed Mark's lead in prefacing the episode with a reference to the future return of the Son of Man in glory (Lk. 9.26; cf. Mk 8.38),

---

[35] See Lindars, *Gospel*, 159.
[36] See especially Keener, who compares Wis. 7.22 here to affirm that Jesus as μονογενής is the 'unique and special object of divine love' (*Gospel*, 416).
[37] As John Ashton comments, the image demanded by the Greek is 'of a father hugging a greatly loved son to his chest', in 'Really a Prologue?', in Christopher Rowland and Catrin H. Williams (eds), *Discovering John: Essays by John Ashton* (Eugene, OR: Cascade Books, 2020), 64-83 (83). For the expression used of God's parental care of Israel, see Schnackenburg, *Gospel*, 280-1.
[38] Matthew adds 'with whom I am well pleased' in 17.5 (so also 2 Pet. 1.17), while Luke prefers 'chosen' (ἐκλελεγμένος) instead of 'beloved' in 9.35. Note further that the third and final instance of ἀγαπητός in Mark is in connection with υἱός in the parable of the vineyard in 12.1-9, where it is clear that the father's 'beloved' son is uniquely the heir (12.6, 7).

twice introduces the word 'glory' into the scene itself. First, in 9.31, he reports that Moses and Elijah appeared with Jesus 'in glory' (ἐν δόξῃ) and, second, in 9.32, he specifically declares that the disciples 'saw his glory' – εἶδαν τὴν δόξαν αὐτοῦ – thereby creating a direct link with the narrative of the Sinai theophany (Exod. 33.18, 22) and, in so doing, articulating a remarkably similar claim to John's ἐθεασάμεθα τὴν δόξαν αὐτοῦ in 1.14.

In conclusion, the aim of this study has been to propose that John's claim in 1.14 that believers have seen the glory of the Father's 'only one' (μονογενής) constitutes a passing reference to the occasion of Jesus's transfiguration narrated in the Synoptics. Taking into account John's familiarity with the apocalyptic visionary tradition and also his tendency to refer in passing to known events, the argument has focused on John's use of the term μονογενής not only in his prologue but also in the kerygmatic 3.16. On this basis, it has proved possible to identify John's reference in 1.14 as a nod to the disciples' revelatory vision according to the Synoptic accounts, in which Luke reports that they saw Jesus's glory and, in Matthew and Mark, God's voice from the cloud declares that Jesus is his 'beloved' – ἀγαπητός or, as John puts it, μονογενής – Son.

12

The identity and destiny of 'all Israel' in Paul's apocalyptic imagination: Revisiting Rom. 11.26

B. J. Oropeza

Not many scholars today doubt that the Apostle Paul was an apocalyptic thinker.[1] He speaks of his own calling and message as revelation (Gal. 1.11-12, 15-16; Rom. 1.17a). He also speaks about his own heavenly ascension (2 Cor. 12.1-9), about struggles with Satan and evil spirits (1 Thess. 2.18; 2 Cor. 2.10-11; 12.7), about sin and death as cosmic forces (Romans 6), and he anticipates future bodily resurrection (1 Cor. 15.12-58), final judgement (2 Cor. 5.10; Rom. 2.16) and the Parousia of Jesus as reigning Messiah (1 Thess. 4.13-17; 1 Cor. 15.20-28). Likewise, he considers the present age as evil and temporal in contrast with the new creation and coming age that is permanent (Gal. 1.4; 1 Cor. 2.6; 3.18; 7.31; 10.11; 15.24-26, 50-55; 2 Cor. 5.17; Rom. 8.18-23; cf. Eph. 1.21). What is not so clear is the role Israel plays in Paul's apocalyptic vision. On the one hand, a judgement of obduracy has fallen on Israel for rejecting Christ, and Paul grieves over Israel's present condition (Rom. 11.7-10; cf. 9.1-3, 30-33; 10.1). On the other hand, Paul anticipates that 'all Israel' will be saved (11.26).[2] This happens after the 'fullness' of the gentiles takes place (11.25).[3] What is the identity of 'all Israel' and when will Israel be saved?

At least several interpretations are possible for identifying 'all Israel', but the two most prominent perspectives in recent years are the so-called eschatological and ecclesiological viewpoints.[4] The first one interprets Israel as ethnic Jews and Israelites

[1] I write this after attending a conference hosted by the Enoch Seminar entitled, 'Was Paul an Apocalyptic Jew?' (25–27 October 2021; University of Michigan). The implied conclusion is a resounding 'yes'.
[2] 1 Thess. 2.14-16 is not really counterevidence. Here judgement seems limited to persecutors in Judea and is not necessarily eternal (2.16: εἰς τέλος may be translated as 'at last' rather than 'forever': cf. T.Lev. 6.11. Alternatively, if translated as 'to the end', this may refer to the Parousia event discussed later in this essay).
[3] In 11.26 καὶ οὕτως can be modal, temporal or both; the events in any case are contextually sequential.
[4] For surveys and evaluations on all the major perspectives, see recently, John K. Goodrich, '"Until the Fullness of the Gentiles Comes In": A Critical Review of Recent Scholarship on the Salvation of "All Israel" (Romans 11:26)', JSPL 6 (2016): 5–32; Eckhard J. Schnabel, Der Brief des Paulus an die Römer (Witten: SCM R.Brockhaus, 2016), 2:500–9; Sarah Whittle, Covenant Renewal and the Consecration of the Gentiles in Romans, SNTMS 161 (Cambridge: Cambridge University Press, 2014), 58–72; Christopher Zoccali, Whom God Has Called: The Relationship of Church and Israel in Pauline Interpretation, 1920 to the Present (Eugene, OR: Pickwick, 2010); Christopher Zoccali, '"And So All Israel Will Be Saved": Competing Interpretations of Romans 11.26 in Pauline Scholarship',

who will be saved *en masse* in the future, normally at or right before the second coming of Christ.[5] The second perspective interprets 'Israel' as all of God's people, both Jews and gentiles, and their salvation is not normally tied in with the Parousia.[6] This position is argued most forcefully by N. T. Wright. My task in this study will be to assess Wright's arguments and his critique of the eschatological perspective. Then I will present what I consider to be the strengths of the eschatological view. Along the way I hope to add some fresh insights; it will turn out that Paul's interpretation of Israel's scriptures, along with his end-time forecast in 2 Thessalonians 2, weigh in to support the position.

The ecclesiological view of N. T. Wright: 'All Israel' as believing Jews and Gentiles

Tom Wright's most thorough and recent treatment of Rom. 9–11 is in *Paul and the Faithfulness of God*.[7] His structural outline of Romans 11 starts with 11.13-15 as the centre, and then it moves outward in a centrifugal pattern to 11.11-12, 11.16-24, 11.1-10 and then 11.25-32.[8]

In 11.13-15, Paul celebrates his gentile ministry with the hope of making Israel jealous and saving some of them, based on Deut. 32.21 (quoted in Rom. 10.19). In Romans 10 Israel failed to submit to God's righteousness and refused to believe

---

JSNT 30 (2008): 289–318; A. Andrew Das, *Solving the Romans Debate* (Minneapolis, MN: Fortress, 2007), 235–60. Space does not permit critiques of the other viewpoints. For the *Sonderweg* or two-covenant view and its critique, see Zoccali and Schnabel. For the Roman mission view (Mark Nanos) and its critique, see Zoccali. For Israel as the elect remnant, see Zoccali, and for critiques, Goodrich, Das and Schnabel. For more on the ecclesiological view, see Schnabel and critiques by Das, Goodrich and Zoccali. For more on the eschatological view, see Goodrich and critiques by Zoccali and Schnabel. Further positions and critiques on the eschatological and elect remnant views are found in Jared Compton and Andrew David Naselli (eds), *Three Views on Israel and the Church: Perspectives on Romans 9–11* (Grand Rapids, MI: Kregel Academic, 2018).

[5] See recently, e.g. Scott Hafemann, *Paul: Servant of the New Covenant*, WUNT 435 (Tübingen: Mohr Siebeck, 2019), 257–66; Douglas J. Moo, *The Letter to the Romans*, NICNT, 2nd edn (Grand Rapids, MI: Eerdmans, 2018), 734–41; Richard N. Longenecker, *The Epistle to the Romans*, NIGTC (Grand Rapids, MI: Eerdmans, 2016), 894–900; John M. G. Barclay, *Paul and the Gift* (Grand Rapids, MI: Eerdmans, 2015), 554–5; B. J. Oropeza, *Jews, Gentiles, and the Opponents of Paul* (Eugene, OR: Cascade, 2012), 191–9. Also, Goodrich, 'Fullness'.

[6] Recently, see e.g. Stanley E. Porter, *The Letter to the Romans*, NTM 37 (Sheffield: Sheffield Phoenix, 2015), 217; Rafael Rodriguez, *If You Call Yourself a Jew: Reappraising Paul's Letter to the Romans* (Eugene, OR: Cascade, 2014), 226; Joshua D. Garroway, *Paul's Gentile-Jews: Neither Jew Nor Gentile, but Both* (New York: Palgrave Macmillan, 2012), 140–9; Dongsu Kim, 'Reading Paul's καὶ οὕτως πᾶς Ἰσραὴλ σωθήσεται (Rom. 11:26a) in the Context of Romans', *CTJ* 45 (2010): 317–34; Bruce D. Chilton, *Rabbi Paul: An Intellectual Biography* (New York: Doubleday, 2004), 234. Also, Schnabel, *Römer*, 2:505–9.

[7] COQG 4 (Minneapolis, MN: Fortress, 2013), 1195–1256; henceforth, *PFG*. For earlier treatments, see N. T. Wright, *The Climax of the Covenant: Christ and the Law in Pauline Theology* (Edinburgh: T&T Clark, 1991), 231–67; N. T. Wright, 'Romans and the Theology of Paul', in David M. Hay and E. Elizabeth Johnson (eds), *Romans*, vol. 3 of *Pauline Theology* (Minneapolis, MN: Fortress, 1995), 56–62; N. T. Wright, 'Romans', in Leander Keck (ed.), *The New Interpreter's Bible Commentary* (Nashville, TN: Abingdon, 2002), 9:317–664 (589–95).

[8] *PFG*, 1197.

the good news about the Messiah. God will thus bring in a 'no-nation' (interpreted as gentiles) whom God will allow to share the covenants, sonship, glory and other privileges once exclusively Israel's (cf. 9.4-5). This will thus provoke Israel to jealousy and 'make Israel itself realize the result of turning away from God'.[9]

Israel's acceptance (referring to its reception after being cast away) means 'life from the dead' (11.15), which for Wright does not refer to a futuristic general resurrection but to baptism. The effect of baptism is that one dies to sin and is raised alive to God (Rom. 6.4, 11; cf. 4.17; Gal. 2.19-20).[10] Paul is speaking of Israelites at this present time that are provoked to jealousy on account of Paul's gentile mission. 'Some' of these Israelites will be saved by believing in Jesus Christ and getting baptized (cf. 1 Cor. 9.19-22). Wright adds,

> How will God *save* them? According to 10.2–13, he will do it by renewing the covenant, as foretold by Moses himself in Deuteronomy 30, a passage drawn on by other second-Temple Jews for exactly this purpose. Paul's interpretation of it is that the covenant is renewed in and for those who confess that Jesus is lord and believe that God raised him from the dead.[11]

In 11.11-12, God works through Israel's turning away to save the world. In this manner, according to Wright, Israel acts out both Adamic trespass and Messianic death and resurrection.[12] For Wright, the Israelites' 'fullness' (πλήρωμα) mentioned in 11.12 is unclear, though Paul is not making predictions about saving a multitude of Israelites at the second coming. Rather, his saving 'some' of them will count as this fullness, the 'full extension' of the small, saved remnant of Israel to which he himself belongs.[13] The remnant will become 'very much larger' if it is to move towards fullness.[14]

In 11.16-24, Wright understands the agricultural imagery of 'firstfruits' in 11.16 as both Messiah and the remnant, whereas the 'lump' is the unbelieving/hardened portion of Israel. The branches in the olive tree are also the remnant, whereas the broken branches are the unbelieving Jews.[15] Jeremiah 11.1-8, 14-19 'resonates closely' with Paul's words. Israel was once described as a green olive tree bearing good fruit, but now its branches will be consumed due to evil practices, and covenant curses echoing Deut. 27.26 are brought on the people.[16]

Paul's olive tree picks up where the prophet left off; the ripped off branches are not the last word. The tree itself is a metaphor for Israel and is, according to Wright, a '*single* family; a family rooted in the patriarchs and the promises God made to them; a family from which, strangely, many "natural branches" have been broken off, but into which many "unnatural branches" have been grafted in'.[17] This engrafting of the

---

[9] Ibid., 1202.
[10] Ibid., 1199–1200.
[11] Ibid., 1201.
[12] Ibid., 1207–9.
[13] Ibid., 1209.
[14] Ibid., 1239.
[15] Ibid., 1212–13.
[16] Ibid., 1215–16 (quote from 1215).
[17] Ibid., 1213–14. All italics in quotes are original.

unnatural branches, the gentiles, incorporates them into *Israel*. Even so, the broken-off branches, hardened Jews, have not been replaced; God is not through with them but 'will undoubtedly want to bring plenty more to faith, too'.[18] They could be re-engrafted into the tree if they believe in Christ according to Rom. 10.6–13. This re-engrafting for Wright refers to saving them through jealousy (11.14), not a last-minute massive re-entry related to the Parousia.

In 11.1–10, Wright observes the distinction between the elect 'remnant' of Israel and 'the rest' of Israel who are hardened in 11.7, interpreting this verse in light of 9.6b: 'not all who are of Israel are Israel'. The elect are the second Israel in that phrase,[19] and God hardens the rest along with those who 'persist in holding God's saving purpose at bay'.[20] In 11.8-10 Paul quotes from Deut. 29.3[4], Isa. 29.10 and Ps. 68.23-24 (LXX), which speak of being stupefied and spiritual blindness. Wright translates διὰ παντός from the Psalm as 'for ever', though he suggests that we do not read too much into this since anyone in the blinded condition of Deuteronomy 29 can move over to Deuteronomy 30 (choosing life and covenant renewal) as described in Rom. 10.6-10.[21] Nevertheless, if Paul wanted to affirm that the hardened condition of the 'rest' was not too bad since it would only be temporary (until the Parousia), then 'he has gone about it in a very strange way'.[22]

In 11.25-32, Wright sees the 'mystery' of 11.25 not as a new revelation but as '*the entire sequence of thought from 11.11 onwards*' that builds on the argument since 9.6 and includes 11.25-27.[23] Although 'until' is a temporal marker for the phrase, 'the fullness of the nations comes in', this word cannot 'tell us what happens to the "hardened" part of Israel once that time is reached'.[24] Scholars assume that Israel's hardening will then be over even though Paul does not actually say this. Rather, for Wright, hardening has to do with God's forbearance, and the alternative of delayed judgement is swift punishment. Paul does not say what will happen to those who do not take that space of opportunity to repent and believe, but 9.1-5, 10.1 and 11.7-10 clue us in. This hardening 'will eventually give way to final judgement'.[25] Also in 11.25, the gentiles 'coming in' refers again to their entrance into the olive tree of Israel. When that fullness is reached, this will cause a '*much greater number of those presently "hardened" to become "jealous" and to swell the present small "remnant" to a fullness out of all proportion to its present diminution*'.[26] Wright affirms a 'hugely increased "remnant", through jealousy/faith'[27] will be saved.

Whereas others interpret 'Israel' in 11.25 as ethnic, Wright suggests instead that Israel here consists of the entire people of God inclusive of Jews presently hardened and the incorporated gentiles. 'All Israel' in 11.26, then, 'must reflect that double

---

[18] Ibid., 1212.
[19] Ibid., 1225.
[20] Ibid., 1227.
[21] Ibid., 1228-9; cf. Wright, *Romans*, 678.
[22] *PFG*, 1228.
[23] Ibid., 1233.
[24] Ibid., 1237.
[25] Ibid., 1239.
[26] Ibid., 1243.
[27] Ibid., 1244.

existence'.²⁸ 'All Israel' thus includes believing gentiles. In the OT quotes from 11.26b-27 the deliverer from Zion establishes a covenant with Jacob 'when' (ὅταν) he takes away the people's sins (cf. Isa. 59.20; 27.9; Jer. 31[38].33). Wright opts instead to translate ὅταν as '*whenever* I take away their sins'. This refers not to a unique futuristic event but something indefinite: 'at whatever time, however frequently repeated, people "turn to the lord"'.²⁹ He also believes that the third 'now' (νῦν) in 11.30-31 is not a scribal insertion but originally from Paul.³⁰ This means that mercy given to Israel is something that is happening in the present; it is not locked to a future event, and thus it pertains to those saved through jealousy (11.14).³¹

Assessing N. T. Wright's interpretation

Although Wright's ecclesiological view is formidable, I do find some weaknesses with it (sorry, Tom!). I now address these according to the same text order he presents.

Regarding Wright's view that 11.13-15 is central to Paul's message, it seems to me that when one follows the trajectory of Romans 9–11 the more natural climactic point turns out to be in 11.26 with all Israel being saved. Its importance is emphasized by the composite quote from scripture that immediately follows; Paul often quotes scripture when wanting to emphasize a point (see e.g. Rom. 1.16-17/Hab. 2.4). Another high point would seem to be when Paul states in 11.32 that God's mercy is for all Jews and gentiles. These verses seem to refer back to and repair the bifurcation of Israel in the thesis of 9.6, which is recalled in 11.7. Namely, the statement 'not all Israel are Israel' is disclosed as a distinction between the 'remnant' and the 'rest' of Israel. It is in 11.25-27 that both the remnant and the rest appear to be once again united as a totality, which suggests 11.25-32 is more properly central to Romans 11 as the climax to this entire section of the letter.

In 11.12 the 'fullness' of Israel would seem to correspond with the 'fullness' of the gentiles in 11.25; both may refer to the respective peoples' collective totality. This language corresponds with the 'all' of 11.32, inclusive of gentiles as 'you' and Israelites as 'they' in 11.30-31. The unqualified 'they' (αὐτοί) for the rest of Israel does not correspond well with Paul's mitigated 'some' that his gentile ministry might save in 11.14. The construction of εἴ + πως + subjunctive or future verb in v. 14 is to be understood as a hesitant expectation. 'if somehow', 'in hope that perhaps', 'whether by any means' or 'possibly' (cf. Rom. 1.10; 1 Cor. 9.27; 2 Cor. 2.7; 9.4; Phil. 3.11).³² Differently, what Paul claims in 11.26 and 11.30-32 is a more assured salvation and mercy involving 'all' (πᾶς), not just 'some' (τινές), of Israel. The tentative 'some' seems

---

[28] Ibid.
[29] Ibid., 1251.
[30] The third 'now' is present in e.g. NRSV, ESV, but missing in ISV, NKJV. NA²⁸ places it tentatively in brackets.
[31] *PFG*, 1252–3.
[32] See John D. Harvey, *Romans*, EGGNT (Nashville, TN: B&H Academic, 2017), 275; Max Zerwick and Mary Grosvenor, *A Grammatical Analysis of the Greek New Testament* (Rome: Biblical Institute, 1974), 484.

to stand at odds with Wright's other claims that the number is 'out of all proportion' and that a 'much greater number' of hardened Israel will become part of the remnant. Wright wants to affirm that 'fullness' (11.12), 'some of them' (11.14) and 'all Israel' all refer to the same salvific thing for Israel.[33] But there is a basic problem here – 'some' plainly does not mean 'all' or 'fullness'.

Regarding the olive tree in 11.16-24, Paul never identifies it as 'Israel'; otherwise, the severed branches could not be 'Israel' in 11.11. They remain identified as wild olive branches rather than the natural branches, and so their distinction from the Israelite branches is maintained. To be sure, the olive tree's roots may be identified as the patriarchs, and the gentiles/nations are promised as offspring of Abraham by faith (Romans 4), but they remain *the nations* without being named 'Israel'. In fact, nowhere in Romans 9–11, nor the entire letter, nor arguably in the entire Pauline corpus, do gentiles ever take on the name 'Israel'.[34]

In 11.10 διὰ παντός is best translated 'continually' or 'always' (non-intermittent) rather than 'forever' (cf. 2 Thess. 2.16; Heb. 2.15; Acts 2.25; 24.16). This distinction may be seen through the continual (διὰ παντός) torment of the demoniac *until* Jesus heals him (Mk 5.5), and the disciples were continually (διὰ παντός) in the temple up to the Day of Pentecost (Lk. 24.53; cf. Acts 1–2). Clearly, groups and individuals in this type of continuity need not remain in that condition forever. This is also the case with hardened Israel.

Several points are worth making regarding 11.25-32. First, 'I don't want you ignorant' suggests that the 'mystery' is something they did not previously know (11.25).[35] The mystery is not best explained, then, by the content from 11.11 onwards. It seems better centred on gentile fullness preceding the 'rest' of Israel's salvation.

Second, it is highly questionable that the 'coming in' of these gentiles refers to their being engrafted into the olive tree. We might expect Paul in this case to use ἐγκεντρίζω again as he does repeatedly in 11.17-24 instead of εἰσέρχομαι. Their being engrafted, moreover, is in the passive voice (11.17, 19, 23a, 24) with God as the subject (11.23b).

---

[33] PFG, 1245–6.

[34] A popular view for scholars is to argue that 'the Israel of God' in Gal. 6.16 includes gentiles, but this is far from clear, especially given that the salutation contains conventional elements of ancient Jewish epistles: 'mercy', 'peace' and a salutation to Israel (see examples in Lutz Doering, *Ancient Jewish Letters and the Beginnings of Christian Epistolography*, WUNT 298 (Tübingen: Mohr-Siebeck, 2012), 207, 412–13, 427, 451, 489–90). Against the gentile view, see Susan G. Eastman, 'Israel and the Mercy of God: A Re-Reading of Galatians 6.16 and Romans 9–11', NTS 56 (2010): 367–95; A. Andrew Das, 'Galatians 6:16's Riddles and Isaiah 54:10's Contribution: Gentiles Joining the Israel of God?', in A. Andrew Das and B. J. Oropeza (eds), *Scripture, Texts, and Tracings in Galatians and 1 Thessalonians* (Lanham, MD: Fortress Academic), forthcoming. Das, *Solving the Romans Debates*, 244, argues that had Paul wanted to equate the Church with 'Israel of God', he should have omitted the second καὶ in 6.16. Even if for the sake of argument we assume Gal. 6.16 implies gentiles, 'the Israel of God' is not the same phrase as 'all Israel', and context, not usage, is decisive for its interpretation. Considering gentile converts as members of a '*christologically redefined Israel*' (italics in the original), Terence L. Donaldson, *Paul and the Gentiles* (Minneapolis, MN: Fortress, 1997), 236–8, supports this claim with Phil. 3.3; Col. 2.11–13; 1 Cor. 10.1; Gal. 6.16; Rom. 11.17-24 and gentile inclusion into Abraham's family (Galatians 3; Romans 4). But the gentiles as part of Abraham's family, along with privileges and adoption pertaining to it, are not the same thing as gentiles being called 'Israel'. Again, we must resort to context as decisive for Rom. 11.26.

[35] Rightly, Goodrich, 'Fullness', 8.

Differently, the active εἰσέλθῃ in 11.25 suggests that the gentiles themselves are doing the action of coming in. That is because their destination has Zion as its object, not the olive tree, as 11.26b-27 clarifies.

Third, it hardly makes good sense for Paul to write about Israel in clearly ethnic terms and then suddenly have gentiles included as 'Israel' in 11.25-26. Would Paul's auditors readily comprehend that the word 'gentiles' refers both to gentiles *and* Israel in these verses? Paul nowhere in this context gives them a clear signal of such double use. Rather, every other time 'Israel' or 'Israelite' appears in this discourse, it refers to ethnic Israel (9.4, 6, 27, 31; 10.19, 21; 11.1, 2, 7, 11), even in 9.6 which is explained in 11.7. Paul's Roman auditors seem to have no other recourse, then, but to think that this same sense is used for Israel in 11.25-26. This sense is confirmed once again in 11.26b when Paul's quote from Isa. 59.20 uses 'Jacob' to identify Israel. In Isaiah, Jacob represents *Israel*, not Israel and the nations. Paul himself refers to Jacob this same way earlier in the text (Rom. 9.10-13).

Fourth, given that the third νῦν in 11.30-31 is omitted in Alexandrian, Western, Byzantine and mixed textual families inclusive of the oldest single witness (p⁴⁶), I personally think a copyist included it.[36] But even if we suppose that this third νῦν were original, these verses do not nullify the claim that gentiles already have received this mercy, and Israel's reception of mercy seems to be after the gentiles' mercy.[37] Perhaps it would imply Paul's belief that the fullness of the gentiles and Parousia is imminent (cf. Rom. 13.11-12; 1 Cor. 7.29-31). He believed himself to be living towards the end of salvific history, and the closing period of this history is the 'now' era.[38] As his gospel ministry will finally reach Spain, he may have surmised that the 'fullness' of the gentiles was all the more imminent (15.19b-29). Alternatively, or in addition, perhaps Israel's reception of mercy would be considered both 'now' (11.14) and 'not yet' (11.26).

Wright's criticisms of the eschatological view

Wright also points out some major weaknesses regarding the eschatological view, to which I now respond.

First, for Wright, the *present* gentile mission that makes Jews jealous and saves some of them, along with Paul's warning that gentiles should not boast against Jews (since God could re-engraft them in based on 10.6-13), militates against a 'last-minute' deliverance of Jews. Wright argues that it makes no sense for Paul to say, 'In effect, that in point of fact no Jews will come to faith until the *parousia*. How would that support his warning and exhortation? It would allow Christian gentiles in Rome to shrug their shoulders, to turn their backs on Jews for the present – which is the very opposite of what Paul is so eager to stress.'[39] But the eschatological viewpoint is not denying the

---

[36] See mss. evidence in Longenecker, *Romans*, 872.
[37] See further Das, *Solving the Romans Debate*, 240–1; Goodrich, 'Fullness', 26–7.
[38] See Frank Thielman, *Romans*, ZECNT (Grand Rapids, MI: Zondervan, 2018), 551.
[39] *PFG*, 1222.

present salvation for some Jews. Paul hopes that some will be presently saved (11.14) *and* that more will be saved in the future (11.26).

Second, Wright asks why Paul is in anguish over Israel (9.1-3; 10.1) if, according to the eschatological view, Israel is going to be saved by a new divine act. If so, 'Paul ought really to have told Tertius his scribe, to throw away these three chapters and start again'.[40] In response, perhaps even though Paul hopes by using the language of imminence for this salvific event, he does not actually know with certainty when this deliverance will take place. Meanwhile, he and his colleagues experience opposition and potential hardships from his compatriots (e.g. 2 Cor. 11.24). These things alone would seem to warrant his anguish and prayers for their salvation, but beyond this, he may have feared that some of them might die in their fallen state before the Parousia would take place.

Third, related to the second point, Wright asks regarding this position, 'What about those who had died in the meantime?'[41] The fullness of the gentiles and Parousia have not taken place, and it has now been almost two thousand years. This is surely a problem, and one wonders whether Paul would have said things differently had he known how long the delay would have lasted.[42] Goodrich responds that 'God's restorative promises were never intended to be enjoyed by every generation of Israel', and the centuries of Jews who lacked such restoration between the prophets and Paul demonstrate this.[43] While this is true, a couple of millennia between Paul and *now* is quite a lot longer wait! It is tempting to side with scholars who opt for a diachronic, not just synchronic, salvation of Israel at the event. But ultimately, we must ask what a just and merciful God might do, hope the amount of 'some' who might presently be saved is a large 'some' and concede to mystery. Paul expresses this himself with his doxology that God's ways are past finding out (11.33-36). Nevertheless, Wright's position is also vulnerable to the same problem since he affirms that a 'very much larger', 'hugely increased' number of the hardened Jews are to be saved on account of the fullness of the gentiles. Has *that* happened in salvation history? Whether 'all Israel' or a 'very much larger' number will be saved, we all must struggle with the long delay.

Fourth and finally, Wright asks how this view escapes arbitrariness (and even coercion if automatic) if all Jews are to be 'converted as Paul had been by a sudden revelation of Jesus'.[44] Scholars from the eschatological position, however, normally affirm that Israel will in fact trust in Christ at that event. If it happens in a way similar to Paul's Damascus experience, this still requires trust and obedience, even as Paul believed and was baptized (Acts 9; Gal 1.15-17). Nothing suggests that Paul could not have said 'no' and reject both his calling and the revelation of Christ. If the religious leaders who rejected Christ and his miracles are an example here, seeing is not necessarily believing if one is not willing to obey (e.g. Mk 3.1-6; Mt. 12.22-32; Lk. 16.29-31).

---

[40] Ibid., 1238.
[41] Ibid., 1245.
[42] E. P. Sanders, 'Paul's Attitude toward the Jewish People', *USQR* 33 (1978): 175–87 (185), raises a similar point.
[43] Goodrich, 'Fullness', 11.
[44] *PFG*, 1245–6.

What might compel Israel to trust in Christ voluntarily at or near the Parousia? If 2 Thessalonians is written by Paul – and I and many other scholars believe that it is – the reason can be readily adduced.[45] Paul believes the 'man of lawlessness' will sit in Jerusalem's temple and present himself as God (2 Thess. 2.2-4).[46] This ultimate form of idolatry would doubtless bring on tribulation for the Judeans who refuse to worship him. But Paul also believes that when Christ returns he will defeat this man and his satanic power (2 Thess. 2.7-8; cf. 1.5-10). Israel will thus be delivered by Christ. It is not too difficult to surmise that Paul anticipates a large number of Israelites willingly accepting Jesus as their Messiah due to these events. Just about a decade and a half earlier a horrible incident like this nearly came to fruition when Emperor Caligula tried to set up an image of himself in that very temple (Josephus *Ant.* 18.257-309). Paul and early Christ followers apparently believed another incident like this would succeed where Caligula's attempt failed. Such an event coincides with a prophecy attributed to Jesus in Mt. 24.15-22 and Mk 13.14-20, and Paul seems to know an oral version of this 'Little Apocalypse' when mentioning a 'thief in the night' in relation to the Parousia (1 Thess. 5.1-3/Mt. 24.43-44). Other early Christ traditions likewise seem to anticipate a restoration of Israel connected with fulfilment of the gentiles' era (Lk. 21.24), the Parousia (Mt. 23.39) or Christ's kingdom reign in the age to come (Mt. 19.28; Acts 1.6-7; cf. Lk. 1.32-33).[47]

Strengths of the eschatological view

Now that we have explored the eschatological view's potential weaknesses, some of its strengths are as follows.

First, what prompts Paul's writing of Romans 9–11 is his insistence that nothing can separate the elect in Christ from God's love (Rom. 8.28-39; cf. 11.2). The implied retort from his interlocutor would be, 'But what about Israel? Are they not God's elect? Yet they are separated from God's love in Christ!' Paul thus assures his audience that God's promises have not failed (9.6), God has not finally forsaken Israel (11.1-2, 11) and all Israel will be saved (11.26). Anything less than the totality of ethnic Israel being saved

---

[45] On the letter's authenticity, see Paul Foster, 'Who Wrote 2 Thessalonians? A Fresh Look at an Old Problem', *JSNT* 35 (2012): 150–75 (170–1): of 111 scholars surveyed, 63 believe it is Paul, 13 do not and 35 are uncertain (special thanks to Nijay Gupta for this source). See also the lucid case for authenticity made by Jeffrey Weima, *1–2 Thessalonians*, BECNT (Grand Rapids, MI: Baker, 2014), 46–54. The burden of proof now rests on those who would deny Pauline authorship.

[46] This man is not metaphorically sitting in the hearts of the church or its people; there is no signal whatsoever from Paul that he is speaking of the 'temple of the Holy Spirit', as in 1 Corinthians 3 and 6. This is a different audience, different message, different genre, and the lawless man's self-presentation (ἀποδείκνυμι: 2 Thess. 2.4) means 'to show forth for public recognition' (BDAG, 108). Paul is referring here to *visible* signs his auditors can rely on that will take place before the end. Also, the emphatic phrase, 'the temple of the God' (τὸν ναὸν τοῦ θεοῦ), could only be understood by an ancient Christ-following audience in 51 CE as Jerusalem's temple. See Weima, *1–2 Thessalonians*, 518.

[47] Although Michael J. Vlach, 'Response to Merkle', in *Three Views*, 209–22 (214–15), references these and other texts, to me, his hermeneutical lens is too narrowly focused as 'literal fulfilments of OT expectations concerning national Israel'.

would seem to demonstrate to the interlocutor that something has indeed separated God's elect from God, and so God's promises to Israel have failed. As such, Paul's assurances in 8.28-39 could not be trusted. I should also point out that the salvation of 'all Israel' probably does not mean that every individual Israelite will be saved, let alone every Israelite of the past (Judas? Ahab? Absalom?). Such universalism would seem to ruin Paul's entire argument in the previous chapters, which teaches, among other things, that sin enslaves Jews and gentiles and elicits God's wrath. By 'all Israel' Paul means *corporate* Israel will be saved, both 'the remnant' and 'the rest' united together as Israel's totality. This corporateness also seems to anticipate the unification of the twelve tribes of Israel, a thought informed by the apostle's use of covenant language from Jer. 31[38].31-34 in Rom. 11.27.[48] The Lord establishing a new covenant with both the 'house of Israel' (the ten northern tribes) and the 'house of Judah' (Judah and Benjamin) (Jer. 31[38].31) – that is, all Israel – will be fully realized at that time.[49] Paul would seem to concur in principle with *Mishnah Sanhedrin* 10. The text declares that 'all Israelites have a share in the world to come', and then it proceeds to name those who are excluded, inclusive of the wilderness generation and other Israelites.

Second, as most scholars agree, the 'firstfruits' (ἀπαρχή) in 11.16 represents the current believing remnant of Israel. The word signifies produce from the beginning of the harvest season that anticipates a greater harvest to come. Paul also uses this imagery to distinguish the risen Christ as the 'firstfruits' and the implied greater harvest to follow as those who will be resurrected at his second coming (1 Cor. 15.20-23). 'What is offered as firstfruits is holy and representative of the quality and character of the entire harvest that must eventually follow' (Exod. 34.22; Lev. 23; Sir. 45.20; Jdt. 11.13; *LetArist.* 40).[50] Who represents the implied larger harvest to follow in 11.16? Paul likely believes this to be the rest of Israel that is presently hardened but will trust in Christ and participate in the future resurrection (11.15). They may represent the larger, holy 'lump' in the analogy.

Third, 'the deliverer' from Zion who cleanses Jacob in Rom. 11.26b/Isa. 59.20-21 is ὁ ῥυόμενος. This single masculine present participle form of ῥύομαι appears only one other time in the NT, and it so happens to be Paul who uses it to identify Jesus at the Parousia (1 Thess. 1.10). I doubt this is coincidental usage; it suggests that Paul considered the event in 11.26b to be associated with Christ's second coming.

---

[48] For the twelve tribes interpretation of 'all Israel', see James M. Scott, '"And Then All Israel Will Be Saved" (Rom 11:26)', in James M. Scott (ed.), *Restoration: Old Testament, Jewish, and Christian Perspectives* (Leiden: Brill, 2001), 489–527; J. Brian Tucker, *Reading Romans after Supersessionism* (Eugene, OR: Cascade, 2018), 187. For a position in which gentiles are mixed with the northern tribes of Israel here, see Brant Pitre, Michael P. Barber and John A. Kincaid, *Paul: A New Covenant Jew: Rethinking Pauline Theology* (Grand Rapids, MI: Eerdmans, 2019), 53–9; Scott W. Hahn, '"All Israel Will Be Saved": The Restoration of the Twelve Tribes in Romans 9–11', *Letter & Spirit* 10 (2015): 65–108; Jason A. Staples, 'What Do the Gentiles Have to Do with "All Israel"? A Fresh Look at Romans 11:25–27', *JBL* 130 (2011): 371–90. A critique of this latter position is given by Goodrich, 'Fullness', 15–22. I generally concur with Scott's variation.

[49] The gentiles' fullness is likewise corporate, a unifying of all the nations together as fulfilling prophetic anticipation of entering into Zion. For the gentiles' fullness as the seventy nations from the Table of Nations in Genesis 10 (cf. Deut. 32.8, 43), see Paula Fredriksen, *Paul: The Pagan's Apostle* (New Haven, CT: Yale University Press, 2017), 161–2.

[50] B. J. Oropeza, *1 Corinthians*, NCCS (Eugene, OR: Cascade, 2017), 206, cf. 199–200.

Fourth, if Paul knows the context of his quotations, he almost surely believes that a prophetic pilgrimage to Zion includes salvation to Israel and the nations, and Israel's hardening at that time would be removed.[51] We see repeatedly in scripture that Israel's restoration includes the nations coming to Zion (Isa. 2.2-3; 43.5-9; 49.6, 22; 66.18-20; Mic. 4.1-5; Mal. 1.11; cf. *Pss. Sol.* 17.30-35; *T.Benj.* 9.2). Perhaps most significantly, in the same context of Paul's quote from Isa. 59.20-21, Israel's blindness comes to an end. No longer will they walk in darkness and grope as blind people with no eyes, for divine light and glory will shine on Jerusalem, the nations will walk in its light and the Lord will restore sight to the blind (Isa. 59.9-10; 60.1-5, 19-21; 61.1-3). The nations come into Zion (60.4-12; 61.5, 11; 62.2), and they bring in their wealth (60.5, 7-10, 13, 16-17; 61.6; cf. Rom. 11.12). We already know that Paul is informed by Isaiah regarding Israel's obduracy (Rom. 11.8/Isa. 29.10; cf. 6.9-10) as well as their deliverance (Rom. 11.26-27/Isa. 59.20-21; cf. 27.9), and I suggest that all Israel being saved is informed further by Isa. 45.17-25, a text Paul will cite in Rom. 14.11 (also Phil. 2.10-11). It seems to me almost inescapable, then, that Paul recognizes Israel's blindness as temporary; it gives way to sight and restoration in the messianic era in which he participates (Isa. 9.1-7; 29.18; 32.3-4; 35.4-5; 60.1-3). Moreover, since this blindness has *not* been removed in Paul's day, he anticipates its removal when the fullness of nations comes into Zion. That is when Christ the deliverer reveals himself to Israel. Romans 11 is thus informed by this anticipated restoration that has Zion reconfigured as the place name for the delivered-in-Christ-community of Jews and gentiles.[52]

Fifth, in 11.29, hardened Israel's restoration seems inevitable since the gifts and calling of God for Israel are irrevocable. That calling connects the delivered 'Jacob' of 11.26-27 with the calling of 'Jacob' whom God loves, mentioned in 9.10-13. The hardened portion of Israel is an enemy and yet beloved of God on account of their forefathers, one of them Jacob who represents all Israel. Israel is God's people whom God has foreknown and not forsaken (11.1-2), a people comprised not only of the remnant (11.3-7) but also of the hardened rest, whom Paul *specifically* and *emphatically* denies have fallen irreparably (11.11). Why? Because he believes they will be saved as collective group.

Finally, in 11.32 both gentiles/the nations ('you') and hardened Israel ('they') were surrendered over to disobedience so that God could have mercy on them all. Back in 1.18-32, gentiles are primarily in view and surrendered over to divine hardening in the form of a debased mind (1.28). But this hardening turned out to be temporary; the nations are now being saved and their fullness is up ahead (11.25, 30). It stands to reason that this same type of reversal applies to Israel as well. They were hardened in 11.7-10, but this hardening will turn out to be temporary; salvation will come to the fullness of them as it did to the gentiles (11.12, 26).

---

[51] Pace Donaldson, *Paul and the Gentiles*, 187–97, who rejects the nations' eschatological pilgrimage claiming, among other things, that it should be precipitated by Israel's restoration (not the other way around). But for Paul Israel *via the remnant* was restored *before* salvation came to the nations; restoration is thus a two-stage process for Israel, already inaugurated by the 'remnant' but not yet consummated by the 'rest'. On this point see further, Scott, 'All Israel', 492–5.

[52] Zion in this reconfigured sense is perhaps also the 'Jerusalem above' in Gal. 4.26.

Conclusion

Although the ecclesiological view of N. T. Wright is stimulating and formidable, 'all Israel' in Rom. 11.26 still seems to be best explained as ethnic Israel. In Paul's apocalyptic imagination, then, Israel is temporarily understood both as a remnant, who believe the gospel about Christ, and the rest who are hardened. Some of the latter group, Paul hopes, will be turning to Christ in the present age. Then, once the gospel reaches all the nations and they trust in Christ, the hardened state of the rest of Israel will be removed, and 'all Israel' will be saved. I have argued in a fresh way and in response to criticisms that that event is likely associated with the Parousia. Paul's view of the Parousia from 2 Thessalonians (which should be considered Pauline) supports that Israel will be saved *en masse*. Likewise, various images from Israel's scriptures, such as language about the firstfruits, Israel's temporary blindness and recovery of sight, both the houses of Judah and northern Israel being restored to a new covenant and the deliverer from Zion interpreted as Jesus Messiah at the Parousia, support this interpretation.

13

The wedding imagery of the Apocalypse and Paul

Lionel North

Apocalypse

Like the Apocalypse as a whole, its final chapters with their wedding imagery are set in a context of vicious persecution and the ever-present possibility of desertion. Before the wedding there had been only violence and fornication. 'The great, strong city Babylon' (16.19; 17.5; 18.2, 10, 21), 'the great harlot' (17.1, 15), the 'mother of harlots' (17.5) may flaunt her purple, scarlet and 'bling' (17.4; 18.16) but she who persecutes and murders the saints (16.6; 17.6; 18.24; 19.2) will soon be destroyed, as will the empire that she contaminated (16.19; 17.2, 18; 18.3, 9; 19.19) and the commerce that kept her in the lap of luxury (18.3, 11–19, 23c). Hallmarks of a civilized society, music-making, handicrafts, farm work and weddings, are things of the past; the wedding lamp (λύχνος) is extinguished and the ecstatic cries of groom and bride (φωνή) are silent (18.22-3b), only tears remain (18.15, 19).

'Spectacular violence' was followed by 'a spectacular wedding'.[1] An appropriate contrast to violence is the exuberant excitement and anticipation of a wedding, culminating in a couple's commitment to each other that guests will witness, with a grand wedding breakfast to follow, thrown by God to celebrate the union of the Lamb and his Bride (19.7, 9, 17). The Lamb, once slain (5.6, 9, 12), now shares God's throne (3.21; 22.1, 3).[2] Unlike the harlot in her finery his Bride is simply dressed, in 'fine linen, bright and pure' (19.7d-8a; 21.2b),[3] code for the righteousness of the martyrs (19.8b), just as 'bride' is code for 'the holy city, the new Jerusalem', the Church, which 'descends from heaven' (21.2a, 9-10) to displace 'Babylon'; 'from heaven' is code for God who orchestrates the proceedings as matchmaker. Light (λύχνος) is restored (21.23-4; 22.5) and like all weddings this one is an occasion of great joy (21.4; 19.7) where the guests join in the Amen Hallelujah! (φωνή, 19.1-9; 22.17). This imagery has influenced its

---

[1] E. Rosenberg, 'Weddings and the Return to Life in the Book of Revelation', in F. S. Tappenden and C. Daniel-Hughes (eds), *Coming Back to Life* (Montreal: McGill UL, 2017), 309–41.
[2] This may be one reason why the *Lamb* shares *God's* throne; on the day of their wedding a Jewish couple was treated as royalty. So as Lamb and groom the Lamb is a doubly royal figure and may very properly occupy the throne of God; Sotah 49a. For Jewish betrothal and wedding customs see S. Krauss, *Talmudische Archäologie* (Leipzig: Fock, 1911), 2.34–43 (37–8).
[3] Unless otherwise stated, all English translations are taken from the RSV.

Christology; titles used of Christ, especially 'faithful and true' (1.5; 3.14; 19.11), reflect the faithfulness the couple promise each other.

The imagery employed in the Apocalypse would have been familiar to Paul too. The sentiments and the language used to express them were already present in the Old Testament. The 'spectacular violence' of persecuting Babylon is very prominent in Jeremiah and the longing of the Song of Solomon can only be the prelude to 'a spectacular wedding'. Paul may have expressed himself more soberly but with no less conviction. Later I will compare the Apocalypse and Paul.

Gospels

In the overwrought language of the Apocalypse some important features of Jewish weddings are missing, especially the matchmaker. The Synoptic Gospels, which often couch the meaning of Jesus's mission in wedding terms, also lack a matchmaker.[4] Matthew who is particularly fond of weddings speaks of the 'groom' (νυμφίος) who may be Jesus and the 'sons of the bride-chamber' (οἱ υἱοὶ τοῦ νυμφῶνος, 'wedding guests' [9.15//Mk 2.19-20//Lk. 5.34-35]); 22.1-14 describes the guests who refused to attend the wedding supper laid on by the host in honour of his son, the groom; in 25.1-13 (*varia lectio* in 25.1 καὶ τῆς νυμφῆς is uncertain), it is the groom's delay and the maidens' need to refill their λαμπάδες (cf. Lk. 12.35-38) that are significant. The feast in Lk. 14.7-14 is probably a wedding breakfast, though P75 omits εἰς γάμους at v. 8. The Fourth Gospel had a matchmaker, present at the marriage at Cana in Galilee, who is John the Baptist, ὁ φίλος τοῦ νυμφίου, one of whose duties was to listen outside the bedroom for the φωνὴ τοῦ νυμφίου, proof that the marriage had been consummated (3.29).[5] Julius Pollux (2 CE) recorded a detail about Greek weddings: one of the groom's friends (τις τῶν τοῦ νυμφίου φίλων καὶ θυρωρός) *was posted* outside the bedroom to stop women entering the bedroom when the bride cried out (βοώσῃ).'[6]

Paul's context

I turn from the Synoptic silence about a matchmaker to examine Paul's image of himself as one, in 2 Cor. 11.2 (ἡρμοσάμην γὰρ ὑμᾶς ἑνὶ ἀνδρὶ παρθένον ἁγνὴν παραστῆσαι τῷ

---

[4] See P. J. Long, *Jesus the Bridegroom: The Origin of the Eschatological Feast as a Wedding Banquet in the Synoptic Gospels* (Eugene, OR: Pickwick, 2012); A. Villeneuve, *Nuptial Symbolism in Second Temple Writings, the NT and Rabbinic Literature: Divine Marriage at Key Moments of Salvation History* (Leiden: Brill, 2016), 38–48, who reviews both the wider background and earlier studies by C. Chavasse, *The Bride of Christ: An Enquiry into the Nuptial Element in early Christianity* (London: Faber & Faber, 1940); and R. Batey, *New Testament Nuptial Imagery* (Leiden: Brill, 1963). Batey also devoted an article to 2 Cor. 11.2 in *Interpretation* 17 (1963): 176–84.

[5] J. McWhirter, *The Bridegroom Messiah and the People of God: Marriage in the Fourth Gospel* (Cambridge: Cambridge University Press, 2006). *The Valentinian Gnostic Theodotus (c. 170) conflated John the Baptist's duties*: ὁ δὲ τοῦ δείπνου μὲν ἀρχιτρίκλινος, τῶν γάμων δὲ παράνυμφος, τοῦ νυμφίου δὲ φίλος (*GCS* 3.128; cf. Jn 2.9; 3.29).

[6] Onomasticon 3.42.

Χριστῷ); this is part of his self-understanding as an apostle (cf. n. 21). But first, in the light of what I will later say about Paul's honesty, I must say something here about misrepresentation. In a different society but still part of Paul's wide Mediterranean experience, matchmakers in Athens could misrepresent their clients' charms. In Aristophanes *Clouds* 41, Strepsiades curses the matchmaker (προμνήστρια), a woman who had misled him about the thriftiness she had claimed for his wife-to-be. On this line Kenneth Dover commented, 'It is surprising that we hear so little about their activity', but Plato had much to say about it. In *Theaetetus* 149a-51c, Socrates claims he has modelled his work as a 'wise man' on his mother's occupation as a midwife and compares his work to intellectual midwifery, bringing wisdom to birth: '[midwives and matchmakers have much in common, the latter are] very wise in knowing what union of man and woman will produce the best possible children'.[7] Xenophon's parallel version is different: here Aspasia informed Socrates, 'Good matchmakers are successful in making marriages only when the good reports they carry to and fro are true; false reports she would not recommend, for the victims of deception hate one another, the matchmaker too' (*Mem.*, 2.6.36). Xenophon is concerned about the repercussions of a bad match, bitterness and recrimination (cf. Strepsiades), Plato about the result of a good one, children.[8]

In early Jewish tradition, there were three stories about someone who could be regarded as a matchmaker; in Genesis 24 Abraham 'sends' Eliezer back to Mesopotamia, under oath to find a wife there for his son Isaac. In the story of Samson's first marriage, to the Philistine woman of Timnath, it is his parents who act as matchmakers and make all the arrangements to implement Samson's own wishes ('get her for me; for she pleases me well' (Judg. 14.4; cf. v. 2)). The Timnites provide Samson with a group of thirty companions and one of their number seems to act as though *he* were the 'best man', but, far from it, Samson did not behave as though he liked him or them. Tobit 6–12 represent the archangel Raphael as a matchmaker acting on God's behalf: though he was not one of Tobias's close friends, simply a relative, also known as Azariah, he encourages Tobias to marry Sarah, reassures him that no harm will ensue and negotiates with her father about the marriage.[9]

In later tradition however the matchmaker, the שדכן, was infamous.[10] What had been an honourable profession, pursued even by rabbis, fell into disrepute. In *The Joys of Yiddish*, Leo Rosten tells many *shadchen* jokes, for example, 'A young man, having patiently and sceptically endured the shadchen's hyperbole, said, "But you left out one

---

[7] προμνήστριαί εἰσι δεινόταται, ὡς πάσσοφοι οὖσαι περὶ τοῦ γνῶναι ποίαν χρὴ ποίῳ ἀνδρὶ συνοῦσαν ὡς ἀρίστους παῖδας τίκτειν.
[8] A. I. Mintz shows that Plato regarded Socrates as a matchmaker: 'The Midwife as Matchmaker: Socrates and Relational Pedagogy', *PEA* (2007): 91–99; A. I. Mintz, 'Damon, Prodicus, and Socratic Matchmaking', *SPE* 36 (2017): 377–9; J. Tomin, 'Socratic Midwifery', *CQ* 37 (1987): 97–102, esp. 101–2.
[9] G. D. Miller, *Marriage in the Book of Tobit* (Berlin: de Gruyter, 2011), mentions the שושבין in nn. 127; 139. Matchmakers do not appear in the Song of Songs or *Joseph and Aseneth*, but the relationships they imply were arranged.
[10] שדכן and שושבין are perhaps best translated 'best man', one's father or best friend.

thing, didn't you?" "Never, what?" "She – limps!" The shadchen protested, "Only when she walks!"[11]

Paul and 2 Cor. 11.2

Paul drew on a wide range of metaphors to define his relationship to 'his' converts, many taken from family life. Usually converts are his 'brethren' (ἀδελφοί) but also 'children' (τέκνα) where he can be their 'mother' ('my children [τεκνία] with whom I am again in labour', Gal. 4.19) and/or their 'nurse' (1 Thess. 2.7). Whether τροφός means wet nurse or nursing mother, it emphasizes the maternal role of someone who jealously breastfeeds her newborn charge (1 Cor. 3.2). Yet he is also their father ('I became your father in Christ Jesus through the gospel') (4.15). As we saw with Samson, one role of a father was to arrange the wedding of his son, particularly to find a suitable bride; he is a 'matchmaker', in post-biblical terms a שׁדכן, a role that combines familial and legal duties.[12]

His predecessors had developed matchmaking language (words compounded with νυμφ-), never the classical word, προμνηστρ-, but Paul chose to use a word with history. The betrothal nuance of ἁρμοζ- goes back to Pindar and Herodotus, and its use in LXX, Philo and Josephus may explain his use of a word with *gravitas* in a serious passage.

As for the context of 2 Cor. 11.2, it is not necessary to go behind chapters 10–13. Chapters 1–7 and 8–9 are blocks which adopt quite a different tone from 10–13, so much so that some scholars see them as two or three separate documents; H. D. Betz devoted a commentary to chapters 8–9 alone. Chapters 10–13 express some very strong, barely controlled, emotions that have affected his language. Paul will speak of himself, in what post-biblical Hebrew will term a שׁדכן, and of his readers as a pure virgin (11.2),[13] but the context reveals a far less promising relationship that does not bode well for his claims. Some of his readers were very critical of Paul: he is two-faced (10.1, 10), acts in a worldly manner (10.2), cuts an unimposing figure and is an ineffective speaker (11.6) (so much for his role as matchmaker!). He can maintain discipline only through weighty letters (3.1-3; 7.8; 10.9-11); he is power mad (10.8; 13), does not belong to Christ (10.7) and had usurped the rights of others to evangelize Corinth (10.13-18). They will just have to 'tolerate' the old 'fool' (11.1). Chapters 11–13 continue in the same vein: he has shocked them into parting with their money (καταναρκ-, 11.9; 12.13-14, 16 (*varia lectio*)), only to con the poor saints in Jerusalem out of the proceeds (ὑπάρχων πανοῦργος δόλῳ ὑμᾶς ἔλαβον; ἐπλεονέκτησα ὑμᾶς) (12.16-18; cf. 6.3; 7.2; 8.20). He has deceived them (12.16), Christ does not speak through him (13.3), so they can rubbish what he does say. For other accusations, about his honesty, see later in the text.

---

[11] Leo Rosten, *The Joys of Yiddish: A Relaxed Lexicon of Yiddish, Hebrew and Yinglish Words Often Encountered in English ... from the Days of the Bible to those of the Beatnik.* (New York: McGraw Hill Book Co., 1968), 332–5.
[12] See Krauss, *Talmudische Archäologie*, 450 n. 246; 458 n. 314; 461 nn. 341–2; 462 n. 345.
[13] H. Danby defined the status of the girl in *Ketubot* 1.3 as '*virgo intacta*' (Oxford, 1933), 245.

But Paul can give as good as he gets. Some of his readers happily 'tolerate' fools and bullies (11.4, 19-20). 'Being tolerated', 'being putting up with' is a common theme (it occurs five times in this one chapter) and clearly had got under Paul's skin. He retorts they are disobedient (10.6); in their self-assessment they adopt inadequate criteria in contrast with Paul's own claim to observe μέτρον ('moderation') (10.12-15). He dismisses them as ὑπερλίαν ἀποστόλοι, 'super-duper' apostles, 'too big for their own boots' (11.5; 12.11).[14]

Fired with divine zeal

This mutual recrimination is depressing. The transition from the acrimonious passage of arms in chapter 10 to the more promising matchmaker metaphor, only to be resumed as soon as it is finished, could not be more extreme. I have wondered if the metaphor itself is in fact 'tongue-in-cheek', part of his 'foolishness'; it is hardly extolling the qualities of the bride, one of the שושבין's principal duties. He may not have thought through the suitability of the metaphor, but it does make four, more positive, contributions to an understanding of these chapters; they concern the divine zeal, the bride's virginity, Paul's honesty and Paul on the Day of Judgement.

11.2 is linked by γάρ to v. 1 to explain why his readers must put up with him; his 'zeal' for them is not his own 'zeal' but the zeal God displays, ζηλῶ γὰρ ὑμᾶς θεοῦ ζήλῳ. The matchmaking context strongly suggests that we are talking about God's jealous passion for his people (cf. Zech. 1.14; 8.2). Chapter 10 had concluded with the stress that the Lord is the only proper object of boasting since it is only his commendation that matters. So in 11.1-2 Paul identifies his own zeal, for which he has probably been criticized, with the zeal of God, quite different from a human שושבין's wish to be the very best possible matchmaker. It is the ζῆλος of the divine שושבין who, according to the fancies of Jewish preachers, plaited Eve's hair in the garden, loaded her with ornaments and conducted her to Adam.[15] Paul's care for the churches is no different from God's care for Eve. He knows that this is foolish, though he calls it only slightly foolish (μικρόν τι) – Paul is not one for conceding too much. Like boasting (nineteen times in chapters 10–12) foolishness is clearly a prominent word, nine times in the same chapters (see further below). As I have suggested, Paul is probably picking up another barb from his opponents' arsenal of criticism of him as a boastful old fool and making what argumentative capital he can out of it, perhaps over against their boastful preoccupation with γνῶσις. Yes, on his own showing Paul's identification of his apostolic fervour with the divine fervour is a silly piece of nonsense, but it conveys something of the intensity he feels about his apostolic and pastoral duty; it is still foolish boasting (11.21b), but

---

[14] Paul coined ὑπερλίαν since λίαν alone did not do justice to his low opinion of his critics' self-opinionated manners (10.18; 11.5; 12.11; cf. Rom. 12.3). A scholiast on Homer, *Iliad* 16.779, defined ὑπερλίαν as πλέον ἢ κατὰ μέτρον; Cyril of Alexandria often contrasted λίαν and μέτρον. Section 5 borrowed a few lines from a piece I have written on Paul's zeal, awaiting publication.

[15] Cf. H. L. Strack and P. Billerbeck, *Kommentar zum Neuen Testament aus Talmud und Midrasch* (München: Beck, 1922), vol. 1, 503–4.

there is the daily pressure upon me of my anxiety for all the churches. Who is not weak and I am not weak? Who is made to fall and I do not fume? (11.28-29)

His anxiety and his 'foolishness' are not flaws in his character for which he could be chided. He feels about things exactly as God does. God's concern is his.

The bride's virginity

Not only does the שושבין discourage haste and wrong motives for betrothal and marriage, not only does he make the arrangements for the betrothal, he also ensures that the couple does not anticipate marriage before the wedding or even during it. Evidence for this slowly accumulated. First, *Ketubot* 1.5 says, 'He who eats with his father-in-law in Judaea without the presence of witnesses cannot raise a complaint regarding the virginity, because he has been alone with her.' A footnote adds, 'and he may have had intimate intercourse with his bride'. How this may have arisen is made clear in the *Gemara*: 'In Judaea they used formerly to leave the bridegroom and the bride alone one hour before their entry into the bridal chamber, so that he may become intimate with her' ('zu einem *tête à tête*').[16] Thus far however there has been no reference to the שושבין, but the *Gemara* goes on: 'In Judaea they used formerly to put up two שושבינין, one for him and one for her, in order to examine the bridegroom and the bride *when* they entered the bridal chamber. In Judaea formerly the שושבינין used to sleep in the house in which the bridegroom and the bride slept.' After the consummation of the marriage the groom called in the bride's שושבין to recover the bloodstained bedding which had to be retained in case of any query later on about the bride's virginity.[17] This was important should a question of divorce arise. Thus, one duty of the שושבין was to ensure that the bride remained a virgin until the bridal chamber door closed behind the couple; during the wedding day itself was not enough, nor even the final hour when they are 'becoming acquainted'.

As any שושבין would, Paul feared that in the interval between betrothal and marriage (which could last for up to a year,[18] for him, the interval between baptism and Parousia), the church, the bride-to-be, in Jewish law already committed, already a wife, has been sweet-talked and seduced by a rival lover, the serpent and his false doctrine (2 Cor. 11.3-4). The thought that the serpent's seduction of Eve is sexual is almost certainly in Paul's mind (or was he thinking of Adam's *first* wife Lilith?),[19] but

---

[16] I. Epstein, *The Babylonian Talmud, Seder Nashim* (London: Soncino, 1936), 3.62-3; cf. 46-7. See Krauss, *Talmudische Archäologie*, 42.
[17] The *signum virginitatis* of Deut. 22.13-21.
[18] See Krauss, *Talmudische Archäologie*, 36.
[19] See R. Adelman, *The Return of the Repressed: Pirqe de-Rabbi Eliezer and the Pseudepigrapha*, SJSJ 140 (Leiden: Brill, 2009), chapter 5: 'Adam, Eve and the Serpent – the First Version of the Fall (PRE 13)'; W. Kosior, 'A Tale of Two Sisters: The Image of Eve in Early Rabbinic Literature and Its Influence on the Portrayal of Lilith in the Alphabet of Ben Sira', *NJJWSFI* 32 (2018): 112–30, especially 119–20 on Eve and the Serpent. See J. R. C. Cousland, 'Adam and Eve, Did Satan Sleep with Eve in the Greek and Latin Lives of Adam and Eve?', *JThS* 71 (2020): 134–57. Contemporary sources bear on this: the *Protevangelium Jacobi* 27(13) speaks of Eve 'defiled' by the serpent

what I have not seen proposed is the possibility that as in some traditions Cain is the child of that union (1 Jn 3.12; cf. Jn 8.44),[20] so the ὑπερλίαν ἀπόστολοι, ψευδοαπόστολοι, ψευδαδέλφοι (2 Cor. 11.5, 13, 26; 12.11) also were children of Eve and the serpent (11.3), bastards spawned from within a complacent church (v. 4) tolerant of any doctrine, whatever its paternity, as long as it was not Paul's. They are described as ἐργάται δόλιοι (v. 13); δόλιοι echoes the serpent's πανουργία (v. 3; cf. Jn 8.41) and ὁ δὲ ὄφις ἦν φρονιμώτατος (LXX Gen. 3.1), repeated in φρόνιμοι (v. 19). It is also echoed in Paul's ironic acceptance of ἄφρων (11.1, 16-7, 19, 21; 12.6, 11). To repeat, they rubbish *his* gospel and substitute a different version (ἄλλον Ἰησοῦν ... πνεῦμα ἕτερον ... εὐαγγέλιον ἕτερον (11.4)) of which probably they are hugely proud, which brings us to honesty.

Paul's honesty

More than once Paul implies that he has been accused of playing fast and loose with the word of God. He insists that he does not mislead nor tinker with nor falsify what is God's word.[21] He is horrified at the thought of 'not telling it like it is' and keeps repeating 'I am telling the truth'.[22] He points out the implications of lying if one misrepresents the resurrection:

> If Christ has not been raised, then our proclamation is in vain and your faith has been in vain. We are even found to be misrepresenting God (ψευδομάρτυρες τοῦ θεοῦ), because we testified of God that he raised Christ, whom he did not raise if it is true that the dead are not raised. (1 Cor. 15.14-15; cf. 1 Jn 5.10)

His defence contrasts his own honesty with the false apostles who are the real 'con artists'. I suggest a שובין-framework lies behind this insistence: *honest* representation is of the essence of his task as an apostle.[23] In Apocalypse terms, a servant of the 'Faithful and True', whose words are faithful and true, could be no other. Misinformation meant a flogging, and perhaps worse, because we move on to Judgement.

(ἐμίανεν); Clement of Alexandria claimed that, correctly aspirated, 'Eve' in Hebrew (חוה) meant a female serpent (thus able to mate with a (male) serpent, in Aramaic חויא) (PG 8.72A); he is followed in the fourth century by Eusebius (PG 21.121B) and elaborated by Epiphanius (PG 42.801A).

[20] *Clementine Homilies*, Epiphanius and Cyril of Alexandria link Cain with 'liar' (PG 2.123A; 41.688A; 42.128B; 69.40A). See Adelman, *Return of the Repressed*, 103–6, for Cain's role in 'Gnostic' Sethianism.

[21] πλάνοι, καπηλεύοντες, δολοῦντες (1 Thess. 2.3-5; 2 Cor. 6.8; 2.17; 4.2).

[22] Rom. 9.1; 2 Cor. 11.31 (cf. 11.10; 12.6; 13.8); Gal. 1.20; 1 Tim. 2.7), something God can corroborate (Rom. 1.8; 2 Cor. 1.22; Phil. 1.8; 1 Thess. 2.5, 9). Cf. J. L. North, 'Paul's Protest That He Does Not Lie in the Light of His Cilician Origin', *JThS* ns 47 (1996): 439–63.

[23] שליח and ἀπόστολος overlap not only each other in certain circumstances (Aquila//LXX-3 Kgs 14.6; cf. Symmachus-Isa. 18.2) but also שובין. Was Paul's understanding of his apostleship indebted to the שובין-concept, not only at 2 Cor. 11.2-3 *but as a whole*? H. L. Strack and P. Billerbeck (n. 13), 3.2-3, list four similar duties for the שליח (on Rom. 1.1, ἀπόστολος).

Paul on the Day of Judgement

I find a fourth place where greater appreciation is achieved if we assume שושבין-thinking in Paul's attitude towards 'his' churches. It relates to a paper I read long ago on 'Paul on the Day of Judgement', never published, where 'on' meant not only 'writing about' but also 'personally present on'. At the Great Assize Paul would be looking to his converts, *his* work as well as the work of God (1 Cor. 9.1-2) as proof that *his* faith and work had been genuine and not ἀδόκιμος (9.27; cf. 2 Cor. 13.3-7; 2 Tim. 2.15). That in part is why he is so concerned for their welfare. His feeling is that if he has faithfully and successfully preached the word and tended the flock, and if its loyalty to Christ remains unimpaired to the end, he can look forward *his own* final acquittal and salvation.

There is never a perfect match between social-cultural and religious realities, but שושבין-thinking may confirm this last point. The Jewish texts imply that one reason for the concern to discharge שושבין duties as well as possible was that one day the שושבין too would be a groom and would look to his שושבין to do for him what he had done for him, the courting, the negotiating, sorting out any problems, making the arrangements, the giving of presents and especially ensuring the virginity of his bride. 'Their [*viz.* שושבינין] services and gifts were *reciprocated* on the occasion of *their* marriages.'[24] If Paul can fight off his rivals with their doctrines that imperil his churches' purity, then he can expect the day of judgement to become his wedding day, when the שושבין who had betrothed the Corinthians to Christ finds himself to be part of the Bride of Christ, the Body of Christ. As I have said, what Paul has done in 2 Cor. 11.2 is apply to himself the image of God as the jealous שושבין of Adam and Eve. Having already spoken of Christ as the last Adam (1 Cor. 15.45) he would have no difficulty in seeing Christ in Gen. 2.22 and the Church in Eve. This enables him to explain *his* behaviour in terms of God's determination to shield the Bride's chastity for Christ (2 Cor. 11.3),[25] protecting the Church for the exclusive enjoyment of the Groom;[26] second, to identify his critics as the sons of the serpent, misbegotten, lying, fratricidal.[27] In this way the Bride

---

[24] *The Babylonian Talmud, Baba Bathra* 145b, Soncino edition, 618 n. 10; 626.

[25] D. A. Kurek-Chomycz defends the originality of καὶ τῆς ἁγνότητος in 'Sincerity and Chastity for Christ: A Textual Problem in 2 Cor. 11:3 Reconsidered', *NovT* 49 (2007): 54–84. Her full treatment of the textual evidence (MSS and Fathers, 55–70) is followed by one on 'intrinsic probability'. She believes 'haplography [after τῆς ἁπλότητος] is the easiest explanation' (for the omission) (83); the similarity of the second syllables (-ΠΛ-/-ΓN-) could easily cause confusion. Another reason for its omission may be the novelty of ἁγνότης; the first extant examples are found in the first century CE, used of Apollo by the Stoic philosopher L. Annaeus Cornutus (Ramelli, 282) and here by Paul. One or other may have coined it completely independently. NT *apparatus critici* probably attests other Pauline words that scribes rejected because of their strangeness.

[26] Like Theodotus with the Baptist (n. 3) other Greek Fathers developed this wedding symbolism: not only is God portrayed as the שושבין who conducts Eve to Adam in the garden (*The Babylonian Talmud, Erubin* 18a-b (Soncino edition, 125), Theodoret describing him as νυμφοστόλος καὶ νυμφευτής, Basil of Seleucia as νυμφαγωγός), and Christ often called a νυμφαγωγός (Chrysostom), but Paul also is frequently a νυμφαγωγός and νυμφοστόλος.

[27] See W. Crouser, 'Satan, the Serpent, and Witchcraft Accusations: Reading Rom. 16:17-20a in the Light of Allusions and Anthropology', *Journal for the Study of Paul and His Letters* 4 (2014): 218–33, especially 218–27. See Adelman, *The Return of the Repressed* for 'bad seed'.

becomes *Paul's own* 'hope [and] joy [and] crown of boasting before our Lord Jesus at his Parousia' (1 Thess. 2.19-20), thus he achieves '[*his own*] salvation with fear and trembling' on the day of Christ (Phil. 2.12, 16; cf. 2 Cor. 1.14).

Conclusion

I finish where I began, with the Apocalypse and, with Paul behind us, with questions about the two presentations of the betrothal-wedding motif. Paul's presentation seems doomed to failure, unbalanced as it is by its unflattering setting in 2 Cor. 10-13. The way he uses the matchmaker metaphor seems misplaced, but the four corollaries of matchmaking that we have examined may rescue it from that criticism; perhaps they are the real reason for his choice of the motif. He speaks of δαιμόνια (1 Cor. 11.2; 10.20-21; cf. 1 Tim. 4.1) and once of ὁ ὄφις who deceived Eve (2 Cor. 11.3) where the erotic overtones of a wedding explain its presence, but Paul has no δεῖπνον, surely sequel to any wedding. John's presentation is richer. He has a divine Groom and a Bride (though no human שושבין) and has entered into the spirit of the occasion by adding a marriage supper (δεῖπνον) to which the Spirit and the Bride invite guests (Rev. 22.17; 19.9, 17). Even the demonology is richer, centring around the '*ancient*' serpent; 'ancient' harks back to Eden in Genesis 3, to temptation, deception (πλαν-; a major function of the serpent, in its conflict with the 'faithful and true'), fall and expulsion. One cannot always recognize the serpent; its aliases are listed ('he who is called the Devil', 'Satan who deceives the whole world') (12.9; 20.2; cf. 2.20); in the guise of 'the great red dragon' it had threatened to devour the child and remains the enemy of the Lamb and his Bride (9.19; 12.3, 9, 14-15; 20.2). The dragon's entourage includes locusts as big and deadly as scorpions (9.3, 5, 7-11). Much more briefly and less graphically, Paul shared the view that the serpent comes in many disguises (μετασχηματιζ-, 2 Cor. 11.13-15), always quick to deceive ([ἐξ]απατ-, 11.3; cf. 1 Tim. 2.14).[28]

As I said, none of this would have been unfamiliar to Paul, nor were he and John at odds with each other; they chose what they needed. Famously, Harold Macmillan is claimed to have said that events can blow governments off course; for a time vicious persecution had blown the Church off course, but Paul and John agree on God's final triumph over the serpent, however disguised, false apostles or the Roman state, *and triumph soon* (Rom. 16.20; Rev. 12.7-9; 20.2-3; 22.6-7)!

---

[28] Cf. Mt. 7.15 and Strack-Billerbeck (n. 13), 1.140-1.

14

David the prophet in the first apocryphal *Apocalypse of John*

Craig A. Evans

Introduction

Several decades ago, Jacques Dupont remarked that the tradition of David as prophet explains the frequent appeal to psalms in the Book of Acts.[1] I believe that he is correct and, furthermore, that this explains also the frequent appeal to David and the Psalter by the author of the first *Apocalypse of John*, an early Christian apocryphal work inspired by the Book of Revelation. In this chapter, I propose to set out the evidence for this claim and thereby to illuminate the reuse of scripture in this little-known apocalyptic writing.

David's prophetic status in Second Temple literature

King David's status as a prophet was firmly established by the late Second Temple period.[2] Without embarrassment or need for proof the early Christian community could assert that 'the Holy Spirit spoke beforehand by the mouth of David, concerning Judas who was guide to those who arrested Jesus' (Acts 1.16) and then quote as fulfilled prophecy passages from the Psalter (Pss. 69.25 and 109.8 in Acts 1.20). Likewise, at the beginning of the Pentecost sermon Peter quotes Ps. 16.8-11 as prophecy (Acts 2.25-28) and then claims that David, 'being therefore a prophet' (προφήτης οὖν ὑπάρχων), 'foresaw [προϊδών] and spoke of the resurrection of the Christ, that he was not abandoned to Hades, nor did his flesh see corruption' (Acts 2.29-31; cf. 13.35; cf. Acts

---

[1] Jacques Dupont, 'L'interprétation des psaumes dans les Actes des Apôtres', in *Études sur les Actes des Apôtres*, LD 45 (Paris: Cerf, 1967), 283-307.
[2] See Joseph A. Fitzmyer, 'David, "Being Therefore a Prophet ..."', *CBQ* 34 (1972): 332-9; George J. Brooke, 'The Psalms in Early Jewish Literature in Light of the Dead Sea Scrolls', in Steve Moyise and Maarten J. J. Menken (eds), *The Psalms in the New Testament* (London: T&T Clark International, 2004), 5-24; J. Samuel Subramanian, 'The Prophetic Reading of the Psalms in Second Temple Jewish Literature', in *The Synoptic Gospels and the Psalms as Prophecy*, LNTS 351 (London: T&T Clark, 2007), 19-44. Subramanian rightly concludes that 'the Psalms were read as prophecies about future events'.

2.34, quoting Ps. 110.1). When Jerusalem's leadership threatens Peter and the apostles, David is once again appealed to as a prophet, whose word is being fulfilled: 'Why did the Gentiles rage, and the peoples imagine vain things? The kings of the earth set themselves ... and the rulers were gathered together, against the Lord and against his Christ' (Acts 4.25-26; cf. Ps. 2.1-2; Acts 13.33).

Elsewhere in the New Testament, Paul, too, presents David as speaking prophetically of those who will oppose the Lord's Christ: 'And David says, "Let their table become a snare and a trap"' (Rom. 11.9-10; cf. Ps. 69.22-23). The author of Hebrews also lists several important figures, concluding with 'David and Samuel and the prophets' (Heb. 11.32), possibly implying that David was numbered with the prophets. This exploitation of David's prophetic status to support early Christian claims about Jesus is seen also in the gospels, in the discussion about the Messiah 'son of David' in Ps. 110.1: 'David himself, inspired by the Holy Spirit [ἐν τῷ πνεύματι τῷ ἁγίῳ], declared, "The Lord said to my Lord, Sit at my right hand"' (Mk 12.36).

The men of Qumran similarly viewed David as an inspired prophet.[3] They believed that the Lord had given him a 'discerning and enlightened spirit', which enabled him to write some 4,050 psalms, including 364 psalms to be sung over the altar daily, 50 songs for the sabbath offerings, 30 songs for the Day of Atonement and 4 songs to speak over the demon possessed. 'All these', we are told, 'he spoke through prophecy [דבר בנבואה]' (11Q5 col. xxvii 2–11).[4] The community may well have thought that it possessed David's Songs of the Sabbath (cf. 4Q400–407; 11Q17; MasŠirŠabb) as well as the four songs of exorcism, one of them being Psalm 91 (cf. 11Q11). David is believed to have spoken of the 'last days': 'for the last days [אחרית הימים], as David said, "Lord do not scold me in anger. Take pity on me, Lord"' (4Q177 frgs. 10+12+13, col. i, line 7; cf. on the heavenly role of the eschatological Melchizedek, 11Q13 ii line 10). Among the apocryphal psalms attributed to David recovered from the Cairo Genizah there is one that says: 'You prophesied by Your spirit [ניבאת ברוחך] through the mouth of Your servant (David)' (*Songs of David* 1.14).[5] Although it is far from certain, these psalms may have originated at Qumran and, along with a copy of the *Damascus Covenant*, made their way to Egypt.[6]

The name David even stands out in the Qumran literature in reference to the contents of authoritative scripture, when 4QMMT speaks of 'the book of Moses, the book[s of the Pr]ophets, and Davi[d ...]' (4Q397 frgs. 14–21 line 10; 4Q398 frgs. 14–17, col. i, lines 2–3). What exactly is meant by 'David' is disputed, but whether it

---

[3] Peter W. Flint, 'The Prophet David at Qumran', in Matthias Henze (ed.), *Biblical Interpretation at Qumran*, Studies in the Dead Sea Scrolls and Related Literature (Grand Rapids, MI: Eerdmans, 2005), 158–67.

[4] This tally may have been inspired by 1 Kgs 5.12: 'Solomon also uttered three thousand proverbs.'

[5] Translation by Geert W. Lorein and Eveline van Staalduine-Sulman, 'Songs of David: A New Translation and Introduction', in Richard J. Bauckham, James R. Davila and Alexander Panayotov (eds), *Old Testament Pseudepigrapha: More Noncanonical Scriptures*, vol. 1 (Grand Rapids, MI: Eerdmans, 2013), 265. The *Songs of David* are preserved in one ms. (Antonin Ms 798) recovered from the Cairo Genizah (Lorein and van Staalduine-Sulman, 'Songs of David', 257). For the Hebrew text, see David M. Stec, *The Genizah Psalms: A Study of MS 798 of the Antonin Collection*, Études sur le Judaïsme Médiéval 57, Cambridge Genizah Studies Series 5 (Leiden: Brill, 2013), 8.

[6] For a succinct assessment, see Lorein and van Staalduine-Sulman, 'Songs of David', 259–62.

refers to the Psalter or to a larger corpus of material, the mere fact that his name stands alongside such weighty classifications as 'book of Moses' and 'books of the Prophets' is quite remarkable. We may have something like this in Luke 24, where the risen Jesus tells his disciples that 'everything written about me in the law of Moses and in the Prophets and Psalms [τοῖς προφήταις καὶ ψαλμοῖς] must be fulfilled' (Lk. 24.44). This language implies a close connection between the Prophets and the psalms, as though the latter is part of the former. And if the psalms are prophetic (and Qumran's *pesharim* on the psalms support this possibility), then their principal writer, David, is prophetic as well.

In Philo (*c.* 20 BCE – 50 CE) David is presented as a prophet, whose inspired utterances are found in the psalms. He 'is not any ordinary person, but a prophet [προφήτης] ... who wrote the psalms' (*De agricultura* 50, quoting LXX Ps. 22.1; cf. *Quis rerum divinarum heres sit* 290, paraphrasing LXX Ps. 83.11; cf. *De plantatione* 29, paraphrasing LXX Ps. 93.9).[7]

Josephus (*c.* 36–100 CE) also regarded David as a prophet. According to the Hebrew Bible, when Samuel the priest and prophet anointed David as Israel's new king, the 'Spirit of the Lord came mightily upon David [תִּצְלַח רוּחַ־יְהוָה אֶל־דָּוִד] / καὶ ἐφήλατο πνεῦμα κυρίου ἐπὶ Δαυίδ]' (1 Sam. 16.13). Shortly thereafter 'the Spirit of the Lord departed from Saul' (v. 14). One can see how saying that the Spirit 'came mightily upon David' could lead to the idea that he was able to prophesy, but alone this affirmation is not enough. After all, the same is said of Samson (Judg. 13.25; 14.6, 19; 15.14, 19) and other Israelite judges (e.g. Judg. 11.29) and none of them attained true prophetic status. However, in his paraphrase of 1 Sam. 16.13 Josephus says, 'and the Deity abandoned Saul and passed over to David, who, when the divine spirit had removed to him, began to prophesy [καὶ ὁ μὲν προφητεύειν ἤρξατο τοῦ θείου πνεύματος εἰς αὐτὸν μετοικισαμένου]' (*Ant.* 6.166). Josephus may have assumed that if Saul acted and spoke as a prophet (1 Sam. 10.11-12; 19.24), David would have also. In his narration of the life of Solomon, Josephus has the famous monarch recall the prophetic insights of his late father, how God 'had shown all things that were to come to pass to David' and how God had disclosed to David that after his death his son 'should build God a temple', which has taken place, 'according to his prophecy [κατὰ τὴν ἐκείνου προφητείαν]' (*Ant.* 8.109-110).[8]

David's prophetic gifts are explicit in the Targum. According to the Aramaic version, he frequently speaks 'in the spirit of prophecy' [ברוח נבואה] (e.g. *Tg.* 2 Sam. 22.1; *Tg.* Pss. 14.1; 18.1; 49.16; cf. *Tg.* Pss. 51.13-14; 103.1; *Tg.* Song 1.1; *Tg.* 2 Sam. 23.2; *Tg.* 1 Chr. 23.27; *Tg.* 2 Chr. 8.14).[9] This tradition of David as a prophet is equally widely

---

[7] See the brief but incisive discussion in Erwin R. Goodenough, *By Light, Light: The Mystic Gospel of Hellenistic Judaism* (New Haven, CT: Yale University Press, 1935), 76–7.

[8] For additional comments, see Christopher T. Begg, *Flavius Josephus: Translation and Commentary. Volume 4: Flavius Josephus Judean Antiquities 5–7* (Leiden: Brill, 2005), 144–5 n. 601.

[9] See the discussion of prophecy in the Psalms Targum in David M. Stec, *The Targum of Psalms: Translated, with a Critical Introduction, Apparatus, and Notes*, ArBib 16 (Collegeville, MN: Liturgical Press, 2004), 5–6. *Tg.* Ps. 54.3 ('Your beauty, O King Messiah, is greater than the sons of men; the spirit of prophecy (רוח נבואה) has been placed on your lips') probably (*contra* the Rabbis) is in reference to the eschatological Messiah, not the historical David.

attested in rabbinic midrash, both early and late. As an example of the former, we learn that the Holy Spirit came upon the house of David because of what it says in Zech. 12.10, 'I will pour upon the house of David … the spirit of grace [רוּחַ חֵן]' (*Mek. Pisha* 13).[10] In a discussion of David's divine election to be king over Israel (with citation of 2 Chr. 13.5), David confesses, 'I am from the prophets [אנכי מן הנביאים] who speak' (*Praefatio* to *Mekilta*).[11] Commenting on Prov. 11.27 ('He who diligently seeks good seeks favour') we are told in the *Midrash on the Psalms* that 'David procured God's favor so that the Holy Spirit came to rest upon him, and thus he was able to bless the children of Israel' (*Midr. Pss.* 1.1).[12] The implication is that David was able to compose and sing his songs because of the Holy Spirit, a view that agrees with the extravagant claims made in 11Q5. Elsewhere in this midrash the Rabbis inquire into the differing word order of the phrases 'A Psalm of David' and 'To David, a Psalm' seen in the Masoretic Text: 'When David sought the Holy Spirit to rest upon him, he summoned it with the words, "A Psalm of David"; but when the Holy Spirit came to him of its own accord, he said, "To David, a Psalm"' (*Midr. Pss.* 24.1 (on Ps. 24.1)).[13]

In the Talmud David is identified as a 'former prophet' [נביאים הראשונים], together with Samuel, and Solomon' (*b. Sotah* 48b; cf. *y. Sotah* 9.24b). In the much later *Seder 'Olam* he is numbered among those in scripture called 'man of God' (cf. 2 Chr. 8.14), men who are also recognized as prophets (*Seder 'Olam* §20). Finally, in the late Middle Ages an *Apocalypse of David* of unknown origin found its way into the Hekhalot literature.[14] At the conclusion of this apocalypse King David appears at the head of a procession of all of his royal successors (§125), during which he recites Ps. 146.10 and then speaks 'hymns and praises that no ear has ever heard' (§126, possibly alluding to Isa. 64.4 and/or the tradition behind *Bib. Ant.* 26.13).

David as prophet in early Christian literature

The foregoing review of Jewish literature makes it clear that David was widely understood to have been a prophet and that his psalms were regarded as prophecies.[15] Building on this foundation, as well as on the numerous references to the prophetic words of David within the New Testament outlined above, several early Christian authors unsurprisingly refer to him in a similar vein as a prophet who spoke of

---

[10] LXX Zech. 12.10 πνεῦμα χάριτος. 'Spirit of grace' is understood as the equivalent of 'Holy Spirit'.
[11] M. Friedmann, *Mechilta de-Rabbi Ismaël* (Vienna: Published by the author, 1870), 2: פתחתא.
[12] Translation based on William G. Braude, *The Midrash on Psalms*, YJS 13 (London: Yale University Press, 1959), 1:3. Lit. 'the Shekinah rested on him' (שהשרה עליו שכינה).
[13] Translation based on Braude, *Midrash on Psalms*, 1:336.
[14] The *Apocalypse of David* is the first of three apocalypses preserved in MS. New York 8128, whose contents are summarized in Peter Schäfer (ed.), *Synopse zur Hekhalot-Literatur*, TSAJ 2 (Tübingen: Mohr Siebeck, 1981), x–xiv. It is also preserved in MS Budapest. In *Hekhalot Rabbati* the *Apocalypse of David* appears as paragraphs §§122–6. (The second and third apocalypses appear in §§130–8 and §§140–51.) For a learned analysis of the *Apocalypse of David* and the mss. in which it appears, see Ulrike Hirschfelder, 'The Liturgy of the Messiah: The Apocalypse of David in Hekhalot Literature', *Jewish Studies Quarterly* 12 (2005): 148–93. For discussion of §126, see 175–8.
[15] See Brooke, 'The Psalms'; James L. Kugel, 'David the Prophet', in James L. Kugel (ed.), *Poetry and Prophecy: The Beginnings of a Literary Tradition* (Ithaca, NY: Cornell University Press, 1990), 45–55.

things fulfilled in the life, death and resurrection of Jesus. As in Acts, so in later Christian literature, for instance, the statement that Israel's great king was a prophet never requires a defence. In the Coptic *Epistula Apostolorum* 19.18-19 Jesus quotes the words of Ps. 3.1-8, which he introduces as 'the prophecy [προφητια] of David the prophet [προφητης] (that) might be fulfilled concerning what he [said] both of my death and of my resurrection' (*Ep. Apost.* 19.18).[16] Elsewhere Jesus tells his disciples, 'Truly I say to you, as the prophet David spoke concerning me ... the prophecy of David will come to pass' (*Ep. Apost.* 35.4-5; cf. Pss. 13.3; 49.18, 19, 20-21).[17]

According to the *Epistle of Barnabas* (in circulation before 130), David uttered the prophetic words of Ps. 110.1, because he anticipated the 'error of sinners' who will assert that the Messiah is only the 'son of David'. Therefore, 'David himself prophesies' (αὐτὸς προφητεύει Δαυίδ), speaking the words of the well-known psalm (*Ep. Barn.* 12.10).[18] Elsewhere David's psalms are referenced as prophecies and David himself, whether named or not, is referred to as 'the one who prophesies' or 'the prophet' (e.g. *Ep. Barn.* 5.13 ὁ προφητεύων ἐπ' αὐτῷ; cf. LXX Ps. 21.21, 17 (in that order); *Ep. Barn.* 6.4 ὁ προφήτης; cf. LXX Ps. 117.22, 24; *Ep. Barn.* 6.6-7 ὁ προφήτης; cf. LXX Ps. 21.17, 19; *Ep. Barn.* 6.16 λέγει γὰρ κύριος πάλιν[19]; cf. LXX Pss. 41.3; 21.23; *Ep. Barn.* 9.1 λέγει κύριος ἐν τῷ προφήτῃ; cf. LXX Ps. 17.45; *Ep. Barn.* 9.2 πάλιν τὸ πνεῦμα κυρίου προφητεύει; cf. LXX Ps. 33.13; *Ep. Barn.* 11.6-7 πάλιν ἐν ἄλλῳ προφήτῃ λέγει; cf. LXX Ps. 1.3-6).

Justin Martyr (*c.* 100–160) also frequently appeals to David as a prophet. Many examples appear in his *First Apology* and in his *Dialogue with Trypho*. After quoting LXX Ps. 21.17 ('they pierced my hands and feet') and LXX Ps. 21.19 ('and cast lots for my clothing') Justin asserts that 'David, the king and prophet [ὁ βασιλεὺς καὶ προφήτης] who said this, suffered none of these things' (*1 Apol.* 35.5-6). The prophecy, therefore, must have been fulfilled in the death of Jesus. David is credited with prophesying many other elements of Jesus's life and death, including his human birth and heavenly exaltation (*Dialogus cum Tryphone* 76.7; cf. LXX Pss. 44.12; 88.37-38; 109.3); his entry into Jerusalem to begin Passion Week (ὁ λόγος ὁ τῆς προφητείας τῆς διὰ Δαβὶδ ἐπᾶραι τὰς πύλας; *Dialogus cum Tryphone* 85.4, alluding to LXX Ps. 117-19); and the coming of the Holy Spirit upon Jesus (*Dialogus cum Tryphone* 88.8, quoting LXX Ps. 2.7; cf. *1 Apol.* 40.1-4, 5; 41.1-4; 45.1-4; *Dialogus cum Tryphone* 28.5).[20] Justin also assures Trypho that 'through David he (God) spoke [διὰ τοῦ Δαβὶδ ἔφη]' the words of LXX Ps.

---

[16] I have quoted the English translation of the Coptic text. The writing is also extant in Ethiopic. See Julian V. Hills, *The Epistle of the Apostles*, Early Christian Apocrypha 2 (Santa Rosa, CA: Polebridge Press, 2009), 45. The Greek loan words that appear in the Coptic text are noted in square brackets.

[17] Here I have quoted the English translation of the Ethiopic text. See Hills, *Epistle of the Apostles*, 63.

[18] The author of the *Epistle of Barnabas* shows that he rightly understood Mk 12.35-37 par. For discussion, see Helmut Köster, *Synoptische Überlieferung bei den apostolischen Vätern*, TU 65 (Berlin: Akademie-Verlag, 1957), 145–6; R. A. Kraft, *The Apostolic Fathers: A Translation and Commentary. Volume 3: Barnabas and the Didache* (New York: Thomas Nelson, 1965), 120–2. See also Ps.-Clementine *Homilies* 18.13, which makes a similar argument with regard to LXX Ps. 109.1.

[19] Here the 'Lord' is understood as speaking the words of David's Psalms (as in *Ep. Barn.* 9.1-2).

[20] Justin's προφητικὸν πνεῦμα, 'prophetic Spirit', reminds us of Philo's τις προφητικὸς ἀνήρ, 'a certain prophetic man' (*Quis rerum divinarum heres sit* 290), a passage noted above.

17:44-45, and that Jesus 'the Lord is called the Christ by the Holy prophetic Spirit [ὑπὸ τοῦ ἁγίου προφητικοῦ Πνεύματος]' (*Dialogus cum Tryphone* 28.5; 32.3), eventually citing LXX Ps. 109.1. It is important to observe that it is the same 'prophetic Spirit' that speaks through other prophets, like Isaiah (cf. *Dialogus cum Tryphone* 43.3; 56.5; 85.1; 87.4) and Moses (*Dialogus cum Tryphone* 56.14).

Later fathers continue to view David as an inspired prophet. Church historian Eusebius (*c*. 250–340) refers to the 'prophets' (οἱ προφῆται) and then cites David as an example (*Eccl. Hist.* 1.3.6). Athanasius (*c*. 296–373) sometimes cites passages from those psalms attributed to David and then alongside cites passages from the Prophets. In one place he cites David (LXX Ps. 92.1) and then says, 'This text in the prophet [τὸ ἄρα παρὰ τῷ προφήτῃ ῥητόν] signifies the coming of the Savior' (*Ep. Serap*. 1.10), clearly implying that David is a prophet. In the same letter Athanasius says that 'the prophet David [ὁ προφήτης Δαυίδ] prayed, saying: "Send out your light and your truth"' (*Ep. Serap*. 1.33, quoting LXX Ps. 42.3). Jerome says the Holy Spirit speaks through the prophecy of David (*Comm. in ep. ad Galatas* 4.5, 'when the prophet says', quoting Ps. 51.10-12; 4.19, 'the prophet recalls', quoting Ps. 139.16; 5.10, 'a prophetic spirit').

In Christian pseudepigraphal literature David enjoys the status of inspired prophet: 'David the prophet says [λέγει Δαυὶδ ὁ προφήτης]: "Do you not know, O blind, that I when living in the world prophesied this saying: Lift up your gates, O you rulers?"' (*Acts of Pilate* 21.2 (5.2)). In the *Apocalypse of Paul* 29 David is introduced as a prophet, and in the Syriac *Apocalypse of Paul* we are told that 'David, the prophet, saw by the spirit, the passion of our Lord, and his crucifixion, saying, "They pierced my hands and my feet"' (quoting Ps. 22.16b).[21] No doubt inspired by the New Testament's Book of Acts, David is mentioned often as a prophet in some of the apocryphal books of Acts (e.g. *Mart. Peter Paul* 8.2; 9.2; *Acts of Philip* 78.6, 9). In the medieval *Palaea Historica* there is reference to an unknown source in which a wise man speaks 'to David your prophet [Δαυὶδ προφήτα τῷ σῷ]' (*Pal. Hist.* 161.16).[22] In the Ethiopic *Epistle of Dionysius the Areopagite to Timothy* 53 we find: 'On this day the words of the prophet David have been fulfilled, saying, "They gave the dead bodies of Thy servants as food for the fowl"' (quoting Ps. 79.2; cf. *Ep. Dion. Areop.* 57, quoting 2 Sam. 18.33).[23] In the Ethiopic *Apocalypse of Peter* Pss. 24.6, 7-9 are quoted as 'fulfilled' (*Eth. Apoc. Pet.* 17). The psalm, of course, is attributed to David.

---

[21] The translation of the Syriac text is from Justin Perkins, 'The Revelation of the Blessed Apostle Paul', *Journal of the American Oriental Society* 8 (1866): 183–212 (186).

[22] For Greek text, see Afanasiĭ Vassiliev, *Anecdota Graeco-Byzantina* (Moscow: Caesarea University, 1893), 287. For English translation and chapter and verse numbering, see William Adler, '*Palaea Historica* ("The Old Testament History"): A New Translation and Introduction', in Richard J. Bauckham, James R. Davila and Alexander Panayotov (eds), *Old Testament Pseudepigrapha: More Noncanonical Scriptures*, vol. 1 (Grand Rapids, MI: Eerdmans, 2013), 668.

[23] The translation is from E. A. Wallis Budge, *The Contending of the Apostles: The Histories of the Lives and Martyrdoms and Deaths of the Twelve Apostles and Evangelists, vol. II. The English Translation* (London: Henry Frowde, 1901), 55.

David's prophetic status in the first apocryphal *Apocalypse of John*

David's role as prophet reaches its zenith in the first apocryphal *Apocalypse of John*. There are four known apocryphal apocalypses of John, all of them to one degree or another inspired by the New Testament Revelation of John. The first apocryphal *Apocalypse* is Greek and may have originated in the early fifth century. Constantine Tischendorf published a text based on several mss.[24] The second apocryphal *Apocalypse of John* dates to the sixth to eighth centuries. The principal ms. (BnF gr. 947), published by François Nau in 1914,[25] attributes it to John Chrysostom. The third apocryphal apocalypse was found in a fourteenth-century codex and was published by Afanasiĭ Vassiliev in 1893.[26] A fourth apocryphal *Apocalypse of John* is extant in an early eleventh-century Coptic ms. It was published by E. A. Wallis Budge in 1913.[27] John Court published all four apocryphal apocalypses, with Greek-English facing pages for the first three and English translation only for the fourth.[28]

Rick Brannan has published a new English translation of the first apocryphal *Apocalypse of John* with introduction (which includes a very helpful updated list of the manuscripts), notes and brief commentary.[29] Little is known of this text. Its first mention is in a ninth-century grammar, where it is described as 'pseudonymous and spurious' (ψευδώνυμον καὶ ἀλλότριον).[30] It is presented as a series of questions and answers mostly concerned with the Antichrist, angels and eschatological judgment.[31] John Court remarks that this text 'imitates the canonical Book of Revelation in many respects'.[32] True enough, but in one important respect it does not imitate its canonical

---

[24] C. Tischendorf, *Apocalypses Apocryphae* (Leipzig: H. Mendelssohn, 1866), 70–94.

[25] François Nau, 'Une deuxième Apocalypse apocryphe grecque de S. Jean', *RB* 23 (1914): 209–21. Nau provides an introduction, Greek text and French translation. The incipit reads: 'Of our father John Chrysostom, archbishop of the city of Constantinople'. The name 'Chrysostom' also appears in 3.1.

[26] Vassiliev, *Anecdota Graeco-Byzantina*, 317–22. The text is from St Mark in Venice Codex 87.

[27] E. A. Wallis Budge, *Coptic Apocrypha in the Dialect of Upper Egypt* (London: Longmans, 1913), 59–74 (Coptic text), 241–57 (English translation). The text is from British Museum Oriental MS 7026.

[28] It is very conveniently laid out in John M. Court, *The Book of Revelation and the Johannine Apocalyptic Tradition*, JSNTSup 190 (Sheffield: Sheffield Academic Press, 2000). Court numbered the four apocryphal apocalypses as *Second Apocalypse of John*, *Apocalypse of John Chrysostom*, *Third Apocalypse of John* and *Coptic Apocalypse of John*. They are also referenced as *1 Apocr. Apoc. John*, *2 Apocr. Apoc. John* and so on. Other writings that are part of the Johannine Apocalyptica include the *Questions of John to Abraham*, the *Mysteries of John*, the *Questions of John*, the *Questions of James to John* and the *Apocryphon of John*.

[29] Rick Brannan, '1 Apocryphal Apocalypse of John', in Tony Burke (ed.), *New Testament Apocrypha: More Noncanonical Scriptures*, vol. 2 (Grand Rapids, MI: Eerdmans, 2020), 378–98. The Greek text and facing English translation appear in Court, *Book of Revelation*, 32–47. Court (48–65) also supplies notes. An older translation is found in Alexander Walker, *Apocryphal Gospels, Acts, and Revelations* (Edinburgh: T&T Clark, 1870), 493–503.

[30] Alfred Hilgard, *Scholia in Dionysii Thracis artem grammaticam*, Grammatici Graeci 3 (Leipzig: B. G. Teubner, 1901), 568; Court, *Book of Revelation*, 30.

[31] Jean-Daniel Kaestli, 'La Figure de l'Antichrist dans l'Apocalypse de Saint Jean Le Théologien (Première Apocalypse Apocryphe de Jean)', in J.-M. Blanchard, B. Pouderon and M. Scopello (eds), *Les forces du Bien et du Mal dans les premiers siècles de l'Église*, ThH 118 (Paris: Beauchesne, 2011), 277–90.

[32] Court (*The Book of Revelation*, 2) draws attention to Heinrich Weinel's comment that the first apocryphal *Apocalypse of John* seems to have been written as a 'completion' (*Ergänzung*) of the

counterpart: The first apocryphal *Apocalypse of John* many times explicitly quotes scripture. The canonical Revelation of John never does; its use of scripture is allusive.[33]

In the first apocryphal *Apocalypse of John* David is referenced and cited formally many times. In the canonical Book of Revelation David's name appears three times, all of which allude to prophecies of Isaiah. In Rev. 3.7 the risen Jesus, speaking to John, prefaces his message to the church of Philadelphia: 'The words of the holy one, the true one, who has the key of David, who opens and no one shall shut, who shuts and no one opens.' The allusion to Isa. 22.22 is unmistakable, though it likely presupposes little of the original Isaianic context. Whatever the original meaning in Isaiah, Jesus now holds the 'key of David', which implies that he has inherited David's authority.[34] In the next two texts the risen Jesus will claim descent from David. In Rev. 5.5 a heavenly elder tells John that Jesus is 'the Lion of the tribe of Judah, the Root of David', and in Rev. 22.16 Jesus identifies himself as 'the root and the offspring of David, the bright morning star'. The epithet 'the Lion of the tribe of Judah' alludes to Gen. 49.9-10 and 'bright morning star' probably alludes to Num. 24.17,[35] while the epithet 'the Root of David [ἡ ῥίζα Δαυίδ]' alludes to LXX Isa. 11.1-10, where twice we hear of ἡ ῥίζα τοῦ Ιεσσαι, 'the Root of Jesse' (vv. 1 and 10). The 'root' (in Hebrew as חֹטֶר, 'shoot', and, especially, צֶמַח, 'branch') of David becomes a messianic title (cf. Jer. 23.5; Zech. 3.8; 6.12; and several texts from Qumran).

In Rev. 5.6 there is also mention of a Lamb that had been slain, which of course refers to the crucified Jesus with Passover ideas.[36] How exactly the images of Lion and Lamb complement one another has been much debated.[37] But for the purposes

---

canonical work. See Heinrich Weinel, 'Die spätere christliche Apokalyptik', in Hans Schmidt (ed.), *EYXAPIΣTHPION: Studien zur Religion und Literatur des Alten und Neuen Testaments. Hermann Gunkel zum 60. Geburtstag, dem 23. Mai 1922 dargebracht von seinen Schülern und Freunden.* 2. Teil: *Zur Religion und Literatur des Neuen Testaments*, FRLANT 19 (Göttingen: Vandehoeck & Ruprecht, 1923), 141-73 (149).

[33] Several scholars have made this observation. See Jon Paulien, 'Elusive Allusions: The Problematic Use of the Old Testament in Revelation', *Biblical Research* 37 (1988): 37–53. It is interesting to note that when it comes to allusions to the Psalter, canonical Revelation seems to follow the Greek, not the Hebrew. See Steve Moyise, 'The Language of the Psalms in the Book of Revelation', *Neot.* 37 (2003): 246–61. The first apocryphal *Apocalypse of John* depends heavily on the Greek Psalter.

[34] See David E. Aune, *Revelation 1-5*, WBC 52A (Nashville, TN: Nelson, 1997), 235-6. In a Coptic magic text (London Oriental MS 5987) the 'key of David' becomes the 'key of deity'. For German translation, with brief introduction, see Viktor Stegemann, *Die Gestalt Christi in den koptischen Zaubertexten* (Heidelberg: S. Bilabel, 1934), 19–21. Stegemann (20) dates the text to the fourth or fifth century. For English translation, see Marvin Meyer and Richard Smith (eds), *Ancient Christian Magic: Coptic Texts of Ritual Power* (Princeton, NJ: Princeton University Press, 1999), 129–33, with quotation from page 132. For the Coptic text, see Angelicus Kropp, *Ausgewählte koptische Zaubertexte*, Bd. I: *Textpublikation* (Bruxelles: Fondation Égyptologique Reine Élisabeth, 1931), 22–5 (24).

[35] On the 'morning star', see the discussion in David E. Aune, *Revelation 17-22*, WBC 52C (Nashville, TN: Nelson, 1997), 1226–7.

[36] Which probably includes the Johannine confession that Jesus is 'the Lamb of God, who takes away the sin of the world' (Jn 1.29).

[37] The complexities and options are well considered in S. Moyise, *The Old Testament in the Book of Revelation*, JSNTSup 115 (Sheffield: Sheffield Academic Press, 1995), 128–35; S. Moyise, 'Intertextuality and the Study of the Old Testament in the New Testament', in Steve Moyise (ed.), *The Old Testament in the New Testament: Essays in Honour of J. L. North*, JSNTSup 189 (Sheffield: Sheffield Academic Press, 2000), 14–41 (26–32).

of the present study it is enough that David appears in canonical Revelation. Jesus is identified as the 'root and offspring of David' and he claims to be in possession of the 'key of David'. Given David's well-established reputation as a prophet, the author of first apocryphal *Apocalypse of John* (hereafter *Apocalypse*) may have believed that it was natural – perhaps necessary – that David uttered many prophecies regarding his exalted and awaited descendant. The author of the new apocalypse has identified and contextualized those Davidic prophecies.

This author arranges his material into a series of questions and answers, a format seen in many other apocalyptic texts. John asks the risen Jesus (the 'Lord') several questions, who usually answers as a 'voice'. David the prophet appears in *Apoc.* 8, 9, 15, 20, 21, 22, 23, 24, 25, 26 and (perhaps) 28. David is by far the *Apocalypse*'s most important prophetic witness. The passages are as follows:

Apocalypse 8. John asks, 'O Lord, how many years will this one be active upon the earth?' The Lord replies that the Antichrist's time will be like three years reduced to three months, which will be reduced to three weeks, which will be reduced to three days, which will be reduced to three hours, which will be reduced to three moments, 'just as the prophet David said [καθὼς εἶπεν ὁ προφήτης Δαυίδ], "His throne you smashed to the ground [τὸν θρόνον αὐτοῦ εἰς τὴν γῆν κατέρραξας]. You diminished the days of his time [ἐσμίκρυνας τὰς ἡμέρας τοῦ χρόνου αὐτοῦ], you covered him with shame [κατέχεας αὐτῷ αἰσχύνην]."'

The prophecy that the time will be shortened from years, to months, to days and so on is based on the dominical assurance expressed in the Synoptic eschatological discourse: 'And if the Lord had not shortened the days, no human being would be saved; but for the sake of the elect, whom he chose, he shortened the days' (Mk 13.20; cf. Mt. 24.22). In *Apocalypse* 8 the days are quite literally shortened.[38]

The first prophecy attributed to David draws upon LXX Ps. 88.45b-46, τὸν θρόνον αὐτοῦ εἰς τὴν γῆν κατέρραξας, ἐσμίκρυνας τὰς ἡμέρας τοῦ χρόνου αὐτοῦ, κατέχεας αὐτοῦ αἰσχύνην. The Greek text is cited verbatim. The promised shortened days of Mk 13.20 match the prophecy of the shortened days in the passage from the Psalter. Appeal to this passage shifts the meaning of the dominical prophecy somewhat, in that what is now promised isn't so much a shortened period of tribulation but a much reduced period of time in which the Antichrist rules.

The Lord tells John that he will send Enoch and Elijah to accuse the Antichrist and prove him to be a liar and a deceiver. Enoch and Elijah should be understood as the two unnamed witnesses mentioned in Rev. 11.1-13. The context suggests that Zerubbabel and Joshua are in view (compare v. 4 with Zech. 3.1–4.14), but there are also allusions to Elijah (compare vv. 5–6 with 2 Kgs 1.10) and Moses (compare v. 6 with Exod. 7.17, 19). Because Moses and Elijah passed from life in a mysterious way (Deut. 34.5-6; 2 Kgs 2.11-12), it was popular to identify them with Revelation's two unnamed witnesses.[39] But the departure from mortal life was also mysterious in the case of Enoch (Gen. 5.21-24), so it should not surprise that Church Fathers (e.g. Irenaeus and

---

[38] As rightly noted in Court, *Book of Revelation*, 51.
[39] For learned discussion, see David E. Aune, *Revelation 6–16*, WBC 52B (Nashville, TN: Nelson, 1998), 598–603, 610–30.

Hippolytus) identified Revelation's two witnesses with Enoch and Elijah,[40] which is what we see here in the first apocryphal *Apocalypse*.[41]

The Lord tells John that the Antichrist will kill Enoch and Elijah 'upon the altar, just as the prophet [ὁ προφήτης] said, "They will offer on your altar calves [ὅτε ἀνοίσωσιν ἐπὶ τὸ θυσιαστήριόν σου μόσχους]."' 'The prophet' is David (and the psalm, both in the Hebrew[42] and in the Greek, is attributed to David). The prophecy is taken verbatim from LXX Ps. 50.21 (= MT 51.19). Foretelling the martyrdom of the two witnesses alludes to Rev. 11.7. It is not obvious why the *Apocalypse* applies LXX Ps. 50.21 to the martyred witnesses. It could be that the martyrdom of the witnesses was understood as a sin offering that facilitates the coming redemption.

Apocalypse 9. John asks what will happen after the martyrdom of the two witnesses. He is told that the whole human race will die, then the angels Michael and Gabriel[43] will sound the trumpet, 'as the prophet David foretold [προεῖπεν ὁ προφήτης Δαυίδ], "with the voice of a horn trumpet [ἐν φωνῇ σάλπιγγος κερατίνης]"'. David's prophecy is a shortened version of LXX Ps. 97.6a, ἐν σάλπιγξιν ἐλαταῖς καὶ φωνῇ σάλπιγγος κερατίνης, 'with metal trumpets and the sound of a horn trumpet' (NETS).

John is told that the sound of the horn will be heard throughout the world and that its sound is so great the earth will shake.[44] This too was prophesied by David: 'just as the prophet foretold, "and by the sound of the sparrow every plant will rise up [καὶ ὑπὸ τὴν φωνὴν τοῦ στρουθίου ἀναστήσεται πᾶσα βοτάνη]"'. David's 'prophecy' appears to be based on Eccl. 12.4, καὶ ἀναστήσεται εἰς φωνὴν τοῦ στρουθίου, 'and he will rise up at the sound of the sparrow'.[45] In the *Apocalypse*'s prophecy, however, it is not a person who rises up (i.e. awakens) at the sound of a sparrow's chirping, it is 'every plant' (πᾶσα βοτάνη).[46] Although the language and imagery of Heb. 6.7 may have influenced the wording of this prophecy,[47] it is likely that what lies behind it is a saying found in the Fourth Gospel: 'Truly, truly, I say to you, unless a grain of wheat falls into the earth and dies, it remains alone; but if it dies, it bears much fruit' (Jn 12.24). In the Johannine context, the seed that dies and falls into the earth is Jesus who dies and is buried, which then results in resurrection. This well suits the context of the *Apocalypse*, which says,

---

[40] The two witnesses are explicitly identified as Enoch and Elijah in *Apoc. Elij.* 4.7-19.

[41] Court, *Book of Revelation*, 51.

[42] And this includes Psalm 51 at Qumran as well (cf. 4QPs^c).

[43] The archangels Michael and Gabriel appear often in Jewish and Christian literature. For Michael, see Dan. 10.13, 21; 12.1; Jude 9; Rev. 12.7; *1 Enoch* 9.1; 10.11; 20.5; 24.6; *3 Bar.* 11.2, 4; 12.1, 7; 13.2-3; *Acts of Andrew and Matthew* 30.3; *Acts of Peter and Andrew* 10.3; *Acts of Philip* 137.2; *Acts of Pilate* 25.1; 26.1; 27.1; for Gabriel, see Dan. 8.16; 9.21; *1 Enoch* 9.1; 10.9; *Jub.* 2.1; 48.1; Lk. 1.19, 26; *T. Sol.* 18.6; *Mart. Bart.* 4.8.

[44] According to Isa. 27.13, 'in that day a great trumpet [τῇ σάλπιγγι τῇ μεγάλῃ] will be blown' and all Israelites scattered throughout the world will return to Jerusalem.

[45] It is curious that the author of the *Apocalypse* appeals to Ecclesiastes for a Davidic prophecy. Ecclesiastes begins by claiming to be 'the words of the Preacher, the son of David' (Eccl. 1.1), which traditionally has been understood as Solomon, son and successor of David.

[46] In MS F (Biblioteca Apostolica Vaticana, Pal. Gr. 364) we find a different reading: 'and from the sound of that horn all the dead of the earth will be raised, just as the prophet David said, "And by the voice of the sparrows" the whole human race (will rise up).' I have cited Brannan, '1 Apocryphal Apocalypse of John', 391 n. b.

[47] 'For land which has drunk the rain that often falls upon it, and brings forth vegetation [τίκτουσα βοτάνην] useful to those for whose sake it is cultivated, receives a blessing from God.'

'This is understood to mean that by voice of the archangel the whole human race will rise up.'

MS E (Biblioteca Nazionale Marciana, gr. II.90) adds: 'They that have gold and silver will throw them into the streets, and into every place in the world, and no one will heed them. They will throw into the streets ivory vessels and robes adorned with stones and pearls; kings and rulers wasting away with hunger.' The longer reading may have been inspired by Ezekiel's grim prophecy of the suffering of those besieged in Jerusalem by the Babylonians:

> They cast their silver into the streets, and their gold is like an unclean thing; their silver and gold are not able to deliver them in the day of the wrath of the Lord; they cannot satisfy their hunger or fill their stomachs with it. For it was the stumbling block of their iniquity.[20] Their beautiful ornament they used for vainglory, and they made their abominable images and their detestable things of it; therefore I will make it an unclean thing to them. (Ezek. 7.19-20)

The longer passage in MS E may also allude to a passage in Isaiah: 'In that day men will cast forth their idols of silver and their idols of gold, which they made for themselves to worship, to the moles and to the bats' (Isa. 2.20).

The *Apocalypse*'s ὑπὸ τὴν φωνὴν ἀρχαγγέλου ('by voice of the archangel'), taken with the earlier reference to ἐν φωνῇ σάλπιγγος ('with sound of the trumpet'), is an unmistakable allusion to 1 Thess. 4.16, 'For the Lord himself will descend from heaven with a cry of command, with the voice of the archangel, and with the sound of the trumpet of God [ἐν φωνῇ ἀρχαγγέλου καὶ ἐν σάλπιγγι θεοῦ]. And the dead in Christ will rise first.'[48] *Apocalypse* 13 will quote 1 Thess. 4.17.

Apocalypse 12. John asks the risen Jesus if the righteous in heaven will give any thought to the things of earth, such as fields or vineyards. The voice of the Lord replies: 'The prophet David affirms (this), saying, "I remembered that we are dust [ἐμνήσθην ὅτι χοῦς ἐσμέν]. Man is as a flower of the field [ἄνθρωπος ὡσεὶ ἄνθος τοῦ ἀγροῦ], thus he blossoms [οὕτως ἐξανθήσει]; for a wind has passed over it [ὅτι πνεῦμα διῆλθεν ἐν αὐτῷ] and it shall be no more [καὶ οὐχ ὑπάρξει], and it shall no longer know its place [καὶ οὐκ ἐπιγνώσεται ἔτι τὸν τόπον αὐτοῦ]."' David's prophecy, with minor variation, is a verbatim quotation of LXX Ps. 102.14b-16. The only significant variant is that the LXX's imperative 'Remember [μνήσθητι] that we are dust' becomes an indicative in the *Apocalypse*, 'I remembered [ἐμνήσθην] that we are dust.' The final line of the quotation, οὐκ ἐπιγνώσεται ἔτι τὸν τόπον αὐτοῦ, 'it shall no longer know its place', answers John's question about whether the righteous will give thought to the things of earth.

---

[48] Paul's language echoes LXX Ps. 46.6, ἀνέβη ὁ θεὸς ἐν ἀλαλαγμῷ, κύριος ἐν φωνῇ σάλπιγγος: 'God went up with a shout, the Lord (went up) with the sound of a trumpet.' Church fathers linked LXX Ps. 46.6 with the ascension and second coming of Christ. For further discussion, see Craig A. Evans, 'Ascending and Descending with a Shout: Psalm 47.6 and 1 Thessalonians 4.16', in Craig A. Evans and James A. Sanders (eds), *Paul and the Scriptures of Israel*, JSNTSup 83, SSEJC 1 (Sheffield: JSOT Press, 1993), 238–53.

The answer is further clarified by yet another prophecy: 'And again, the same one (i.e., the prophet David) said, "His breath [τὸ πνεῦμα αὐτοῦ] will depart, and he will return to his earth; in that very day all his designs will perish."' This time the 'prophecy' is from LXX Ps. 145.4. The quotation is verbatim with the exception of the personal pronoun in the last clause. Whereas the LXX reads 'all their designs' (πάντες οἱ διαλογισμοὶ αὐτῶν), the *Apocalypse* reads 'all his designs' (πάντες οἱ διαλογισμοὶ αὐτοῦ), which fits the verse better grammatically. The idea is that at death a man returns to the earth (or the 'dust', as in the first quotation) and his 'designs' (or 'reasonings') perish. The implication is that he will have no more thoughts of the earth. John Court wonders if the point of *Apocalypse* 12 is to exclude 'the possibility of stray recollections that can be used as proof for reincarnation, and any theory of anamnesis such as Plato developed in the dialogues of Socrates'.[49]

Apocalypse 15. The risen Jesus explains to John that it is necessary to purify the earth so that it might become white as snow. When the purification is finished, the earth will cry out to Jesus: 'I am a virgin before you, O Lord, and there is no sin in me; as the prophet David said of old, "You will sprinkle me with hyssop, and I shall be cleansed; you will wash me, and I shall be whiter than snow."' The *Apocalypse* has quoted LXX Ps. 50.9 verbatim. The passage from the Psalter has justified the earlier promise that the earth will be purified and made 'white as snow', a prophecy that may also allude to Isa. 1.18 (though here it is in reference to the nation of Israel). Of course, the passage from LXX Psalm 50 was originally understood to apply to the repentant David, not to the earth. Perhaps the *Apocalypse* understands the words of David as offering an analogy, not a prophecy as such. The image of the sinless virgin is inspired by the chaste women of Rev. 14.4.

Jesus also promises John that the earth will be made flat 'as a table' (ὡς ἡ τράπεζα). There will be no more crooked places, which the ancients without benefit of modern transportation found difficult, tiresome and sometimes dangerous. Jesus again appeals to David, who says, 'Every valley shall be filled, and every mountain and hill shall be brought low, and the crooked shall be made straight, and the rough ways shall be made smooth; and all flesh shall see the salvation of God.' The prophecy comes from LXX Isa. 40.5-6, but the quotation is actually based on Lk. 3.5-6. The author of the *Apocalypse* probably did not know that the prophecy comes from Isaiah and therefore has no connection to David.[50] It is possible that the reference to 'crooked' (σκολιός) brought to mind LXX Ps. 77.8, where the Psalmist complains of a 'crooked generation' (γενεὰ σκολιά), which is faithless and whose heart is not right towards God. Many times in the Psalter God is praised and thanked for his salvation (σωτήριον). Perhaps linguistic overlaps like these explain the passage's link to David.

The appeal to LXX Ps. 50.9 and Isa. 40.4-5 (i.e. Lk. 3.5-6) is for the purpose of clarifying and confirming Rev. 21.1, in which the seer says, 'Then I saw a new heaven and a new earth; for the first heaven and the first earth had passed away, and the sea was no more.' The author of the *Apocalypse* could have appealed to Isa. 65.17 ('behold,

---

[49] Court, *Book of Revelation*, 54.
[50] MS D (Bibliothèque nationale de France, gr. 1034) corrects the text, to read, 'Again, another prophet has said', meaning a prophet other than David; see Court, *Book of Revelation*, 56.

I create new heavens and a new earth; and the former things shall not be remembered or come into mind'; cf. 66.22), but there is no firm evidence that this author was familiar with Isaiah. The appearance of Isa. 40.4-5 here in *Apocalypse* 15 is really a quotation of Lk. 3.5-6, and the appearance of an allusion to Isa. 66.24 ('the worm does not die') in *Apocalypse* 24 derives from dominical tradition (cf. Mk. 9.48). Therefore, to speak of a renewed, purified earth, as the author of the *Apocalypse* envisions it, we find appeals to texts that either speak of personal renewal (as in LXX Psalm 50) or of divine assistance given captive Israel to facilitate return to the homeland (as in Isaiah 40). Neither text originally had anything to do with the eschatological renewal of the earth.

Apocalypse 20. When John learns that the first beings to be punished in the day of judgement are unclean spirits, he asks Jesus where they are located. The voice of Jesus tells him that the pit of Hades, in which they are held, is so deep that even a large stone cast into the pit will not reach its bottom after falling for twenty years. This is 'just as the prophet David foretold, "And he made darkness his hideaway [καὶ ἔθετο σκότος ἀποκρυφὴν αὐτοῦ]"'. The *Apocalypse* has quoted LXX Ps. 17.12 verbatim. The logic is that a very deep pit would be very dark. True enough, but LXX Ps. 17.12 has nothing to do with Hades (or Sheol) or with a deep pit. The psalm speaks of dark storm clouds, whose darkness hides God. The idea that Hades is dark is found in *1 En.* 10.4 (apparently alluded to in Mt. 22.13; cf. *1 En.* 103.7). In Job 10.21-22 the realm of the dead is described as 'the land of gloom and deep darkness'. In Rev. 9.1-2 a plague rises up from a 'bottomless pit' (τοῦ φρέατος τῆς ἀβύσσου).

Apocalypse 21. John asks Jesus which peoples will be sent to Hades and he is told that it will be those who are idolatrous, including the Hellenist (ὁ ἑλληνισμός), and who have not confessed the Father, the Son and the Holy Spirit. 'I will send these to Hades, just as the prophet David foretold, "Let sinners be turned away to Hades, all the nations that keep forgetting God."' The *Apocalypse* has quoted LXX Ps. 9.18 verbatim. The passage is a good choice, for the psalm calls out for protection from and judgement upon the nations, which 'have sunk in the pit which they made' (v. 16 [v. 15]), an image that coheres with the theme expressed in *Apocalypse* 20.

The *Apocalypse* buttresses its point with another prophecy: 'And again the same one said, "Like sheep they were placed in Hades [ἐν ᾅδῃ]; Death shall be their shepherd."' This time LXX Ps. 48.15 has been quoted verbatim. The 'same one' (ὁ αὐτός) is of course David. In this instance the author of the *Apocalypse* apparently understands the meaning of LXX Psalm 48 (MT Psalm 49) close to its original sense. The psalm assures the faithful that the wicked, even if wealthy and powerful, will face judgement, and like helpless sheep the wealthy will be sent to Hades, where Death will be their shepherd. Lying behind the appeal to this verse is no tradition of evil sheep destined for judgement; it is simply the teaching of the passage itself that accommodates the point the *Apocalypse* wants to make here.

It is possible that the *Apocalypse* understands Death (θάνατος) in a personified sense, which is why I have presented the word as a name. Death appears as a personification in other later Jewish and Christian texts, especially the *Testament of Abraham*, where God and Abraham take turns speaking to Death (*T. Abr.* A 16–20).[51]

---

[51] In the *Acts of John* 84.1 the apostle John addresses Death: 'O Death [ὦ θάνατε], exulting in those who are yours!' In the *Martyrdom of Bartholomew* a frightened demon confesses that Jesus 'put to

Apocalypse 22. John asks the risen Jesus who next will be punished. Jesus tells him that next to be judged will be the unbelieving Hebrews, including those who nailed him to the tree like a criminal. John then asks what their punishment will be and he is told: 'They will go away into Tartaros, just as the prophet David foretold: "They cried out to the Lord, and there was no one to save, and he did not listen to them."' The *Apocalypse* has quoted LXX Ps. 17.42 verbatim. Originally the psalm was an expression of celebration and thanks to God for a military victory, in which the enemy was defeated. One would assume that because the psalm is Hebrew and royal, the enemy would be a gentile people. Yet, we are told that 'They' (the enemy) 'cried out to the Lord' (ἐκέκραξαν ... πρὸς κύριον / עַל־יְהוָה ... יְשַׁוְּעוּ). Does this mean that *gentiles* cried out to Yahweh? Or does this verse point to intramural conflict within Israel, perhaps David against Saul or David against Absalom? Whatever the explanation,[52] the psalm accommodates the interests of the author of the *Apocalypse*, who applies this to future judgement of the Hebrew people. The unit ends with an appeal to Paul's teaching in Rom. 2.12, 'All who have sinned without the law will also perish without the law, and all who have sinned under the law will be judged by the law.' Those 'who have sinned without the law' applies to the gentiles of *Apocalypse* 21 and those 'who have sinned under the law' applies to the Hebrews of *Apocalypse* 22. Both groups will be judged with respect to their response to Jesus.

Apocalypse 23. John asks Jesus about those who have been baptized. Jesus assures him that angels will gather up 'the race of Christians' (τὸ γένος τῶν Χριστιανῶν) from among the sinners,[53] 'just as the prophet David foretold: "because the Lord shall not allow the rod of the sinners over the allotment of the righteous"'. Apart from the insertion of the 'Lord' (κύριος), the *Apocalypse* has quoted LXX Ps. 124.3 verbatim. The psalm is understood as offering assurance that the righteous will not be moved from their inheritance and that evil will not reign over them. This interpretation is seen in the comment that follows: 'And all the righteous will be placed by my right (hand) and they will shine like the sun.' We have here an allusion to dominical tradition: 'Then the righteous will shine like the sun in the kingdom of their Father' (Mt. 13.43;[54] cf. 25.33-34, 'he will place the sheep at his right hand ... the King will say to those at his right hand, "Come, O blessed of my Father, inherit the kingdom prepared for you from the foundation of the world"').

Apocalypse 24. John inquires further about all Christians on the day of judgement, ranging from kings, high priests, priests, patriarchs, rich and poor, even to slaves. Jesus

---

death Death himself, our king [αὐτὸν τὸν θάνατον τὸν βασιλέα ἡμῶν ἐθανάτωσε], and he bound our prince in chains of fire; and on the third day, having conquered death and the devil, rose in glory, and gave the sign of the cross to his apostles, and sent them out into the four quarters of the world' (6.2). Of course, one thinks of Paul's use of Hos. 13.14 in 1 Cor. 15.55: 'O death, where is thy victory? O death, where is thy sting?'

[52] For discussion of this complex and difficult Psalm 18 (MT), see H.-J. Kraus, *Psalms 1–59: A Continental Commentary* (Minneapolis, MN: Fortress Press, 1993), 252–66, esp. 264.

[53] Christians are called τὸ γένος, 'the race', 'in the sense of the "third race" after pagans and Jews', as rightly stated by Court, *Book of Revelation*, 61. As examples, Court cites 1 Pet. 2.9; *Mart. Pol.* 3.2; 14.1; 17.1; *Diogn.* 1; Hermas, *Sim.* 9.17.5; Clement, *Stromata* 6.5.

[54] The statement that 'the righteous will shine like the sun' may also reflect Dan. 12.3: 'those who are wise shall shine like the brightness of the firmament.'

begins his response by appealing to what was foretold by the prophet David, who said, 'The endurance of the needy shall not perish forever.' The *Apocalypse* has quoted LXX Ps. 9.19b almost verbatim. The last phrase, εἰς τέλος (lit. 'to the end'), in the LXX is εἰς τὸν αἰῶνα (lit. 'to the age'). Both phrases can be translated 'forever'. LXX Ps. 9.19 is a strange passage to appeal to, for it does not support well the point that is being made, which is that those who may call themselves Christians, whether kings or priests, who have sinned will be punished. It is not clear how assurance of the endurance of the needy clarifies the idea. At best, the passage assures God's true people that they will not be forgotten.

Sinners will be judged and sentenced according to 'the proportion of each of their own transgressions'. Punishment options include placing 'some in the river of fire [ἐν τῷ πυρίνῳ ποταμῷ], some with the worm that does not sleep [εἰς τὸν σκώληκαν τὸν ἀκοίμητον], and others in the seven-mouthed pit of punishment [ἐν τῷ ἑπταστόμῳ φρέατι τῆς κολάσεως]'. The first, the 'river of fire', probably alludes to a passage in *1 Enoch*, where the patriarch says, 'And we came up to a river of fire [ποταμοῦ πυρός], in which the fire ran down as water' (*1 En.* 17.5). The second place of punishment, inhabited by the worm that does not sleep, as already mentioned, alludes to the last verse of Isaiah: 'for their worm shall not die [ὁ γὰρ σκώληξ αὐτῶν οὐ τελευτήσει] and their fire shall not be quenched' (Isa. 66.24). The undying worm is associated with hell and punishment in the afterlife in a number of texts (e.g. Jdt. 16.17; Sir. 7.17; *Apoc. Paul* 42, where we are told the worm is large and has two heads). The *Apocalypse of Paul* 41 offers an approximate parallel to the 'seven-mouthed pit' place of punishment. Paul says that 'the angel took me from these punishments and made me stand above a pit, which had on its mouth seven seals [ὃ εἶχεν ἐπὶ τοῦ στόματος αὐτοῦ σφραγῖδας ἑπτά]'. The 'seven-mouth pit' of the *Apocalypse* could well be the pit described in the *Apocalypse of Paul* said to have a mouth that requires seven seals.

The appearance of a class of Christians called 'Levites' may strike us as out of place, but in the Byzantine Church Hebrew terminology, such as 'patriarchs' (πατριάρχαι), 'high priests' (ἀρχιερεῖς), 'priests' (ἱερεῖς), 'elders' (πρεσβύτεροι) and 'Levites' (Λευῖται) – in reference to deacons – was employed.[55]

Apocalypse 25. John now asks Jesus where the righteous will dwell. The voice (of Jesus) tells John: 'Then shall paradise be revealed; and the whole world and paradise shall be made one, and the righteous shall be on the face of all the earth with my angels, as the Holy Spirit foretold through the prophet David: "The righteous shall inherit the earth, and dwell therein for ever and ever."'

John is told that 'paradise' (ὁ παράδεισος) and 'the whole world' (ὁ κόσμος ὅλος) will be made 'one' (ἕν) or, as we might say, will merge. Therefore the righteous will live on earth (not up in heaven), which has become paradise. The word paradise is Persian and originally referred to a garden (cf. Gen. 2.8, where παράδεισος translates גן). Jesus promises the man who sympathized with him on the cross, 'Truly, I say to you, today you will be with me in Paradise [ἐν τῷ παραδείσῳ]' (Lk. 23.43). Paradise presumably is in heaven, where Jesus is standing or seated at the right hand of God (Acts 7.56; cf.

---

[55] Court (*Book of Revelation*, 62) cites *Apostolic Constitutions* 2.26.3 as an example of 'Levite' in reference to a deacon. The text reads: 'and your Levites, who now are deacons'.

Mk 14.62). Speaking of his own heavenly experience, Paul says that 'this man was caught up into Paradise [ἡρπάγη εἰς τὸν παράδεισον] ... and he heard things that cannot be told, which one may not utter' (2 Cor. 12.3-4).[56] In Revelation the risen Jesus promises the faithful believer that he will be able to 'eat of the tree of life, which is in the paradise of God [ἐν τῷ παραδείσῳ τοῦ θεοῦ]' (Rev. 2.7). The paradise envisioned here is on the earth. It will be at the time when 'the holy city, new Jerusalem' comes down from heaven (Rev. 21.1, 10) and when God will dwell on the earth (Rev. 21.2). Paradise, on earth, will be restored; or, in the words of *Apocalypse* 25, 'the whole world and paradise will be one'.

David's prophecy this time is drawn from LXX Ps. 36.29 verbatim. The psalm is attributed to David and is concerned with justice. The purpose of the psalm is to assure the righteous that justice will prevail and that the wicked and their schemes will come to naught. The verse that is quoted comes from a small unit that exhorts the people to 'turn from evil and do good, so that you will abide forever' (v. 26). Whereas the righteous shall be kept safe, the lawless will be chased away (v. 28). The theme concludes with the verse quoted in *Apocalypse* 25: 'The righteous shall inherit the earth, and dwell therein for ever and ever', a verse that now has an eschatological nuance.

We find a similar perspective at Qumran, where Psalm 37 (= LXX Psalm 36) is interpreted in reference to the elect and the future judgement that will befall the wicked (cf. 4QpPs^a).[57] Commenting on our verse, the pesher says the faithful 'will live for a thousand generations in safety; and to them will belong all the inheritance of Adam and to their seed forever' (frgs. 1–10, col. iii, lines 1–2).[58] This shows that the eschatological perspective of the *Apocalypse* in its interpretation of this psalm is not unique.

Apocalypse 26. John abruptly asks about the number of angels and the number of humans and which is the greater. Jesus answers that they are equal in number and then appeals to what 'the prophet says'. This time a passage is quoted from LXX Deut. 32.8 (= Odes 2.8) verbatim: 'He fixed boundaries of nations according to the number of the angels of God.' Given the frequent reference to David as 'the prophet', the reference here to 'the prophet' (ὁ προφήτης) most likely means David. The author of the *Apocalypse* may have associated this passage from Deuteronomy with David because of its appearance in the collection of the Odes, songs and hymns that he assumed were composed by Israel's famous king.

The *Apocalypse* concludes with the assurance that sin and sorrow will cease (alluding to Rev. 21.4, 25) as the Good Shepherd (implied) of John 10 gathers his sheep into one

---

[56] Paul's testimony probably does not contradict what *Apocalypse* 25 asserts, for the latter's prophecy that someday paradise and the world will become 'one' will be fulfilled in the future. Until then, one may speak of paradise as in heaven above, as Paul implies in 2 Cor. 12. In 1 Thess. 4.16-17 Paul says Jesus will descend from heaven and the faithful will be 'caught up' (ἁρπαγησόμεθα) to meet him as he descends. The returning Jesus will bring paradise to earth.

[57] For critical discussion, see Maurya P. Horgan, 'Psalm Pesher 1', in James H. Charlesworth et al. (eds), *The Dead Sea Scrolls: Hebrew, Aramaic, and Greek Texts with English Translations. Volume 6B: Pesharim, Other Commentaries, and Related Documents*, The Princeton Theological Seminary Dead Sea Scrolls Project (Tübingen: Mohr Siebeck; Louisville, KY: Westminster John Knox Press, 2002), 6–23. Like the other *pesharim*, 'the thrust of the interpretation of Psalm 37 is eschatological' (6).

[58] Translation from Horgan, 'Psalm Pesher 1', 15.

fold (*Apoc.* 27, quoting Jn 10.16). The final word of the risen Jesus is a beatitude drawn, as we would expect, from one of the psalms: 'Blessed are those who guard justice and do righteousness' (*Apoc.* 28, quoting LXX Ps. 105.3). It is not clear that this beatitude is understood as a prophecy. Even so, it seems only appropriate that the last passage from Old Testament scripture quoted in the *Apocalypse* is drawn from the Psalter.

Conclusion

This investigation has confirmed Dupont's insight about the significance for early Christian interpreters of the long Jewish tradition of David's prophetic status. This heritage underpins the frequent reference in the first apocryphal *Apocalypse of John* to David and the Psalms. It may well be that this author, as part of his effort to expand or even 'complete' the canonical Book of Revelation, desired to make explicit what he believed was implicit in the canonical book. Of all figures in Israel's sacred scriptures it was David who was the most important for understanding Jesus, for Jesus is the fulfilment of the prophecy that someday the 'root of David' will appear and bring judgement, righteousness and Paradise to earth, which is the ultimate message of both the canonical Revelation of John and the first apocryphal *Apocalypse of John*. For our author it was important that the prophecies of this David, whose descendant the risen Jesus is, should be heard.[59]

---

[59] It is a pleasure to offer this essay in appreciation of Steve Moyise and his excellent work on the Book of Revelation and biblical intertextuality.

Bibliography

Adelman, Rachel. *The Return of the Repressed: Pirqe de-Rabbi Eliezer and the Pseudepigrapha*. SJSJ 140. Leiden: Brill, 2009.
Adler, William. '*Palaea Historica* ("The Old Testament History"): A New Translation and Introduction'. In *Old Testament Pseudepigrapha: More Noncanonical Scriptures*, Vol. 1, edited by Richard J. Bauckham, James R. Davila and Alexander Panayotov, 585–672. Grand Rapids, MI: Eerdmans, 2013.
Aldhelm, 'Epistola ad Acircium'. In *Aldhelm: The Prose Works*, translated by Michael Lapidge and Michael Herren, 35. Woodbridge: D. S. Brewer, 2009.
Allen, David M. *Deuteronomy and Exhortation in Hebrews: A Study in Narrative Re-presentation*. WUNT 2.238. Tübingen: Mohr Siebeck, 2009.
Allen, Garrick V. 'Textual Pluriformity and Allusion in the Book of Revelation: The Text of Zechariah 4 in the Apocalypse', *ZNW* 106 (2015): 136–45.
Allen, Garrick V. 'Scriptural Allusions in the Book of Revelation and the Contours of Textual Research 1900–2014: Retrospect and Prospects', *CBR* 14 (2016): 319–39.
Allen, Garrick V. *The Book of Revelation and Early Jewish Textual Culture*. SNTSMS 168. Cambridge: Cambridge University Press, 2017.
Allen, Garrick V. 'An Anti-Islamic Marginal Comment in the Apocalypse of "Codex Reuchlin" GA 2814 and Its Tradition'. In *Der Codex Reuchlins zur Apokalypse: Byzanz – Basler Konzil – Erasmus*, edited by M. Karrer, 193–8. MB 5. Berlin: de Gruyter, 2020.
Allen, Garrick V. *Manuscripts of the Book of Revelation: New Philology, Paratexts, Reception*. Oxford: Oxford University Press, 2020.
Andrieu, Michel. Les *Ordines Romani* du Haut Moyen Age, Vol. 2, Les Textes (Ordines I–XIII). Louvain: Spicilegium, 1971: 467–526.
Andrieu, Michel. Les *Ordines Romani* du Haut Moyen Age, Vol. 3, Les Textes (Ordines XIV–XXXIV). Leuven: Peeters, 2006: 23–41.
Ashton, John. *Understanding the Fourth Gospel*. 2nd edn. Oxford: Oxford University Press, 2007.
Ashton, John. 'Intimations of Apocalyptic: Looking Back and Looking Forward'. In *John's Gospel and Intimations of Apocalyptic*, edited by Catrin H. Williams and Christopher Rowland, 3–35. London: Bloomsbury T&T Clark, 2013.
Ashton, John. 'Really a Prologue?' In *Discovering John: Essays by John Ashton*, edited by Christopher Rowland and Catrin H. Williams, 64–83. Eugene, OR: Cascade Books, 2020.
Atherstone, Andrew. *An Anglican Evangelical Identity Crisis: The Churchman-Anvil Affair of 1981–1984*. London: Latimer Trust, 2008.
Augustine. *De Genesi Contra Manichaeos* 1.23.40 (J. P. Migne, *Patrologiae cursus completus, Series latina*. Paris: Garnier Frères, 1844–64 (hereafter PL), 34.190–3).
Aune, David E. *Revelation 1–5*. WBC 52A. Dallas, TX: Word, 1997.
Aune, David E. *Revelation 6–16*. WBC 52B. Dallas, TX: Word, 1998.
Aune, David E. *Revelation 17–22*. WBC 52C. Dallas, TX: Word, 1998.
Bailey, Kenneth. *Jesus through Middle Eastern Eyes*. London: SPCK, 2008.

Balz, Horst R., and Gerhard Schneider. *EDNT*. Grand Rapids, MI: Eerdmans, 1990.
Bannister, Henry Marriott (ed.). *Missale Gothicum I, A Gallican Sacramentary, MS. Vatican. Regin. Lat. 317*. London: Henry Bradshaw Society, 1917.
Barclay, John M. G. *Paul and the Gift*. Grand Rapids, MI: Eerdmans, 2015.
Barney, Stephen, W. J. Lewis, J. A. Beach and Berghof, Oliver (eds). *The Etymologies of Isidore of Seville*. Cambridge: Cambridge University Press, 2006.
Barr, David L. 'Waiting for the End That Never Comes: The Narrative Logic of John's Story'. In *Studies in the Book of Revelation*, edited by Steve Moyise, 101–12. Edinburgh: T&T Clark 2001.
Barrett, C. K. *The Gospel According to St John: An Introduction and Commentary with Notes on the Greek Text*. 2nd edn. London: SPCK, 1978.
Bartelmus, Rüdiger. '"Schriftprophetie" außerhalb des corpus propheticum – eine unmögliche Möglichkeit? Das Mose-Lied (Ex 15,1–21) als deuterojesajanisch geprägtes "eschatologisches Loblied"'. In *Schriftprophetie (Festschrift Jörg Jeremias)*, edited by Friedhelm Hartenstein and Jutta Krispenz, 55–82. Neukirchen-Vluyn: Neukirchener Verlag, 2004.
Barton, John. *The Nature of Biblical Criticism*. Louisville, KY: Westminster John Knox Press, 2007.
Batey, Richard A. *New Testament Nuptial Imagery*. Leiden: Brill, 1963.
Batey, Richard A. 'Paul's Bride Image: A Symbol of Realistic Eschatology', *Interpretation* 17 (1963): 176–84.
Bauckham, Richard. *The Climax of Prophecy*. Edinburgh: T&T Clark, 1993.
Bauckham, Richard. *The Theology of the Book of Revelation*. Cambridge: Cambridge University Press, 1993.
Bauer, Walter. *Orthodoxy and Heresy in Earliest Christianity*. Edited by Robert A. Kraft. London: SCM, 1972.
Beale, G. K. *The Use of Daniel in Jewish Apocalyptic Literature and in the Revelation of St. John*. Lanham, MD: University of America Press, 1984 (repr. Eugene, OR: Wipf and Stock).
Beale, G. K. 'The Origin of the Title "King of Kings and Lord of Lords" in Revelation 17.14', *NTS* 31 (1985): 618–20.
Beale, G. K. 'A Reconsideration of the Text of Daniel in the Apocalypse', *Biblica* 67 (1986): 539–43.
Beale, G. K. 'Positive Answer to the Question Did Jesus and His Followers Preach the Right Doctrine from the Wrong Texts? An Examination of the Presuppositions of Jesus' and Apostles' Exegetical Method'. In *The Right Doctrine from the Wrong Text? Essays on the Use of the Old Testament in the New*, edited by G. K. Beale, 387–404. Grand Rapids, MI: Baker, 1994.
Beale, G. K. 'Revelation'. In *It Is Written: Scripture Citing Scripture*, edited by D. A. Carson and H. G. M. Williamson, 318–36. Cambridge: Cambridge University Press, 1998.
Beale, G. K. *John's Use of the Old Testament in Revelation*. JSNTSup166. Sheffield: Sheffield Academic Press, 1998.
Beale, G. K. *The Book of Revelation: A Commentary on the Greek Text*. NIGTC. Cambridge: Eerdmans, 1999.
Beale, G. K. 'Questions of Authorial Intent, Epistemology, and Presuppositions and Their Bearing on the Study of the Old Testament in the New: A Rejoinder to Steve Moyise', *IBS* 21 (1999): 152–80.
Beale, G. K. 'A Response to Jon Paulien on the Use of the Old Testament in Revelation', *AUSS* 39 (2001): 23–34.

Beale, G. K. *Handbook on the New Testament Use of the Old Testament*. Grand Rapids, MI: Baker, 2012.
Beale, G. K. 'The Old Testament in Colossians: A Response to Paul Foster', *JSNT* 41 (2018): 261-74.
Beale, G. K., and D. A. Carson. *Commentary on the New Testament Use of the Old Testament*. Grand Rapids, MI: Baker, 2007.
Beale, G. K., and D. A. Carson. 'Introduction'. In *Commentary on the New Testament Use of the Old Testament*, edited by G. K. Beale and D. A. Carson, xxiii-xxviii. Grand Rapids, MI: Baker/ Nottingham: Apollos, 2007.
Begg, Christopher T. *Flavius Josephus: Translation and Commentary. Volume 4: Flavius Josephus Judean Antiquities 5-7*. Leiden: Brill, 2005.
Benito, Marconcini. 'L'utilizzazione del T.M. nelle citazioni Isaeiane dell'Apocalisse', *RivBib* 24 (1976): 113-36.
Bennema, Cornelis. 'The Sword of the Messiah and the Concept of Liberation in the Fourth Gospel', *Biblica* 86 (2005): 35-58.
Bietenhard, Hans, 'The Millennial Hope in the Early Church', *SJT* 6.1 (1953): 12-30.
Billett, Jesse D. *The Divine Office in Anglo-Saxon England 597 - c.1000*. Woodbridge: Boydell Press, 2014.
Black, Matthew. *The Book of Enoch or 1 Enoch: A New English Edition with Commentary and Textual Notes in Consultation with James C. VanderKam*. SVTP 7. Leiden: Brill, 1985.
Blenkinsopp, Joseph. *Opening the Sealed Book: Interpretations of the Book of Isaiah in Late Antiquity*. Grand Rapids, MI: Eerdmans, 2006.
Blount, Brian K., *Revelation: A Commentary*. 1st edn, NTL. Louisville, KY: Westminster John Knox, 2009.
Boccaccini, Gabriele (ed.). *Enoch and the Messiah Son of Man: Revisiting the Book of Parables*. Grand Rapids, MI: Eerdmans, 2007.
Bolton, W. F. *A History of Anglo-Latin Literature, 597-1066*. Vol. 1. Princeton, NJ: Princeton University Press, 1967.
Bonner, Gerald, *Saint Bede in the Tradition of Western Apocalyptic Commentary*. Newcastle upon Tyne: Jarrow Lecture, 1966.
Boring, Maynard Eugene. 'The Voice of Jesus in the Apocalypse of John', *NovT* 34 (1992): 334-59.
Bovon, François. *Luke 1: A Commentary on the Gospel of Luke 1:1-9:50*. Hermeneia. Minneapolis, MN: Fortress, 2002.
Boxall, Ian. *Revelation: Vision and Insight*. London: SPCK, 2002.
Boxall, Ian. *The Revelation of Saint John*. BNTC. London: Continuum, 2006.
Boxall, Ian, and Richard Tresley (eds). *The Book of Revelation and Its Interpreters*. Lanham, MD: Rowman and Littlefield, 2016.
Boyarin, Daniel. 'The Gospel of the *Memra*: Jewish Binitarianism and the Prologue to John', *HTR* 94 (2001): 243-84.
Brannan, Rick. '1 Apocryphal Apocalypse of John'. In *New Testament Apocrypha: More Noncanonical Scriptures*, Volume 2, edited by Tony Burke, 378-98. Grand Rapids, MI: Eerdmans, 2020.
Braude, William G. *The Midrash on Psalms*, YJS 13. London: Yale University Press, 1959.
Brent, Allen. 'History and Eschatological Mysticism in Ignatius of Antioch', *Ephemerides Theologicae Lovanienses* 65.4 (1989): 309-29.

Brooke, George J. 'The Psalms in Early Jewish Literature in Light of the Dead Sea Scrolls'. In *The Psalms in the New Testament*, edited by Steve Moyise and Maarten J. J. Menken, 5–24. London: T&T Clark International, 2004.
Brown, George Hardin. *A Companion to Bede*. Woodbridge: Boydell Press, 2009.
Brown, George Hardin, and Frederick M. Biggs. *Bede, Part 2. Bible: Commentaries. Fascicles 1–4*. Amsterdam: Amsterdam University Press, 2016.
Bultmann, Rudolf. *History and Eschatology: The Gifford Lectures 1955*. Edinburgh: Edinburgh University Press, 1957.
Bultmann, Rudolf. *The Gospel of John*. Translated by G. R. Beasley-Murray. Oxford: Basil Blackwell, 1971.
Burkitt, F. Crawford (ed.) *The Book of Rules of Tyconius*. Cambridge: Cambridge University Press, 1894.
Cabaniss, Alan. 'Wisdom 18.14ff.: An Early Christmas Text', *VC* 10 (1956): 97–102.
Caird, George B. *The Revelation of St John the Divine*. London: A & C Black, 1966.
Campbell, Constantine. *Paul and the Hope of Glory*. Grand Rapids, MI: Zondervan, 2020.
Carson, D. A. *The Gagging of God*. Grand Rapids, MI: Zondervan, 1996.
Charles, R. H. *The Book of Enoch or 1 Enoch*. Oxford: Clarendon, 1912.
Charles, R. H. *Apocrypha and Pseudepigrapha of the Old Testament*. 2 Vols. Oxford: Clarendon Press, 1913.
Charles, R. H. *The Revelation of St. John, Vol. 1*. ICC. Edinburgh: T&T Clark, 1985.
Charles, R. H. *The Revelation of St. John. Vol. II*. ICC. Edinburgh: T&T Clark, 1980.
Chavasse, Claude. *The Bride of Christ: An Enquiry into the Nuptial Element in Early Christianity*. London: Faber & Faber, 1940.
Chilton, Bruce D. *Rabbi Paul: An Intellectual Biography*. New York: Doubleday, 2004.
Colgrave, Bertram, and R. A. B. Mynors, eds. *Bede's Ecclesiastical History of the English People*. Oxford: Clarendon Press, 1969.
Collins, John J. *The Scepter and the Star: Messianism in Light of the Dead Sea Scrolls*. 2nd edn. Grand Rapids, MI: Eerdmans, 2010.
Collins, John J. *The Apocalyptic Imagination*. 3rd edn. Grand Rapids, MI: Eerdmans, 2016.
Compton, Jared, and Andrew David Naselli, eds. *Three Views on Israel and the Church: Perspectives on Romans 9–11*. Grand Rapids, MI: Kregel Academic, 2018.
Court, John M. *The Book of Revelation and the Johannine Apocalyptic Tradition*, JSNTSup 190. Sheffield: Sheffield Academic Press, 2000.
Cousland, J. R. C. 'Adam and Eve, Did Satan Sleep with Eve in the Greek and Latin Lives of Adam and Eve?', *JThS* 71 (2020): 134–57.
Crawford, Sidnie White, *Rewriting Scripture in Second Temple Times*. Studies in the Dead Sea Scrolls and Related Literature. Grand Rapids, MI: Eerdmans, 2008.
Crouser, Wesley. 'Satan, the Serpent, and Witchcraft Accusations: Reading Rom. 16:17–20a in the Light of Allusions and Anthropology', *JSPL* 4 (2014): 218–33.
Cubitt, Catherine. 'Apocalyptic and Eschatological Thought in England around the Year 1000'. *TRHS*, 25 (2015): 30.
Danby, Herbert. *The Mishnah*. Oxford: Oxford University Press, 1933.
Daniélou, Jean. *Sacramentum Futuri*. Paris: Beauchesne, 1950.
Daniélou, Jean. 'L'Étoile de Jacob et la mission chrétienne à Damas', *VC* 11 (1957): 121–38.
Daniélou, Jean. *Primitive Christian Symbols*. Translated by Donald Attwater. Baltimore, MD: Helican Press, 1964.
Darby, Peter. 'Apocalypse and Reform in Bede's De die iudicii'. In *Apocalypse and Reform from Late Antiquity to the Middle Ages*, edited by M. Gabriele and J. T. Palmer, chapter 4. London: Routledge, 2018.

Das, A. Andrew. *Solving the Romans Debate*. Minneapolis, MN: Fortress, 2007.
Das, A. Andrew. 'Galatians 6:16's Riddles and Isaiah 54:10's Contribution: Gentiles Joining the Israel of God?'. In *Scripture, Texts, and Tracings in Galatians and 1 Thessalonians*, edited by A. Andrew Das and B. J. Oropeza. Lanham, MD: Fortress Academic, forthcoming.
Davila, James R. *Liturgical Works*. Eerdmans Commentaries on the Dead Sea Scrolls. Grand Rapids, MI: Eerdmans, 2000.
Davis, Dale Ralph. 'The Relationship between the Seals, Trumpets and Bowls in the Book of Revelation', *JETS* 16.3 (1973): 149–58.
DeGregorio, Scott. 'Bede's *In Ezram et Neemiam* and the Reform of the Northumbrian Church', *Speculum* 79 (2004): 1–25.
DeGregorio, Scott. 'Bede, the Monk, as Exegete: Evidence from the Commentary on Ezra-Nehemiah', *Revue Bénédictine* 115.2 (2005): 357–9.
Delamarter, Steve. *A Scripture Index to Charlesworth's the Old Testament Pseudepigrapha*. Sheffield: Sheffield Academic/Continuum, 2002.
De Lubac, Henri. *Medieval Exegesis, Volume 2: The Four Senses of Scripture*. Grand Rapids, MI: Eerdmans; Edinburgh: T&T Clark, 2000.
De Moor, J. C., and E. Van Staalduine-Sulman. 'The Aramaic Song of the Lamb', *JSJ* 24 (1993): 266–79.
Dempsey, G. T. 'Aldhelm of Malmesbury and the Irish', *PRIA*, 99C. 1 (1999): 1–22.
DiTomasso, Lorenzo. 'Apocalypticism in the Contemporary World'. In *The Cambridge Companion to Apocalyptic Literature*, edited by Colin McAllister, 316–42. Cambridge: Cambridge University Press, 2020.
Docherty, Susan E. *The Use of the Old Testament in Hebrews: A Case Study in Early Jewish Bible Interpretation*. WUNT 2/260. Tübingen: Mohr Siebeck, 2009.
Docherty, Susan E. 'New Testament Scriptural Interpretation in Its Early Jewish Context', *NovT* 57 (2015): 1–19.
Dodd, C. H. *The Parables of the Kingdom*. London: Nisbet, 1935.
Doering, Lutz. *Ancient Jewish Letters and the Beginnings of Christian Epistolography*. WUNT 298. Tübingen: Mohr-Siebeck, 2012.
Doering, Lutz. 'Gottes Volk: Die Adressaten als "Israel" im Ersten Petrusbrief'. In *Bedrängnis und Identität: Studien zu Situation, Kommunikation und Theologie des 1. Petrusbriefes*, edited by David S. du Toit, 81–114. BZNW 200. Berlin: de Gruyter, 2013.
Donaldson, Terence L. *Paul and the Gentiles*. Minneapolis, MN: Fortress, 1997.
Doyle, A. I. 'A Fragment of an Eighth-Century Northumbrian Office Book'. In *Words, Texts and Manuscripts: Studies in Anglo-Saxon Culture. Presented to Helmut Gneuss on the Occasion of His Sixty-Fifth Birthday*, edited by Michael Korhammer, Karl Reichl and Hans Sauer, 11–27. Cambridge: D. S. Brewer, 1992.
Dupont, Jacques. 'L'interprétation des psaumes dans les Actes des Apôtres'. In *Études sur les Actes des Apôtres*, 283–307. LD 45. Paris: Cerf, 1967.
Easley, Kendall H. *Revelation*. Holman NT Commentary. 12. Nashville, TN: Broadman & Holman, 1998.
Eastman, Brad J. 'Name'. In *Dictionary of the Later New Testament and Its Developments*, edited by R. P. Martin and P. H. Davids, 785–7. Downers Grove, IL: InterVarsity, 1997.
Eastman, Susan G. 'Israel and the Mercy of God: A Re-reading of Galatians 6.16 and Romans 9–11', *NTS* 56 (2010): 367–95.
Ellis, E. Earle, *Paul's Use of the Old Testament*. Grand Rapids, MI: Baker, 1957.
Epstein, Isidore (ed.). *The Babylonian Talmud, Seder Nashim*. London: Soncino, 1936.

Estelle, Bryan. *Echoes of Exodus*. Downers Grove, IL: IVP, 2018.
Evans, Craig A. 'Ascending and Descending with a Shout: Psalm 47.6 and 1 Thessalonians 4.16'. In *Paul and the Scriptures of Israel*, edited by Craig A. Evans and James A. Sanders, 238–53. JSNTSup 83, SSEJC 1. Sheffield: JSOT Press, 1993.
Fabiny, Tibor. *The Lion and the Lamb: Figuralism and Fulfilment in the Bible, Art and Literature*. Basingstoke: Macmillan, 1992.
Farrer, Austin. *A Rebirth of Images*. Westminster: Dacre Press, 1949.
Fee, Gordon D. *Paul's Letter to the Philippians*. NICNT. Grand Rapids, MI: Eerdmans, 1995.
Fee, Gordon D. *Revelation*. NCCS. Eugene, OR: Cascade, 2011.
Fekkes, Jan. *Isaiah and Prophetic Traditions in the Book of Revelation*. Sheffield: Sheffield Academic Press, 1994.
Fenske, Wolfgang. '"Das Lied des Mose, des Knechtes Gottes, und das Lied des Lammes" (Apokalypse des Johannes 15,3f): Der Text und seine Bedeutung für die Johannes-Apokalypse', *ZNW* 90 (1999): 250–64.
Fishbane, Michael. *Biblical Interpretation in Ancient Israel*. Oxford: Clarendon, 1985.
Fitzmyer, Joseph A. 'David, "Being Therefore a Prophet …"', *CBQ* 34 (1972): 332–9.
Fitzmyer, Joseph A. *The Interpretation of Scripture: In Defense of the Historical-Critical Method*. New York: Paulist Press, 2008.
Fletcher, Michelle. *Reading Revelation as Pastiche: Imitating the Past*. LNTS 571. London: T&T Clark, 2018.
Flint, Peter W. 'The Prophet David at Qumran'. In *Biblical Interpretation at Qumran*, edited by Matthias Henze, 158–67. SDSSRL. Grand Rapids, MI: Eerdmans, 2005.
Foot, Sarah. 'Anglo-Saxon "Purgatory"'. *SCH* 45 (2009): 87–96.
Foster, Paul. 'Who Wrote 2 Thessalonians? A Fresh Look at an Old Problem', *JSNT* 35 (2012): 150–75.
Foster, Paul. 'Echoes without Resonance: Critiquing Certain Aspects of Recent Scholarly Trends in the Study of the Jewish Scriptures in the New Testament', *JSNT* 38 (2015): 96–111.
Fredriksen, Paula. 'Apocalypse and Redemption in Early Christianity: From John of Patmos to Augustine of Hippo', *VC* 45.2 (1991).
Fredriksen, Paula. *Paul: The Pagan's Apostle*. New Haven, CT: Yale University Press, 2017.
Frey, Jörg. 'God's Dwelling on Earth: "Shekhina-Theology" in Revelation 21 and in the Gospel of John'. In *John's Gospel and Intimations of Apocalyptic*, edited by Catrin H. Williams and Christopher Rowland, 79–103. London: Bloomsbury T&T Clark, 2013.
Frey, Jörg. *The Glory of the Crucified One: Christology and Theology in the Gospel of John*. Translated by Wayne Coppins and Christoph Heilig. Waco, TX: Baylor University Press, 2018.
Friedmann, M. *Mechilta de-Rabbi Ismaël*. Vienna: Published by the author, 1870.
Frye, Northrop. *The Great Code: The Bible and Literature*. London: Routledge & Kegan Paul, 1982.
Fuchs, Guido, and Hans Martin Weikmann. *Das Exsultet: Geschichte, Theologie und Gastaltung der österlichen Lichtdanksagung*. Regensburg: Verlag Friedrich Pustet, 1992.
Fudge, Edward. 'The Eschatology of Ignatius of Antioch: Christocentric and Historical', *JETS* 15.4 (1972): 231–7.
Gallus, Laszlo. 'The Exodus Motif in Revelation 15–16: Its Background and Nature', *AUSS* 46 (2008): 21–43.

García Ureña, Lourdes. *Narrative and Drama in the Book of Revelation: A Literary Approach*. Translated by Donald Murphy. SNTSMS 175. Cambridge: Cambridge University Press, 2019.

Garroway, Joshua D. *Paul's Gentile-Jews: Neither Jew Nor Gentile, but Both*. New York: Palgrave Macmillan, 2012.

Goodenough, Erwin R. *By Light, Light: The Mystic Gospel of Hellenistic Judaism*. New Haven, CT: Yale University Press, 1935.

Goodrich, John K. '"Until the Fullness of the Gentiles Comes In": A Critical Review of Recent Scholarship on the Salvation of "All Israel" (Romans 11:26)', *JSPL* 6 (2016): 5–32.

Gorman, Michael. *Reading Revelation Responsibly*. Eugene, OR: Cascade/Wipf and Stock, 2011.

Goulder, Michael D., and M. L. Sanderson. 'St. Luke's Genesis', *JThS* 8.1 (1957): 12–30.

Grant, Jamie. 'Review of the Psalms in the New Testament edited by Steve Moyise and Maarten J. J. Menken', *Themelios* 32.2 (2006): 93–5.

Grant, Robert M. 'Scripture and Tradition in St. Ignatius of Antioch', *CBQ* 25 (1963): 322–35.

Gray, John. *Black Mass: Apocalyptic Religion and the Death of Utopia*. London: Penguin, 2008.

Greene, Thomas. *The Light in Troy: Imitation and Discovery in Renaissance Poetry*. Yale: Yale University Press, 1982.

Grocock, Christopher, and I. N. Wood (eds). *Abbots of Wearmouth and Jarrow*. Oxford: Clarendon Press, 2013.

Grogan, Geoffrey W. *Psalms*. THOTC. Grand Rapids, MI: Eerdmans, 2008.

Gryson, Roger (ed.). *Bedae Presbyteri, Expositio Apocalypseos ad fidem codicum manuscriptorum edidit adnotationibus criticis instruxit prolegomenis munivit*. Turnhout: Brepols, 2001.

Guiver, George. *Company of Voices: Daily Prayer and the People of God*. London: SPCK, 1988.

Gurtner, Daniel M. *Introducing the Pseudepigrapha of Second Temple Judaism*. Grand Rapids, MI: Baker Academic, 2020.

Haddan, Arthur W., and William Stubbs (eds). *Councils and Ecclesiastical Documents Relating to Great Britain and Ireland*. 3 vols. Oxford: Clarendon Press, 1869–78.

Hafemann, Scott. *Paul: Servant of the New Covenant*. WUNT 435. Tübingen: Mohr-Siebeck, 2019.

Hahn, Scott W. 'All Israel Will Be Saved: The Restoration of the Twelve Tribes in Romans 9–11', *Letter & Spirit* 10 (2015): 65–108.

Hall, J. R. 'Some Liturgical Notes on Aelfric's *Letter to the Monks at Eynsham*', *DR* 93 (1975): 297–303.

Hardin, Les. 'A Theology of the Hymns in Revelation', *Stone-Campbell Journal* 17 (2014): 233–45.

Harrington, Wilfred J. *Revelation*. SP 16. Collegeville, PA: Liturgical Press, 2008.

Hartenstein, Friedhelm. '"Wach auf, Harfe und Leier, ich will wecken das Morgenrot" (Psalm 57,9). Musikinstrumente als Medien des Gotteskontakts im Alten Orient und im Alten Testament'. In *Musik, Tanz und Gott. Tonspuren durch das Alte Testament*, edited by Michaela Geiger and Rainer Kessler, 101–27. SBS 207. Stuttgart: Verlag Katholisches Bibelwerk, 2007.

Hartman, Lars. *Asking for Meaning: A Study of 1 Enoch 1–5*. ConBNT 12. Lund: Gleerup, 1979.

Harvey, John D. *Romans*, EGGNT. Nashville, TN: B&H Academic, 2017.
Hauerwas, Stanley. *A Community of Character: Toward a Constructive Christian Social Ethic*. Notre Dame, IN: University of Notre Dame Press, 1981.
Hawkes, Jane. 'The Rothbury Cross: An Iconographic Bricolage', *Gesta* 35.1 (1996): 77–94.
Hays, Richard B. *Echoes of Scripture in the Letters of Paul*. New Haven, CT: Yale University Press, 1989.
Hays, Richard B. *First Corinthians*. Interpretation. Louisville, KY: John Knox, 1997.
Hemer, Colin J. *The Letters to the Seven Churches of Asia in Their Local Setting*. JSNTSup 11. Sheffield: Sheffield Academic Press, 1986.
Hilgard, Alfred. *Scholia in Dionysii Thracis artem grammaticam*. Grammatici Graeci 3. Leipzig: B. G. Teubner, 1901.
Hills, Julian V. *The Epistle of the Apostles*. ECA 2. Santa Rosa, CA: Polebridge Press, 2009.
Hirsch, E. D. *Validity in Interpretation*. New Haven, CT: Yale University Press, 1967.
Hirsch, E. D. *The Aims of Interpretation*. Chicago: University of Chicago Press, 1976.
Hirschfelder, Ulrike. 'The Liturgy of the Messiah: The Apocalypse of David in Hekhalot Literature', *JSQ* 12 (2005): 148–93.
Horbury, William. 'Septuagintal and New Testament Conceptions of Church.' In *A Vision for the Church: Studies in Early Christian Ecclesiology in Honour of J. P. M. Sweet*, edited by Markus N. A. Bockmuehl and Michael B. Thompson, 1–17. Edinburgh: T&T Clark, 1997.
Horgan, Maurya P. 'Psalm Pesher 1'. In *The Dead Sea Scrolls: Hebrew, Aramaic, and Greek Texts with English Translations. Volume 6B: Pesharim, Other Commentaries, and Related Documents*, edited by James H. Charlesworth, 6–23. The Princeton Theological Seminary Dead Sea Scrolls Project. Tübingen: Mohr Siebeck; Louisville, KY: Westminster John Knox Press, 2002.
Huffman, Douglas S. 'A Two-Dimensional Taxonomy of Forms for the NT Use of the OT', *Themelios* 46.2 (2021): 306–18.
Hurtado, Larry W. *The Earliest Christian Artifacts: Manuscripts and Christian Origins*. Grand Rapids, MI: Eerdmans, 2006.
Jauhiainen, Marko. 'Revelation and Rewritten Prophecies'. In *Rewritten Bible Reconsidered: Proceedings of the Conference in Karkku, Finland August 24–26 2006*, edited by A. Laato and J. van Ruiten, 177–97. Winona Lake, IN: Eisenbrauns, 2008.
Jenkins, Fred W. *The Old Testament in the Book of Revelation*. Grand Rapids, MI: Baker Book House, 1972.
Johnson, David H. 'Blessing'. In *Dictionary of the Later New Testament and Its Developments*, edited by R. P. Martin and P. H. Davids, 129–30. Downers Grove, IL: InterVarsity, 1997.
Kaestli, Jean-Daniel. 'La Figure de l'Antichrist dans l'Apocalypse de Saint Jean Le Théologien (Première Apocalypse Apocryphe de Jean)'. In *Les forces du Bien et du Mal dans les premiers siècles de l'Église*, edited by J.-M. Blanchard, B. Pouderon and M. Scopello, 277–90. ThH 118. Paris: Beauchesne, 2011.
Kannengiesser, Charles. *Handbook of Patristic Exegesis: The Bible in Ancient Christianity*. Leiden: Brill, 2006.
Karkov, Catherine E. *The Art of Anglo-Saxon England*. Woodbridge: Boydell Press, 2011.
Karrer, Martin. *Die Johannesoffenbarung als Brief. Studien zu ihrem literarischen, historischen und theologischen Ort*. FRLANT 140. Göttingen: Vandenhoeck & Ruprecht 1986.

Karrer, Martin. 'Von der Apokalypse zu Ezechiel: Der Ezechieltext der Apokalypse'. In *Das Ezechielbuch in der Johannesoffenbarung*, edited by D. Sänger, 84–120. Neukirchen-Vluyn: Neukirchener, 2004.
Karrer, Martin. 'Scriptural Quotations in the Jesus Tradition and Early Christianity: Textual History and Theology'. In *Ancient Readers and Their Scriptures: Engaging the Hebrew Bible in Early Judaism and Christianity*, edited by G. V. Allen and J. A. Dunne, 98–127. Leiden: Brill, 2019.
Karrer, Martin, Siegfried Kreuzer and Marcus Sigismund (eds). *Von der Septuaginta zum Neuen Testament: Textgeschichtliche Erörterungen*. Berlin: de Gruyter, 2010.
Keener, Craig S. *The IVP Bible Background Commentary: New Testament*. Downers Grove, IL: InterVarsity, 1993.
Keener, Craig S. *Revelation*. NIVAC. Grand Rapids, MI: Zondervan, 1999.
Keener, Craig S. *The Gospel of John: A Commentary*. Vol. 1. Peabody, MA: Hendrickson, 2003.
Kendall, Calvin B., and Faith Wallis. *Bede: On the Nature of Things and on Times*. Liverpool: Liverpool University Press, 2010.
Kim, Dongsu. 'Reading Paul's και ούτως πας Ισραηλ σωθήσεται (Rom. 11:26a) in the Context of Romans', *CTJ* 45 (2010): 317–34.
Kingston-Smith, Andy. 'Migrants, Justice and Border Lives'. In *Carnival Kingdom: Biblical Justice for Global Communities*, edited by Marijke Hoek et al., 101–24. Gloucester: Wide Margin, 2013.
Klaiber, Walter. *Die Offenbarung des Johannes*. BNT. Göttingen: Vandenhoeck & Ruprecht, 2019.
Knoebel, Thomas L. (ed.). *Isidore of Seville De Ecclesiasticus Officiis*. New York: Newman Press, 2008.
Koester, Craig R. *Revelation and the End of All Things*. 2nd edn. Grand Rapids, MI: Eerdmans, 2018.
Koester, Craig R. *Revelation: A New Translation with Introduction and Commentary*. AB 38A. New Haven, CT: Yale University, 2014.
Konrad, Ulrich. 'Apocalypsis cum figuris musices. Musikalische Annäherungen an die Offenbarung des Johannes'. In *Die Apokalypse in der Bibel und in den Künsten*, edited by Erich Garhammer, 33–71. Bildmontagen: Schnell & Steiner, 2013.
Kosior, Wojciech. 'A Tale of Two Sisters: The Image of Eve in Early Rabbinic Literature and Its Influence on the Portrayal of Lilith in the Alphabet of Ben Sira', *NJJWSFI* 32 (2018): 112–30.
Kostenberger, Andreas J. 'The Use of Scripture in the Pastoral and General Epistles and the Book of Revelation'. In *Hearing the Old Testament in the New Testament*, edited by S. E. Porter, 230–54. Grand Rapids, MI: Eerdmans, 2006.
Köster, Helmut. *Synoptische Überlieferung bei den apostolischen Vätern*. TU 65. Berlin: Akademie-Verlag, 1957.
Kowalski, Beate. *Die Rezeption des Propheten Ezechiel in der Offenbarung des Johannes*. SBB 52. Stuttgart: Verlag Katholisches Bibelwerk, 2004.
Kowalski, Beate. 'Die Ezechielrezeption in der Offenbarung des Johannes und ihre Bedeutung für die Textkritik', *SNTU.A* 35 (2010): 51–77.
Kowalski, Beate. 'Prophetie und die Offenbarung des Johannes? Offb 22,6–21 als Testfall'. In *Prophets and Prophecy in Jewish and Early Christian Literature*, edited by Joseph Verheyden and Korinna Zamfir, 253–93. WUNT II/286. Tübingen: Mohr Siebeck, 2010.

Kowalski, Beate. '"Let My People Go, That They May Serve Me" (Ex 10:3). Exodus Motifs of Liberation as Key to Understanding Worship in Revelation of John', *Henoch* 38 (2016): 32–53.

Kowalski, Beate. 'Selective versus Contextual Allusions: Reconsidering Technical Terms of Intertextuality'. In *Methodology in the Use of the Old Testament in the New: Context and Criteria*, edited by David Allen and Steve Smith, 86–102. London: T&T Clark, 2020.

Kraft, Robert A. *The Apostolic Fathers: A Translation and Commentary. Volume 3: Barnabas and the Didache*. New York: Thomas Nelson, 1965.

Kraus, Hans-Joachim. *Psalms 1–59: A Continental Commentary*. Minneapolis, MN: Fortress Press, 1993.

Krauss, Samuel. *Talmudische Archäologie*. Leipzig: Fock, 1911.

Kreitzer, Larry. *The New Testament in Fiction and Film: On Reversing the Hermeneutical Flow*. Sheffield: Sheffield Academic Press, 1993.

Kreitzer, Larry. *Pauline Images in Fiction and Film: On Reversing the Hermeneutical Flow*. Sheffield: Sheffield Academic Press, 1999.

Kristeva, Julia. *Desire in Language: A Semiotic Approach to Literature and Art*. Translated by Leon S. Roudiez. Oxford: Blackwell, 1980.

Kropp, Angelicus. *Ausgewählte koptische Zaubertexte*, Bd. I: *Textpublikation*. Bruxelles: Fondation Égyptologique Reine Élisabeth, 1931.

Kugel, James L. 'David the Prophet'. In *Poetry and Prophecy: The Beginnings of a Literary Tradition*, edited by James L. Kugel. Ithaca, NY: Cornell University Press, 1990.

Kurek-Chomycz, Dominika A. 'Sincerity and Chastity for Christ: A Textual Problem in 2 Cor. 11:3 Reconsidered', *NovT* 49 (2007): 54–84.

Laato, A. *A Star Is Rising: The Historical Development of the Old Testament Royal Ideology and the Rise of the Jewish Messianic Expectations*. Atlanta, GA: Scholars Press, 1997.

Labahn, Michael. 'Griechische Textformen in der Schriftrezeption der Johannesoffenbarung? Eine Problemanzeige zu Möglichkeiten und Grenzen ihrer Rekonstruction anhand von Beispielen aus der Rezeption des Ezechielbuchs'. In *Die Septuaginta – Entstehung, Sprache, Geschichte*, edited by S. Kreuzer, M. Meiser and M. Sigismund, 529–60. Tübingen: Mohr Siebeck, 2012.

Ladd, George Eldon. *A Commentary on the Revelation of John*. Grand Rapids, MI: Eerdmans, 1972.

Lampe, G. W. H., and K. J. Woollcombe. *Essays on Typology*. SBT 27. London: SCM Press, 1957.

Lange, Armin, and Matthias Weigold. *Biblical Quotations and Allusions in Second Temple Jewish Literature*. JAJS 5. Göttingen: Vandenhoeck & Ruprecht, 2011.

Lapidge, Michael, and Paolo Chiesa (eds). *Beda: Storia degli Inglesi*. Vol.1. Rome: Fondazione Lorenzo Valla, 2008.

Lincoln, Andrew T. *The Gospel According to St John*. BTNC, 4 London: Hendrickson, 2005.

Lindars, Barnabas. *The Gospel of John*. NCB. London: Marshall, Morgan and Scott, 1972.

Long, Phillip J. *Jesus the Bridegroom: The Origin of the Eschatological Feast as a Wedding Banquet in the Synoptic Gospels*. Eugene, OR: Pickwick, 2012.

Longenecker, Richard N. '"Who Is the Prophet Talking About?" Some Reflections on the New Testament's Use of the Old', *Themelios* 12 (1987): 4–8.

Longenecker, Richard N. *The Epistle to the Romans*. NIGTC. Grand Rapids, MI: Eerdmans, 2016.

Lookadoo, Jonathan. 'Ignatius of Antioch and Scripture', *ZAC* 23.2 (2019): 201–27.

Lorein, Geert W., and Eveline van Staalduine-Sulman. 'Songs of David: A New Translation and Introduction'. In *Old Testament Pseudepigrapha: More Noncanonical Scriptures*,

vol. 1, edited by Richard J. Bauckham, James R. Davila and Alexander Panayotov, 257–71. Grand Rapids, MI: Eerdmans, 2013.
Lux, Rüdiger. ' "Man lobt dich in der Stille" Ps 65,2. Ein biblisches Essay über Gott und das Schweigen in den Psalmen', *leqach* 9 (2009): 7–19.
Maiani, Brad, 'Readings and Responsories: The Eighth-Century Night Office Lectionary and the Responsoria Prolixa', *Journal of Musicology* 16.2 (1998): 254–82.
Maier, Harry. *Apocalypse Recalled*. Minneapolis, MN: Fortress Press, 2002.
Malik, Peter, and Edmund Gerke. 'Marginalglossen in GA 2323: Edition und Übersetzung'. In *Studien zum Text der Apokalypse III*, edited by M. Sigismund and D. Müller, 371–415. Berlin: de Gruyter, 2020.
Marsh, Clive. *Cinema and Sentiment: Film's Challenge to Theology*. Paternoster: Carlisle, 2004.
Martin, Lawrence T. (ed.). *Bede, The Venerable Bede, Commentary on the Acts of the Apostles*. Kalamazoo: Cistercian Studies, 1989.
Martin, Lawrence, and D. Hurst (eds). *Bede the Venerable: Homilies on the Gospels*. 2 Vols. Kalamazoo: Cistercian Studies, 1991.
McHugh, John F. *John 1–4: A Critical and Exegetical Commentary*. London: Bloomsbury T&T Clark, 2014.
McLean, B. H. *Biblical Interpretation and Philosophical Hermeneutics*. Cambridge: Cambridge University Press, 2012.
McWhirter, Jocelyn. *The Bridegroom Messiah and the People of God: Marriage in the Fourth Gospel*. SNTSMS 138. Cambridge: Cambridge University Press, 2006.
Merton, Thomas. *The Seven Storey Mountain*. New York: Harcourt Brace, 1968.
Merton, Thomas. *The Power and Meaning of Love*. La Vergne: SPCK, 2021.
Meyer, Marvin W., and Richard Smith (eds). *Ancient Christian Magic: Coptic Texts of Ritual Power*. Princeton, NJ: Princeton University Press, 1999.
Michelli, Perette, 'What's in the Cupboard? Ezra and Matthew Reconsidered'. In *Northumbria's Golden Age*, edited by Jane Hawkes and Susan Mills, 345–58. Stroud: Sutton, 1999.
Miller, Geoffrey David. *Marriage in the Book of Tobit*. Berlin: de Gruyter, 2011.
Mintz, Avi. I. 'The Midwife as Matchmaker: Socrates and Relational Pedagogy', *PEA* 2 (2007): 91–9.
Mintz, Avi. I. 'Damon, Prodicus, and Socratic Matchmaking', *SPE* 36 (2017): 377–9.
Moberley, R. W. L. *The Old Testament of the Old Testament: Patriarchal Narratives and Mosaic Yahwism*. Minneapolis, MN: Fortress, 1992.
Mohlberg, Leo Cunibert. *Das fränkische Sacramentarium Gelasianum in alamannischer Überlieferung* (Codex Sangall. no. 348). *St. Galler Sakramentar-Forschungen I*. Münster: Aschendorff, 1918.
Moloney, Francis J. *The Gospel of John*. SP 4. Collegeville, PA: Michael Glazier, 1998.
Moo, Douglas J. *The Letter to the Romans*. NICNT. 2nd edn. Grand Rapids, MI: Eerdmans, 2018.
Moore, Stephen D. *Revelation: Book of Torment, Book of Bliss*. London: T&T Clark, 2021.
Morgenthaler, Robert. *Statistik des Neutestamentlichen Wortschatzes*. 3rd edn. Zürich: Gotthelf-Verlag, 1982.
Morin, Germain, and Antonio Casamassa (eds). *Miscellanea Agostiniana: Testi E Studi, Pubblicati a Cura Del-l'Ordine Eremitano Di S. Agostino Nel XV Centenario Dalla Morte Del Santo Dottore*. Rome: Tipografia Poliglotta Vaticana, 1930.
Mounce, Robert H. *The Book of Revelation*. NICNT. Grand Rapids, MI: Eerdmans, 1977.
Moyise, Steve. 'Does the NT Quote the OT Out of Context?', *Anvil* 11 (1994): 133–43.

Moyise, Steve. *The Old Testament in the Book of Revelation*. JSNTSup 115. Sheffield: Sheffield Academic Press, 1995.
Moyise, Steve. 'The Language of the Old Testament in the Apocalypse', *JSNT* 76 (1999): 97–113.
Moyise, Steve. 'The Old Testament in the New: A Reply to Greg Beale', *Irish Biblical Studies* 21 (1999): 54–8.
Moyise, Steve. 'Intertextuality and the Study of the Old Testament in the New Testament'. In *The Old Testament in the New Testament: Essays in Honour of J. L. North*, edited by Steve Moyise, 14–41. JSNTSup 189. Sheffield: Sheffield Academic Press, 2000.
Moyise, Steve. 'Authorial Intention and the Book of Revelation', *AUSS* 39 (2001): 35–40.
Moyise, Steve. 'Does the Lion Lie Down with the Lamb?' In *Studies in the Book of Revelation*, edited by Steve Moyise, 181–94. Edinburgh: T&T Clark, 2001.
Moyise, Steve. 'Does the Author of Revelation Misappropriate the Scriptures', *AUSS* 40 (2002): 3–21.
Moyise, Steve. 'The Language of the Psalms in the Book of Revelation', *Neot* 37 (2003): 246–61.
Moyise, Steve. 'Singing the Song of Moses and the Lamb: John's Dialogical Use of Scripture', *AUSS* 42 (2004): 347–60.
Moyise, Steve. 'The Wilderness Quotation in Mark 1.2–3'. In *Wilderness: Essays in Honour of Frances Young*, edited by R. S. Sugirtharajah, 78–87. London: Continuum/T&T Clark, 2005.
Moyise, Steve. *Evoking Scripture: Seeing the Old Testament in the New*. London: T&T Clark, 2008.
Moyise, Steve. 'Ezekiel and the Book of Revelation'. In *After Ezekiel, Essays on the Reception of a Difficult Prophet*, edited by Andrew Mein and Paul M. Joyce, 45–57. LHBOTS 535. New York: T&T Clark, 2011.
Moyise, Steve. 'Genesis in Revelation'. In *Genesis in the New Testament*, edited by Maarten J. J. Menken and Steve Moyise, 166–79. LNTS 466. London: Bloomsbury, 2012.
Moyise, Steve. *The Later New Testament Writers and Scripture*. London: SPCK, 2012.
Moyise, Steve. 'Models for Intertextual Interpretation of Revelation'. In *Revelation and the Politics of Apocalyptic Interpretation*, edited by Richard B. Hays and Stefan Alkier, 31–46. Waco, TX: Baylor University Press, 2012.
Moyise, Steve. 'A Response to Currents in British Research on the Apocalypse'. In *The Book of Revelation: Currents in British Research on the Apocalypse*, edited by Garrick V. Allen, Ian Paul and Simon P. Woodman, 281–8. WUNT 2/411. Mohr Siebeck: Tübingen, 2015.
Moyise, Steve. *The Old Testament in the New: An Introduction*. 2nd edn. London: Bloomsbury, 2015.
Moyise, Steve. 'Dialogical Intertextuality'. In *Exploring Intertextuality: Diverse Strategies for New Testament Interpretation of Texts*, edited by B. J. Oropeza and Steve Moyise, 3–15. Eugene, OR: Cascade Books, 2016.
Moyise, Steve. 'Concluding Reflection'. In *Methodology in the Use of the Old Testament in the New: Context and Criteria*, edited by David Allen and Steve Smith, 178–86. LNTS 579. London: T&T Clark, 2019.
Moyise, Steve, and Maarten J. J. Menken (eds). *The Psalms in the New Testament*. London: Continuum/T&T Clark, 2004.
Müller, Darius, and Peter Malik. 'Rediscovering Paratexts in the Manuscripts of Revelation', *Early Christianity* 11 (2020): 247–64.

Müller-Fieberg, Rita. 'Song of Moses, Song of the Lamb: The Reception of Exodus in the Revelation of John'. In *Reception of Exodus Motifs in Jewish and Christian Literature: 'Let My People Go!'*, edited by Beate Kowalski and Susan E. Docherty, 334–49. TBN 30. Leiden: Brill, 2021.

Nau, François. 'Une deuxième Apocalypse apocryphe grecque de S. Jean', *RB* 23 (1914): 209–21.

Newman, Judith H. *Praying by the Book: The Scripturalization of Prayer in Second Temple Judaism*. SBLEJL 14. Atlanta, GA: Society of Biblical Literature, 1999.

Nickelsburg, George W. E. 'Son of Man'. In *The Anchor Bible Dictionary Volume 6*, edited by David N. Freedman, 137–50. New York: Doubleday, 1992.

Nickelsburg, George W. E. 'Scripture in *1 Enoch* and *1 Enoch* as Scripture'. In *Texts and Contexts: Biblical Texts in Their Textual and Situational Contexts. Essays in Honour of Lars Hartman*, edited by Tord Fornberg and David Hellholm, 333–54. Oslo: Scandinavian University Press, 1995.

Nickelsburg, George W. E. *1 Enoch: A Commentary on the Book of 1 Enoch*. 2 vols. Hermeneia. Minneapolis, MN: Augsburg Fortress, 2001.

North, J. Lionel. 'Paul's Protest That He Does Not Lie in the Light of His Cilician Origin', *JThS* 47 (1996): 439–63.

North, Wendy E. Sproston. *The Lazarus Story within the Johannine Tradition*. JSNTSup 212. Sheffield: Sheffield Academic Press, 2001.

North, Wendy E. Sproston. *What John Knew and What John Wrote: A Study in John and the Synoptics*. Interpreting Johannine Literature. Lanham, MD: Lexington Books/Fortress Academic, 2020.

Norton, Jonathan D. H. *Contours in the Text: Textual Variation in the Writings of Paul, Josephus and the Yahad*. LNTS 430. London: T&T Clark, 2011.

Nussbaum, Emily. '"Years and Years" Forces Us into the Future,' *The New Yorker*, 22 July 2019. https://www.newyorker.com/magazine/2019/07/29/years-and-years-forces-us-into-the-future, accessed 31 October 2021.

Ó Carragáin, Eamonn, 'Conversion, Justice, and Mercy at the Parousia: Liturgical Apocalypses from Eighth-Century Northumbria, on the Ruthwell and Bewcastle Crosses', *Literature and Theology* 26.4 (2012): 367–83.

Oropeza, B. J. *Jews, Gentiles, and the Opponents of Paul*. Eugene, OR: Cascade, 2012.

Oropeza, B. J. *1 Corinthians*. NCCS. Eugene, OR: Cascade, 2017, 206; cf. 199–200.

Parker, D. C. *The Living Text of the Gospels*. Cambridge: Cambridge University Press, 1998.

Paul, Ian. 'The Use of the Old Testament in Rev 12'. In *The Old Testament in the New Testament*, edited by Steve Moyise, 256–78. JSNTS 189. Sheffield: Sheffield Academic Press, 2000.

Paul, Ian. 'Source, Structure, and Composition in the Book of Revelation'. In *The Book of Revelation: Currents in British Research on the Apocalypse*, edited by Garrick V. Allen, Ian Paul and Simon P. Woodman, 41–54. WUNT 2/411. Tübingen: Mohr Siebeck, 2015.

Paul, Ian. *Kingdom, Hope and the End of the World*. Cambridge: Grove Books, 2016.

Paul, Ian. *Revelation*. TNTC. London: IVP, 2017.

Paulien, Jon. *Decoding Revelation's Trumpets: Literary Allusions and the Interpretation of Revelation 8:7–12*. Berrien Springs, MI: Andrews University Press, 1987.

Paulien, Jon. 'Elusive Allusions: The Problematic Use of the Old Testament in Revelation', *BR* 37 (1988): 37–53.

Paulien, Jon. 'Dreading the Whirlwind: Intertextuality and the Use of the Old Testament in Revelation', *AUSS* 39 (2001): 5–22.

Paulsen, Henning. *Studien zur Theologie des Ignatius von Antiochien*. Göttingen: Vandenhoeck & Ruprecht, 1978.
Pearce, Philippa. *Tom's Midnight Garden*. Oxford: Oxford University Press, 1958.
Perkins, Justin. 'The Revelation of the Blessed Apostle Paul', *JAOS* 8 (1866): 183–212.
Perrin, Norman. *The Kingdom of God in the Teaching of Jesus*. London: SCM Press, 1963.
Peterson, Eugene H. *Reversed Thunder: The Revelation of John and the Praying Imagination*. 1st edn. San Francisco, CA: Harper & Row, 1988.
Pitre, Brant, Michael P. Barber and John A. Kincaid. *Paul: A New Covenant Jew: Rethinking Pauline Theology*. Grand Rapids, MI: Eerdmans, 2019.
Plummer, Charles (ed.). *Venerabilis Baedae opera historica*. 2 vols. Oxford: Clarendon Press, 1896.
Porter, Stanley E. *The Letter to the Romans*. NTM 37. Sheffield: Sheffield Phoenix, 2015.
Reddish, Mitchell. 'The Genre of the Book of Revelation'. In *The Oxford Handbook to the Book of Revelation*, edited by Craig R. Koester, 21–36. Oxford: Oxford University Press, 2020.
Reventlow, Henning Graf. *History of Biblical Interpretation Volume 1: From the Old Testament to Origen*. Atlanta, GA: Society of Biblical Literature, 2009.
Reynolds, Benjamin E. *John among the Apocalypses: Jewish Apocalyptic Tradition and the 'Apocalyptic' Gospel*. Oxford: Oxford University Press, 2020.
Robertson, Archibald T. *Word Pictures in the New Testament*. Nashville, TN: Broadman, 1933.
Robinson, David C., and Francis X. Gumerlock (eds). *Tyconius, Exposition of the Apocalypse*. Fathers of the Church: A New Translation. Washington, DC: Catholic University of America Press, 2017.
Rodriguez, Rafael. *If You Call Yourself a Jew: Reappraising Paul's Letter to the Romans*. Eugene, OR: Cascade, 2014.
Rogers, Bret A. *Jesus as the Pierced One: Zechariah 12:10 in John's Gospel and Revelation*. Eugene, OR: Pickwick, 2020.
Roloff, Jürgen. *Die Offenbarung des Johannes*. ZBK 18. Zürich: Theologischer Verlag, 1984.
Roloff, Jürgen. *A Continental Commentary: The Revelation of John*. Minneapolis, MN: Fortress, 1993.
Rosenberg, Eliza. 'Weddings and the Return to Life in the Book of Revelation'. In *Coming Back to Life*, edited by Frederick S. Tappenden and Carly Daniel-Hughes, 309–41. Montreal: McGill UL, 2017.
Rosten, Leo. *The Joys of Yiddish: A Relaxed Lexicon of Yiddish, Hebrew and Yinglish Words Often Encountered in English ... from the Days of the Bible to Those of the Beatnik*. New York: McGraw-Hill Book Co., 1968.
Rowland, Christopher. *The Open Heaven: A Study of Apocalyptic in Judaism and Early Christianity*. London: SPCK, 1982.
Ruiz, Jean-Pierre. *Ezekiel in the Apocalypse: The Transformation of Prophetic Language in Revelation 16.17–19.10*. Frankfurt: Peter Lang, 1989.
Ryan, Sean Michael. 'In Animate Praise. The Heavenly Temple Liturgy of the Apocalypse and the Songs of the Sabbath Sacrifice', *ScrB* 42.1 (2012): 13–25.
Sanders, E. P. 'Paul's Attitude toward the Jewish People', *USQR* 33 (1978): 175–87.
Sargent, Benjamin. 'The Narrative Substructure of 1 Peter', *ET* 124.10 (2013): 485–90.
Sargent, Benjamin. *David Being a Prophet: The Contingency of Scripture upon History in the New Testament*. BZNW 207. Berlin: de Gruyter, 2014.

Sargent, Benjamin. '"Interpreting Homer from Homer": Aristarchus of Samothrace and the Notion of Scriptural Authorship in the New Testament', *TynBul* 65.1 (2014): 125–39.
Sargent, Benjamin. 'The Exegetical Middah דבר הלמד מענינו and the New Testament', *NovT* 57.4 (2015): 413–17.
Sargent, Benjamin. *Written to Serve: The Use of Scripture in 1 Peter*. LNTS 547. London: T&T Clark/Bloomsbury, 2015.
Sargent, Benjamin. *Written for Our Learning: The Single Meaning of Scripture in Christian Theology*. Eugene, OR: Cascade, 2016.
Sargent, Benjamin. 'The Typological Interpretation of Scriptural Quotations in the New Testament: A Test Case for the Bible in the Academy'. In *The Exegetical and Ethical: The Bible and the Academy in the Public Square: Essays for the Occasion of Professor John Barton's 70th Birthday*, edited by H. Clifford and M. Daffern. BIS 197. Leiden: Brill, 2022.
Schäfer, Peter (ed.). *Synopse zur Hekhalot-Literatur*. TSAJ 2. Tübingen: Mohr Siebeck, 1981.
Scharneck, Rudolph. 'The Song of Moses Which Is Not (Also) the Song of the Lamb: An Investigation into the Number of Songs at Play in Rev. 15', *JECH* 9 (2019): 59–73.
Schedtler, Justin Jeffcoat. *A Heavenly Chorus: The Dramatic Function of Revelation's Hymns*. WUNT II/381. Tübingen: Mohr Siebeck, 2014.
Schelkle, K. H. *Die Petrusbriefe, der Judasbrief*. HThKNT. Freiburg: Herder, 1970.
Schlatter, Adolf. *Das alte Testament in der johanneischen Apokalypse*. Gütersloh: Mohn, 1912.
Schlier, Heinrich. *Religionsgeschichtliche Untersuchungen zu den Ignatiusbriefen*. BZNW 8. Geißen: Alfred Töpelmann, 1929.
Schnabel, Eckhard J. *Der Brief des Paulus an die Römer*. Witten: SCM R. Brockhaus, 2016.
Schnackenburg, Rudolf. *The Gospel According to St John*. Vol. 1. Translated by Kevin Smyth. Tunbridge Wells: Burns & Oates, 1990.
Schoedel, William R. 'Ignatius and the Archives', *HTR* 71 (1978): 97–106.
Schuller, E. 'Psalms, Apocryphal'. In *The Eerdmans Dictionary of Early Judaism*, edited by J. J. Collins and D. C. Harlow, 1105. Grand Rapids, MI: Eerdmans, 2010.
Schüssler Fiorenza, Elisabeth. *Revelation: Vision of a Just World*. Minneapolis, MN: Fortress Press, 1991.
Schweitzer, Albert. *The Quest of the Historical Jesus*. 2nd edn. London: A & C Black, 1936.
Scott, James M. '"And Then All Israel Will Be Saved" (Rom 11:26)'. In *Restoration: Old Testament, Jewish, and Christian Perspectives*, edited by James M. Scott, 489–527. Leiden: Brill, 2001.
Self, Will. *Revelation: The Canon Pocket Bible Series*. Edinburgh: Canongate, 1998.
Sheridan, Ruth. 'John's Prologue as Exegetical Narrative'. In *The Gospel of John as Genre Mosaic*, edited by Kasper Bro Larsen, 171–90. SAN 3. Göttingen: Vandenhoeck & Ruprecht, 2015.
Simonetti, Manlio. *Biblical Interpretation in the Early Church: An Historical Introduction to Patristic Exegesis*. Translated by John A. Hughes. Edinburgh: T&T Clark, 1994.
Smalley, Stephen S. *The Revelation to John: A Commentary on the Greek Text of the Apocalypse*. Downers Grove, IL: InterVarsity, 2005.
Shaw, J. F. (trans.). *St Augustine: On Christian Doctrine*. Buffalo: The Christian Literature Co., 1887; Mineola, NY: Dover, 2009.
Smith, J. H. *The New Treasury of Scripture Knowledge*. Nashville, TN: Thomas Nelson, 1992.

Smith, Steve. *The Fate of the Jerusalem Temple in Luke-Acts: An Intertextual Approach to Jesus' Lament over Jerusalem and Stephen's Speech*. LNTS 553. London: T&T Clark, 2018.
Smith, Steve. 'The Use of Criteria: A Proposal from Relevance Theory'. In *Methodology in the Use of the Old Testament in the New: Context and Criteria*, edited by David Allen and Steve Smith. LNTS 579. London: T&T Clark, 2019.
Smyth, Marina. 'The Seventh-Century Hiberno-Latin Treatise *Liber de ordine creaturarum*. A Translation', *JML* 21 (2011): 137–222.
Smyth, Marina. 'Monastic Culture in Seventh-Century Ireland', *JASIMS* 12 (2019): 64–101.
Sommer, Michael. 'Von politischen Räumen … Das Lied des Mose und die Apokalypsen des frühen Judentums und frühen Christentums'. In *Mosebilder. Gedanken zur Rezeption einer literarischen Figur im Frühjudentum, frühen Christentum und der römisch-hellenistischen Literatur*, edited by Erik Eynikel and Elisabeth Hernitscheck, 299–317. WUNT 390. Tübingen: Mohr Siebeck, 2017.
Stanley, Christopher D. *Paul and the Language of Scripture: Citation Technique in the Pauline Epistles and Contemporary Literature*. SNTSMS 69. Cambridge: Cambridge University Press, 1992.
Staples, Jason A. 'What Do the Gentiles Have to Do with "All Israel"? A Fresh Look at Romans 11:25–27', *JBL* 130 (2011): 371–90.
Stare, Mira. 'Das neu gesungene Lied des Mose (Offb 15,3b-4)'. In *Führe mein Volk heraus. Zur innerbiblischen Rezeption der Exodusthematik (FS Georg Fischer)*, edited by Simone Paganini and Claudia Paganini, 121–38. Frankfurt: Lang, 2004.
Staubli, Thomas. 'Musikinstrumente und musikalische Ausdrucksformen', *WuB* 46 (2007): 7–39.
Stec, David M. *The Targum of Psalms: Translated, with a Critical Introduction, Apparatus, and Notes*. ArBib 16. Collegeville, PA: Liturgical Press, 2004.
Stec, David M. *The Genizah Psalms: A Study of MS 798 of the Antonin Collection*, ÉJM 57; CGSS 5. Leiden: Brill, 2013.
Stegemann, Viktor. *Die Gestalt Christi in den koptischen Zaubertexten*. Heidelberg: S. Bilabel, 1934.
Steinhauser, Kenneth B. *The Apocalypse Commentary of Tyconius: A History of Its Reception and Influence*. Frankfurt am Main: Peter Lang, 1987.
Stewart-Sykes, Alistair. *The Lamb's High Feast: Melito, Peri Pascha and the Quartodeciman Paschal Liturgy at Sardis*. Leiden: Brill, 1998.
Steyn, Gert. J. *A Quest for the Assumed Septuagint Vorlage of the Explicit Quotations in Hebrews*. FRLANT 235. Göttingen: Vandenhoeck & Ruprecht, 2011.
Strack, Hermann L., and Paul Billerbeck. *Kommentar zum Neuen Testament aus Talmud und Midrasch*. München: Beck, 1922.
Stuckenbruck, Loren T. *1 Enoch 91–108*. CEJL. Berlin: de Gruyter, 2007.
Subramanian, J. Samuel. 'The Prophetic Reading of the Psalms in Second Temple Jewish Literature'. In *The Synoptic Gospels and the Psalms as Prophecy*, LNTS 351. London: T&T Clark, 2007.
Sweet, John. *Revelation*. London: SCM, 1979.
Swete, Henry Barclay. *The Apocalypse of St. John*. 2nd edn. Classic Commentaries on the Greek NT. New York: The Macmillan Company, 1906.
Taft, Robert. *The Liturgy of the Hours in East and West: The Origins of the Divine Office and Its Meaning for Today*. Collegeville, PA: Liturgical Press, 1986.
Tangl, Michael (ed.). *Die Briefe des heiligen Bonifatius und Lullus*. Berlin: Ficker, Gerhard, 1916 [1919].

Thacker, Alan. 'Bede's Ideal of Reform'. In *Ideal and Reality in Frankish and Anglo-Saxon Society: Studies Presented to J. M. Wallace-Hadrill*, edited by Patrick Wormald, Donald Bullough and Roger Collins, 130–53. Oxford: Basil Blackwell, 1983.
Thielman, Frank. *Romans*. ZECNT. Grand Rapids, MI: Zondervan, 2018.
Thomas, John Christopher, and Frank D. Macchia. *Revelation*. Grand Rapids, MI: Eerdmans, 2016.
Tiller, Patrick A. *A Commentary on the Animal Apocalypse of 1 Enoch*. SBLEJL 4. Atlanta, GA: Scholars, 1993.
Tischendorf, C. *Apocalypses Apocryphae*. Leipzig: H. Mendelssohn, 1866.
Tomin, Julius. 'Socratic Midwifery', *CQ* 37 (1987): 97–102.
Toniste, Külle. *The Ending of the Canon: A Canonical and Intertextual Reading of Revelation 21–22*. LNTS 526. London: T&T Clark, 2016.
Tonstad, Sigve. *Revelation*. Commentaries on the New Testament. Paideia: Baker, 2019.
Tooman, William A. *Gog of Magog: Reuse of Scripture and Compositional Technique in Ezekiel 38–39*. FAT 52. Tübingen: Mohr Siebeck, 2011.
Tooman, William A. 'Scriptural Reuse in Ancient Jewish Literature: Comments and Reflections on the State of the Art'. In *Methodology in the Use of the Old Testament in the New: Context and Criteria*, edited by David Allen and Steve Smith, 23–39. London: T&T Clark, 2020.
Trafton, Joseph L. *Reading Revelation: A Literary and Theological Commentary*. Rev. edn. Macon: Smyth & Helwys, 2005.
Trevett, Christine. 'The Other Letters to the Churches of Asia: Apocalypse and the Letters of Ignatius of Antioch', *JSNT* 37 (1989): 124–30.
Tucker, J. Brian. *Reading Romans after Supersessionism*. Eugene, OR: Cascade, 2018.
Utley, R. J. *Hope in Hard Times – the Final Curtain: Revelation*. Study Guide Commentary Series 12. Marshall: Bible Lessons International, 2001.
Vall, Gregory. *Learning Christ: Ignatius of Antioch and the Mystery of Redemption*. Washington, DC: Catholic University of America Press, 2013.
Van der Pas, Sarah, and John Litteral (eds). *Alcuin of York: On Revelation, Commentary and the Questions and Answers Manual*. West Monroe, LA: Consolamini, 2016.
Van Schaik, A. 'De Apocalyps als Tekstmozaïek', *Schrift* 114 (1987): 231–4.
VanderKam, James C. 'The Theophany of 1 Enoch 1:3b-7, 9', *VT* 23 (1973): 129–50.
Vanhoozer, Kevin J. *Is There a Meaning in This Text?* Grand Rapids, MI: Zondervan, 1998.
Vanhoye, Albert. 'L'utilisation du livre d'Ézéchiel dans l'Apocalypse', *Bib* 43 (1962): 436–76.
Vanni, Ugo. 'Liturgical Dialogue as a Literary Form in the Book of Revelation', *NTS* 37 (1991): 348–72.
Vassiliev, Afanasiĭ. *Anecdota Graeco-Byzantina*. Moscow: Caesarea University, 1893.
Villeneuve, André. *Nuptial Symbolism in Second Temple Writings, the NT and Rabbinic Literature: Divine Marriage at Key Moments of Salvation History*. Leiden: Brill, 2016.
Vlach, Michael J. 'Response to Merkle'. In *Three Views on Israel and the Church: Perspectives on Romans 9–11*, edited by Jared Compton and Andrew David Naselli, 209–22. Grand Rapids, MI: Kregel Academic, 2018.
Vreugdenhil, Gerrit C. *Psalm 91 and Demonic Menace*. OtSt 77. Leiden: Brill, 2020.
Walker, Alexander. *Apocryphal Gospels, Acts, and Revelations*. Edinburgh: T&T Clark, 1870.
Wallis, Faith (ed.). *Bede: The Reckoning of Time*. Liverpool: Liverpool University Press, 1999 [republished 2004].

Wallis, Faith (ed.). *Bede: Commentary on Revelation*. Liverpool: Liverpool University Press, 2013.
Wallis, Faith. 'Why Did Bede Write a Commentary on Revelation?' In *Bede and the Future*, edited by Peter Darby and Faith Wallis, 23–45. Farnham: Ashgate, 2014.
Wallis Budge, E. A. *The Contending of the Apostles: The Histories of the Lives and Martyrdoms and Deaths of the Twelve Apostles and Evangelists, vol. II. The English Translation*. London: Henry Frowde, 1901.
Wallis Budge, E. A. *Coptic Apocrypha in the Dialect of Upper Egypt*. London: Longmans, 1913.
Ward, Benedicta. *The Venerable Bede*. London: Geoffrey Chapman, 1990.
Watson, Francis. *Paul and the Hermeneutics of Faith*. London: T&T Clark, 2004.
Watts, James W. *Psalm and Story: Inset Hymns in Hebrew Narrative*. LHBOTS 139. Sheffield: JSOT Press, 1992.
Watts, James W. 'Biblical Psalms Outside the Psalter'. In *The Book of Psalms: Composition and Reception*, edited by Peter W. Flint and Patrick D. Jr Miller, 288–309. VTSup 99. Leiden: Brill 2005.
Weima, Jeffrey. *1–2 Thessalonians*. BECNT. Grand Rapids, MI: Baker, 2014.
Weinel, Heinrich. 'Die spätere christliche Apokalyptik'. In *ΕΥΧΑΡΙΣΤΗΡΙΟΝ: Studien zur Religion und Literatur des Alten und Neuen Testaments. Hermann Gunkel zum 60. Geburtstag, dem 23. Mai 1922 dargebracht von seinen Schülern und Freunden. 2. Teil: Zur Religion und Literatur des Neuen Testaments*, edited by Hans Schmidt, 141–73. FRLANT 19. Göttingen: Vandehoeck & Ruprecht, 1923.
Whittle, Sarah. *Covenant Renewal and the Consecration of the Gentiles in Romans*. SNTMS 161. Cambridge: Cambridge University Press, 2014.
Whittock, Martyn. *The End Times, Again?* Eugene, OR: Wipf and Stock, 2021.
Williams, Catrin H. *John's Gospel and Intimations of Apocalyptic*. London: Bloomsbury T&T Clark, 2013.
Williams, Catrin H. 'Patriarchs and Prophets Remembered: Framing Israel's Past in the Gospel of John'. In *Abiding Words: The Use of Scripture in the Gospel of John*, edited by Alicia D. Myers and Bruce G. Schuchard, 187–212. SBLRBS, 81. Atlanta, GA: SBL Press, 2015.
Wilson, David M. *Anglo-Saxon Art: From the Seventh Century to the Norman Conquest*. London: Thames and Hudson, 1984.
Wilson, Mark. *Charts on the Book of Revelation: Literary, Historical, and Theological Perspectives*. Kregel Charts of the Bible and Theology. Grand Rapids, MI: Kregel Academic & Professional, 2007.
Witherington, Ben. *Revelation*. NCBC. Cambridge: Cambridge University Press, 2003.
Wright, N. T. *The Climax of the Covenant: Christ and the Law in Pauline Theology*. Edinburgh: T&T Clark, 1991.
Wright, N. T. *The New Testament and the People of God*. London: SPCK, 1992.
Wright, N. T. 'Romans and the Theology of Paul'. In *Romans, Vol. 3 of Pauline Theology*, edited by David M. Hay and E. Elizabeth Johnson, 56–62. Minneapolis, MN: Fortress, 1995.
Wright, N. T. 'Romans'. In *The New Interpreter's Bible Commentary*, edited by Leander Keck, 9:317–664. Nashville, TN: Abingdon, 2002.
Wright, N. T. *Paul and the Faithfulness of God*. Christian Origins and the Question of God 4. Minneapolis, MN: Fortress, 2013.
Wright, N. T. *The Day the Revolution Began: Rethinking the Meaning of Jesus' Crucifixion*. London: SPCK, 2016.

Wright, N. T. *History and Eschatology*. London: SPCK, 2019.
Years and Years. StudioCanal, 2019.
Young, Frances. 'Typology'. In *Crossing the Boundaries: Essays in Biblical Interpretation in Honour of Michael D. Goulder*, edited by Stanley E. Porter, Paul Joyce and David E. Orton, 29–48. Leiden: Brill, 1994.
Young, Frances. *Biblical Exegesis and the Formation of Christian Culture*. Cambridge: Cambridge University Press, 1997.
Young, Frances. '*Theotokos*: Mary and the Pattern of Fall and Redemption in the Theology of Cyril of Alexandria'. In *The Theology of Cyril of Alexandria: A Critical Appreciation*, edited by Thomas G. Weinandy and Daniel A. Keating, 55–74. London: T&T Clark, 2003.
Young, Frances. *Exegesis and Theology in Early Christianity*. Farnham: Ashgate, 2012.
Young, Frances. *Construing the Cross: Type, Sign, Symbol, Word, Action*. Didsbury Lecture Series. Eugene, OR: Cascade Books, 2015; London: SPCK, 2016.
Zahn, Theodor. *Ignatius von Antiochen*. Gotha: Perthes, 1873.
Zerwick, Max, and Mary Grosvenor. *A Grammatical Analysis of the Greek New Testament*. Rome: Biblical Institute, 1974.
Zoccali, Christopher. ' "And So All Israel Will Be Saved": Competing Interpretations of Romans 11.26 in Pauline Scholarship', *JSNT* 30 (2008): 289–318.
Zoccali, Christopher. *Whom God Has Called: The Relationship of Church and Israel in Pauline Interpretation, 1920 to the Present*. Eugene, OR: Pickwick, 2010.
Zumstein, Jean. *L'Évangile selon Saint Jean 1–12*. CNT. Deuxième Série IVa Genève: Labor et Fides, 2014.

Index of Modern Authors

Adelman, R. 188–90
Adler, W. 198
Allen, D. M. 25
Allen, G. V. 25, 28, 36, 38, 148
Andrieu, M. 123, 128
Ashton, J. 161, 168
Atherstone, A. 42
Aune, D. E. 47, 60, 67, 68–74, 76, 77, 79, 109, 200, 201

Bailey, K. 110
Balz, H. R., 74, 77
Bannister, H. M. 122
Barber, M. P. 180
Barclay, J. M. G. 172
Barney, S. W. J. 121
Barr, D. L. 139
Barrett, C. K. 167
Bartelmus, R. 94
Barton, J. 45
Batey, R. A. 184
Bauckham, R. 2, 11, 12, 19–22, 49, 57, 59, 102, 104, 107, 111–13, 194, 198
Bauer, W. 48
Beale, G. K. 2, 3, 25–37, 39, 41–5, 50
Begg, C. T. 195
Benito, M. 96
Bennema, C. 162
Berghof, O. 121
Bietenhard, H. 118
Billerbeck, P. 187, 189, 191
Billett, J. D. 122
Black, M. 148, 151, 153–5
Blenkinsopp, J. 70
Blount, B. K. 55
Boccaccini, G. 157
Bolton, W. F. 124
Bonner, G. 118
Boring, M. E. 83
Bovon, F. 73
Boxall, I. 56, 107, 122, 125

Boyarin, D. 165
Brannan, R. 199, 202
Braude, W. G. 196
Brooke, G. J. 193, 196
Brown, G. H. 118, 119
Bultmann, R. 18, 19, 161
Burkitt, F. C. 124

Cabaniss, A. 48
Caird, G. B. 106, 107
Campbell, C. 108
Carson, D. A. 34, 42, 44, 103
Casamassa, A. 120
Charles, R. H. 21, 47, 69, 70, 72–4, 77, 79–81, 103, 106, 151, 153–5
Chavasse, C. 184
Chiesa, P. 118
Chilton, B. D. 172
Colgrave, B. 120, 122, 126
Collins, J. J. 65, 69, 70, 101
Compton, J. 172
Court, J. M. 199, 201, 202, 204, 206, 207
Cousland, J. R. C. 188
Crawford, S. W. 62
Crouser, W. 190
Cubitt, C. 124

Danby, H. 186
Daniélou, J. 12, 48
Darby, P. 118, 124
Das, A. A. 172, 176, 177
Davila, J. R. 69, 194, 198
Davis, D. R. 106
DeGregorio, S. 123, 124, 128
Delamarter, S. 148, 150, 153, 154
de Lubac, H. 118
de Moor, J. C. 56
Dempsey, G. T. 117
Docherty, S. E. 36, 166
Dodd, C. H. 17, 18
Doering, L. 46, 176

Donaldson, T. L. 176, 181
Doyle, A. I. 122
Dupont, J. 193, 209

Easley, K. 67
Eastman, B. J. 78
Eastman, S. G. 176
Ellis, E. E. 53
Estelle, B. 113
Evans, C. A. 203

Fabiny, T. 14
Farrer, A. 11, 12, 21, 107
Fee, G. D. 71, 79
Fekkes, J. 26
Fenske, W. 54, 58
Fishbane, M. 2, 14, 15, 21
Fitzmyer, J. A. 45, 193
Fletcher, M. 3, 25, 59–63, 148
Flint, P. W. 99, 194
Foot, S. 126
Foster, P. 26, 149, 179
Fredriksen, P. 125, 180
Frey, J. 162-4, 166
Friedmann, M. 196
Fuchs, G. 122
Fudge, E. 49

Gallus, L. 54, 57
García Ureña, L. 61
Garroway, J. D. 172
Gerke, E. 37
Goodenough, E. R. 195
Goodrich, J. K. 171, 172, 176-8, 180
Gorman, M. 105, 106
Goulder, M. D. 13, 48
Grant, J. 67
Grant, R. M. 49
Greene, T. 42, 44
Grocock, C. 119, 122
Grogan, G. W. 71
Grosvenor, M. 175
Gryson, R. 125
Guiver, G. 128
Gumerlock, F. X. 126
Gurtner, D. M. 147

Haddan, A. W. 119
Hafemann, S. 172

Hahn, S. W. 180
Hall, J. R. 128
Hardin, L. 54
Harrington, W. J. 69–71
Hartenstein, F. 93, 94
Hartman, L. 150, 152, 157
Harvey, J. D.. 175
Hauerwas, S. 137
Hawkes, J. 119, 124
Hays, R. B. 1, 44, 46, 84, 148
Hemer, C. J. 47
Hilgard, A. 199
Hills, J. V. 197
Hirsch, E. D. 32, 34, 42, 43
Hirschfelder, U. 196
Horbury, W. 58
Horgan, M. P. 208
Huffman, D. S. 66
Hurst, D. 121
Hurtado, L. W. 36

Jauhiainen, M. 36
Jenkins, F. W. 84
Johnson, D. H. 72

Kaestli, J.-D. 199
Kannengiesser, C. 118
Karkov, C. E. 119
Karrer, M. 35–8, 84
Keener, C. S. 70, 71, 77, 79, 165, 167, 168
Kendall, C. B. 120, 121, 124
Kim, D. 172
Kincaid, J. A. 180
Kingston-Smith, A. 139
Klaiber, W. 69–71, 74, 79, 80
Knoebel, T. L. 127
Koester, C. R 58, 62, 69, 71, 76, 78–80, 102, 106, 107, 109
Konrad, U. 93
Kosior, W. 188
Kostenberger, A. J. 65, 66, 81
Köster, H. 197
Kowalski, B. 35, 37, 84, 94, 97, 99
Kraft, R. A. 49, 197
Kraus, H-J. 206
Krauss, S. 183, 186, 188
Kreitzer, L. 131
Kristeva, J. 1, 29, 42
Kropp, A. 200

Kugel, J. L. 196
Kurek-Chomycz, D. A. 190

Laato, A. 70
Ladd, G. E. 70
Lampe, G. W. H. 12
Lange, A. 72, 148, 151, 154
Lapidge, M. 117, 118
Lewis, J. A. 121
Lincoln, A. T. 133, 165
Litteral, J. 118
Long, P. J. 184
Longenecker, R. N. 41, 42, 50, 172, 177
Lookadoo, J. 49
Lorein, G. W. 194
Lux, R. 99

Macchia, F. D. 55, 56
Maiani, B. 122
Maier, H. 109
Malik, P. 37
Marsh, C. 143
Martin, L. 118, 121, 124
McHugh, J. F. 164-7
McLean, B. H. 45
McWhirter, J. 184
Merton, T. 95
Michelli, P. 124
Miller, G. D. 185
Mintz, A. I. 185
Moberley, R. W. L. 14
Mohlberg, L. C. 122
Moloney, F. J.. 164
Moo, D. J. 172
Moore, S. D. 131
Morgenthaler, R. 167
Morin, G. 120
Mounce, R. H. 69, 74, 75, 78-81
Moyise, S. 3, 5, 6, 11, 25-7, 29-37, 39, 41-5, 47, 48, 50, 53, 57, 58, 60, 63, 64, 65-8, 70, 76, 78, 79, 81, 83, 84, 101-4, 108, 111, 114, 139, 147, 148, 159, 162, 200, 209
Müller, D. 37
Müller-Fieberg, R. 94
Mynors, R. A. B. 120, 122, 126

Naselli, A. D. 172
Nau, F. 199

Newman, J. H. 156
Nickelsburg, G. W. E. 148-58
North, J. L. 189
North, W. E. S. 162, 165
Norton, J. D. H. 28

Ó Carragáin, E. 119
Oropeza, B. J. 172, 180

Parker, D. C. 36
Paul, I. 101, 102, 104, 105, 107-9, 111, 112
Paulien, J. 26, 33, 34, 41, 43, 44, 200
Paulsen, H. 47
Pearce, P. 104
Perkins, J. 198
Perrin, N. 18
Peterson, E. H. 58
Pitre, B. 180
Plummer, C. 118
Porter, S. E. 13, 172

Reddish, M. 102
Reventlow, H. G. 118
Reynolds, B. E. 161, 162, 164
Robertson, A. T. 70
Robinson, D. C. 126, 127
Rodriguez, R. 172
Rogers, B. A. 28
Roloff, J. 69, 70, 76, 79, 81
Rosenberg, E. 183
Rosten, L. 185, 186
Rowland, C. 19, 132
Ruiz, J-P. 26
Ryan, S. M.. 99

Sanders, E. P. 178
Sanderson, M. L. 48
Sargent, B. 41, 45, 46
Schäfer, P. 196
Scharneck, R. 55, 56
Schedtler, J. J. 99
Schelkle, K. H. 46
Schlier, H. 48
Schlatter, A. 27
Schnabel, E. J. 171, 172
Schnackenburg, R. 163, 164, 167, 168
Schneider, G 74, 77
Schoedel, W. R. 48
Simonetti, M. 48

Schuller, E. 65
Schüssler Fiorenza, E. 57
Schweitzer, A. 17
Self, W. 131
Sheridan, R. 163
Shaw, J. F. 124
Smalley, S. S. 54, 55, 57
Smith, J. H. 70
Smith, S. 25, 63
Smyth, M. 117, 126
Sommer, M. 94
Stanley, C. D. 53
Staples, J. A. 180
Stare, M. 94
Staubli, T. 92
Stec, D. M. 194, 195
Stegemann, V. 200
Steinhauser, K. B. 125
Stewart-Sykes, A. 16
Steyn, G. J. 75, 77, 148
Strack, H. L. 187, 189, 191
Stubbs, W. 119
Stuckenbruck, L. T. 155-6
Subramanian, J. S. 193
Sweet, J. 103, 109
Swete, H. B. 76

Taft, R. 122, 123
Tangl, M. 128
Thacker, A. 124
Thielman, F. 177
Thomas, J. C 55, 56
Tiller, P. A. 158
Tischendorf, C. 199
Tomin, J. 185
Toniste, K. 114
Tonstad, S. 55
Tooman, W. A. 28, 37, 148
Trafton, J. L. 58
Trevett, C. 47
Tucker, J. B. 180

Vall, G. 47, 48
Vassiliev, A. 198, 199
Van der Pas, S. 118
Van Schaik, A. 84
Van Staalduine-Sulman, E. 56, 194
VanderKam, J. C. 148, 149, 157
Vanhoozer, K. J. 31, 32
Vanhoye, A. 27, 97
Vanni, U. 83
Villeneuve, A. 184
Vlach, M. J. 179
Vreugdenhil, G. C. 152

Walker, A. 199
Wallis, F. 117-22, 124, 125, 127
Wallis Budge, E. A. 198, 199
Ward, B. 118, 122, 123, 128
Watson, F. 46
Watts, J. W. 99
Weigold, M. 72, 148, 151, 154
Weikmann, H. M. 122
Weima, J. 179
Weinel, H. 199, 200
Whittle, S. 171
Whittock, M. 103
Williams, C. H. 164, 165
Wilson, D. M. 119
Wilson, M. 70
Witherington III, B. 56
Wood, I. N. 119, 122
Woollcombe, K. J. 12
Wright, N. T. 6, 16, 18, 22, 32, 33, 71, 132, 172-8, 182

Young, F. 11, 13, 16

Zahn, T. 48, 49
Zerwick, M. 175
Zoccali, C. 171, 172
Zumstein, J. 167

Scripture Index

HEBREW BIBLE/LXX

Genesis
1.5	153
1.9–10	149
2.8	207
2.22	190
3	20, 191
3.1	189
5.21–24	201
6.1–2	148
6.4	148
10	180 n.49
22.2	166, 167
22.12	166, 167
22.16	166
37.7	48
37.9	41, 47, 48
49.9	19
49.9–10	200

Exodus
1.16–17	164
7.17	201
7.19	201
12.46	17
14.31	22, 57
15	3, 22, 57 nn.18 and 20, 58 n.24, 61, 64
15.1	58
15.1–18	56
15.11	57 n.18
15.20	61
19–20	21
19.4	109 n.35
19.16	22, 91
19.18	157
19.19	93
24.15–18	164
25.8	164
29.45–46	164
28.2	74 n.52
32.32–33	149
33–34	6, 163
33.9–11	164
33.18	164, 169
33.18–23	164
33.20	165
33.22	169
34.5	164
34.6	164
34.22	180
34.29–30	168
34.29–35	164
38.26 LXX	57
40.34–35	164

Leviticus
11.7	158
23	180

Numbers
12.7–8	57 n.23
23.7–24.24	152
24.2–4	152
24.15–16	152
24.17	48, 200
33.5–49	112

Deuteronomy
11.8–32	150
14.8	158
27.15–28	150
27.26	173
28.12	149
28.63	154
29	174
29.3 LXX	174
29.4	174
30	173
30.1–20	150
31.21	58

32	3, 57 n.18, 58 n.24, 61, 73	1 Kings (LXX 3 Kingdoms)	
32.1	155 n.28	5.12	194 n.4
32.1–43	56	6.7	99
32.4	58, 69 n.15, 73, 74 n.48, 78 n.71	6.20	111
		10.1–29	154
32.8	180 n.49, 208	14.6 LXX	189 n.22
		17.1	112 n.50
32.10	155	18.1	112 n.50
32.11	109 n.35	19.11	157
32,14	149	19.12	99
32.17	149	2 Kings (LXX 4 Kingdoms)	
32.21	172	1.10	201
32.43	58, 180 n.43	2.11–12	201
32.44 LXX	58	21 LXX	73
33.2	157		
33.3	69 n.18	1 Chronicles	
34.5–6	201	17.24	73 n.42
Joshua		2 Chronicles	
1.2	57 n.23	3:1	14
1.7	57 n.23	5.2–6.42	93
3–5	14	8.14	196
		9.22	75
Judges		13.5	196
5.4–5	157	33	72
11.29	195		
13.25	195	Esther	
14.2	185	1.1	91
14.4	185		
14.6	195	Job	
14.19	195	5.1	69 n.18
15.14	195	10.21–22	205
15.19	195	26.10-12	155
		38.8–11	155
Ruth		38.22	149
2.12	151		
		Psalms	
1 Samuel		1.3 LXX	197
10.11–12	195	1.5	150
17.43	56	1.6 LXX	197
16.13	195	2	68, 79 n.82, 81, 157
19.24	195	2.1	79 nn.77 and 82
		2.1–2	194
2 Samuel (LXX 2 Kingdoms)		2.1–5	79 n.82
7.25 LXX	73 n.42	2.2	77 n.65, 79 n.82, 151, 157
7.27 LXX	73 n.42		
18.33	198	2.4	154
22.16	149	2.5 LXX	79 nn.77 and 82

2.6	77 n.65	19	151 n.14
2.7	157, 197	19.4–5	151 n.14
2.8	79	19.9	78 n.70
2.9	79 n.82	19.10	154
2.12	79 n.82	19.14	152
3 LXX	81	20–21 LXX	81
3.1–8	197	20.2 LXX	71
3.7	149	20.6–7 LXX	75, 76
3.9 MT	76	21.17 LXX	197
3.9 LXX	75, 76 n.62	21.19 LXX	197
4.19	198	21.21 LXX	197
5.10	198	21.23 LXX	197
7.7 LXX	79	21.28 LXX	70
7.12–13	149	21.29 LXX	77
8.4	162 n.3	22	156
8.6 LXX	74	22.1 LXX	195
9 LXX	81	22.12	158
9.3 LXX	71	22.16	198
9.5 LXX	78, 80	23.1–2	158
9.8	80 n.83	24.1	196
9.9 LXX	80	24.2	149
9.16 LXX	205	24.6	198
9.18 LXX	205	24.7–9	198
9.19 LXX	207	25.2	149
9.37 LXX	79 n.78	25.8 LXX	80
10.7 LXX	78	27.8 LXX	76
11.2	69 n.15	27.8–9	156
11.7	78 n.69	31	156
13.1	156	31.11 LXX	71
13.3	197	32–33 LXX	81
13.7 LXX	71	32.1–2 LXX	72
16.8–11	193	32.2–3 LXX	69 n.16
17 LXX	81	32.3 LXX	67 n.11
17.2 LXX	75	32.8 LXX	69
17.3 LXX	75 n.57	32.21 LXX	71 n.36
17.8	151, 155	33 LXX	81
17.8 LXX	79	33.2	72 n.37
17.9 LXX	80	33.10 LXX	69
17.12 LXX	205	33.13 LXX	197
17.23 LXX	78	34.9 LXX	71 n.36
17.42 LXX	206	34.10 LXX	69–70
17.44–45 LXX	197–8	34.12	155
17.45 LXX	197	35.26	149
18	206 n.52	36.7	151
18.7	157	36.26 LXX	208
18.8 LXX	75 n.55	36.28 LXX	208
18.10–11	153	36.29 LXX	208
18.14–15	149	36.30 LXX	75 n.55
18.49	153	37 LXX	208

37	150	61.4	151
37.9	150	61.13 LXX	76
37.11	150	62.3 LXX	74
37.13	154	62.12	149
37.22	150	62.13 LXX	76
37.29	150	63.7	151
38.16	149	67	156
38.23 MT	76 n.62	67.4 LXX	81
39.4 LXX	67 n.11	68.2	157
39.17 LXX	71 n.36	68.7	157
40.14 LXX	72	68.17	157
41	72	68.23–24 LXX	174
41.3 LXX	197	69.17	156
41.14 MT	72 n.39	69.22–23	194
42–43	156	69.25	193
42.3 LXX	198	69.28	149
42.12MT	76 n.62	71.2 LXX	80
43.5MT	76 n.62	72	154
44	156	72.2	80 n.82
44.5 LXX	78	72.10	154
44.7 LXX	77	72.17	151
44.7–8 LXX	77 n.66	72.18–19	72 n.41
44.12 LXX	197	74	156
45.7	77 n.66	74.1	158
46	156	74.2	150
46.6 LXX	203 n.48	76.19 LXX	89–91
46.9 LXX	79, 80	77.8 LXX	204
47.8–9	79 n.77	77.17–18	149
48 LXX	205	77.20	158
48.4 LXX	75 n.55	77.60 LXX	80
48.15 LXX	205	78	152
49.18	197	78.2–3	152
49.19	197	79	156
49.20–21	197	79.2	198
50 LXX	204, 205	79.13	158
50.8 LXX	75 n.55	80	156
50.9 LXX	204	80.5–13	158
50.21 LXX	202	81.17	149
51	201 n.42	83.2 LXX	80
51.5	156	83.11 LXX	195
51.10–12	198	85 LXX	81
51.16	156	85.9 LXX	70
51.19	156, 202	85.16 LXX	76
56	156	86	66, 68, 81, 156
56.8	149	86.8	58 n.28
57	156	86.8–10	58 n.27, 69 n.15, 70 n.23
57.1	151		
58.6	149	86.9	69 n.15, 70 nn.23 and 25
60	156		

Scripture Index

88 LXX	81	99.4 LXX	71
88.15 LXX	78	100.3	158
88.37–38 LXX	197	102.2	156
88.45–46 LXX	201	102.14 LXX	77 n.67
89	67, 68, 81	102.14–16 LXX	203
89 LXX	58 n.24, 81	102.19 LXX	77
89.1–4	151	102.26	154
89.6	69 n.18	102.28	154
89.8	69 n.18	103–104 LXX	81
89.9	155	103.1	156
89.12 LXX	75 n.55	103.5	109 n.35
89.15 LXX	78 n.73	103.7 LXX	89, 90
89.52	72 n.41	103.19–20	77 n.67
91	152, 194	103.24 LXX	75 n.55
91.4	151	104 LXX	75
91.6	152	104–6 LXX	71
91.6 LXX	69	104.2	153
91.13	152	104.3	153
92.1 LXX	198	104.4	150
93.1	79 n.77	104.5–9	155
93.9 LXX	195	104.9	149
95	17	104.22	75 n.55
95–98 LXX	81	105.3 LXX	209
95.2–3 LXX	76	105.26	57 n.23
95.3 LXX	76 n.64, 80	105.29	155
95.7 LXX	74	105.48 LXX	72
95.7	158	106	72, 81
95.11 LXX	81 n.85	106.9	155
95.13 LXX	78	106.27 LXX	75 n.55
96.1 LXX	67 n.11, 71, 79	106.36–37	149
96.2 LXX	78	106.48	72 nn.40, 41
96.6 LXX	78	107	155
96.13	78 n.74, 157	107.23–30	155
97.1	79 nn.77 and 79	109.1 LXX	198
97.1 LXX	67 n.11, 69	109.3 LXX	197
97.2	78 n.73	109.8	193
97.2 LXX	58	110 LXX	81
97.4 LXX	72	110.1	194, 197
97.5	157	110-18 LXX	71
97.6 LXX	202	110.1	158
97.9 LXX	78, 80	110.2 LXX	69, 80
98	79 n.77	110.10 LXX	75 n.55
98 LXX	72	111.2	58, 69 n.15
98.1 LXX	79	112–117 LXX	81
98.2	69 n.15	112.1 LXX	71
98.9 LXX	72, 94	113 LXX	81
98.9	78, 157	113.2 LXX	77
99	72 n.38, 156	113.2–3	156
99.1	79 nn.76 and 81	113.21 LXX	80

114.4	151	145–150 LXX	71, 81
114.6	151	145.4 LXX	204
115.13 MT	80	145.10 LXX	79 n.80
116–118 LXX	81	145.11–14	77 n.68
116.1 LXX	71	145.17	69 n.15, 78
117 LXX	73	146.1 LXX	71
117–119 LXX	197	146.5 LXX	75
117.14 LXX	75	146.10	196
117.22 LXX	197	147.4	153
117.24 LXX	72, 197	147.14	149
117.25 LXX	73 n.43	148 LXX	81
117.26 LXX	73	148.1–4 LXX	71
117.27 LXX	73 n.43	148.7 LXX	71
118 LXX	81	149.1 LXX	67
118.12 LXX	78, 81	149.1	67 n.11, 150
118.64 LXX	78	150 LXX	81
118.68 LXX	78	150.1 LXX	71
118.121 LXX	78		
118.137 LXX	78 n.70	Proverbs	
118.160 LXX	78	7.2	155
119–33 LXX	4, 81	8.22–31	157
119.103	154	8.23–29	149
119.137	78 n.70	8.23–39	149
119.176	158	8.29	155
124.3 LXX	206	11.27	196
134–35	71	16.24	154
134–135 LXX	81	21.15	73
134.1 LXX	71	24.12	149
134.3 LXX	71	24.13–14	154
135.4 LXX	80	24.17	149
135.9	149		
136.2–3	156	Ecclesiastes	
136.6	149	1.1	202 n.43
137.7	158	12.4	201
138.14 LXX	69		
139.14	69 n.15	Isaiah	
139.16	149, 198	1.18	204
142	156	2.2–3	181
143.7	156	2.20	203
143.9 LXX	67 n.11	6	72 n.38
144 LXX	81	6.1–3	153
144–146 LXX	81	6.3	72, 94
144.2 LXX	81	6.9–10	181
144.4–5 LXX	74	9.1–7	181
144.7 LXX	72	11.1	19, 157
144.11 LXX	77	11.1–5	157
144.12 LXX	77	11.1–10 LXX	200
144.17 LXX	58, 69 n.15, 73, 74 n.48, 78 n.71	11.4	77 n.66, 80 n.82
		18.3	93

Scripture Index

22.22	37 n.74, 200	65.9	150
24	96	65.15–16	150, 157
24.8	96	65.17	204
24.23	79 n.80	65.17–25	14
26.21	157	66.18–20	181
27.9	175, 181	66.22	205
27.13	201 n.43	66.24	205, 207
29.10	174, 181		
29.18	181	Jeremiah	
32.3–4	181	5.22–24	155
35.4–5	181	10.6–7	69 n.15
40	205	10.7	58 n.28
40.4	157	10.11	92
40.4–5	204, 205	11.1–8	173
40.5–6	204	11.14–19	173
40.6–7	163	12.10	158
40.26	153	17.10	76 n.60
40.31	109 n.35	23.1–4	158
42.1	157	23.5	200
43.5–9	181	25.31	157
45.14	70 n.25, 154	31.31	180
45.17–25	181	31.33	175
49.1–7	157	31.31–34	180
49.6	181	39.19	73 n.42
49.22	181	50.6	158
49.23	70 n.25		
50.2	155	Ezekiel	
51.9–11	14	1.4–28	153
53.6	158	1.13	22, 91
55.1–3	154	1.24	89, 90
58.1	90	3.12	92
59.9–10	181	7.19–20	203
59.20	175, 177	26	96
59.20–21	180, 181	26.13	96, 97
60.1–3	181	26.22	97
60.1–5	181	26–27	96
60.4–12	181	27	96
60.5	181	34	158
60.7–10	181	37.11–24	96
60.13	181	38.19	92
60.14	70 n.25	43.7	164
60.16–17	181	48.35	97
60.19–21	181		
61.1–3	181	Daniel	
61.5	181	2.28	103
61.6	181	4.14	69 n.18
61.11	181	7	26 n.4, 27, 70, 158, 162 n.3
62.2	181		
64.4	196	7.9–10	153

7.9–14	157	2.10MT	76 n.62
7.13	73, 112 n.52, 161, 162 n.3	Micah	
7.21	69 n.17	1.3	157
7.25	111, 112 n.50, 113	1.4	157
8.16	201 n.43	4.1–5	181
9.21	201 n.43	7.8	149
10	27		
10.6	90, 91	Nahum	
10.13	201 n.43	1.5	157
10.21	201 n.43	3.5	73 n.42
12.1	108 n.30, 149, 201 n.43	Habakkuk	
12.3	206 n.54	2.3	73 n.45
12.4	102	2.3–4	73
12.7	111, 113	2.4	175
12.9	102	2.20	97 n.15, 98
12.11	111	3.6	157
Hosea		Zephaniah	
11.10	90	1.7	97 n.15
12.6	73 n.42	1.11	97 n.15
13.14	206 n.51		
		Zechariah	
Joel		1.14	187
3.21	79 n.80	2.8	155
		2.13	97 n.15
Amos		2.17	98
1	108	3.1–4.14	201
2	108	3.8	200
3.8	90	6.12	200
3.13	58, 73 n.42	8.2	187
4.13	58, 69 n.15, 73 n.42	10.3	73 n.42, 158
5.8	58, 73 n.42	11.3–17	158
5.14	73 n.42	12.10	167 n.30, 196 n.10
5.14-16	59		
5.15	73 n.42	13.7	158
5.16	73 n.42, 108	14.5	69 n.18
5.18	108	14.14	154
5.25–26	39 n.77		
5.26	39	Malachi	
5.27	73 n.42	1.11	69 n.15, 181
6.1	108		
9.5	73 n.42	NEW TESTAMENT	
9.6	73 n.42	Matthew	
9.15	73 n.42	2.2	48
		5.5	150
Jonah		5.8	78 n.69
1.4–5	155	8.5–13	163 n.12

9.15	184	16.15	76 n.64
9.23	93		
11.3	73	Luke	
12.22–32	178	1.19	201 n.43
13.43	206	1.26	201 n.43
17.1–8	168	1.32–33	179
17.2	168	1.64	156
17.5	168 n.38	2.14	81
19.28	179	3.5–6	204, 205
21.9	73	4.16–19	110 n.41
22.1–14	184	4.25	112 n.50
22.13	205	5.34–35	184
23.39	73, 179	7.2–10	163 n.12
24.15–22	179	7.12	167
24.22	201	7.19–20	73
24.30	112 n.52	8.42	167
24.43–44	179	9.26	168
25.1	184	9.28–36	168
25.1–13	184	9.29	168
25.6	120	9.35	168 n.38
25.33–34	205	9.38	167
28.19	76 n.64	11.22	75
		12.35–38	184
Mark		13.35	73
1.11	168	14.7–14	184
1.15	110	14.26–27	137
2.19–20	184	16.29–31	178
3.1–6	178	19.38	73
3.31–33	137	21.24	179
5.5	176	23.43	207
8.38	168	24	195
9.2	168	24.44	195
9.2–8	168	24.53	176
9.4–5	168		
9.7	168	John	
9.31	169	1.5	163
9.32	169	1.9–10	163
9.48	205	1.9–13	163
10.29–30	137	1.11	163
11.9	73	1.12–13	163
12.1–9	168 n.38	1.13	165
12.6	168 n.38	1.14	5, 74, 162–5, 168, 169
12.7	168 n.38	1.18	165, 168
12.35–37	197 n.18	1.36	112
12.36	194	2.9	184 n.5
12.37	45	2.23	162 n.5
13.14–20	179	3	168
13.20	201	3.2	162 n.5
14.62	208	3.16	5, 165, 166–9

3.16–21	165	19.37	167 n.30
3.18	165, 166	20.21	76 n.64
3.24	162	20.24	162
3.29	184 n.5	20.30–31	162
4.46–53	163 n.12		
5	162	Acts	
5.21–24	161	1–2	176
5.25–29	161	1.6–7	179
5.27	161	1.8	76 n.64
5.39	46	1.16	193
6.2	162 n.5	1.20	193
6.14	73	2.17	110
6.39	162	2.25	176
6.40	162	2.25–28	193
6.44	162	2.29–31	45, 193
6.53–58	162 n.5	2.34	45, 193–4
6.54	162	4.25–26	194
6.66–71	162	7.42–43	39
6.67	162	7.56	207
6.70–71	162	9	178
7.35	163 n.12	9.13	69 n.17
7.37	162 n.5	13.33	194
7.41	162 n.5	13.35	193
8.41	189	14.22	108
8.44	189	21.4	99
10	208	24.16	176
10.16	208	27.14–20	155
11.24	162		
11.33	162	Romans	
11.38	162	1.8	189 n.21
11.43–44	162	1.10	175
11.43	162	1.16–17	175
11.52	165	1.17	171
12.13	73	1.18–32	181
12.20	163 n.12	128	181
12.23	163 n.12	2.6	149
12.24	201	2.12	206
12.27	162	2.16	171
12.31	113	4	176
12.48	162	4.17	173
13.11	162	5.8	166
13.18–19	162	6	171
13.21	162	6.4	173
13.23	168	6.11	173
16.33	108	8.18–23	171
18.11	162	8.28–39	179, 180
18.28	16	8.32	166
19.14	16	8.35–39	166
19.31	17	9–11	6, 172, 176, 179

9.1	189 n.21	11.27	180
9.1–3	171, 178	11.29	181
9.1–5	174	11.30	181
9.4	177	11.30–31	175, 177
9.4–5	173	11.30–32	175
9.6	174, 175, 177, 179	11.32	175, 181
9.10–13	177, 181	12.2	142
9.27	177	12.3	187 n.13
9.31	177	12.13	69 n.17
9.30–33	171	13.11–12	177
10	172	14.11	181
10.1	171, 174, 178	15.4	46, 49
10.6–10	174	15.11	71 n.33
10.6–13	177	15.19–29	177
10.13	110	15.29	75
10.19	172, 177	16.20	191
10.21	177		
11	172, 175, 181	1 Corinthians	
11.1	177	1.20	142
11.1–2	179, 181	1.24	74
11.1–10	172, 174	2.6	171
11.2	177, 179, 181	3	179 n.46
11.3–7	181	3.2	186
11.7	174, 175, 177	3.18	171
11.7–10	171, 174, 181	3.19	142
11.8	181	4.15	186
11.8–10	174	5.7	17
11.9–10	194	5.10	171
11.11	176, 177, 179, 181	5.17	112
11.11–12	172, 173	6	179 n.46
11.12	173, 175, 176, 181	7.29–31	177
		7.31	142, 171
11.13–15	172, 175	9.1–2	190
11.14	174–8	9.19–22	173
11.15	173, 180	9.27	175, 190
11.16	173, 180	10.1	176 n.34
11.16–24	172, 173, 176	10.1–11	46
11.17	176	10.2–13	173
11.17–24	176 n.34	10.11	171
11.19	176	10.20	149
11.23	176	11.23–34	17
11.24	176	11.33–36	178
11.25	171, 174–7, 181	15.14–15	189
11.25–26	177	15.20–23	180
11.25–27	174, 175	15.20–28	171
11.25–32	172, 174–6	15.24–28	171
11.26	6, 171, 174, 175, 176 n.34, 177–82	15.45	190
		15.50–55	171
11.26–27	175, 177, 181	15.55	206 n.51

2 Corinthians		11.13	189
1–7	186	11.13–15	191
1.1	69 n.17	11.19	189
1.14	191	11.21	187, 189
1.16–17	189	11.24	178
1.22	189 n.21	11.26	189
2.7	175	11.28–29	188
2.10–11	171	11.31	189 n.21
2.17	189 n.20	12	208 n.56
3.1–3	186	12.1–9	171
3.2–3	189 n.22	12.3–4	208
3.12–16	46	12.6	189 n.21
4.2	189 n.20	12.7	171
9.4	175	12.11	187 n.13, 189
5.10	149		
5.17	171	12.13–14	186
6.3	186	12.16	186
6.8	189 n.20	12.16–18	186
7.2	186	13.3–7	190
7.8	186	13.8	189 n.21
8–9	186		
8.20	186	Galatians	
10	187	1.4	171
10–12	187	1.11–12	171
10–13	186, 191	1.15–16	171
10.1	186	1.15–17	178
10.2	186	1.20	189 n.21
10.6	187	2.19–20	173
10.7	186	3	176 n.34
10.8	186	4.3	142
10.9–11	186	4.19	186
10.10	186	4.24–25	42
10.12–15	187	4.26	181 n.52
10.13	186	6.14	142
10.13–18	186	6.16	176 n.34
10.18	187 n.13		
10.20–21	191	Ephesians	
11.1	186, 187, 189	1.21	171
11.1–2	187		
11.2	6, 184, 186, 187, 190, 191	Philippians	
		1.8	189 n.21
11.2–3	189 n.22	2.8–11	77 n.67
11.3	189, 190, 191	2.10–11	181
11.3–4	188	2.11	74
11.4	187, 189	2.12	191
11.5	187 n.13, 189	2.16	191
11.6	186	3.3	176 n.34
11.9	186	3.11	175
11.10	189 n.21	4.3	149

Colossians		11.17	167
2.11–13	176 n.34	11.32	194
1 Thessalonians		James	
1.10	180	5.17	112 n.50
2.3–5	189 n.20		
2.5	189 n.21	1 Peter	
2.7	186	1.10–12	46, 49
2.9	189 n.21	2.9	206 n.53
2.14–16	171 n.2		
2.18	171	2 Peter	
2.19–20	191	1.17	168 n.38
4.13–17	171	1.17–18	168
4.15–16	127	1.19–21	46
4.16	203		
16–17	208 n.56	1 John	
4.17	203	1.1–3	166
5.1–3	179	2.7	167 n.34
		3.1	165
2 Thessalonians		3.2	78 n.69, 167 n.34
1.5–10	179	3.11	166
1.10	78 n.74	3.12	189
2	172	3.21	167 n.34
2.2–4	179 n.46	4.1	167 n.34
2.4	179	4.7	167 n.34
2.7–8	179	4.11	167 n.34
2.16	176	4.9	166 n.25
		5.10	189
1 Timothy			
1.17	74 n.52	3 John	
2.7	189 n.21	1	167 n.34
2.14	191	2	167 n.34
4.1	191	5	167 n.34
6.16	74 n.52	11	167 n.34
2 Timothy		Jude	
2.15	190	9	201 n.43
Hebrews		Revelation	
1.1	115	1	26 n.4, 60
1.7	150	1–19	97
1.8–9	77 n.66	1.1	103, 140
2.6	162 n.3	1.2	140
2.13	75 n.57	1.3	104
2.15	176	1.4	94
4.7	45	1.5	65 n.1, 110, 140, 184
4.12–13	46	1.6	94, 110, 112
6.7	201	1.7	1, 94, 112 n.52, 167 n.30
10.37	73		

1.8–20	27	5.9	54, 94, 183
1.9	104 n.16, 113, 140	5.9–10	55, 94
1.9–10	107	5.9–14	54, 68
1.10	84, 85, 89, 90, 92, 93, 162	5.11	68, 84, 85
		5.11–12	68, 84, 94
1.12	85	5.11–14	140
1.12–13	162	5.12	74, 75, 85, 140, 183
1.13	162	5.12f	74
1.14	126 n.65	5.13	74–7, 79, 80, 94
1.15	85, 89, 90	5.13–14	68
2.1–3.22	83, 97, 136	5.14	75, 94
2.2	104 n.16	6	106
2.3	104 n.16	6–8	125
2.7	208	6.1	84, 86, 89
2.18	126 n.65	6.1–8.1	97
2.19	104 n.16	6.3–8	125
2.21	104	6.4	126
2.23	76 n.60	6.5	126
2.26	79 n.82	6.6	84, 86
2.28	221	6.7	84, 86, 126
3.5	149	6.9	84
3.7	37 n.74, 200	6.10	86
3.9	70 n.25	6.11	104
3.10	104 n.16, 142	6.12	85
3.14	184	6.15	79 n.82
3.18	126 n.65	6.16–17	127
3.20	85	7	106 n.25, 110
3.21	183	7.2	84, 86
4–5	26 n.4, 29	7.9	110, 140, 141
4.1	84, 86, 89, 92	7.9–10	68, 94
4.2	67, 93	7.9–12	68
4.2–3	79 n.76	7.7–17	140
4.5	22, 84, 85, 90, 91	7.10	73 n.43, 76, 79, 80, 84, 86
4.6–9	68		
4.8	59, 67, 72, 73, 94	7.11–12	67, 68, 94
4.8–11	68	7.12	74–7
4.9	74	7.15	164
4.9–10	79 n.76	8–9	106
4.9–11	94	8:1	4, 97–9
4.10	93	8.2	92
4.10–11	67, 68	8.5	22, 84, 85, 90, 91, 126 n.65
4.11	72, 74		
5	2	8.6	92
5.2	84, 85	8.6–11.19	97
5.5	200	8.7	126 n.65
5.5–6	19, 20	8.8	126 n.65
5.6	183, 200	8.13	84, 86, 92, 109
5.8	92, 93	9.1–2	205
5.8–10	67, 68	9.3	191

9.5	120 n.21, 191	12.10	74, 76–7, 81, 84, 88, 113
9.7–11	191	12.10–12	68, 94, 104
9.9	85, 86	12.11	110
9.12	109	12.12	81 n.85, 104, 109, 111, 164
9.13	73 n.43, 84, 86		
9.14	92	12.14	104 n.19, 109 n.35, 110
9.19	191		
10	104, 110	12.14–15	191
10.1	84	12.17	110, 140
10.2	84	12.19	142
10.3	85, 87, 89, 90	13	26 n.4
10.3–4	85	13.1–18	83, 97
10.4	84, 86	13.5	110, 112
10.6	104	13.6	164 n.17
10.7	86	13.8	141, 142, 149
10.8	84, 87	13.10	104 n.16
10.12	84	13.18	37, 38 n.75, 39
11	104, 110, 111	14–15	60 n.32
11.1–10	105 n.20, 111	14.1	92, 109
11.1–13	201	14.2	84, 87–90
11.2	110	14.3	54 n.5, 55, 56, 67, 68, 94, 110
11.3	110, 113		
11.5	126, 127	14.4	204
11.8	104	14.6	76 n.64, 84
11.12	87	14.7	87
11.13	22, 85	14.8	71 n.33
11.14	109	14.9	84, 87
11.15	37, 68, 77, 79 nn.78 and 80, 84, 87, 94, 120 n.21, 142	14.10	126 n.65
		14.12	104 n.16, 140
11.15–18	68	14.13	84, 88
11.15–19	98	14.14	162
11.16–17	94	14.15	84, 87, 88
11.16–18	67, 68	14.18	84, 88
11.17	59, 72–4, 79 n.77	15	56–8, 61, 63, 64, 78 n.75
11.18	79 nn.77 and 82, 80, 104		
		15–16	57, 106
11.19	22, 83, 85, 86, 90, 92	15.1	61
		15.1–2	58
12	47 n.22, 105 n.20, 110, 111	15.2	53 n.3, 56, 57, 61, 69, 92, 93
12.1	41, 47, 111	15.2–4	94
12.1–6	46, 104	15.2–6	56, 59–62
12.3	191	15.2–8	62
12.5	71 n.33, 79 n.82	15.3	22, 54, 55, 57, 73, 78, 79, 94
12.6	110, 113		
12.7	201 n.43	15.3–4	1, 3, 53–7, 58 nn.27 and 28, 59 n.29, 60–4, 67–9, 70 n.23, 78, 94
12.7-9	47 n.22, 191		
12.9	20, 104 n.19, 191		

15.4	57 n.18, 58, 61, 69, 71 n.33, 73 n.48	18.15	183
		18.16	109, 183
15.5	57, 69, 164 n.17	18.19	109, 183
15.6	57, 61	18.21	183
15.8	57	18.22	85, 92, 93, 95–7
5.9	94	18.22–23	83, 95, 96, 97, 183
5.13–14	67, 79, 80	18.23	71 n.33, 86, 95, 97, 183
16	57		
16.1	84, 88	18.24	183
16.1–21	98	19.1	70, 74, 76, 83, 87, 89, 90
16.5	73 n.48, 74, 78, 80, 94		
16.5–6	67, 68	19.1–2	70, 94
16.5–7	68	19.1–3	67, 68
16.6	183	19.1–4	68, 127
16.7	59, 67, 68, 72, 73, 78, 94	19.2	78, 80, 183
		19.3	70, 80, 94
16.14	142	19.4	67, 68, 70, 72 n.40, 94, 122
16.16	106		
16.17	88, 89	19.5	67, 71, 80 n.84, 89
16.18	85, 86, 90, 92		
16.18–21	22	19.5–6	79 n.79, 84
16.19	183	19.5–8	68
17	26 n.4, 60	19.6	71–3, 84, 88, 89, 90
17–18	84		
17.1	183	19.6–7	71
17.1–18	140	19.6–8	68, 70, 94
17.2	183	19.7	71, 74, 183
17.3	93	19.9	183, 191
17.4	183	19.9–21.1	106
17.5	183	19.10	140
17.6	140, 183	19.11	184
17.8	141, 142, 149	19.11–16	78 n.74
17.14	140	19.15	79 n.82
17.15	183	19.17	84, 88, 183, 191
17.16	142	19.18	142
17.17–21	98	19.19	79 n.82, 183
17.18	79 n.82, 183	19.20	126 n.65
18	60, 61	19.21	142
18.1	96	20.2	120 n.21, 191
18.1–3	67, 18	20.2–3	191
18.2	83, 88, 183	20.3	104
18.3	71 n.33, 183	20.4	117, 140
18.4	83, 89	20.5	117
18.4–8	67	20.10	126 n.65
18.8	72, 75, 80	20.12	141, 149
18.9	183	20.13	149
18.10	109, 183	20.14	126 n.65
18.11–13	96	20.15	126 n.65, 149
18.11–19	183	20.20	191

21–22	21	Wisdom of Solomon	
21.1	127, 139, 204, 208	7.22	168 n.36
21.1–22.7	83, 97	18.14	98, 99
21.2	208	18.14–19	48
21.3	84, 89, 162, 164 n.17		
21.3–4	68, 80	Sirach	
21.4	208	7.17	207
21.7	149	14.17–18	163
21.8	126 n.65	17.22	155
21.9	102	23.3	149
21.9–22.5	105 n.20	24.8	164
21.10	93, 208	43.14	149
21.20	120 n.21	43.17	89, 90
21.22	44, 97	45.20	180
21.25	208		
22	21	Baruch	
22.1	183	3.1	73 n.42
22.1–2	139	3.4	73 n.42
22.3	183	4.7	149
22.5	97		
22.6	97, 102, 103, 140	1 Maccabees	
22.6–7	191	4.36–61	93
22.10	104		
22.16	200	PSEUDEPIGRAPHA	
22.17	191	*1 Enoch*	
22.20	140	1–36	147, 158
22.21	140	1.2–3	152
		1.4	157
APOCRYPHA		1.4–9	157
1 Ezra (1 Esdras)		1.6	157
4.40	77	1.9	157
4.45	158	5.5–9	150
4.59–60	75	5.6–7	150
		5.7	150
4 Ezra (2 Esdras)		6–11	147
8.22	150	6.1–7.6	148
8.52	21 n.44	9.1	201 n.43
11.7–8	109 n.35	9.4	156
		9.4–11	156 n.33
Tobit		10.4	205
3.1–6	156	10.9	201 n.43
3.11–15	156	10.11	201 n.43
6–12	185	10.21	153
12.22	58	11.2	148
		14.8	153
Judith		14.20	153
9.1–14	156	17.1	150
11.13	180	17.2	149
16.17	207	17.5	207

18.1–2	149	69.12	152
18.5	150	69.16–21	156
19.1	149	69.17	149
20.5	201 n.43	69.21	153
24.6	201 n.43	69.23	149
28.13	149	69.29	158
37–71	147, 157, 158	71.12	152
		71.13–14	157
38.1	150–1	72–82	158
38.2	151	72.1–5	149
38.4	150	81.5	148
39–40	147	82.3	154
39.4–8	151	84.2–6	156
39.7	151	84.6	156
39.8	151	85–90	158
39.9	156	86–88	147
41.4–5	149	89.12	158
41.6	151	89.12–90.38	158
43.1	153	89.28	158
45–49	147	89.58	154
45.1	150	92–105	158
45.3	158	94.10	154
46.1–5	157	95.5	149
46.4	149	96.5	149
46.8	150	96.8	155
47.3	149	100.5	155
48.2–7	157	101.4–9	155
48.3	153	101.7	155
48.8	157	103.2	149
48.10	151, 157	103.7	205
49.3	157	104.1	149
49.3–4	157	106–107	147
51.4	148, 151–2	106.3	155–6
52.4	157	106.5–6	156
52.6	157	106–11	155–6
52.9	154	108.3	149
53.1	153–4	108.7	149
53.5	157	108.9	156
53.6	150	110.7	149
55.4	158		
56.5–8	147	*3 Baruch*	
60.12–21	149	11.2	201 n.43
61.8	158	11.4	201 n.43
62–63	147	12.1	201 n.43
62.2	157, 158	12.7	201 n.43
62.8	150	13.2–3	201 n.43
62.16	154		
63.12	150	*Apocalypse of Elijah*	
65–68	147	4.7–19	202 n.40

Jubilees		DEAD SEA SCROLLS	
2.1	201 n.43	1QM	
2.2	150	I	28 n.17
30.20	149	IV, 5	72 n.37
37.20	158		
48.1	201 n.43	1QS	
		5.20	151
Letter Aristeas			
40	180	4Q85 (4QPs^c)	202 n.42
3 Maccabees		4Q171	
2.1–20	156		150
3.23	99	Ii.5	151
6.1–15	156		
		4Q177	
Odes of Solomon		frgs. 10+12+13, col. i, line 7	194
2	73		
2.4	74	CD	
2.8	208	VII	39 n.77
12	73, 81		
12.1	73	4Q381	
14	81		65 n.2
Prayer of Azariah		4QMMT (4Q394–99)	
	156		194
Liber Antiquitatum Biblicarum			
32.1-18	62	4Q397	
51.3–6	62	frgs. 14–21 line 10	194
Psalms of Solomon		4Q398	
2.16	149	frgs. 14–17, col. i, lines 2–3	194
2.34	149		
10.5	74	4Q400–407	
17.16	151		194
17.30–35	181		
		11QPs^a (11Q5)	
Testament of Abraham		XXVI, 10–11	78 n.73
A 16–20	205	XXVII.2–11	194
Testament of Levi		11Q11	
6.11	171 n.2		152, 194
Testament of Benjamin		11Q17	
9.2	181		194
Testament of Solomon		11Q13	
18.6	202 n.43	ii line 1	194

MasŠirŠabb
                        194

THE CAIRO GENIZAH
Songs of David
1.14   194

Damascus Covenant
                        194

TARGUM
Tg. 2 Samuel
22.1   195

Tg. Psalms
14.1   195
18.1   195
49.16   195
51.13-14   195
54.3   195 n.9
103.1   195

Tg. Song of Songs
1.1   195

Tg. 2 Samuel
23.2   195

Tg. 1 Chronicles
23.27   195

Tg. 2 Chronicles
8.14   195

TALMUD
Gemara
                        188

b. Sotah
48b   196
49a   183 n.2

b. Sheb.
15b   152

y.Reub
10.11   152

y. Sotah
9.24b   196

MISHNAH
Ketubot
1.5   188

Sanhedrin
10   180

OTHER RABBINIC LITERATURE
Mek.Pisha
13   196

Midrash on the Psalms
1.1   196
24.1   196

Seder 'Olam
§20   196

Apocalypse of David
§125   196
§126   196

PHILO
De agricultura
50   195

De plantatione
29   195

Quis rerum divinarum heres sit
290   195

JOSEPHUS
Antiquities
6.166   195
8.109–110   195
18.257–309   179

CHRISTIAN PSEUDEPGRAPHA
Acts of Andrew and Matthew
30.3   202 n.43

Acts of Peter and Andrew
10.3   202 n.43

Acts of John
84.1   205 n.51

Acts of Pilate
5.2   198
21.2   198
25.1   202 n.43
26.1   202 n.43
27.1   202 n.43

Acts of Philip
78.6   198
137.2   202 n.43
78.9   198

Apocalypse of John
             199–200
8   201–2
9   201, 202–3
12   203–4
13   203
15   201, 204–5
20   201, 205
21   201, 205, 206
22   201, 206
23   201, 206
24   201, 206–7
25   201, 207–8
26   201, 208
27   209
28   201, 209

Apocalypse of Paul
29   198

Apocalypse of Peter
17   198

Apostolic Constitutions and Canons
2.26.3   207 n.55

Epistle of Dionysius the
Areopagite to Timothy
53   198
57   198

Epistula Apostolorum
19.18   197

19.18-19   197
35.4–5   197

Martyrdom of Bartholomew
4.8   202 n.43
6.2   205–6 n.51

Martyrdom of Peter and Paul
8.2   198
9.2   198

Palaea Historica
161.16   198

EARLY CHRISTIAN WRITINGS
Epistle of Barnabas
6.4   197
6.6–7   197
6.16   197
9.1   197
9.2   197
11.6–7   197
12.10   197

Athanasius
Epistulae ad Serapionem
1.10   198
1.33   198

Eusebius
De ecclesiastica theologia
1.3.6   198

Jerome
Commentariorum in Epistulam ad Galatas
4.5   198

Justin Martyr
1 Apol.
35.5–6   197
40.1–4   197
40.5   197
41.1–4   197
45.1–4   197

Dialogus cum Tryphone
28.5   197, 198
32.3   198
43.3   198

56.5	198	85.4	197
76.7	197	87.4	198
85.1	198	88.8	197

www.ingramcontent.com/pod-product-compliance
Lightning Source LLC
Chambersburg PA
CBHW051518230426
43668CB00012B/1655